WHEN WORLDS COLLIDE

INDO-EUROPEANS & PRE-INDO-EUROPEANS

Linguistica Extranea, *Studia 19*

When Worlds Collide:

The Indo-Europeans and the Pre-Indo-Europeans

*The Rockefeller Foundation's
Bellagio Study and Conference Center
Lake Como, Italy*

February 8-13, 1988

Presented by:
T. L. Markey & John A. C. Greppin

1990

KAROMA PUBLISHERS, INC.

Karoma Publishers, Inc.
3400 Daleview Drive
Ann Arbor, Michigan 48105 USA

Copyright © **1990** *by*
Karoma Publishers, Inc.
All Rights Reserved
ISBN 0-89720-090-X

COVER COLLAGE
Top: Detail from scabbard from Hallstatt, Grave No. 994, 400-350 BC (Vienna, Naturhist. Museum, Inv. Nr. 51244). Bottom and left-hand side: Gold ring from Erstfeld (Uri, Switzerland), 420-350 BC (Zurich, Schweizerisches Landesmuseum, Inv. Nr. 3192-98). Photographic scene: Detail of Stanley Marsh's "Cadillac Ranch," near Amarillo, Texas. Photograph by Steve Douglass, Amarillo Globe-News, by the artist's permission. Marsh, creator of the "ranch," a self-proclaimed eccentric and a multimillionaire in reality, buried ten cadillacs from the 50s and 60s nose-down at the precise angle of the pyramids as a moument to the finest achievements of Western civilization.

CONFERENCE PARTICIPANTS, February 8th - 13th, 1988

Seated from left to right: Nino Gamkrelidze, Daniel Zohary, Colin Renfrew, Alice Harris, Eric P. Hamp, Antonio Gilman, John A. C. Greppin.

Standing from left to right: Thomas V. Gamkrelidze, Roger J. Mercer, Charles Burney, Karl Horst Schmidt, Francisco Villar, Timothy Champion, Edgar C. Polomé, Stefan Zimmer, Thomas L. Markey.

Participants who attended, but were not photographed: Giancarlo Bolognesi, Heiner Eichner, Patricia P. Markey, Marek Zvelebil.

Invited participants who were unable to attend, but who contributed to this volume: Igor M. Diakonoff, Gevork B. Djahukian, Marija Gimbutas, and Clive Ruggles.

CONTENTS

Welcome Remarks: When Cultures Collide - The Indo-Europeans and Pre-Indo-Europeans
Thomas Markey 1

On the Problem of an Asiatic Original Homeland of the Proto-Indo-Europeans
Thomas V. Gamkrelidze 5

Archaeology and Linguistics: Some Preliminary Issues
Colin Renfrew 15

Did Armenians Live in Asia Anterior Before the Twelfth Century B.C.?
Gevork B. Djahukian 25

Domestication of Plants in the Old World: The Emerging Synthesis
Daniel Zohary 35

The Indo-European Impact on the Hurrian World
Charles Burney 45

Language Contacts in the Caucasus and the Near East
Igor M. Diakonoff 53

Kartvelian Contacts with Indo-European
Alice C. Harris 67

The Inception of Farming in the British Isles and the Emergence of Indo-European Languages in NW Europe
Roger J. Mercer 101

Astronomical and Geometrical Influences on Monumental Design: Clues To Changing Patterns of Social Tradition?
Clive Ruggles 115

The Mafia Hypothesis
Antonio Gilman 151

The Collision of Two Ideologies
Marija Gimbutas 171

The Postulated Pre-Indo-European Substrates in Insular Celtic and Tocharian
Karl Horst Schmidt 179

The Make-Up of the Armenian Unclassified Substratum
John A. C. Greppin 203

The Indo-European Horse
Eric P. Hamp 211

Arménien et Iranien: Une Théorie Linguistique Passée Inaperçue
Giancarlo Bolognesi 227

Agricultural Transition, "Indo-European Origins" and the Spread of Farming
Marek Zvelebil and Kamil V. Zvelebil 237

Types of Linguistic Evidence for Early Contact: Indo-Europeans and Non-Indo-Europeans
Edgar C. Polomé 267

The Pre-Indo-European Language of Northern (Central) Europe
Eric P. Hamp 291

The Investigation of Proto-Indo-European History: Methods, Problems, Limitations
Stefan Zimmer 311

Gift, Payment and Reward Revisited
Thomas L. Markey 345

Indo-Européens et Pré-Indo-Européens dans la Péninsule Ibérique
Francisco Villar 363

DISCUSSION 395

WHEN CULTURES COLLIDE: THE INDO-EUROPEANS AND PRE-INDO-EUROPEANS

Welcome remarks
Thomas Markey (Bellagio, February 8-13, 1988)

It is an exclusive pleasure for John A.C. Greppin and myself to welcome so many friends, who also happen to be professional colleagues, to this week-long discussion----*symposium* seems far too inflated a term for this event, while *conference* is even more inappropriate, though perhaps the *convegno* of our host country is, after all, most apt for an inviting setting in which we hope to accomplish much.

In welcoming you, I wish to provide, however fragmentarily, both some foregrounding and some scaffolding.

First, the conveners must thank the Rockefeller Foundation, whose villa hosts but some thirty such gatherings each year, and this particular gathering marks, we understand, a first : The first time linguists and archaeologists and anthropologists have met together here, and we would hope that this might provide a precedent for similar gatherings here and elsewhere in the future.

But why, as we asked in our proposal for this gathering to the Rockefeller Foundation, this topic and why now?

If the 19th century was, and I for one am thoroughly convinced that it was, concerned with origins, then the present century is an era that has increasingly looked for roots. A quest for origins and a search for roots are not the same and not to be confused. The quest for origins focuses on "whatness," while the search for roots focuses on "whoness." The issue of origins is typically centered around natural ancestry, and Darwin provided the brand name for his age. In contrast, the quest for roots is essentially concerned with probing a cultural heritage, defining the fibres of an ethnicity, mapping ideational stratigraphies. The origins issue is characteristically a biological matter, while that of roots is generally intellectual in scope. The topic we are to address here in Bellagio is, indeed, fundamentally a question of roots. Having been assigned a biological past by the Victorians, we now want to discover mental cultivations within that past. The quest to know a Pre-Indo-European vs. an Indo-

European setting, the effort to question cultural confrontation, is a quest for roots, a search for a definition of one's intellectual self. It is the puzzle of roots, not of origins, that has made our discussion topic so timely. Just how timely, how very popular, and how very open to commercialization the matter of roots has become may not be so obvious to us as scholars who naturally shun or who, perhaps out of professional or personal aesthetic necessity, must shun popular culture.

"Roots" has become big business. A recent spate of films with the archaeologist as hero such as *Raiders of the Lost Ark*, *Romancing the Stone*, and *Indiana Jones*, has made it abundantly clear just how enormous the size of that business can be. Another clear sign of that bigness is the staggering popularity of Jean M. Auels engaging on-going series, *Earth's Children*, which began with *The Clan of the Cave Bear*. Ms. Auel has recently informed me that she is now hard at work on the fourth book in this projected six volume set. The popular acclaim of her writing is evidenced by the fact that ABC's *20/20 Program* featured her and her work (April 17, 1986) and by the fact that such national attention might well have encouraged or at least have smoothed the way for the acceptance of Randall White as guest curator of the "Dark Caves, Bright Visions" exhibit, a "roots" display that was chronicled by no less an observer of the anthro-scene that John E. Pfeiffer in the *Smithsonian Magazine* (October, 1986). Ice Age Europe was never so "in," never so irresistible as now. It was also during the recent past that Alexander Marschack's extraordinary technical proficiency brought those bright visions to light, and the photographic record of cave art was intentionally packaged for mass consumption. The "roots" of writing have been brought to far wider public attention during the past decade by the notable efforts of Denise Schmandt-Besserat, e.g. her article in *Science* 211 (16 January 1981), pp. 283-5. The portrayal of a Great Goddess as earth-mother, as prime life-force, great diviner, and directive matriarch by Marija Gimbutas has engendered a feminist following that has provided its own intriguing quest for roots, its own interpretation of the artifactual record. Note, for example, Riane Eisler's recent *The Chalice and the Blade. Our History, Our Future* (New York: Harper and Row, 1987). In yes, Ms. Eisler sees Gimbutas' Old Europe as representing a so-called "*gylanic*" chalice-half Europe where reverence and celebration of life were symbolized by the Goddess' religion, a half that was pitted against the warlike patriarchy of the intrusive Indo-Europeans. Then, too, Donna Wilshire (Plainfield, New Jersey) now gives performances that are collages of song, dance, dramatized verse, and spoken history, contemporaneous ritual if you will that is based on recent scholarship about the Great Goddess.

The archaeologist, in comparison with the linguist, has clearly played stage-center in the "roots" business. Indeed, it seems as if the linguist has been rudely shoved aside, although an apparent exception seems to be Colin Renfrew's *Archaeology and Language* (1987), about which we shall hear much more later at this gathering. Nevertheless, there has not been total media silence on the linguistic front, and the comparativist has not been excluded from all of this great fun. Nostratic theory has been given a North American revival Vitaly Shevoroshkin, and this catharsis was covered by John Noble Wilford this past fall in *The New York Times* (*Science Times*, Tuesday, Nov. 24, 1987). So, the search for a unified proto-language, however distant in time and unrealistic in design, has also fired the "roots" imagination. Also within the linguistic realm is a work that I personally could not fail to mention, namely Derek Bickerton's *Roots of Language* (1981), a study which, in its perhaps abortive attempt to see creole-like origins and a definite, well-articulated bioprogram for all lingual genesis, attracted vast amounts of mass-media attention for a number of years.

Then, too, the origins people, the evolutionists, particularly the neo-darwinians, have hardly been silent either, as evidenced by *Newsweek's* (January 11, 1988) coverage of the pros and cons of the mitochondrial mother, the original Ayla and Great Goddess, a common female ancestor for the species, quite possibly out of Africa.

If you think that the "roots" phenomenon is some particularly American misadventure or aberration, then you are quite wrong and an imperceptive observer of your own time. Anglophones have hardly cornered the market. Michel Foucault (b. 1926 - d. 1984) obviously sought "an archaeology of knowledge," merely another label for "roots," and his *Les mots et les choses* (1966) was not only a best-seller in France, but also, as, *The Order of Things*, in the English-speaking world. There, Foucault devotes electrifying attention to the journey of historical linguistics from an alchemy of verbiage to principled insights about the arsenal of minor morphemes we recognize as the basis of an Indo-European speech, if not language, community. Foucault's countryman, Michel Serres, has run a parallel course in his search for the common roots of Western science and yes. And far from France or German bookstores laden with best sellers discussing how a band of *spater bekannt als Indo-German* (naturally), would conquer the world, we note that the Japanese, too, have embraced "roots": how and why were the original Jomon replaced by the Yayoi and with whom are these intruders to be linked, culturally and/or linguistically? As if in preparation to answer these and related questions, Japanese linguistics has recently shown a new awareness of an interest in Indo-European studies. As precursors of the current Japanese, were the Yayoi designed from Austro-Tai stock, as Paul K. Benedict has compellingly asserted, or where they some lost ribe of Uralic wanderers as Roy Andrew Miller has steadfastly and simplistically maintained?

So it is that "rootism" holds pervasive fascination for an era, a fascination that spans gulfs between disciplines and encircles the globe. It is possibly entirely natural that the question of "whatness" should precede the question of "whoness," that is, that the issue of roots should trail in the wake of the subject origins. No matter, rootsism is now a nuclear concern, and a particular manifestation of that ism is our topic of the Indo-Europeans and the pre-Indo-Europeans, whether a cataclysmic cultural onslaught or quiet hybridization, a massive invasion or a virtually imperceptible swarming effect, wholesale colonization or gradual, integrated accommodation, violent patriarchal herdsmen vs. passive matriarchal planters. The crux, it seems to me, of our topic is the proper definition of process. We are here to consider the modalities of evidence in forging a definition, quite possibly a redefinition, from the linguistic, material, and social artifacts at our disposal. We seek inferences about the margins of disruption. We may advance parallels from a recent past to enlighten a remote relationship: What might subjugation of the agricultural Guanas by the fierce Paraguayan Mbayas have to say about the topic at hand? What valid social glosses are actually permitted by the artifactual evidence? What data can be used to delineate a North European community prior to its Indo-Europeanization, or define a pre-Greek cultural sphere? What kinds of evidence do we have or can we use to show that knowledge partitioning distinguishes cultural and/or ethnic units? Was, for example, "megalithic science" transferable, or was this a form of knowledge that was socially tied to a particular cultural context? What ritualizations can be read into what kinds of knowledge evidenced by material and linguistic debris?

The fanciful speculations that I often find characteristic of the past couple of decades are now being increasingly curtailed by advances in technology. Correspondingly, compelling and credible hypothesizing has become far less diffuse, but also perhaps far less thrilling for the popular mind. Such progress over previously highly imaginative assessment has been admirably exemplified by the detective work conducted by Don Robbins and Anne Ross on Lindow Man, the victim of an identifiable ritual act practised by a particular ethnic group. This is a far cry from the scrutiny first accorded Piltdown Man. Those V-inscribed Balkan figurines may be related to some sort of fertility exercise, but to design a Great Goddess to accommodate them is mere wishful thinking.

In welcoming you here, I hope to have shown just how timely and central the topic of this *convegno* is. The further interpretation of this topic may well become heated, for it is a well known complementarity of scholarship that the more elusive the facts, the less objective and more personal their interpretation. This has certainly been the case in the heated debate over the demise of the dinosaurs: Extra-terrestrial intervention vs. natural causes, that is, Luis Alvarez and his meteorite hypothesis vs. the paeleontologists, an outsider vs. the members of a discipline. What we hope to accomplish here, however, is an interdisciplinary conversation where there can be no outsiders.

ON THE PROBLEM OF AN ASIATIC ORIGINAL HOMELAND OF THE PROTO-INDO-EUROPEANS

Ex Oriente Lux.
Thomas V. Gamkrelidze (Tbilisi, Georgia, USSR)

A revision and reformulation of the basic structure of Proto-Indo-European and a formal-semantic reconstruction of the Common Indo-European vocabulary according to new phonological patterns in our recent publication* necessitate, as a consequence, to advance a new look at the areal and ethno-cultural problems pertaining to the distribution of the ancient Indo-European dialects, the original localization of the Proto-Indo-European speakers and their prehistoric migrations to the territories of their historical habitation.

The picture of areal affinities drawn from the study of grammatical, phonological, and lexical isoglosses among dialects of a proto-language provides a way of determining how dialectal differentiation of the proto-language proceeded and hence of establishing what contacts took place among speakers of the dialects. In other words, purely linguistic facts make it possible to establish extra-linguistic factors such as historical interactions among speakers of the linguistic systems.

Of particular value and significance for linguistically based reconstruction of non-linguistic historical and social relations is formal semantic analysis of the dialect lexicons, since they can reflect all essential aspects of the historical existence of their speakers. The historical existence of the speakers includes the ecological environment (fauna, flora, geographical surroundings, climate) and human habitation and migration in the environment, as well as culture in the broadest sense (including both material and spiritual culture). Semantic reconstruction of relevant lexemes from the daughter languages gives us a general representation (although sometimes only a fragmentary one) of the speakers' historical existence. In such reconstructions, linguistic facts are a source of information on prehistoric culture and its historical evolution.

Thus, comparative semantic analysis of words from separate daughter dialects of a proto-language and text fragments in separate daughter traditions, together with the method that may be called "linguistic paleontology of culture," makes it possible to reconstruct a semantic lexicon of the proto-language and a picture of the protoculture of the speakers of the proto-language or its dialect groups. This points to a possible original homeland and suggests routes of migration by which speakers of the proto-language or its dialects may have reached their historical territories.

Semantic analysis of the reconstructed vocabulary and its implications for the ecological environment and the material and spiritual culture of tribes speaking ancient Indo-European dialects places the center of diffusion of these dialects, and consequently the Proto-Indo-European homeland, somewhere in the broad area extending from the Balkans in the west to northern Mesopotamia and the Iranian plateau in the east, in the fifth to fourth millennia B.C. Numerous lexical items shared among Proto-Indo-European, Proto-Semitic, South Caucasian, and sometimes other ancient Near Eastern languages, further narrow down the potential homeland to a particular area in southwest Asia. This posited homeland necessitates a complete revision of the received view of the Proto-Indo-European speakers' migrations to their historical locations on the Eurasian continent.

The main question associated with the problem of the actual existence of a common Indo-European proto-language in space and time is the question of chronology and the territory occupied by the Proto-Indo-European language, the break-up of which led to the formation of related historical dialects. The lower chronological limit for establishing the period of existence of a proto-language is deduced first of all on the basis of the dating of written evidence from the various historical languages deriving from it. In the case of Proto-Indo-European, this lower chronological limit *post quem non* is the turn of the third to the second millennium B.C., when we find the earliest evidence of Hittite and other Anatolian languages.

It may be concluded from Anatolian onomastics of the Cappadocian tablets dating from the turn of the third to the second millennium B.C. that the various Anatolian languages underwent an extremely long period of development and formation after they had become distinct from one another; this period postdates the time when the Anatolian family had become differentiated from Proto-Indo-European.

To the same direction points a recent revelation made by Professor Henning who identifies the *Gutians* or *Kutians* and *Tukres* of the ancient Near East that occur in the cuneiform inscriptions of the end of the 3rd millennium B.C. with historical Kuchi-Tocharians, this being the earliest appearance of Indo-Europeans in history (cf. W. Henning, the first Indo-Europeans in history, "Society and History." *Essays in Honour of Karl August Wittfogel*, ed. by A.L. Ulmen, The Hague, Paris, N.Y. 1978:216-229).

This means that the differentiation of the Anatolian and Tocharian family of languages from the Indo-European proto-language, and thus the beginning of the break-up of the proto-language, must be dated to a period not later than the fourth millennium B.C., and possibly much earlier.

Evidence about the differentiation of other dialectal communities from the proto-language also concurs with the dating of the Proto-Indo-European language deduced from the Anatolian and Tocharian languages. The Indo-European linguistic community that remained after the emergence from the proto-language of a common Anatolian and a corresponding Tocharian linguistic community, which are combined into a single group by the scheme of dialect classification, began the same time to break down into dialect groups, which subsequently produced the respective historical dialects. In particular, one should date the emergence of the Greek-Armenian-Aryan dialect community, later differentiated into the Indo-Iranian dialect group and the Greek and Proto-Armenian dialects to about the same time.

The original area inhabited by the speakers of Proto-Indo-European may be regarded as that geographic region which, in this period, corresponded in its ecological, geographic, and cultural-historical features to the picture of the habitat which emerges on the basis of a linguistic reconstruction, and a semantic analysis, of the common vocabulary of the proto-language.

The first point which may be stated with sufficient assurance with regard to the homeland of the Proto-Indo-European language is that it was a region with a mountainous landscape. This is indicated primarily by the numerous Indo-European words designating 'high mountains' and 'heights.' This picture of the "original" Proto-Indo-European landscape naturally rules out those flat regions of Europe where there are no large mountain ranges, that is, the northern part of central Eurasia and the whole of eastern Europe, including the region north of the Black Sea.

Data about Indo-European names for trees and plants which agree with the characteristics of a mountain landscape for the original Indo-European homeland, situate it in the comparatively more southern regions of the Mediterranean area in the broad sense, which includes the Balkans and the northern part of the Near East (Asia Minor, the mountain regions of Upper Mesopotamia, and adjoining areas).

This relatively southern character of the ecological environments of the original Indo-European homeland, proposed on the basis of data on the geographic landscape and plant life, is supported by an analysis of the Proto-Indo-European names for animals.

The conclusion that the original homeland could not have been in central and eastern (excepting southeastern) Europe as deduced on the basis of evidence about the landscape and ecological habitat concurs with cultural and historical data on domestic animals and cultivated plants with which the ancient Indo-Europeans must have been acquainted. The terminology of agriculture is persuasive evidence supporting the possible location of the Indo-European group in regions with highly developed (in the fourth millennium B.C. and earlier) agriculture, that is, in the southern territories extending from the Balkans to Iran. The presence of a developed terminology for agriculture and viticulture rules out the more northern regions of Europe.

An especially valuable indicator for establishing the original place where the ancient Indo-Europeans lived and locating the original Indo-European homeland is Indo-European terminology for transportation - the names of wheeled vehicles. The names of metal ('bronze'), necessary for making wheeled vehicles from the hardwoods of the mountain forests, and draught power ('horse') - which one must postulate for the period of the Proto-Indo-European language, that is, in the fourth millennium B.C. This entire complex of data again restricts the territory of the original distribution of the Indo-European language to the region from the Balkans to the Near East and the Transcaucasus, up to the Iranian plateau and southern Turkmenia. According to archaeological data, the manufacture of wheeled vehicles dates from around the fourth millennium B.C. The original area of their distribution is accepted to be the area from the Transcaucasus to Upper Mesopotamia. Wheeled vehicles spread from the place of their inception in the Near East to the Volga-Ural region, the region north of the Black

Sea, the Balkans, and Central Europe. This time also marks the beginning of the Bronze Age in the Near East. The very same territory is one of the possible regions where the horse was domesticated or, in any case, to which the domesticated horse and its use as a draught animal had spread. The extensive Proto-Indo-European terminology for transport vehicles, harnesses, and their parts, as well as 'horse' and 'bronze' are grounds for locating the original Indo-European homeland in the fourth millennium B.C. within the area indicated, from the Balkans (including the Near East and the Transcaucasus) as far as southern Turkmenia.

A reconstructed Proto-Indo-European lexicon for different semantic groups expressing fauna, flora, economy, and material culture allows us to outline the approximate geographical area within which the original Indo-European homeland might have been situated and from which the migration of the Indo-European tribes, leading to their distribution throughout the vast territory of Eurasia in historical times, must have begun. Evidence of another order, such as elements of spiritual culture reconstructed on the basis of linguistic data, as well as lexical borrowings and evidence of interaction of the Indo-European language with other languages, enables us to narrow this vast region of the possible original homeland of the Indo-Europeans even further, and to limit it to a more compact area. The Proto-Indo-European linguistic area should be located in that part of the region outlined above where interaction and contact between the Proto-Indo-European language and the Semitic and South Caucasian languages were possible, since these languages contain a whole stratum of lexical elements borrowed from one language to the other, and many complex structural features suggesting interaction between them over a long period of time.

The interaction of Proto-Indo-European with Proto-Semitic and Proto-Kartvelian (Caucasian) as well as certain ancient Near Eastern languages suggests a specific area in southwest Asia as the original Indo-European homeland where these contacts could have come about; this, of course, rules out the Balkans as a possible territory for the original distribution of Proto-Indo-European.

Territorial contacts between Proto-Indo-European and the Semitic and Kartvelian languages revealed in material on lexical borrowings fit in well with the time and space distribution of the Semitic and Kartvelian proto-language systems. The existence of Proto-Semitic must be dated to a period not later than the fourth millennium B.C., since by the middle of the third millennium B.C. the Semitic dialects (Akkadian, Eblaite) are already apparent and completely differentiated and developed. The Proto-Semitic area in the Near East must have been a specific region, where contacts of the Semitic languages with both the Indo-European proto-language system and the southern Caucasian system (Kartvelian) could have taken place.

A semantic analysis of the Proto-Indo-European lexicon and text fragments enables us to reconstruct the culture and social relations of the community which spoke Proto-Indo-European. The entire nature of Proto-Indo-European culture and social relations indicates that this culture was close to the ancient Eastern civilizations. This is an additional argument in favor of the thesis that the Proto-Indo-European homeland was in southern Asia, where the culture of the Proto-Indo-European community formed and developed in contact and in close interaction with the cultural areas of the peoples of the ancient Near East.

The Proto-Indo-European lexicon and reconstructed fragments of texts enable us to establish a relatively high level of material culture.

Various manifestations of a rather high level of spiritual activity can be reconstructed, in particular the metric forms and poetic language, as well as the ritual represented in the mythology and broad priestly terminology.

Not only is Proto-Indo-European mythology similar in type to the ancient Eastern mythological traditions, but its mythological motifs and imagery also have analogues in ancient Eastern mythologies, whose influence must have helped to shape the Proto-Indo-European mythological tradition. The presence of typological parallels and coincidences compel one to draw the conclusion that close interrelationships existed between the different mythological traditions within a common cultural area.

In the fourth and fifth millennia B.C., in which we have hypothetically dated the existence of the Indo-European proto-language and, accordingly, of Proto-Indo-European society, before the beginning of the major migrations, this entire set of cultural and socio-economic features was typologically characteristic of the early civilizations of the ancient Near East. Proto-Indo-European culture belongs typologically to the family of archaic Near Eastern civilizations.

The determination of the area of the original distribution of the Proto-Indo-European language, and, correspondingly, the tribes who spoke it, raises the question as to which archaeological culture in southwest Asia might be identified with the Proto-Indo-European culture.

It should be noted at the outset that the original area of distribution indicated for the Proto-Indo-European language in the fourth - fifth millennia B.C. does not have an archaeological culture which might be identified in any explicit way with Proto-Indo-European. One can only speak of possible connections, direct or indirect, between Near Eastern Archaeological cultures of that period and the Indo-European. These ties between ancient archaeological cultures and reconstructed attributes of Proto-Indo-European spiritual and material culture might serve as indirect evidence of the possible identity between these cultures. It seems to us that within the outlined areas in southwest Asia corresponding to the area of original distribution of the Proto-Indo-European language in the fifth to fourth millennia B.C. and earlier, a number of archaeological cultures are found, which in some of their features are very similar to the Proto-Indo-European culture reconstructed on the basis on linguistic material.

It is very revealing that these conclusions about the original homeland of the Proto-Indo-Europeans in southwest Asia reached mainly on linguistic grounds, on the basis of a semantic analysis of the proto-lexemes by the method of "linguistic paleontology of culture," have been fully corroborated and enhanced by solid archaeological evidence furnished by Professor Colin Renfrew in his recent book on *Archaeology and Language. The Puzzle of Indo-European Origins*, London, 1987. Professor Renfrew argues that the Proto-Indo-Europeans should be located in ancient Anatolia at an early date (around the VII millennium B.C.) with their later westward and eastward expansions as a result of the population growth caused by the development of farming.

That the Proto-Indo-Europeans were good farmers can be demonstrated on the evidence of their reconstructed language and vocabulary, and Colin Renfrew suggests that it was the Indo-Europeans who brought farming culture to Europe.

However, I cannot share Colin Renfrew's skepticism concerning the possibility of a cultural and material reconstruction mainly on linguistic and lexical evidence, if the linguistic analysis is properly carried out and all extralinguistic factors taken duely into account.

The coincidence of our views concerning the original homeland of the Indo-Europeans and the Indo-European origins is a clear demonstration of the validity of both linguistic and archaeological approaches to the problem of the original habitat of the peoples with richly documented linguistic evidence.

The migrations of the speakers of the different dialects into new habitats may have taken place both in the form of a gradual penetration of the new ethnic element in comparatively small groups into the local population, as well as by the conquest of new areas and subjugation of the local population. The dialects brought by the migrating tribes to their new habitats may either have become absorbed by the languages of the local populations, leaving a few traces of their structure and vocabulary as a superstratum in the surviving, old languages of the autochtonous population; or they may have supplanted the ancient local languages of the autochtonous population and become the language of the land. In the latter case, the vestiges of local dialects of the autochtonous population appear as a substratum, leaving traces, sometimes very considerable, throughout the entire structure and lexicon of the new dialects brought by the tribes who had migrated to the new habitat.

The substrata influences can bring about considerable transformations in the original structure and phonetic composition of the dialects brought into the new regions, causing them to diverge from their original structure. In similar instances, where a new language spreads into areas that had been occupied by migrating tribes, the old local population with which the newly arrived tribes have assimilated will, practically speaking, adopt this new language.

Another instance of the diffusion of a new language into areas to which its speakers have migrated would be the expulsion of the local population from its ancient habitat and the settling of the vacated lands by the speakers of the new languages. Each of these types of interaction between languages is correlated with analogous types of culture and anthropological contact between the speakers of these dialects and, in particular, with the mixing or supplanting of certain anthropological types. Thus, for example, in cases where languages spread into new territories and the old local population is expelled we see a simple penetration of the new cultural and anthropological type into these regions from the regions originally inhabited by the speakers of these languages, while when the newly arrived population is assimilated by the previous local inhabitants this process will be less explicitly reflected in cultural and anthropological innovations.

The historical distribution and routes of migration of the principal ancient Indo-European ethnic groups who first appear in ancient written records - the Hittite-Luwians, Indo-Iranians, and Greeks (the Mycenaean Greeks and the Achaeans of Hittite sources) - can be explained more easily if one assumes that the territory of the original Indo-European homeland coincided with a region contained within eastern Anatolia, the southern Caucasus, and northern Mesopotamia in the fourth to fifth millennia B.C.

The most ancient linguistic community to become differentiated from the Proto-Indo-European language and to continue an independent existence in isolation from the latter must be considered the Anatolian dialectal group and Tocharian, as is evident from the pattern of dialectal division of the original Proto-Indo-European language. The displacement of the Proto-Anatolian group relative to the original territory of the Proto-Indo-European language was comparatively minor. This also accounts for the exceptionally archaic features of the Anatolian languages. In the historical period, Anatolian languages (Cuneiform Hittite, Luwian, and Palaic) were already widely spread in Asia Minor in the central regions of Anatolia.

This distribution of Anatolian dialects in the central regions of Anatolia was apparently the result of the movement of speakers of Anatolian dialects from east to west. At the beginning of the historical period, the movement of the Hittites from east to west (and later from north to south) may be assumed on the basis of Hittite historical sources.

After the differentiation of the Proto-Anatolian and Tocharian dialectal groups from the Proto-Indo-European language, the Greek-Armenian-Aryan dialectal group must have emerged from the Proto-Indo-European language system, and then later have broken up into the Greek, Proto-Armenian, and Indo-Iranian dialects. The extensive migrations of tribes which affected this dialectical community evidently began after it had broken up into separate dialects and Greek, Armenian, and Indo-Iranian had emerged as discrete Indo-European dialects. The break-up of this linguistic community evidently began with the formation of an Aryan dialectal area within the Proto-Indo-European language system while Armenian-Greek dialectal unity still persisted.

After the separation of Indo-Iranian from the Greek-Armenian-Aryan dialectal area, the Greek-Armenian dialect remained for a time in its old territory, and may have come in contact there with other Indo-European dialects, in particular with Tocharian and Ancient European. It may have been during this same period, when the Greek-Armenian community existed as an independent entity, that the structural and lexical isoglosses common to Greek and Armenian emerged.

The hypothesis that the original homeland of the Indo-European language was in southwest Asia naturally defines the direction of migration of the speakers of Greek dialects across Asia Minor to their historical habitats in the Peloponnesus and the islands of the Aegean Sea. If it is assumed that the migration of the speakers of the Greek dialects was across Asia Minor, traces of these early migrations might be found in early data on the Greeks in Miletus and Ahhijawa. Evidence of this is also provided by connections discovered between archaeological cultures in western Asia Minor, on the one hand, and the Peloponnesus and the Aegean Island, on the other.

The hypothesis that the Greeks came to mainland Greece from the east across Asia Minor also puts the question of the Greek "colonies" in Asia Minor, and especially the problem of Miletus, in a new light. In the light of the eastern hypothesis, these "colonies" may be regarded as very early Greek settlements established along the path of migration of the Greek tribes to their historical habitat on the Aegean Island and the mainland Greece.

If we assume a southwest Asian homeland for the Indo-Europeans, there was presumably a comparatively minor displacement of Proto-Armenian within the area of

Asia Minor, where it might have come in contact with the Anatolian languages. Subsequently, Proto-Armenian spread into historical Armenia, into the Armenian uplands, and became superimposed on a Hurrian-Urartian substratum.

The eastern borderlands of the Proto-Indo-European territory - the northern part of the Iranian plateau must have been a historical territory of the Indo-Iranian language. According to archaeological data, the appearance of Indo-Iranian tribes in the north of Iran must date from the first half of the third millennium B.C. The gray pottery which appears in this period in northern Iran is comparable to the gray Minyan pottery from western Anatolia. The first waves of Aryans must have passed from here through Afghanistan and then further eastward into northwestern India.

It must be assumed that various Aryan dialects, one of which has been documented in Mitannian Aryan in the middle of the second millennium B.C., were spread out south of the Caucasus in the original territory of the Indo-European tribes as early as the end of the fourth and in the third millennium B.C. The speakers of these dialects, who had chariots and horses, could make the long migrations both to the east, which brought some of them to Afghanistan and historical India, and to the west (the Mitannian Aryans), north, and south. The northern migrations may also have brought some Aryan tribes across the Transcaucasus to the northern Caucasus.

The archaic hymns of the Rigveda provide evidence of the differentiation of a special dialect group which later constituted the beginnings of the Iranian languages, alongside other groups within the Indo-Iranian linguistic community. These hymns contain several Iranian hydronyms and toponyms of southeastern Iran and Afghanistan and proper names which already have specifically Iranian phonetic characteristics.

The Iranian-speaking tribes, especially the eastern Iranians, made intensive migrations across Central Asia and the norther Caspian steppes. The earliest evidence of migrations of Iranian-speaking tribes across Central Asia toward the north and west may be seen in the numerous loanwords in the Finno-Ugric languages. These Finno-Ugric words should be interpreted as early Iranian, and not as Aryan or even less as Old Indic loans. A phonetic analysis of these Finno-Urgic forms links them to the linguistic features characteristic of the early Iranian dialect directly after it became differentiated from the Aryan dialectal group.

The early Iranian borrowings in Finno-Urgic indicate that the Iranian-speaking tribes became differentiated from Proto-Indo-Iranian at a quite early period, evidently as early as the end of the third millennium B.C., and that some of these tribes moved in a northwesterly direction along a path which the Iranian-speaking tribes were later to travel a number of times, leaving their traces in the late Iranian loan words in the Finno-Ugric languages (cf. Middle Iranian and Late Iranian loan words). These early migrations of the Iranian-speaking tribes to the north and then to the northwest followed their migrations from an original region of habitation in Central Asia, whence they must have spread further to the north and northwest, and also perhaps to the south toward Afghanistan.

The dialects of tribes speaking Tocharian became differentiated rather early from Proto-Indo-European and continued to exist along with other dialects of the Indo-European linguistic community in the original territory of the Indo-European tribes in southwest Asia (cf. the later Kutians and Tukres). It was in this period that the isoglosses of Tocharian may have emerged, linking it to the dialect areas comprising

Anatolian, Italic, and Celtic. However, even before Italic and Celtic became differentiated from the proto-language, the Tocharian dialect area must have become differentiated from the Anatolian as a result of the migrations of the speakers of the Tocharian dialects from their original habitations toward the east in the direction of Central Asia. The Tocharian dialects were evidently the first and earliest waves of migrations (preceding even the Indo-Iranian migrations) toward the east from the original homeland of the Proto-Indo-European language in southwest Asia.

The early presence of speakers of the Tocharian dialects in the East, in the region of Central Asia, on their way to eastern Turkestan, is attested by several Tocharian loanwords in the Finno-Urgic languages. This route is assumed to have been traversed also by the speakers of the Ancient European dialects - Celto-Italic, Germanic, and Balto-Slavic. All these languages have a number of lexical isoglosses in common with Tocharian which are very difficult to explain without assuming contacts, probably in process of joint migrations of the speakers of these languages together with the speakers of the Tocharian languages.

The speakers of the Tocharian dialects from Central Asia later moved further to the east toward eastern Turkestan and are found there when these languages begin to be recorded. The remaining "Ancient European" dialects moved across Central Asia and the Volga region toward the west into historical Europe. This eastern route of migrations of the "Ancient European" dialects also accounts for certain lexical ties between the western group of Indo-European languages and the Altaic group, from which they borrowed some specific terms such as, e.g., *mork$^{/h/}$ - 'horse.'

Evidence of the migration of speakers of the Ancient European dialects across Central Asia toward the west is provided, evidently, by the presence of Indo-European lexical borrowings in Finno-Ugric, the source of which may be considered to be the "Ancient European" dialects. The "Ancient European" dialects must have been a language group which was still poorly differentiated into individual dialects during the period of migration of their speakers and in the process of their movement westward from Central Asia. This group was characterized by a number of lexical innovations in comparison to other Indo-European dialects which had already become differentiated by this time. Such innovations of "Ancient European" dialects have to do basically with lexical semantics. They are manifested in the use of ancient words in new meanings specific to this dialect group, and in the appearance of certain new words not represented in the other Indo-European dialects.

The movement of the "Ancient European" dialects across Central Asia with a subsequent orientation toward western Eurasia evidently took place in the form of repeated waves of migrations from the east to western Eurasia, where these tribes later settled and populated some common territory. The newly arrived tribes united with the tribes already settled on this territory and thus formed a common interim area for the Indo-European tribes who migrated from the east and later populated the more westerly regions of Europe. This common interim area became a region for contacts and the reassociation of Indo-European dialects which had earlier become partly separated from one another.

This interaction may be seen as an example of the emergence of a second language union among originally related dialects. The spread of dialects from this second common area (in certain sense, the second interim homeland of tribes who spoke the various dialects) to a new territory in Central and Western Europe laid the basis for the gradual emergence of discrete languages (Italic, Celtic, Germanic, Balto-Slavic).

Consequently, the area north of the Black Sea region and the Volga steppes may be considered the basic common (although secondary) homeland for the "Ancient European" languages. The theory of Marija Gimbutas which situates the original home of the Indo-Europeans in this region thus takes on new import as a hypothesis concerning the homeland of the western group of Indo-European languages. This interim area of joint habitation for tribes who spoke ancient Indo-European dialects may have served as a region through which various waves of migrations of Indo-Europeans passed. It was here that the secondary isoglosses were formed and superimposed on the old ones, uniting these dialects with other Indo-European languages whose speakers had migrated from their original habitations in other directions.

These views on the Proto-Indo-European habitat in southwest Asia and the Indo-European migrations have been put forth by us as early as 1972* and later elaborated upon in diverse publications.** Our work in this direction is summed up in the aforementioned joint monograph of 1984 which contains also a semantic vocabulary of the reconstructed Common-Indo-European lexemes. This semantic vocabulary served as a substantive basis for inquiry into the problems of the original homeland, areal contacts, and possible prehistoric migrations of the Proto-Indo-European speaking tribes.

---

*S. our joint two-volume monograph: Th. V. Gamkrelidze, V.V. Ivanov, *Indo-European and the Indo-Europeans*. A Reconstruction and historical typological analysis of a Protolanguage and a Proto-Culture (in Russian), 2 vols., Tbilisi 1984; an English translation is forthcoming in Mouton de Gruyter.

*cf. Th.V. Gamkrelidze, V.V. Ivanov, Problema opredelenija pervonacal, noj territorii obitanija i putej migracij nositelej dialektov obsceindoevropejskogo jazyka (<<Konferencija po Sravnitel' no-Istoriceskoj grammatike Indoevropejskix jazykov, 12-14 dekabrja. Predvaritel' nye materialy, Moskva 1972): On the problem of localization of the original homeland and determination of migrations of the speakers of Proto-Indo-European dialects (Conference on the Historical Comparative Grammar of the Indo-European Languages. Moscow 1972).

**cf. T.V. Gamkrelidze, V.V. Ivanov, Near Eastern linguistic and historico-cultural data on the Proto-Indo-European language, its time of use and area of diffusion ("Vestnik Drevney Istorii", 1980, N3:3-27); Migrations of the Indo-European speaking tribes from their homeland in the Near East to the historical places of their habitation in Eurasia ("Vestnik Drevney Istorii", 1981, N2:11-33). The English translation of these articles appeared in 1983 in "Soviet Studies in History." The Indo-European problem: Recent Soviet contributions (Guest editor: Marvin A. Powell, Northern Illinois University), v.XXII, N1-2, Summer. Fall 1983:7-52 and 53-95.

ARCHAEOLOGY AND LINGUISTICS: SOME PRELIMINARY ISSUES

Colin Renfrew

Many historical linguists will feel it inappropriate - an impertinence even - that someone from another discipline, someone not well versed in the field of linguistics, should challenge some of the central tenets widely held by various specialists in the field of what has come to be known as Indo-European studies.

It was one of the outstanding inter-disciplinary features of the Bellagio Conference that this view was certainly not expressed. Indeed, while it may privately have been felt by a few of those present, an entirely different spirit prevailed, one in which basic assumptions could be re-appraised. Certainly I came to see more clearly some of the difficulties in the linguistic field for the alternative thesis which I have been propounding. In this short resume, however, it will be more appropriate to develop, concisely, some of the points set out in *Archaeology and Language*[1]. Many of them were taken up in discussion and will no doubt be examined again in the other papers.

There are several general points which merit, I believe, thorough re-examination. In a sense these are more important, certainly of wider validity, than the specific thesis which I offer on the Indo-European problem: namely the correlation of the distribution of an early Proto-Indo-European language with a "wave of advance" spread of a farming economy from Anatolia. These points are (a) the autonomy of the linguistic data, (b) the need for an accompanying historical reality, (c) the problem of chronology in the linguistic field, (d) the appropriate use of archaeology to aid in the reconstruction of the needed historical reality, (e) the risk that the products of research in the field of mythology may come into conflict with that "historical reality," and the appropriate resolution of this conflict.

A. The autonomy of the linguistic approach

A central problem in the field of historical linguistics is the autonomy, the independence of the linguistic data: they prove difficult to relate to other data that are not themselves purely linguistic.

Relations between languages can be asserted and defined, and language groups may be established through studies of phonology and grammar as well as vocabulary. In order, however, to set these observations into a historico-linguistic framework, it is necessary to make various assumptions. Indeed a necessary preliminary is to employ some model for linguistic change. One model has dominated this field for more than a century, and especially since the Neo-Grammarian formulation of Brugmann. This model has the great merit of establishing a clear methodology for linguistic reconstruction. By assuming that a significant change is mainly of one kind - through divergence from a shared common ancestor - a clear program is established for the historical linguist of recreating that ancestral tongue through the 'comparative method.' In doing so, other processes of change are not denied: loan words can be accommodated within the model and phenomena of convergence, for instance through the emergence of chance similarities, and the development of others through contact, are permissible. But seen from the standpoint of neo-grammarian historical linguistics, these are in effect secondary phenomena.

This situation, it might be argued, sets the pattern for all subsequent discussion. Indeed I am very much aware that it has set the pattern for my own. It would have been a more radical approach on my part, and perhaps a more constructive one, to break out of the mold of this kind of historical linguistics which seems inseparable from the primacy of a *Stammbaum* model. In my book I referred briefly to the proposal by Trubetzkoy of an alternative approach where *convergence* rather than divergence would be the dominant process and where the *Stammbaum* model would be relegated to a secondary position. Interestingly enough this point has been among those most brusquely dismissed by the critics of my book. As one of these (P. Baldi[2]) has put it:

> "This paper by the otherwise redoubtable Trubetzkoy was a footnote to a distinguished career as a theoretical phonologist and general linguist, and it cannot be taken to represent anything but his own thoughts on the matter.
>
> What Renfrew fails to recognize is that linguistic convergence theories are not scientifically provable because they cannot be put to the test of the comparative method. That is not to say that convergence doesn't happen but to point out that the methodologies by which such theories are addressed are quite different."

This comment underlines how far the comparative method (which seems inseparable from a family tree model for linguistic change) has come to dominate thought, to the extent that other approaches are 'not scientifically provable' because they are incompatible with it. Of course it is not my intention to belittle the work that has indeed been undertaken using other models for change, not least the wave model. It is precisely here that important developments may come. But despite such work I am not aware of any coherent historical scenario in the field of Indo-European linguistic studies which offers in the last analysis an alternative to the *Stammbaum* model. That model carries with it the inescapable accompaniment of an *Ursprache* and an *Urheimat*. I count it among the greatest limitations of my own position that I have escaped neither. For although the socio-cultural models for change which I have set out (see below) are, I hope, somewhat more coherent than the rather naive migration model which they seek to replace, they do not escape reliance upon this dominant model of historical linguistics whereby the primary process of linguistic change is divergence of family tree type.

Of course it is precisely the limitations of a non-linguist which restrict me to the use of the dominant existing model. But this should not blind one to the opportunities which remain for an explanation much closer in spirit to that of Trubetzkoy. It is, for instance, well established that most of the areas of Europe and Asia were inhabited already in Upper Palaeolithic times. A coherent explanation in terms of convergence might seek to reflect the underlying cultural unities in the Upper Palaeolithic occupation over much of this area in linguistic terms also. Successive phases of interaction over thousands of years would account for many of the linguistic features observed. Such a view would not need to rule out episodes of migration, nor the working of *divergence processes* alongside the primary explanatory elements of community of origin in the Upper Palaeolithic (note, again, the hint of *Urvolk* and *Ursprache* contained there), and of *convergence processes* over several millennia. (The chronological issues raised are touched on in (c) below).

But for an archaeologist to attempt such a task would be even more foolhardy than my own modest attempt, which ultimately succumbs to the dominant position of the comparative method and its *Stammbaum Theorie* implications. Models of linguistic change must be developed by linguists - that is also implied by the term "autonomy." But until such models escape the stigma of the view that "linguistic convergence theories" are not scientifically (or epistemologically) different we shall have to continue to work within a divergence framework and thus maintain the quest for both *Ursprache* and *Urheimat*.

B. The need for an accompanying historical reality

It is helpful, I believe, to see that the linguistic realm just mentioned, and the concrete historical reality of real persons living in determined places at different times, are different worlds. Both are constructs, reached by processes of inference from data observed in the present.

Naturally the archaeologist will see the methods of archaeology as the most appropriate for reaching the "historical reality" in question. That point is considered further in (D) below. But we should not forget that the methods of archaeological reconstruction were not applied in this field until about the time of Kossinna (in 1902). Moreover, it is not inaccurate to say that in the field of Indo-European studies all the historical models hitherto employed have been of a rather simplistic migrationist nature.

The more general point is that, whether or not we are relying heavily upon the methods of archaeology, we are entitled to ask that whatever reconstruction is offered be expressed in coherent historical terms - we are entitled to ask *where* and *when*. Certainly previous archaeological explanations, such as those of Childe and Gimbutas, have been very positive in these respects. But others have been much more vague, and sometimes this vagueness has, at least superficially, added to the plausibility of their explanations.

This criticism could no doubt be levelled at a number of historical linguists. But it is particularly of the work of the late Georges Dumezil and his followers that I am thinking. His vast edifice of mythological reconstruction is based upon the assertion of a shared common origin for the greater part of the mythology (and social structure) for most Indo-European-speaking peoples. But nowhere does he come out and say *where* and *when* this shared experience is to be situated. If he had in fact done so, the implausibility of any of the resulting scenarios which he might have offered would have done damage to his credibility. Instead he appears to have operated in a different world again, separate from a concrete notion of where and when, whose properties are determined solely by the myths and by the social structures which he is considering. It is a dream world standing apart from the constraints and the minutiae of the here and the now (or the there and the then), which has with it some of the timelessness of the Arthurian legend, or of "the fable" in the perspective of the poet Edwin Muir. But while such a perception is illuminating in the work of a poet, to ask from a scholar for more concrete particulars within what purports to be a scholarly discipline is not mere pedantry.

It is no reproach to the historical linguist that the relations and conclusions established by his or her discipline are primarily linguistic: each discipline operates first within its own autonomous field. But the next stage must be to relate this by some explicit means to a more concrete historical reality. Chronology is a central issue.

C. The problem of chronology in the linguistic field

Historical linguistics is about linguistic relationships. In favorable cases it may be possible to arrange these within some temporal sequence. But it should be noted that in most cases such a conclusion can only be reached by making prior assumptions (such as the almost ubiquitous acceptance of the comparative method and the accompanying *Stammbaum* model). There seems nothing, however, in the patterns of linguistic change which would allow the establishment of any kind of absolute chronology.

The contrary, of course, was asserted with dramatic effect by Morris Swadesh, whose exposition of glottochronology had so great an impact in the 1960s. But the notion that all formerly homogeneous languages diverge, once separation has occurred, at a determined and absolute rate has since been almost universally criticized. And one can see why. There is absolutely no prior expectation that such a uniformity should exist. It does not achieve authority by being deduced from some larger explanatory framework, as do many of the laws of physics. But if it is merely an empirical generalization it has two limitations. First, it has not been demonstrated on the basis of a large number of well-argued cases. And secondly, if it is merely a generalization from a few cases, without an accompanying framework of reasoning, there is no special reason to expect it to apply in other cases also.

These epistomological criticisms have always seemed to me so self-evident that demonstration by counter-example of the fallaciousness of the Swadesh "law" is almost superfluous. Why on earth *would* languages diverge at so uniform a rate?

These criticisms have been widely expressed, and so far no critic of my own book has rallied to the defense of glottochronology. Indeed some have argued that in criticizing it I have been in effect flogging a dead horse, and could better have omitted reference to so discredited a field.

Yet there is a curious phenomenon here which merits very close attention. For in some cases it is those same austere critics of glottochronology who make objection to the hypothesis which I have formulated precisely upon chronological grounds. I think that this apparent contradiction would repay further examination.

My own hypothesis proposes the existence of a Proto-Indo-European language in central and eastern Anatolia as early as 7,000 BC, and the transmission of a form of this language to Greece by 6,500 BC through the slow spread of a farming economy carried by individuals, none of which needs to have travelled more than 20 or 30 kilometers on land (although some did indeed have to make the sea crossing of the Aegean). The comparable movements of successive generations of the growing population of farmers would have carried a farming economy, and a form of Proto-Indo-European language to the shores of Britain by about 4,000 BC. This hypothesis, as noted above, while avoiding mass migrations and long-distance movements, does not avoid the basic *Stammbaum* formulation of the comparative method. And it puts an early date upon the divergences involved. The Proto-Celtic language would be separate from Proto-Greek or Proto-Anatolian by 4,000 BC, and so forth. Of course, when neighboring territories are in question, there need not be so early a date of divergence, and the interaction of the Proto-Greek with the Proto-Anatolian languages could be almost indefinitely prolonged. But when we are speaking of more remote areas and language-speakers (e.g. Celts and Tocharians) the implications are clear.

Now one very interesting aspect of the reactions to this view is that many linguists have commented that these proposed dates of separation are "too early." But how, in the light of the foregoing discussion, and of their own almost universal condemnation of glottochronology, do they know this, or judge this?

There are, of course, some who base their conclusions upon the findings of linguistic palaeontology, when reliance upon various key words selected from the reconstructed Proto-Indo-European proto-lexicon, such as those for 'wheel' or 'horse' can indeed, when related to the archaeological data, offer a date in absolute years. But the date comes from the archaeology not from the linguistics. Yet many linguists today look with considerable caution (and very properly so) upon the small congeries of terms which forms the nub of the paleontological argument[3].

There appear to be unstated assumptions, made by many linguists, about unspecified regularities in the rates of innovation and change among dialects or languages formerly homogeneous but subsequently isolated one from another. It may indeed be plausible that language A, which separated early (at time t_1)

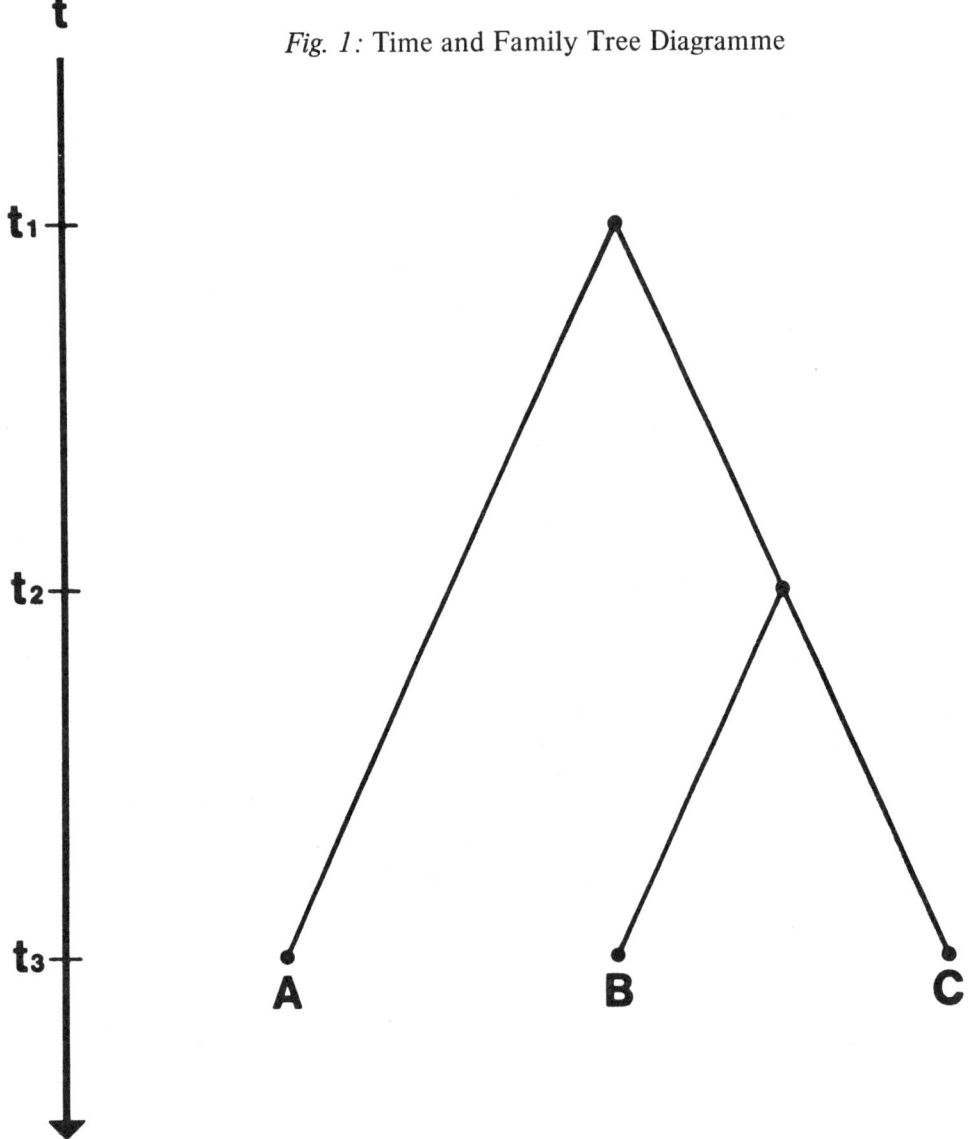

Fig. 1: Time and Family Tree Diagramme

should differ more from language C than does language B. Such a prediction is based on notions of relative similarity and difference rather than of an absolute rate of change which mars glottochronology. But in fact the *relative* chronology itself depends on assumptions of constant rate as much as would an absolute one. For if language A has evolved slowly between t_1 and t_3 and language C likewise between t_2 and t_3 while language B has undergone rapid change between t_2 and t_3, the converse could be true, and C could be more closely similar to A than it is to B. If we abandon assumptions about approximately constant rates of language change, then such assertions, even relative ones, are not necessarily valid. Of course it may appear entirely reasonable to suggest that languages which are very close in their vocabularies have only recently become isolated one from another. But given the widespread rejection of glottochronology *per se*, to accept this without examining the underlying assumptions appears to lack rigor.

D. The appropriate use of archaeology

In my book I argue that the earlier equation:

culture = people (ethnos) = language

should be abandoned. The archaeological 'culture' is an artificial construct, and 'ethnicity' is not lightly to be assumed.

Instead I argue that we can seek to investigate the relationship between:

change in material culture	social and demographic change	language change

It is desirable to be explicit about the kinds of change envisaged. More specifically I argue that *language replacement* within a given area can be approached using a number of models. All homeland models for a given group of languages (and therefore all *Stammbaum* models for such groups) assume language replacement (unless the territories in question were not populated at all prior to the dispersal of the Proto-language).

The principal models for social/demographic change which are offered as likely to accompany language displacement are:

(i)   subsistence/demography model

(ii)   elite dominance

(iii)   system collapse.

But others could be offered, including the development of a pidgin language as a tribe language over a wide tract of country, and its subsequent foundation for the emergence of a number of related creole languages[4].

It is my argument that the use of this kind of reasoning is the only way by which the archaeologist may reach toward the kind of historical reality which could also be intelligible in linguistic terms. Instead, I would go so far as to say that without some such reasoning of this kind, some clear awareness of the *kind* of archaeological evidence which we may be seeking, there can be no hope of arriving at a coherent view of Indo-European origins.

In my book I apply one specific version of the subsistence/demography model, namely the Wave of Advance model proposed by A. Ammerman and L. Cavalli-Sforza. Some commentators have observed that the use of a single model of this kind is an over-simplification. But there need be no disagreement on that point: it is the function of a model to simplify and, in a sense, to oversimplify. What I have tried to do is to explain in this way the very widespread distribution in Europe of the Indo-European languages. To explain in detail all the particularities of the linguistic map would require a series of subsidiary explanations depending, it may well be, upon other models also.

That rejoinder is not, of course, a reply to those archaeologists who feel that the Wave of Advance model is less appropriate for western and northern Europe than it is for central and southeastern Europe. Nor does it deal with the central objection to my proposal, namely that the various broad relationships between the principal Indo-European language groups do not conform well geographically to the spatial relationships generated by the Wave of Advance. That seems to me a substantial and significant problem. But it is a difficulty which applies also to earlier explanations for the Indo-European language distribution.

But I would continue to argue that there can be no alternative to the use of coherent and explicit models. For the processes of change involved have to be faced, and therefore they have to be made explicit. That is all that model-building would claim to do.

E. Mythology and historical reality

The field of mythology like that of historical linguistics has difficulties with chronology. The point has been made earlier that a grasp of the underlying historical reality is essential. Although Dumezil evidently saw no need of a firm chronological framework within which to set the origin of the supposed relationships which he proposed, his whole edifice of inference without such a grasp is set upon shaky foundations.

It is, however, with another point in the field of mythology, introduced by Professor Marija Gimbutas at the Bellagio Conference, that I wish to deal. This is the supposed hiatus in linguistic as well as mythological terms between the neolithic and chalcolithic of South East Europe on the one hand and the succeeding bronze age on the other. Professor Gimbutas has drawn attention with very good effect to the rich symbolic complex seen in the neolithic and chalcolithic archaeology of Greece, Bulgaria, Romania, Yugoslavia, Hungary and the Ukraine. With particular emphasis upon the terracotta figurines, she has coined the term "Old Europe" for the complex. She contrasts it with the succeeding early bronze age in these areas, which has indeed a different character. The latter she explains by the incursion from the east of her

"Kurgan" people, the supposed bearers of the Proto-Indo-European language, with its accompanying culture and mythology.

One may note first that in Pan-European terms these are relatively localized phenomena. But my own points here are different ones. They are, first, that a change in iconography does not necessarily betoken a profound change in the underlying belief system. And second that a change in belief system in no way need correlate with a change in language. So that while Professor Gimbutas may well be right in regarding the language of her Kurgan people as "Indo-European," there is no logic in the inference that the belief system of the previous "Old Europe" phase need be non Indo-European simply because its iconography is different from what follows. The term "Indo-European" is surely with propriety applied to languages. As soon as we use it as a classificatory term for belief systems, for mythologies, we are embarking upon a serious category error.

This point came through to me with particular clarity in a recent consideration of the prehistoric Aegean religions.[5] For many years archaeologists have stressed the various similarities between the religions of the Minoan and Mycenaean worlds. And while I, myself, would distinguish sharply between them, there are indeed relationships between the iconographies. Both show a predominance of female anthropomorphic images (only slightly rectified by the recent find of male figurines at Phylakopi in Melos). These have at times been regarded by Professor Gimbutas and others as the descendants of the allegedly female-oriented belief system of "Old Europe." But if so, what are we to make of the revelation that the Mycenaeans spoke an Indo-European (i.e. Greek) language?

In *The Archaeology of Cult*[5] I have suggested that we can see in the Aegean a whole series of religious *transformations* in which the iconography, and perhaps the underlying belief system, was re-structured. A series of such transformations can lead us from the early neolithic through to the religion of Classical Greece. And we may note in passing that succeeding transformations have brought the Christian religion from the Near East to Greece and modified it in various ways. It is now as securely "Indo-European" in its linguistic expression as its predecessor: while the Old Testament was first set in writing in a Semitic language, the New Testament was first written in Greek.

The underlying idea of religious and iconographic transformation - whether or not accompanied by outside influences - is the crucial one here. It merits closer consideration both from the religious and the iconographic standpoint. Without it we cannot expect the development of myths or of mythological systems to be understood properly. In particular it is difficult to see how a specific iconography or belief system can properly be designated as "non-Indo-European" without reliable *prior* information about the languages spoken by its adherents. Thus while I feel that Professor Gimbutas has greatly added to our knowledge of the period by her publication of the rich material of "Old Europe," it is for me difficult to see that her observations on this material bear significantly upon the Indo-European question. These are, of course, controversial matters, but that makes it all the more appropriate to concentrate upon the underlying methodology, the framework of inference. The Indo-European question is primarily a linguistic one, and can only be approached constructively if sufficient weight is accorded to the principle of linguistic autonomy asserted earlier. I have tried to discuss how the archaeological data may be brought into appropriate relationship with the linguistic data, and the task is evidently not an easy one. A comparable caution must surely be exercised when the rich field of mythology is to be used, either in relation to language or to archaeology. Until the appropriate methodology is established, assertions about either language or historical reality which are based upon data from the field of mythology cannot be regarded as well founded.

In conclusion I would like to remark that a very positive feature of the Bellagio Conference was a willingness to re-examine previously unquestioned assumptions. It is perhaps fair to say that the enterprise of relating linguistic data to archaeological data is a more difficult one than has hitherto been appreciated. Each field of enquiry has its own methodology, its own rigor indeed, well established after decades of research. But the task of moving with assurance from one field to the other has not yet been undertaken with sufficient caution or sufficient rigor. Real progress was made at the Conference towards recognizng and re-defining these problems. This may prove to be its lasting contribution in this difficult, indeed perilous, field.

FOOTNOTES

1. C. Renfrew, *Archaeology and Language: The Puzzle of Indo-European Origins*. London, Jonathan Cape 1987; New York, Cambridge University Press, 1988.
2. P. Baldi, CA Book Review of *Archaeology and Language* in *Current Anthropology* 29, 1988, 447.
3. R. Coleman has written (CA Book Review of *Archaeology and Language* in *Current Anthropology* 29, 1988, 450): "From all this it looks as if 'wheel' was not in the proto-lexicon and the various words for it were created independently after the dispersal, in some areas no doubt by loan-translation from adjacent Indo-European dialects/languages... . Here we might infer that the proto-lexicon contained several words for the animal [horse].... or that the animal was known only in some areas of Proto-Indo-European speech and the original word *ekwos* perhaps, was therefore dialectical and the others innovatory after the dispersal..... . A single root across the languages would be conclusive for the proto-lexicon; a multiplicity of roots is inconclusive either way."
4. See A. Sherratt, CA Book Review of *Archaeology and Language* in *Current Anthropology* 29, 1988, 461.
5. C. Renfrew, 1985, *The Archaeology of Cult, the Sanctuary at Phylakopi*, London, British School at Athens and Thames and Hudson.

Did Armenians Live in Asia Anterior Before the Twelfth Century B.C.?

Gevork B. Djahukian

(Linguistics Institute, Yerevan)

1. During the 19th century and the first decades of the 20th century the dominating view was that at the end of the 13th century and the beginning of the 12th century Armenians, among other "maritime peoples," most probably with Phrygians, came to Asia Minor from the Balkan peninsula, lived there till the 6th century B.C. and later settled in the area of Historical Armenia. On the basis of many facts and considerations an amendment was later made to this view that Armenians settled in the western part of Historical Armenia as early as the 12th-11th centuries B.C. Yet this correction also fails to account for some existing facts. There arises a necessity to reconsider the view that Armenians had appeared in Asia Anterior only at the end of the 13th century or in the beginning of the 12th century B.C.

2. On the basis of this view it is difficult to answer, for example, the following questions: (a) Is the similarity of the forms $Armanam^{KI}$, $Armanim^{KI}$ in the inscriptions of the third millennium of the Akkadian King Naram-Suen and that of $Armi^{KI}$ in the Ebla inscriptions with Urartian *Arme* and the form of *Armina* in the Bihistun inscription of Dareus the First completely accidental? (b) Why are Armenians not mentioned among maritime peoples? (c) Were Armenians close to Phrygians, as is supposed on the basis of the antique authors' data, and if so, why does the present-day science not reveal a close kinship of Armenian and Phrygian to the extent of forming one linguistic group?

3. The Hittite sources of the 14th-13th centuries B.C. mention a certain country Hayasa which presented a significant military force at the south-eastern borders of the Hittite state. Three different opinions concerning the tribes that had inhabited Hayasa come forth: (a) Hayasians were the ancestors of Armenians, and the name of their country was preserved in that of Armenians (K. Roth, K. Forrer, P. Kretchmer, G. Ghapantsian et al.); (b) Hayasians had nothing in common with Armenians, and the Armenian selfname *hay* originated from the form *Ḫate* (I.M. Diakonoff); (c) Hayasians spoke a Hittite-Luvian language, which has been

preserved as a substratum of Armenian (G. Djahukian). The recent examination of the Hayasian proper names led the author to the conclusion that the main inhabitants of Hayasa were Armenians.

In the Hayasian list consisting of about 40 items, there are anthroponyms, theonyms, and toponyms the Armenian parallels of which are rather convincing, being phonetically transitional between Indo-European forms and those occurring in Armenian dialects. In this case, too, the author holds the contention that while the presence of Hittite-Luvian, Hurrian, and, presumably, other language elements in Hayasian proper names is not enough evidence to prove the presence of the tribes speaking those languages (these elements might merely be accounted for by language contacts and borrowings), the presence of Armenian language elements can be explained only by the presence of Armenian tribes. Here certain parallels of the type are given together with the corresponding Indo-European archetypes: (1) *toponyms*: Hayas. *Hay(aša)* (*-aša* is the Hittite-Luvian toponyms) – Arm. *hay* < IE **poti-* 'master'; Hayas. *Az(z)i* – Arm. *az-* 'dry' (in the toponym *Azord* and the reduplicative forms *azazil* 'to dry' and *azazum* 'dried out') < IE **az-ĝh-* (from the root **as-* 'to burn'; cf. Gr. ἄζος 'dry' in the hydronym Ἄζων); Hayas. *Arziya* – Arms. *arc-* (in the words *arcatʻ* 'silver,' *arcarcel* 'to inflame,' *arcnel* 'to do poker-work,' and the toponyms *Arcak, Arcapʻ, Arcn, Arckē; Arziya* reveals correspondence with *Arcn*) < IE**arĝ-* 'white, bright'; Hayas. *Ingalawa* – Arm. *ən-kal ənd-kal-* (in the verb *ənkalul* 'to receive,' dial. 'to close,' 3rd p. aorist *ənkalaw*) **anti + *gwьl-* fr. IE **geu-* 'to bend') or *angł* (if *Ingalawa* corresponds to the name *Angł*); Hayas. -*hila* (in the toponym *Lahirhila*; cf. Hitt. *Haršanhila, Lumanhila, Paršanhila*, etc., as well as *Hilama, Hilamatiya*; along with the place names *Hulaniya, Hulanta, Hulina, Hularu, Aparhulu*, etc., it seems plausible that the Hitt. word *hila-* 'yard' is a borrowing from Armenian) – Arm. *hił, heł, hiwł* fr. *xuł* 'hut' (<**khu-lo-* fr. IE **keu-* 'to cover'); (2) *anthroponyms*: Hayas. *Aišiya* – Arm. *ayci* 'goat' (fr. IE **aiĝiyā* fr. **aiĝ-*; cf. *ayc* 'goat'); Hayas. *Aniya* – Arm. *hani* 'ancestor' (> Georg. *hani* 'ancestor'), later 'grandmother' (< [H]*aniya* Hayas. *Mariya* – Arm. *mari* 'she-bird' (< **mьriyā* or **mьriyā-* which is, perhaps, borrowed in Hurr. *Marianni* 'governor,' Urart. *mare* 'a nobleman'; the Hayasian word is likely to have had the same source); (3) *theonyms*: Hayas. *Terityituni* – Arm. *eri* < IE **tru-* 'three' and *ttun* 'tail' (**erttun* 'three-tailed'); Hayas. *Sililil* –

Arm. *siłeł* 'lover' (fr. **kei-i-* fr. IE **kei-* 'to lie; beloved,' the source of Arm. *sēr* 'love,' *sireli* 'beloved').

4. Different investigators, namely G. Ghapantsian, J. Shultheiss, G. Djahukian, J.A.C. Greppin, have revealed some Hittite-Luvian borrowings in Armenian that could not be explained merely by the influence of the Hittite-Luvian languages preserved after the 12th century B.C. and especially by Hieroglyphic Luvian. Quite recently we succeeded in showing some words of Hittite whose source might have been the Armenian (resp. Hayasa) language. All these facts are in favor of plausible direct contacts between Armenians and Hittite-Luvians before the 12th century B.C.

The source of the following Armenian words may be considered Hittite-Luvian languages: *brut* 'potter,' *brteay* 'made of clay,' *brtin* (dial.) 'clay' – Hitt. *purut* 'clay'; *cux, -oy* 'smoke'[1] – Hitt. *tuḫḫu(wa)i-* 'smoke'?; *dandiṙn* 'sepulchral darkness' (or 'putrescence'?) – Hitt. *dandu-* 'death'; *gorg* 'carpet' – Hitt. *kurka-* 'cover(ing)'l *hat-anel* 'cut (off)' – Hitt. *ḫattai-* 'cut (off); split'; *kštambel* (*kštamb* Instr. Case of *kuštn*) 'to reproach, to reprimand' M Hitt. *kušduwai-* 'to reproach, to reprimand'; *pʿax* 'flight, escape,' *pʿaxnul* 'to run away, to escape' M Hitt. *parḫ-* 'drive, chase,' *parḫanu-* 'chase'; *pʿšur* 'crumb, piece' – Hitt. *paršulli-* 'crumb, piece'; *šełj* (**selyo-*) 'heap (of grain)' – Hitt. *šeli-* 'heap of grain'; *xalam* 'animal scull' (*xalamovin* 'with the head') – Hitt. *ḫalanta* 'head'; *xaṙn* 'mixed,' *xaṙnel* 'to mix' – Hitt. *ḫarna-* 'to mix'; *xołxołel* 'to kill' – Hitt. *ḫulḫuliya-* 'to kill in war'; etc. The Arm. proper name *Mušeł* is an obvious borrowing from *Muršiliš*.

In the following cases the source of the Hittite words might have been the Armenian language: Arm. *art* 'field' (< **arc-* < **acr-* < IE **aǵros*) – Hitt. *arziya-* 'cultivated land,' Luv. *arziyašši-* "(name of a landpiece in Cappadocian texts)"; Arm. *asr* 'wool; fleece' (IE **pokur*) – Hitt. *ešri-* (*eššari-*) 'wool; fleece'; Arm. *hacʿ* 'bread' (**pokʷtu-* fr. IE **pekʷ-*) –

---

1. H. Adjarian (*HAB*) was not right suggesting a "Caucasian source for the Armenian word: Georg. *çuxwa* 'to grieve' and *mçuxri* 'twilight, dusk,' which express entirely different notions.

Hitt. *haz(z)it/da-* (a kind of pastry); Arm. *luc* 'yoke; weight, burden; hard labor' (IE **yugom*) – Hitt. *luzzi-* 'forced labour'; etc.

Along with mutual Hittite-Luvian-Armenian borrowings there is a considerable quantity of proper names in Hittite texts, having obvious Armenian parallels, which testifies to the presence of Armenians in Asia Minor and on its eastern borders. The assumption that the Armenian words *šant'/d* 'lightning' (**kwnti-* fr. IE *keu-* 'to shine; bright') and *loys*, Gen. *lusoy* 'light' (IE **leuk-*) form the base of the Asia-Minor deities *Šantaš* and *Lušiti-* is plausible; if the name of the deity *Zanduza* has the stem *Šand-*, as supposes E. Laroche (1947), the Arm. word *šant'oc'* can be reconstructed for it. It seems likely that the following deities, too, have Armenian origin: *Andaliya* (Earth God) – Arm. *and* 'field' (IE **andh-*), *andel* 'to till, to cultivate'; *Ḫuzziya* – *xuc'* 'cell' (**khu-sko-* fr. IE **(s)keu-* 'to cover'); *Šulutta* – Arm. *šołot* 'radiant' fr. *šoł* 'ray' (**kuol-* fr. IE **keu-* 'to shine; bright'); *Zukki* – Arm. *juk-n* 'fish' (IE **ǵhu-*); etc.

The following proper names may be of Armenian origin: *Aliwašu* – Arm. *ałues, -u* 'fox' < IE **əlōpeku-*; *Anni* (cf. Hayas. *Anniya*); *Arziuta* – Arm. *arciw, arcui* 'eagle' < IE **r̂ǵipiyo-*; the Armenian word was borrowed also in Urartian (*Arṣibedini* - a deity), Georgian (*arçiwi* 'eagle') and other Caucasian languages; *Tatta* – Arm. *t'at'* 'hand, paw,' as well as *T'a'* a proper name (also *T'at'ik, T'at'ul*), etc.

In the toponyms of Hittite texts the Armenian layer is considerable, too. Besides the above-mentioned Arm. *šant'/d* 'lightning' and *loys*, Gen. *lusoy*, that are met in certain toponyms principally via the corresponding theonyms (*Šantašara, Šantima, Tapašanta, Zarašantiya, Luša, Lušna, Tapiluša, Ziḫluša*), there are many parallels in hydronyms, oronyms and other toponyms, based on Armenian appellatives (esp. if the latter are of IE origin) or those borrowed by Armenian.

Hydronyms: *Alt/da, Alt/dani* – Arm. *ałt* 'dirt' (**ḷ-d-* fr. IE **el-*) or *aɫ-t* 'salt' (IE **sal-d-*), *Anzali* – *anc'* 'passage'; *Ululi* – Arm. *ołoł* 'flood' (IE **pel-*); *Wettiḫu* – Arm. *get* 'river' (IE **wed-* before the shift **w > g*), etc.

Oronyms: *Kapakapa* – Arm. *kap* 'tie, bond; connection; communication,' *kapan* 'pass, gorge, defile,' dial. *kap(a)kapel* 'to tie'; *Karna* – Arm. *K'ar*, pl. *k'arink'* 'stone' (IE **kar-* or **(s)ker-?*); *Kuntiya* – Arm. *kunt/d* 'bald' (IE **(s)ken-d-*); *Šunara* M Arm. *snar* 'mountain peak; nape; pillow' (**sunar*), etc.

Names of populated places: *Alatra* – Arm. *aṫal* 'to grind'; there is an Armenian toponym *Aṫori-kʻ* with a late shift *aw > o*); *Ankaliya* – Arm. *angł* 'vulture' (cf. the Arm. toponyms *Angł, Angełtun*); *Artuš, Artuk* – Arm. *art, -oy* 'field' (IE **aǵros*); *Aruna* – Arm. *ariwn* 'blood' (IE **esr̥-*; cf. the Arm. toponyms *Arun, Aruni, Arunkʻ*); *Hazka* M Arm. *hacʻ* 'bread' (**pokʷti-* fr. IE **pekʷ*; cf. the Arm. toponyms *Hacʻik, Hacʻkni*); *Karkar* – Arm. *karkaṙ* 'stone pile'; *Katarka* – Arm. *katar* 'summit, top'; *Kawarna* – Arm. *kawaṙn* 'channel, trench' (IE **geu-?*); *Palapalaša* – Arm. *płpłakʻar* 'big stone' (IE **bel-*); *Tala* – Arm. *tʻal* 'district, block'; *Tuḫupiya* – Arm. *tʻuxp* 'cloud'; *Urma* – Arm. *orm* 'wall' (**ork-mo-* along IE **arek-?*); *Zunaḫara* – Arm. *jiwn(a)har* 'snowbeaten' fr. *jiwn* 'snow' (IE **ǵhiiōm*) and *har-ul* 'to beat' (IE **per-*); etc.

5. Armenian has borrowed from Hurrian the words *anag* 'tin' (Hurr. *anagi* along Assyr. *anaku* and Sumer. *niggi, naggu*), *xnjor* 'apple' (Hurr. *ḫinzuri*), *nuṙn* 'pomegranate' (Hurr. *nuranti* fr. Akkad. *nurimdu*), etc. It is possible to suppose certain connection between the Hurr. *ḫai-* 'small' (along the proper Hurr. *zugi-* 'small') and the Arm. *hayk* 'small.'

6. A certain layer may be separated in the Armenian language directly or indirectly tracing back to the Akkadian language. Taking into consideration the fact that Old Akkadian has had no influence upon Armenian, we may date the Akkadian-Armenian contacts to XX-VII centuries B.C. Two sources of borrowings may be separated: the Akkadian colonies in Asia Minor. These Colonies must have been especially influential in the period when the country Hayasa existed. This will appear more probable if the proper name *Kamax*, supposedly attested in the Hayasian *Kamł*, really originates from the Akkad. *kimaḫ(ḫ)u(m)* (*gimāḫu*) 'grave' (there were graves of Armenian kings in Kamax), as suggested by H. Adjarian (2, 605); this word is preserved in the Arm. *kmax-kʻ* 'remains' and *kmaxi-kʻ* 'funeral cry.' From the other Akkadian borrowings in Armenian the following words are worth mentioning: *anawtʻ* 'vessel, furniture, instrument, weapon' (NAssyr. *anūtu(m)* along *unūtu(m), enūtu(m)* 'instrument, device; belonging; furniture'), *gagatʻn* 'peak' (Akkad. *k/qaqqadu(m)* 'head; upper part,' *knik* 'seal' (Akkad. *kanīku(m)* 'sealed document,' *kunukku(m)* 'seal'), *kšiṙ* 'scales; weight' Akkad. *gišrinnu(m)* 'scales'), *pʻox* 'loan' (Akkad. *pūḫ(m)* 'loan; substitution'), etc.

There are some Armenian borrowings in Akkadian. The Akkadian word for apricot and apricot-tree *armannu(m)* obviously goes back to the name of Armenian tribes (cf. the Syriac word for apricot *hazzūrā armənāyā* 'Armenian apple.' If the Arm. *xucʻ* 'cell' goes back to the *khu-sko- fr. IE *(s)keu- 'to cover' (cf. also *xuł* 'hut' fr. *khu-lo-) and *bołk* 'radish' goes back to the IE *bhel- 'to sprout,' which is also the source of *boł(ik)* 'sprout, bud' and *bołboj* 'bud,' it may be supposed that they were borrowed into Akkadian: *huṣṣu(m)* 'cane hut' and *pugla* 'radish' (cf. Aram. *pugla*).

7. The existence of a few Old Indic borrowings in Hurrian brought the scholars to the presumption that in the middle of the 2nd millennium B.C. Indian tribes lived in Asia Anterior. This gave rise to controversial opinions (cf. Mayrhofer, 1966; Kammenhuber, 1968; Diakonoff, 1970, 39-63; Mayrhofer, 1974). The above-mentioned borrowings, in connection with the Hayas. *Mariya*, Hurr. *mariyanni* 'nobleman' and Urart. *mare* 'nobleman' belong to this type. If Hayasian was a language where Old Indic words had penetrated and really is the oldest state of Armenian, Armenian words going back to Old Indic must have been preserved independently of Iranian. One of such words is, first of all, the Arm. *marmin* 'body' (OInd. *marman-* 'part of the body' originating from the IE *mel-*; the shift *l > r is not characteristic of Armenian). The words *jamb* 'food' and *jambel* 'to cut the food; to feed' should be included in this group, too (cf. OInd. *jámbha-* 'tooth; swallowing,' *jámbhatē* 'to snap at'). To this group belong also the words that, according to W. Porzig, had been borrowed in the middle of the 2nd millennium B.C. on the Northern coast of the Black Sea.

8. The famous Kartvelist H. Vogt contended that there were no Armenisms in Common Kartvelian and Georgio-Zanian, consequently in those periods there were no contacts between Armenians and Kartvelians, and Armenians still lived off the Caucasus. Glottochronological investigations show that the Common Kartvelian broke down approximately by the 19th century B.C., while the Georgio-Zanian unity broke down approximately by the 8th century B.C. [Klimov, 1964, 85]. A more detailed analysis shows that Vogt's contention is rather weak.

There is a considerable number of lexical correlations between Armenian, Georgian, and Zanian, which, at least partly, can be ascribed to the period of Georgio-Zanian unity, i.e. to the 18th-9th centuries B.C. There is also a small number of words common in Armenian, Georgian, Zanian, and Swanian, but it is impossible to date them in the full conviction at least partly to the period of Common Kartvelian, i.e. to the 19th century B.C.

We shall first consider the words common for Armenian and Georgio-Zanian. The first layer consists of original Armenian words that have penetrated into Georgio-Zanian (Georgian and Zanian): Arm. *arcat‛* 'silver' (IE *$ar\hat{g}\partial to$-?)–GZ *$werc^1x\mathit{l}$-, also Avar. *harac*, Lak. *arcu*, Darg. *arc*, Tab. *ars*, Arch. *ars* (for *we*- cf. Arm. *orj* 'male,' *yorj* 'wether' and GZ *$werd^{zl}$-* 'wether'); Arm. *burd*- 'wool' (dial. 'p;umage') and *brdel* 'to cut to pieces' (IE *$bherdh$-) – Gz *$burd\gamma a$-* 'plumage'; Arm. *gini*, Gen. -*woy* 'wine' (IE *$winiyo$-) – GZ *$\gamma wino$-* 'wine'; Arm. *orb*, Gen. -*oy* 'orphan' (IE *$orbho$-) – GZ *$obol$-*, also Abkg. -*iba*, Kab. *ibe*, Chech. *bo* 'orphan'; Arm. *orj* 'male,' *yorj* 'wether' – GZ *$werd^{zl}$-* 'wether'; etc.

The second layer of Armenian-Georgio-Zanian lexical coincidences comprises Georgio-Zanian borrowings in Armenian: GZ *con-* 'to weigh' – Arm. *canr*, Gen. *canu* 'heavy'; GZ *$\dot{c}^1ebo$-* 'to glue,' $\dot{c}^1ebo$- 'glue' – Arm. *cep‛*, Gen. -*oy* 'moulding'; GZ *$\dot{k}rt$-$w\eta$-* 'to look for sth with the beak; pluck,' *ni-$\dot{k}ar\dot{t}$*- 'beak' – Arm. *ktuc‛* 'beak'; etc.

There are quite a few Armenian-Kartvelian coincidences – Armenian borrowings in the Kartvelain: Arm. *arciw*, *arcui* 'eagle' (IE *$\dot{r}\hat{g}ipiyo$-) – Georg., Zan., Swan. *arçiwi* 'eagle,' also Chech. *ärzu*, Ingush. *ärzi* and Urart. *Arṣibini*; Arm. *tiz* 'tick' (IE *$di\hat{g}h$-) – Kartv. *$\dot{t}iz^1$- 'louse' (Georg. $\dot{t}il$-, Megr. $\dot{t}i(j)$-, Chan. $m\dot{t}i$-, Swan. $\dot{t}i\check{s}$-).

The probability of Armenian-Kartvelian language contacts in the period of Hayasa, taking into account the geographical position of Hayasa, is rather high. The Luv. word *t/dawi*- is probably a borrowing from a Kartvelian source: Georg. *twal*-, Megr., Chan. *tol*-, Swan. *te*-/*ter*- 'eye.'

BIBLIOGRAPHY

Adjarian, Hr. (Աճառյան, Հր.)
  1971-1979. Հայերեն արմատական բառարան. 1-4. Yerevan: Yerevan University Press.
Del Monte, G.F. and J. Tischler.
  1978. *Die Orts- und Gewässernamen der hethitischen Texte.* Wiesbaden.
Djahukian, G.B. (Ջահուկյան, Գևորգ Բ., Джаукян, Геворк б.)
  1961. "The Hayasa Language and its Relation to the Indo-European Languages." *Archiv orientálini.* 29. 363-405.
  1964. Хайасский язык и его отношение к тндоевропейским языкам. Yerevan: Press of the Armenian Academy of Sciences.
  1970. Հայարանը եվ հնդեվրոպական հին լեզուներբբ. Yerevan: Press of the Armenian Academy of Sciences.
  1987. Հայոց լեզվի պատմություն: Նախագրային ժամանակաշրջան. Yerevan: Press of the Armenian Academy of Sciences.
Diakonoff, I.M. (Дьяконов, И. М.)
  1968. Предистория армянского народа. Yerevan: Press of the Armenian Academy of Sciences. (Reprint, Delmar, New York: *The Pre-history of the Armenian People.* Caravan Books. 1984.
  1970. "Арицй на ближем востоке: конец мифа" ВДИ 4. 39-63.
Forrer, E.
  1931. "Hayasa-Azzi." *Caucasica.* 9.
Friedrich, J.
  1952 (+ 1957, 1961, 1961). *Hethitisches Wörterbuch* (+ 1-3 *Ergänzungshefte*). Heidelberg.
Ghapantsian G.A.
  1931-1933. *Chetto-armeniaca.* Yerevan.
  1946. Хайаса—колыбель армян: Этногенез армян и их началная история. Yerevan: Press of the Armenian Academy of Sciences.
Klimov, G. A. (Климов, Г. А.)
  1964. Этимологический словарь картвельских языков. Moscow: Press of the

USSR Academy of Sciences: Institute of Linguistics.

Greppin, J.A.C.

    1975. "Hitt. -z(a), Arm. z-, and the Theory of Armeno-Hittite loan words." *Journal of Indo-European Studies*. 3.

    1978. "Armeno-Luvica." *Revue des études arméniens*. 13.

    1980. "'Hittite' Loan Words in Armenian." *Lautgeschichte und Etymoligie*. Wiesbaden.

Kammenhuber A.

    1968. *Die Arier in Vorderen Orient*. Heidelberg.

Kretschmer, P.

    1932. "Die nationale Name der Armenier Haikh." *Anzeiger der Akad. der Wiss. in Wien. Phil.-hist*. Klasse 1-7.

Laroche, E.

    1947. *Recherches sur les noms des dieux hittites*. Paris.

    1959. *Dictionnaire de la langue louvite*. Paris.

    1966. *Les noms des Hittites*. Paris.

Mayrhofer, M.

    1966. *Die Indo-Arier im alten Vorderasien*. Wiesbaden.

    1974. *Die Arier im Vorderen Orient—ein Mythos?* Wien.

Schultheiss, T.

    1961. "Hethitisch und Armenisch." *KZ*. 77.

Tischler, J.

    1977-1988. *Hethitisches etymologisches Glossar*. 1-3.

    1977. *Kleinasiatische Hydronymie*. Wiesbaden.

Vogt, H.

    1937. "Arménien et Caucasique du sud." *Norsk Tidsskift for Sprogvidenskap*. 9.

    1961. "Arménien et géorgien." *Handes amsorya*. 75.

Zgusta, L.

    1964. *Kleinasiatische Personennamen*. Prague.

    1984. *Kleinasiatische Ortsnamen*. Heidelberg.

DOMESTICATION OF PLANTS IN THE OLD WORLD: THE EMERGING SYNTHESIS

Daniel Zohary

Department of Genetics
The Hebrew University
Jerusalem, 91904, Israel

INTRODUCTION

South West Asia, Europe, and the Nile Valley (the "Old World") are unique today as to the extent of their archaeobotanical exploration. In the last 30 years hundreds of prehistoric sites have been excavated all over these territories. Plant remains in many sites have been expertly determined, culturally associated and radiocarbon dated. The finds already identified the plants that started agriculture in the Old World, and established (in general terms) where and when their domestication could have taken place.

Parallel progress has been achieved in the study of the living plants. The wild progenitors of almost all the principal food crops of the Old World have been soundly identified by comparative morphology and by genetic tests. Comparisons between the wild-types and their cultivated counterparts revealed the evolutionary changes which were brought about by domestication. The geographic distributions of the wild progenitors provided clues where their domestication could have taken place.

As a result of these achievements, the Old World emerges as the first major part of the Earth in which the combined evidence from the archaeology and the living plants permits a new synthesis of crop plant domestication. Such an assessment was recently made by Zohary and Hopf (1988)[1], and this paper summarizes the main conclusions arrived at by these authors. For a more detailed, crop-wise survey of what is known on the origin and spread of cultivated plants in West Asia, Europe and Egypt the reader is referred to this recent publication. Furthermore, it was felt unnecessary to list again the numerous reports and publications cited in the Zohary and Hopf book. In this paper references are given only when amendments were made or when new facts were incorporated.

THE NEAR EAST NEOLITHIC CROP ASSEMBLAGE

The first definite signs of plant cultivation in the Old World appear in a string of early Neolithic farming villages that developed in the Near East in the 8th and 7th millennia bc. (Pre-Pottery Neolithic A and Pre-Pottery Neolithic B cultures). The initiation of food production in this "nuclear area" is based on the domestication of a relatively small number (8-9 species) of local wild grain plants. The start of plant cultivation in the Near East was accompanied by domestication of several animals. Sheep and goat were the first to be brought under human control, and they were soon followed by cattle and swine. Three cereals, namely emmer wheat *Triticum turgidum subsp. dicoccum*, barley *Hordeum vulgare* and einkorn wheat *Triticum monococcum* (and in this order of importance) were the main founder crops of the Near East Neolithic agriculture. Diagnostic morphological traits (non-brittle ears, plump kernels) traceable in the archaeological finds indicate that by 7800-7500 bc emmer wheat and barley were intentionally sown and harvested in the Near East.[2] Very likely einkorn wheat was domesticated in the same time. Yet definite indications on the cultivation of this wheat are available, at present, only from the end of the 8th millennium bc. Map 1 shows the main early Neolithic Near East sites from which remains of these three cereals were uncovered.

In both emmer wheat and barley one faces rapid development under domestication. Already in one or two sites dated to the 7th millennium bc, one finds traces of more "modern" derivatives of these crops. Cultivated emmer wheat, with its characteristic invested grains, gave rise to free threshing *durum*-type forms in which threshing releases the naked grains. Cultivated hulled two-rowed barley gave rise to six-rowed cultigenes and again also to varieties with naked grains.[3]

Several additional grain crops appear as constant companions of wheats and barley. Most frequent in the early Neolithic Near East contexts are lentil *Lens culinaris*, pea *Pisum sativum* and flax *Linum usitatissimum*. Remains of two other legumes namely chickpea *Cicer arietinum* and bitter vetch *Vicia ervilia* were uncovered as well, but they are more sporadic in their appearance (for orientation on sites from which lentil, pea and flax were retrieved consult Map 1).

In contrast to the cereals, remains of pulses and flax usually lack morphological features by which initial stages of domestication can be recognized. Clear indication of lentil cultivation is now available from 6800 bc.[4] Definite signs of flax, pea, chickpea and bitter vetch cultivation appear only at about 6000 bc. Yet probably all these four grain crops were taken into cultivation somewhat earlier, either together with wheats and barley or soon after the domestication of these cereals. The origin of another important Old World pulse, namely the broad bean *Vicia faba*, has not yet been satisfactorily clarified. But a recent discovery of a hoard of seed in a Pre-Pottery Neolithic B site in North Israel indicates that broad bean, too, may have been a member of the Neolithic Near East crop assemblage.

WILD PROGENITORS

The wild ancestors of the majority of the food plants grown in West Asia, Europe, and the Nile valley are already well identified. The distribution areas and the main ecological preferences of most of these wild progenitors are also well elucidated. Comparison of this evidence with the archaeological information reveals that with practically all early crops the first signs of cultivation appear in the same general areas where the wild ancestral stock abound today.

The geographic distribution of the wild progenitors of the Neolithic grain crops is indeed significant. Apart from flax and barley the wild ancestors of the founder crops have a rather limited distribution. Wild emmer wheat, wild chickpea and wild bitter vetch are endemic to the Near East. Assuming that their distribution did not change drastically during the last ten millennia, the domestication of these crops could only have taken place in this restricted area. Wild forms of einkorn wheat, lentil and pea have a somewhat wider distribution, but all, as well as barley, are centered in the Near East, i.e. the region in which the earliest farming villages have been discovered.

THE SPREAD OF THE NEAR EAST CROPS

A most remarkable feature of the Neolithic agriculture is the rapid expansion it underwent soon after its establishment in the Near East nuclear area. The quality and quantity of the archaeobotanical evidence varies considerably from region to region. Comprehensive information is available from the Balkan countries, and from central and western Europe, but there is much sparser and frequently incomplete documentation from Russia, Central Asia, and the Indian subcontinent. In Africa, critical data on plant remains are available only from Egypt. In spite of such uneven documentation, the following main features of the diffusion seem apparent.

The spread of agriculture from its nuclear area to Europe and Central Asia was based on the Near East plants. The same crops that started food production in the Near East "arc" also initiated agriculture in these vast territories. Map 2 summarizes the expansion of the six most important Near East crops: emmer wheat (including its free threshing derivatives), einkorn wheat, barley, lentil, pea and flax. From the data assembled on this map it is evident that the crops domesticated in the Near East were also the starting elements of food production in Europe, Central Asia, the Indus basin, and the Nile valley. The earliest farming cultures all over these vast regions always contain wheats and barley. One, two or more other Near East founder crops are frequently present in the sites as well.

38 When Worlds Collide

The spread of the Near East crop assemblage both westwards (to Europe) and eastwards (to Central Asia and to the Indian subcontinent) was a quick process (Map 2). Already in the beginning of the 6th millennium bc, agriculture (based on the Near East crop assemblage) appeared in Greece. By the end of the 6th millennium bc, these crops were grown in Starcevo in the Danubian basin, in Merimde in the Nile Valley, in Chokh in the Caspian Sea basin and in Mehrgarh in Pakistan. Less than 800 years later the Danubian (Bandkeramik) culture was already firmly established in loess soil regions all over central Europe, extending west to north France. At more or less the same time (and perhaps somewhat earlier) farming villages of the Impressed Ware (Cardial) culture appeared on the shores of the west Mediterranean Sea and reached south Spain. All over those vast areas the start of food production depended on the same crops.

EARLY DOMESTICATION OUTSIDE THE NUCLEAR AREA

Signs of additional domesticates start to appear soon after the introduction of the Near East agriculture to Europe, Central Asia and the Nile Valley. The addition of some of these crops obviously took place outside the Near East but within the already established cultivation of the Near East crop assemblage. The poppy *Papaver somniferum*, provides a well documented example for such domestication. Both the area of distribution of the wild poppy and the archaeological finds indicate that *P. somniferum* was brought into cultivation in West Europe. The poppy was locally added to the Near East grain crop assemblage after the latter was established in West Europe. Chufa *Cyperus esculentum*, provides a similar example of an early local addition, this time in the Nile Valley. Its dry tubers were found in large quantities in Egypt from predynastic times on. Grass pea *Lathyrus sativus*, is obviously a Neolithic minor crop but probably not a Near East domesticate. A recent study[5] showed that the more definite early signs of its cultivation come from 6th and 5th millennia bc Greece. The early appearance of the common millet *Panicum miliaceum*, in the Caspian basin (5th millennium bc), might indicate another local addition. However, since the archaeological evidence from central and east Asia is still inadequate, it is impossible to decide whether *P. miliaceum* was locally added to the expanding Near East agriculture after it reached central Asia, or whether this cereal represents an east Asiatic domestication - independent of the Near East diffusion.

Another Neolithic development outside the nuclear area was the emergence of breadwheat *Triticum aestivum*, which today is economically the most important wheat crop. Breadwheat is an independent wheat species which originated, under domestication, by hybridization between cultivated emmer or durum forms of *Triticum turgidum* with a wild wheat grass *Aegilops squarrosa* (for details on origin consult Zohary and Hopf 1988, p. 45 and Table 2). The earliest signs of breadwheat come from the 5th millennium bc Transcaucasia.

BEGINNINGS AND SPREAD OF HORTICULTURE

Olive *Olea europaea*, grape vine *Vitis vinifera*, fig *Ficus carica* and date palm *Phoenix dactylifera* seem to have been the first principal fruit crops domesticated in the

Old World. Definite signs of olive, grape vine[6] and date palm cultivation appear in Chalcolithic sites (3700-3500 bc) in Israel and Jordan, and by the 4th millennium bc date palm cultivation seems to have been practised also in lower Mesopotamia. Also the fig was most probably taken into cultivation in the Levant in the same time. Except for Palestine, the archaeobotanical information on 4th millennium bc sites in other parts of the Levant is insufficient and we still know very little how extensive horticulture was in Chalcolithic times. The picture changes in the Early Bronze Age (first half of the 3rd millennium bc). From this time on olives, grapes and figs emerge as important additions to grain agriculture in the Levant and somewhat later also in Greece. The extensive cultivation of olives and grapes in the late Bronze Age is reflected by the appearance of numerous presses and remains of storage facilities for olive oil and for wine. Contemporarily, dates were cultivated on the southern fringes and the warm river basins of the Near East "arc." Somewhat later the cultivation of dates appears also in the Nile Valley and dates become very common in Egyptian Kingdom contexts. New Apple *Malus pumila*, pear *Pyrus communis*, plum *Prunus domestica* and cherry *Prunus avium* seem to have been added to the Old World horticulture much later. Definite signs of their cultivation appear only in the 1st millennium bc. Their culture is based almost entirely on grafting. Very likely they could have been domesticated and successfully cultivated only after the introduction of this sophisticated method of vegetative propagation.

The available archaeobotanical evidence on the beginning of fruit crop domestication is also supported by information on the wild relatives. Wild olive, grape, fig and date are widely distributed over the Mediterranean basin and southwest Asia. Because they have a wide geographic distribution, they do not provide critical clues for a precise delimitation of the place of origin of their respective crops. Yet it is assuring to know that forms from which the cultivated clones could have been derived thrive in wild niches in the east Mediterranean basin. Thus the evidence from the living plants complements the archaeological finds. Most probably olive, grape vine, date, fig, as well as pomegranate *Punica granatum* and almond *Amygdalus communis* were first brought into cultivation in the same *general area* which several millennia earlier saw the successful establishment of grain agriculture in the Old World. Chalcolithic and Bronze Age cultures in the east Mediterranean basin are characterized not only by the use of copper and bronze; 4th millennium bc human societies in that region had also mastered horticulture.

VEGETABLES

This is the least known group among the cultivated plants of the Old World. Vegetable material, brought home, consists almost entirely of perishable soft tissues. Such elements stand meager chances to char and thus to survive in archaeological contexts. Thus only scant remains of vegetable crops have been detected in archaeological excavations. The only exception is Egypt. In this arid country vegetables placed in pyramids and graves commonly survived by desiccation. These remains show that garlic *Allium sativum*, onion *Allium cepa*, leek *Allium porrum*, melon *Cucumis melo*, watermelon *Citrullus lanatus*, lettuce *Lactuca sativa*, beet *Beta vulgaris* and chufa *Cyperus esculatum* were cultivated in the Nile Valley in the 2nd and the 1st millennia bc;

and that vegetable gardens constituted an important element of food production in dynastic Egypt.

Outside Egypt there is almost no early archaeobotanical evidence of vegetable crops. It seems, however, that by the 2nd millennium bc vegetable gardens flourished in several agricultural provinces in southwest Asia. The distribution areas of the wild plants indicate that some of the Egyptian domesticates (e.g. garlic or onion) are not native in the Nile Valley. They had to be introduced from West Asia. In addition, several early documents and linguistic considerations point to the early use of vegetables in Mesopotamia. But we do not know how extensive gardening was, which were the main vegetable crops, and when and where they were brought into cultivation.

LATE COMERS

A major wave of new crops arrived to the near East in the first millennium bc. It brought into this region both Asiatic and African elements.

Warm weather crops comprise the largest group among these immigrants. They include sorghum *Sorghum bicolor*, sesame *Sesamum indicum*, rice *Oryza sativa* and Old World cotton *Gossypium arboreum*. These crops started in the Mediterranean countries the tradition of summer crops, which since classical times, became an integral element of food production in these territories. Archaeobotanical evidence indicates that rice, sorghum, sesame and cotton were part of Indian agriculture already in the second millennium bc. All appear in Harappan sites. However, while rice and sesame are south and east Asiatic elements, sorghum is not. Very likely the latter was taken into cultivation in East Africa. It was first introduced from there to the Indian subcontinent and only from India it was eventually transported to the Near East.

A second group of later comers arriving from the east comprises several fruit trees. Prominent among them are the apricot *Armeniaca vulgaris* and the peach *Persica vulgaris*. Both are cool climate elements that appeared in the Near East and the Mediterranean basin only at the end of the 1st millennium bc. Another, even earlier, immigrant is the citron *Citron medica*. This is the first representative of the southeast Asiatic citrus fruits to arrive in the Mediterranean basin.[7]

FOOTNOTES

1. Zohary, D. and M. Hopf (1988). *Domestication of Plants in the Old World.* Oxford: Oxford University Press. 249 pp.
2. The earliest signs of emmer wheat cultivation come from Tell Aswad, 30 km South East of Damascus, see: Zeist, W. van and J.A.H. Bakker-Heeres (1985). Archaeobotanical studies in the Levant I. Neolithic sites in the Damascus basin: Aswad, Ghoraife, Ramad. *Palaeohistoria* 24 (1982), 165-256. Here numerous plump *dicoccum*-type grains were uncovered already in the lower habitation level dated 7800-7600 bc. This without any sign wild-type *dicoccoides* remains. Wild emmer does not grow today in the Damascus basin (the climate is far too dry for its survival). Very probably it did not occur in this xeric basin also in early Neolithic times. Thus as van Zeist and Bakker-Heeres argue it is reasonable to assume that emmer wheat was introduced into Tell Aswad as a cultivated crop. The earliest remains of non-brittle barley, i.e. forms that could survive only under cultivation come from Pre-Pottery Neolithic A Netiv Hagdud, North of Jericho, see: Kislev, M.E., O. Bar-Yosef and A. Gopher (1986). Early Neolithic domesticated and wild barley from the Netiv Hagdud region in the Jordan valley. *Israel Journal of Botany* 35, 197-201. Here numerous remains of non-brittle two-rowed barley still mixed with brittle *spontaneum*-type material were uncovered and dated to 7750 bc.
3. It is noteworthy that although emmer wheat and durum wheat belong to the same biological species and are genetically closely related, they were traditionally recognized as two independent crops and called different names. Very likely farmers regarded them as different crops because their processing is different. Such naming repeats itself in numerous crops.
4. Garfinkel, Y., M.E. Kislev and D. Zohary (1988). "Lentil in Pre-Pottery Neolithic B. Yiftah'el: Additional Sign for Its Early Domestication." *Israel Journal of Botany* 37, 49-51.
5. Kislev, M.E. (1986). "Archaeobotanical Finding on the Origin of *Lathyrus sativus* and *L. cicera*." In: *Lathyrus and Lathyrism*, A.K. Kaul and D. Combes (eds), 46-51. New York: Third World Medical Research Foundation.
6. Zohary and Hopf (1988) (see footnote 1) reported that only for the olive and the date palm there is already satisfactory archaeobotanical evidence to conclude that they were under cultivation in Chalcolithic times. Grapevine and fig were only suspected to be part of this early horticulture. Since then, R. Neef, Biologisch-Archaeologisch Instituut, University of Groningen, The Netherlands (pers. comm.) uncovered grape vine pips in chalcolithic Shuna North, Jordan and established also this fruit crop as a member of the 4th millennium bc Near East horticulture.
7. Several additional warm weather crops seem to have arrived even later. Prominent among them are the sugar cane, banana, lemon and eggplant. All these crops seem to have originated in southeast Asia. They reached the Mediterranean basin only in Byzantine or Arab times.

EXPLANATIONS TO MAPS

Map 1: Summary of the available archaeobotanical evidence on the six main "founder crops" in the early Neolithic sites (8th and 7th millennia bc) in the Near East. A short whisker indicates that the crop is relatively rare, and a long whisker that it is relatively common among the excavated plant remains. After Zohary and Hopf (1988) (see footnote 1).

Map 2: Summary of available archaeobotanical evidence on the spread of the Near East Neolithic crops to Europe, West Asia and the Nile Valley. After Zohary and Hopf (1988). For details on the various sites and for references consult Table 6, p. 211 in their publication.

MAP 1

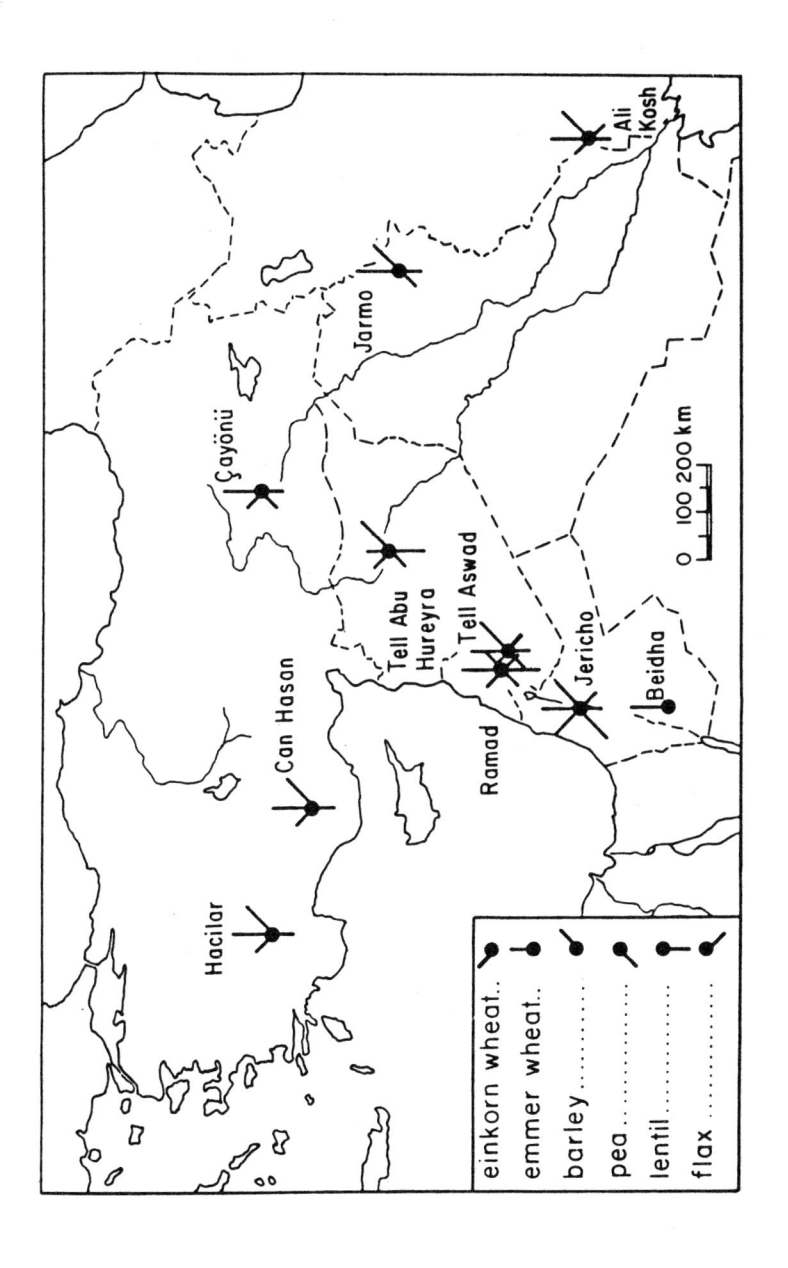

44 When Worlds Collide

MAP 2

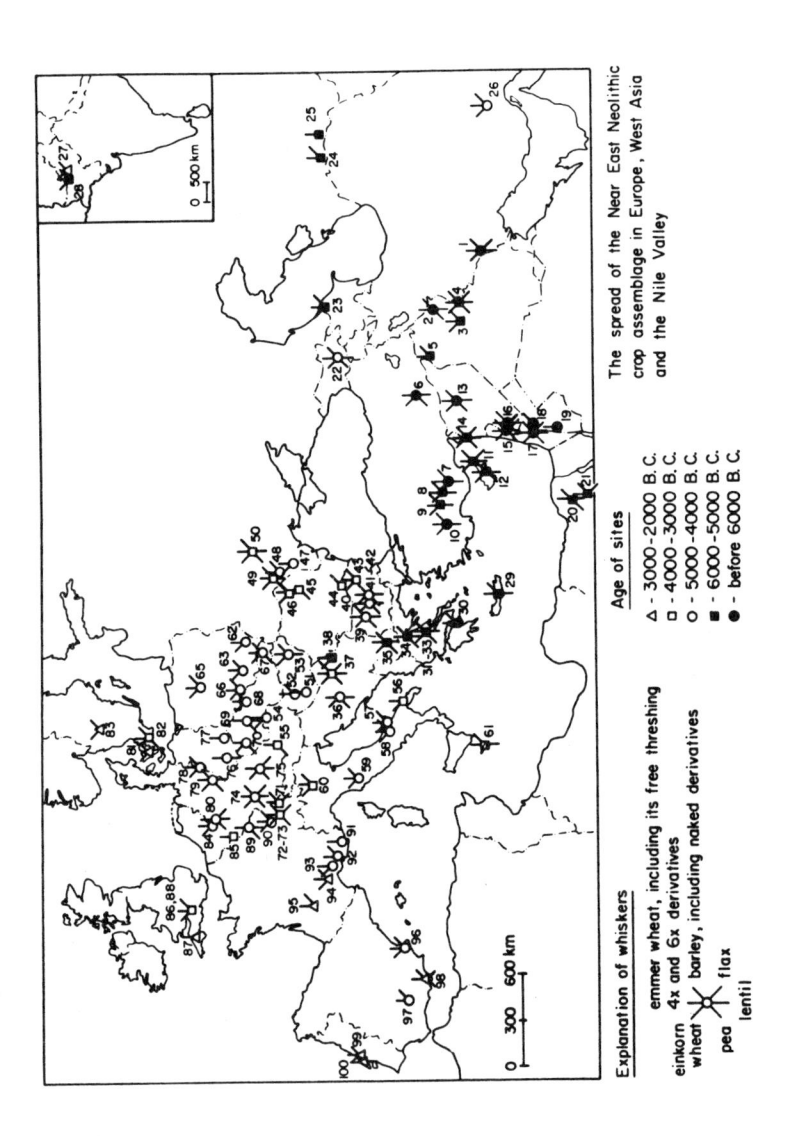

The spread of the Near East Neolithic crop assemblage in Europe, West Asia and the Nile Valley

Age of sites

△ – 3000–2000 B.C.
□ – 4000–3000 B.C.
○ – 5000–4000 B.C.
■ – 6000–5000 B.C.
● – before 6000 B.C.

Explanation of whiskers

emmer wheat, including its free threshing 4x and 6x derivatives
einkorn wheat
barley, including naked derivatives
pea   flax
lentil

THE INDO-EUROPEAN IMPACT ON THE HURRIAN WORLD

by Charles Burney

For the purposes of this contribution to the Bellagio meeting[1], the Hurrian world may be delineated both in space and in time, the dimensions being perhaps rather wider than might be expected by some. The views represented here are of course essentially those of an archaeologist, but of one prepared, hopefully, to learn much from the opportunity provided by the Bellagio symposium to compare approaches to problems of common interest with linguists whose training has necessarily been very different from my own. When one is no longer prepared to listen, then is the time to retire from the fray. At the time when this paper was delivered, early in the program, it was already becoming clear that much would be gained from this meeting of minds. One could not help envying those speaking later, who would thus have the benefit of more contributions on which to draw for any fine tuning! The interpretation of the Hurrian role in the ancient Near East is my own: certainly it will not command unanimous support. Any such popular consensus would not be worth the paper it was printed on.

At its maximum geographical extent the Hurrian world stretched from the Caucasus to northern Mesopotamia; westward into northern Syria and towards the eastern marches of central Anatolia; and eastward into the Urmia basin and northwestern Iran. The evidence for this wide distribution of Hurrians is of course not all of one and the same period. In time-span the Hurrian world emerges in the early to middle fourth millennium B.C., on one interpretation in the Georgian S.S.R., where the settlement of Shulaveri, not far from Tbilisi, has revealed round houses dating well back into the fifth millennium B.C., possible prototypes of ETC round houses; and where local pottery may be seen as leading into that of the ETC I sub-period.[2] The Hurrian world persists until the obscure time of the fall of the kingdom of Urartu (Van) (c.590 B.C.).[3] One school of thought would argue the survival of Hurrians in the disguise of Armenians, though that controversial and complex question cannot be pursued here.[4]

The weight of archaeological and linguistic evidence indicates an Indo-European impact on the Hurrian world at various periods across an arc from west through north to east, but at no time from the south. Frankly speaking, the notion of an Proto-Indo-European homeland in the north of Syria-Mesopotamia in the region once forming - during the sixth millennium B.C. - the habitat of the well-known Halaf culture, whose most significant excavated site is Tell Arpachiyah close to Mosul, will not bear serious scrutiny.[5] The general indications of the archaeological evidence favor the belief that the Sumerians most probably settled in Mesopotamia at least from the sixth millennium B.C., making them the earliest settlers in the south: Diakonoff's suggestion that the Sumerians arrived in the early fourth millennium B.C., implying their association with the advent of the Uruk culture, seems untenable, and probably finds fewer adherents than it would have done a generation ago.[6]

Archaeological and historical evidence of any significant Indo-European impact from the west, i.e. through or from central Anatolia, is minimal until the twelfth century B.C., with the raids by the Mushki[7] (affecting only the southwestern areas of the Hurrian world) and the arrival of the Armenians in the seventh-sixth centuries B.C. It was more a question of the Hurrian impact on central Anatolia, especially in the period of the *karum* of Kanesh,[8] and on the Hittite court, dynasty and religion.[9] It is in Cilicia - Kizzuwatna (Late Bronze Age), Que (Iron Age), when the hill country along the foot of the Taurus was designated Hilakku - that it seems possible to discern an Indo-European (Luvian) element settling in the Early Bronze III period, around the mid-third millennium B.C., with ceramic parallels with northwestern Anatolia, such as the Troy V-type red-cross bowls, long recognized as a diagnostic form.[10] Then, however, in the Cilician Middle Bronze Age, from not later than c. 2100 B.C., painted pottery of north Syrian type, very non-Anatolian in character, seems to indicate the arrival of elements from the east, plausibly to be seen as being of Hurrian origin, and having affinities with pottery from Tell Atchana (Alalakh) in the Amuq plain.[11] This will explain the undoubted Hurrian presence in Cilicia (Kizzuwatna) in the time of the Hittite New Kingdom or Empire, when Pudu-Hepa, the queen of Hattusilis III, introduced Hurrian cultic traditions to the imperial court at Hattusha. Yet there, it seems, the royal family itself was of Hurrian extraction, adopting Indo-European (Hittite) names only on accession.[12] The one king not to do so, Urhi-Teshub, was perhaps significantly deposed by his uncle. Is there here a hidden hint of Indo-European-Hurrian friction? This is unlikely ever to be known.

An Indo-European impact from the north, penetrating the Near East through the Caucasus, may possibly be discernible in the adoption of barrow (*kurgan*) burial in the northern part of the vast Early Trans-Caucasian (ETC) cultural zone,[13] argued by the writer to have been the Hurrian homeland.[14] This does not require acceptance of the tenets of what may be termed "Kurganology."[15] Gimbutas is, however, quite correct in emphasizing the lack of archaeological support for any ethnic movement at this time from south to north, as proposed by Gamkrelidze and Ivanov.[16] There is also evidence, albeit hardly conclusive, of intrusive elements of northern origin in the ETC zone during the third millennium B.C.: at a symposium in Los Angeles (1982) the writer argued for a possible Indo-Iranian presence in northwestern Iran during the third millennium B.C., as a tentative suggestion.[17] Unless the traditional theory of the arrival of the Hittites from the Caucasus into central Anatolia (c.2000 B.C.) is adhered to, a theory by now surely outdated,[18] the next Indo-European impact from the north took the form of movements of Cimmerians and Scyths (c.715-612 B.C.), long known as being of Iranian stock and continuing the devotion to *kurgan* burial, introduced throughout much of Anatolia by the Phrygians.[19]

Indo-European impact on the Hurrian world from the east took different forms, and is harder to distinguish in some respects. In the mid-second millennium B.C. pottery of the type now termed "Urmia ware"[20] penetrated, by whatever mechanism, into the Van region,[21] perhaps at about the same time as the long-known Indo-European *maryannu* and ruling class, with their Indic language, appear in the kingdom of Mitanni.[22] Archaeological evidence of that movement is lacking. It must have penetrated from Iran, perhaps more or less simultaneously with the expansion of the Iranian tribes from the northeast (Gurgan and parts of Khorassan) and possibly also through the Caucasus, marking the start of the Iron I period (c.1500-1100 B.C.) in Iran:[23] the distinctive Iron I grey ware does not, to the writer's knowledge, occur in Mitanni, although it has been found at sites in the Mus plain, just west of lake Van.[24] In the obscure period preceding the emergence of the kingdom of Urartu (Van), northwestern Iran seems to have witnessed a mingling of Indo-European with Hurrian elements, the Mannaeans being Hurrian-related. The Medes were of course beginning to come within the purview of the Assyrian kings, from the reign of Shalmaneser III onwards.[25] Iranian elements may be detected in the formative phase of Urartu during the later ninth century B.C., notably in the links with the city of Musasir and in the long list of offerings to deities, headed by Haldi followed by Tesheba and Shivini, in the rock inscription of Mehr Kapisi ("Mithra's Gate") close to the later Rusa-Citadel, better known as Toprakkale.[26] Iranian elements have likewise been detected at Musasir, perhaps the home city of the new dynasty established by Sarduri I at Van: with Musasir was closely associated the cult of Haldi. There are, moreover, indubitable links between Hasanlu IV and Urartu (c.800 B.C.).[27] As for the Hasanlu gold bowl, which the writer had the privilege of drawing directly after its excavation (1958), Edith Porada's interpretation of the complex iconography in terms of the Hurrian epic of Kummarbi seems irrefutable.[28]

Given the links, albeit not quite as direct as once supposed, between the Hurrian and Urartian languages,[29] the artistic clues (e.g. deities standing on animals or mythical creatures) and the lack of any evidence of a break in the continuity of the Hurrian occupation of their old (ETC) homeland, Urartu may surely be safely considered essentially Hurrian, with Assyrian external influences the strongest. Horse-riding and irrigation engineering were the Urartian achievements especially admired by Sargon II (714 B.C.).[30] To attribute all or even most equestrian skills in the ancient Near East to Indo-European elements simply on the evidence of the Kikkuli text would be absurd.[31] The Hurrians were clearly equally proficient. What too of the famous Mari tablet wherein Bahdi-Lim, the vizier, rebukes Zimri-Lim the king for riding on horseback in public instead of merely in a chariot?[32] That must have come well before the Indo-European element arrived in Mitanni.

Migrations must have played their part, whatever current archaeological doctrine at some great universities may be! Is it really credible that migrations were of only slight significance in prehistoric times, yet played so prominent a part in the decline and fall of the Roman empire and its sequel? What of the Scyths, the

Sarmatians, the Goths or the Huns?[33] What can be said is that migrations are very hard to prove on archaeological data alone. "Kurganology" requires an element of faith to be accepted. Yet its rejection need not even imply uncritical acceptance of symbolism and ranking or peer-polity exchange as major factors in prehistoric societies in the Near East or elsewhere. It goes without saying that all these ideas merit close examination, in a strictly empirical approach: they are not to be adopted uncritically, in a spirit intolerant of widely differing approaches or demanding adherence to fashionable thinking. Theology and archaeology are uneasy bedfellows: after the Bellagio gathering it would be unjust and ungracious to suggest that there is a comparable gulf between archaeology and linguistics. Certainly creditable efforts were made to narrow this divide.[34]

As this contributor made clear in the discussions conducted at Bellagio, it seems quite an untenable proposition to identify a Proto-Indo-European substratum extending over the whole highland zone of the Near East by c.7000 B.C., i.e. in Neolithic times,[35] with a Semitic homeland in Saudi Arabia. This would imply a Hurrian occupation of Indo-European held territories in what later became the Early Trans-Caucasian zone, from the mid-fourth to the end of the third millennium B.C. Attractive as may be the notion of a Proto-Indo-European substratum, in due course overlaid by Hurrian incomers, this remains a construct of those involved in research into proto-lexicons, a model for which there is as yet no evidence whatsoever on the ground. Since the discussion revolves around a period millennia before the appearance of written records, archaeology alone can provide the required evidence, and archaeology is silent.[36] How much significance should be attached to the juxtaposition of distinct ethnic groups cohabiting, or at least co-existing, at Catal Huyuk in the seventh millennium B.C.? These comprise Proto-Mediterraneans (c.59%), Eurafricans (c.17%) and Armenoids (c.24%).[37] Are we to see the last group as Proto-Indo-Europeans? There seems to be general agreement that the two other groups represent direct descendants of Upper Palaeolithic communities. One thing stands out clearly: the population of the Anatolian plateau was already in the seventh millennium B.C. very mixed. This must surely make the task of locating the Proto-Indo-European homeland, there or elsewhere, that much more difficult.

The final stages of the Indo-European impact on Urartu and thus on the Hurrian world must be mentioned briefly. In northwestern Iran the Scyths have left their name in that of the town of Sakkiz, recalling the Sakai; and twenty miles away stands the massive Mannaean fortress of Ziwiye (Izibia in the Assyrian records), best known for the rich contents of a bronze tub, buried c.600 B.C. or slightly earlier, including couchant stags and other motifs related to the so-called "Animal Style" and thus to the steppes north of the Caucasus.[38] Not far southwest of Lake Urmia, the tumuli of Se Girdan ("three mounds") provide another hint of the presence, however fleeting, of northern nomads of Indo-European affinity.[39] Discoveries in a 1978 survey around Meshkinshahr, west of Ardebil and not far south of the River Araxes, included the major stronghold of Arjaq Qale, on the evidence of surface pottery probably dating to the sixth century B.C. Here there were also earlier stelae, of a type attributed by some Soviet archaeologists to the Cimmerians, although on rather uncertain evidence.[40]

Particularly intriguing is the question of the arrival in Urartu of the Armenians. There seems no reason to discount the Classical sources associating the Armenian language with Phrygian.[41] Infiltration by small Armenian groups into the western provinces of Urartu during the seventh century B.C., before the fall of the kingdom, seems perfectly possible. It is regrettable that only rather meager written records survive from the long and active reign of Rusa II (c.685-645 B.C.).[42] Intermarriage with the indigenous Hurro-Urartian majority population would be fully compatible with the imposition of Armenian as the spoken language, just as Turkish was later imposed throughout Anatolia. This is not the occasion to enter into the thorny arguments of language versus race. Suffice it to say that the Indo-European legacy to the modern Armenians is essentially linguistic.

Perhaps it was inevitable that a very recent book attempting to present a new interpretation of Indo-European origins, employing both archaeological and palaeolinguistic approaches, should find itself, with its author, the center of much of the debate at Bellagio.[43] Had this book not appeared after the Bellagio symposium had been announced, one might have been forgiven for seeing an intended connection between the two! The conclusions set out in Colin Renfrew's *Archaeology and Language: the Puzzle of Indo-European Origins* found enthusiastic support from the leading proponent of a Proto-Indo-European homeland somewhat further to the east from that proposed by Renfrew, namely, in eastern Anatolia or just to the south, in north Syria-Mesopotamia.[44] This contributor to the Bellagio symposium found himself the one representative Near Eastern archaeologist, and as such unable to accept many of Renfrew's or Gamkrelidze's suggestions. Models for prehistoric societies or maps for the geographical distribution of proto-languages have their uses, but only within the discipline imposed by the available evidence.

THE INDO-EUROPEAN IMPACT ON THE HURRIAN WORLD: FOOTNOTES

1. The meeting was held at Bellagio, near Como, under the direction of Thomas L. Markey (Ann Arbor) and John A.C. Greppin (Cleveland), with the support of the Rockefeller Foundation, 8-13 February 1988, under the title of *When Worlds Collide: Indo-Europeans and Pre-Indo-Europeans*.
2. Antonio Sagona (University of Melbourne), personal communication.
3. R.D. Barnett: "Urartu" (*Cambridge Ancient History III*, Part 1) (1982), especially pp. 364-5 and bibliography.
4. (a) I.M. Diakonoff: *The Prehistory of the Armenian People*, English translation, Caravan Books (Delmar, New York, 1984).

    (b). C.A. Burney and D.M. Lang: *The Peoples of the Hills* (London, 1971), pp. 177-80.

    (c). B.B. Piotrovsky: *Vanskoe Tsarstvo (Urartu)* (Moscow, 1959).
5. James Mellaart: *The Neolithic of the Near East* (London, 1975), pp. 156-70, for a general discussion of the Halaf culture.
6. I.M. Diakonoff: "Language Contacts in the Caucasus and the Near East" (contribution to *When Worlds Collide ...*)
7. LAR I, para. 221, for the earliest dated appearance of the Mushki (Tiglath-Pileser I)
8. (a). Paul Garelli: *Les Assyriens en Cappadoce* (Paris, 1963), pp. 155-8, for Hurrian onomastica, with the suggestion of Hurrian aristocracies in central Anatolia and the Hurrian affinities of the name of Annum-Hirbi, king of Mamma.

    (b). H.G. Guterbock: "Kanes and Nesa" (*Eretz Israel* 5 (1958), pp. 46-ff) for the Indo-European impact.
9. H.G. Guterbock: "The Hurrian element in the Hittite empire" *(Journal of World History* 2 (1954), pp. 383ff.).
10. (a). James Mellaart: "The end of the Early Bronze Age in Anatolia and the Aegean" (*AJA* 62 (1958), especially pp. 23-4), largely superseded but still stimulating.

    (b). *Peoples of the Hills*, pp. 48-9.
11. C.L. Woolley: *Alalakh-- An Account of the Excavations at Tell Atchana in the Hatay 1937-1949* (Oxford, 1955), especially Levels XVI-VIII.
12. See note 9.
13. *Peoples of the Hills*, pp. 78-85.
14. *Ibid.*, pp. 47-51.
15. Among the abundant literature see articles in *JIES* and also D.W. Anthony: "The "Kurgan Culture," Indo-European Origins and the Domestication of the Horse: A Reconsideration" *Current Anthropology* 27 (1986), pp. 291-314, including counter-comment by Marija Gimbutas.
16. Marija Gimbutas: "Primary and secondary homeland of the Indo-Europeans" (*JIES* 13 1985, pp. 185-202 especially pp. 188-9).

17. Marija Gimbutas: *Bronze Age Cultures in Central and Eastern Europe* (The Hague, 1965), p. 536 (fig. 357), for one parallel cited, in the context of the "Proto-Scythian" Timber-Grave Culture.
18. James Mellaart: "The End of the Early Bronze Age in Anatolia and the Aegean" (*AJA* 62 (1958), pp. 9-33).
19. Best documented at Gordion. Rodney S. Young & E.L. Kohler (ed.): *Three Great Early Tumuli (Gordion Excavations Final Reports I)*, Pennsylvania Museum (Philadelphia, 1981).
20. Michael Edwards: "'Urmia Ware' and Its Contribution in North-western Iran in the Second Millennium B.C.: A Review of the Results of Excavations and Surveys" (*Iran* XXIV (1986), pp. 57-77).
21. Altan Cilingiroglu: "The Second Millennium Painted Pottery Tradition of the Lake Van Basin" (*AS*. XXXV (1985), pp. 129-39).
22. *Cambridge Ancient History* II, Part 1 (3rd. edition) (1973), pp. 419-21.
23. (a). T.C. Young: "The Iranian Migration into the Zagros" (*Iran* V (1967), pp. 11-34). (b). *Peoples of the Hills*, pp. 116-7.
24. *Ibid.*, p. 116.
25. LAR I, par. 581 (Year 24).
26. UKN no. 27 (Mehr Kapisi).
27. *pace* Inna Medvedskaya: "Who Destroyed Hasanlu IV?" (*Iran* XXVI (1988), pp. 1-15).
28. Edith Porada: "The Hasanlu bowl" (*Expedition* I/3 (1959). pp. 19-22).
29. Current opinion is not too far removed from that of I.M. Diakonoff as expressed in his monograph (trans. from Russian) *Hurritisch und Urartaisch (Munchener Studien 2, Sprachwissenschaft n.f. Bh.6* (Munich, 1971) rather than his later opinion that Hurrian and Urartian were essentially one and the same language.
30. LAR II, paras. 158, 160 (8th. campaign).
31. (a). *Cambridge Ancient History* II, Part 1 (3rd. edition) (1973), p. 493.
    (b). A. Kammenhuber: *Hippologia Hethitica* (Wiesbaden, 1961).
32. *Archives Royales de Mari* VI, no. 76 (ed. J.R. Kupper) (Paris, 1954).
33. Explained by Colin Renfrew in discussion as having lived in a very different world from that of prehistoric Europe, a world dominated by the Roman empire and its impact on surrounding regions.
34. See (*inter alia*) two of the contributions to the Bellagio symposium: (a). H. Eichner: "Evidence for language contact in Anatolia." (b). Edgar C. Polome: "The Types of Linguistic Evidence for Early Contact."
35. See notes 43 (especially pp. 173-4 and 269-70) and also 44 below.
36. James Mellaart: *The Neolithic of the Near East* (London, 1975), pp. 195-207.
37. (a). D. Ferembach: "Les hommes du gisement neolithique de Catal Huyuk (*VII Turk Tarih Kongresi 1970* (Ankara, 1972), pp. 15-21. (b). *The Neolithic of the Near East*, p. 99.
38. (a). For the primary report, A. Godard: *Le Tresor de Ziwiye (Kurdistan)* (Haarlem, 1950). (b). Among the extensive literature may be mentioned T. Sulimirski: "The Background of the Ziwiye Find and Its Significance in the

Development of Scythian Art" *Bulletin of the Institute of Archaeology, London* 15 (1978), PP. 7-33.

39. O.W. Muscarella: "The Tumuli at Se Girdan" (*Bulletin of the Metropolitan Museum of Art* II (1969))
40. M.L. Ingraham & G.D. Summers: "Stelae and Settlements in the Meshkin Shahr Plain, Northeastern Azerbaijan" *Archaeologische Mitteilungen aus Iran* Band 12 (1979), pp. 67-102.
41. (a). *Peoples of the Hills*, Chapter V, note 135. (b). Herodotus VII, 73. (c). Strabo XI, 14, 12.
42. UKN no. 278 (Adilcevaz).
43. Colin Renfrew: *Archaeology and Language: the Puzzle of Indo-European Origins* (Jonathan Cape) (London, 1987).
44. (a). T.V. Gamkrelidze and V.V. Ivanov: *Indo-European and the Indo-Europeans....* in Russian (2 vols.) (Tbilisi, 1984). English trans. forthcoming (Mouton de Gruyter). Not yet seen by the writer. (b). T.V. Gamkrelidze: "Ex Oriente Lux: On the Problem of an Asiatic Original Homeland of the Proto-Indo-Europeans" (contribution to the Bellagio symposium).

LIST OF ABBREVIATIONS IN FOOTNOTES:

AJA	*American Journal of Archaeology*
AS	*Anatolian Studies*
JIES	*Journal of Indo-European Studies*
LAR	Luckenbill: *Ancient Records of Assyria and Babylonia* (Chicago 1926-7)
Peoples of the Hills	C.A. Burney and D.M. Lang: *The Peoples of the Hills -- Ancient Ararat and Caucasus* (Weidenfeld & Nicolson) (London, 1971)
UKN	G.A. Melikishvili: *Urartskie Klinobraznye Nadpisi* (Moscow, 1960).

LANGUAGE CONTACTS IN THE CAUCASUS AND THE NEAR EAST

by Igor M. Diakonoff
(Oriental Institute, Leningrad, USSR)

I confess I do not quite understand the title of the symposium: "When Worlds Collide." Webster's Dictionary explains "collide" as "to strike or dash against each other, to meet in shock; to meet in opposition or antagonism;" and the Oxford Dictionary explains "collision" as "violent encounter of moving body with another or with fixed object." A collision of worlds one envisages as an Armageddon of huge clashing armed forces. However, I do not believe in collision of worlds in the primitive and ancient societies (what kind of worlds? Ethnic? Cultural? Linguistic?). Alexander's Graeco-Macedonian army *traversed* the Ancient Oriental world, but the Greek and Oriental *worlds* did not *clash*; Alexander's conquest was followed by a slow and peaceful process of Occidental - Oriental contacts. An Attila, a Jenghiz Khan, a Hitler all belong to typologically later periods. If we are to speak of ancient mankind, a more suitable title would have been "When Worlds Come into Contact." Appropriately, I have been requested to read a paper on "Language Contacts in the Caucasus and the Near East." But language contact occurs always as the result of extralinguistic factors; therefore, if we are to study the meaning of language contact, we must also understand the historical, cultural and anthropological contacts which may be involved.

Ethnic contacts are of different kinds, *e.g.*:

(1) Total annihilation of the local inhabitants by an invading ethnic entity. To make such an event possible, both the level of development and the numbers of the contacting populations must be quite incommeasurable. Obviously, such an event cannot occur in a world still living under archaic conditions.

(2) Total displacement of the local inhabitants to another territory by the immigrating ethnic entity. Such an event is also less than probable in an archaic world

and, besides, to achieve such a displacement, one has to have at disposal sufficient extra space to which the weaker ethnic group could be displaced.

(3) Partial infiltration of a new ethnic entity, while the old one continues in residence in the same territory. This, as I think, was the typical case during the epoch of ancient mankind. The local population could either absorb the newcomers also linguistically, or it could adopt their language; whether the one or the other event occurred, depends on strictly definable historical circumstances. The biological features of the population, in any case, change but very slightly.

I should like to draw the attention of my colleagues to the very frequent misuse of the migration hypothesis. One is apt to explain by population change any, or at least any major change in the pottery which is diagnostic of an archaeological culture; too little weight is sometimes ascribed to inner development and to spontaneous changes in technology as well as in fashions. But as I have just stated, a total population change practically never occurred in antiquity, and even partial population change should not be hypothesized without very good grounds.

But it is exactly major population movements, *viz.* migrations of tribes and peoples in a body over thousands and thousands of miles, that have been commonly assumed as the reason for the spread of linguistic families. Such migrations have been imagined on the pattern and scale of the Great Migration of Peoples during the early Middle Ages, or of the invasion of Turko-Mongol tribes toward the West in the early second millennium A.D. The analogy, however, does not hold water. Thus, neither the early Indo-Europeans nor the early Semites were nomads (the latter fact having been established by the work of Pelio Fronzaroli). Stock rearing was important to both, but their economy can by no means be compared to that of the early Turko-Mongols. As to the Great Migration of the early Middle Ages, it did not bring about a biological and linguistic change in the Western European population, with the only exception of England.*[1]

In the nineteenth and twentieth century it was mainly the linguists who dealt in migrations, but it should be obvious that a migration is primarily a problem for the historian. In order to postulate that a migration has taken place, one has to answer a number of questions that are essentially historical, as follows.

First question: What was the reason of and the impulse to the migration? To my knowledge, there have been, in the Ancient World, only two reasons for mass migration: (a) catastrophic drought on a major scale; in the Mediterranean region such was the case in the sixth-fifth millennium B.C., when the proto-civilization of Catalhuyuk etc. was brought to an end, and in the late third-early second millennium B.C., when contacts were apparently lost between the Fertile Crescent and south Arabia; and (b), a dramatic growth in food production leading to a fall in child mortality and a rise in the population increase above the usual much less than 1% *per annum*. A migration is induced by a relative scarcity of land resources. This applies to the agricultural and agricultural-*cum*-stock raising tribes at the period of the Neolithic "revolution," and, in a quite different context, to the period of the Great Greek Colonization. The spread of the Indo-European speaking tribes - I would not use the term migration - was apparently due to the rise in the production of vegetables, milk and meat under the favorable conditions of the deciduous Eastern European forests in the moist fourth and third millennia B.C.

Second question, or, better, the second group of questions: Did the migration involve the whole population or only the males (the latter was the case of the Cimmero-Scythian migrations)? Did one walk on foot or did one use some means of transportation, and if the latter case is assumed, what were the means? Were they actually available?

Let me cite an example. In one of the latest variants of their theory of Indo-European migrations, Vyacheslav Ivanov and Thomas Gamkrelidze suggest that the Indo-Iranians, whose supposed *Ur-Heimat* was in Iranian Azerbaijan, passed to Middle Asia by ships over the Caspian. However shipping on the Caspian is not attested until very much later, and necessary timber is nowhere available along the coast, except for the inaccessible subtropical forests of Talish and Mazanderan, out of the way of any possible major migration. The mountain passes across the Greater Caucasus although accessible to groups of pedestrians, or of riders without women (like the Cimmerians and the Alani), were not suited for crossing in wagons on primitive wheels, with families and household goods.

Third group of questions: What kind of population did one meet in the path of the migration? What happened to that population? Was it massacred? Was it ousted? Was it assimilated? Or, perhaps, did it itself assimilate the newcomers, culturally and biologically, although adopting the language of the newcomers?

Unless these questions can be satisfactorily answered, I should refuse to discuss any tribal or popular migration *en masse*.

What actually happens in history, can be illustrated by a linguistic 'migration' which occurred in historical times, namely, the spread of the Turkic languages. The late eminent Russian anthropologist L.V. Oshanin studied the stability of certain genes in the different Turkic speaking populations. It is well known that in a biologically stable population the recessive and the dominant genes will be maintained in the same proportion. The first historically attested Turkic tribes were anthropologically Mongoloid and hence had the typical Mongoloid feature of the epicanthic fold of the eyelid, depending upon a dominant gene. If the movement of the Turkic languages from the borders of modern China to those of modern Turkey were actually a mass population movement, then the percentage of the epicanthus in the speakers of Turkish, Azerbaijani, Turkmen, Uzbek, Kazakh and Qyrghyz would be approximately identical. The actual measurements, however, show the retention percentage of epicanthic fold to be, in males, 51% for the Qyrghyz, 22% for the Kazakhs, 11% for the Uzbeks, 6% for the Turkmens, and below 2% for the Azerbaijanis; and in females, 83% for the Qyrghyz, 53% for the Kazakhs, 18% for the Uzbeks, and 10% for the Turkmens. For Turks, the retention percentage for both sexes tends toward zero. This means, of course, that the Turkic language was adopted each time by a certain local population from the newcomers, and was then passed on to the next population; intermarriage of the local and immigrating population, and inclusion of local tribes in the general nomadic ethnic entity, also played their role. The farther West the wave of migration passed, the less it included individuals who were bearers of the original genes. Moreover, Oshanin could show that the modern Turkic-speaking Turkmens, - as far as biological features were concerned, and discounting the above mentioned 10% of gene retention, - differed in no way from the Scythian (Iranian) speaking Massagetae who lived in Turkmenia 25 centuries earlier.

The same must be true of the spread of Indo-European languages, especially if we take into account the fact that, as distinct from the Turks, the Indo-European speakers were not nomads.

This 'relay-race' type spread of languages and linguistic families must be regarded as typical: catastrophic invasions with complete change of population being rather unusual in history. It is only by the 'relay-race' type spread of languages that we can explain why the blond Norwegian or Lithuanian speaks an Indo-European language just as do the very black-skinned Singhalese of Sri Lanka. We can safely relegate to the realm of myth the masses of Indo-Iranians crossing the Caspian in ships from Iranian Azerbaijan to Turkmenia, or, for that matter, any simultaneous mass emigration of an entire Indo-European speaking population from one country to another. The same is true of any other agricultural tribe: a peasant does not leave his land unless driven by dire necessity.

It is my considered opinion that the Indo-European language speakers never left their homeland, wherever it may have lain. What happened, was the constant spread of an increasing population to neighbouring peripheral territories, where the aborigines were usually less numerous and often were on a lower level of production culture; the new settlers intermarried and intermixed with the locals, a common culture and a common (Indo-European) language arose, and was spread by the same procedure further onward.

Another misconception must also be touched upon. This is the misconception of a *Herrenvolk* forcing its language upon a conquered population. This is something which cannot be substantiated historically. None of the ancient empires forced their language upon the conquered people. The Near East emerged after its conquest by the Assyrian and later the Babylonian empire linguistically united, but the common language was not Akkadian of the conquerors but the Aramaic, and from the dominion of Urartu Eastern Anatolia emerged Armenian speaking; the common language of all peoples in the eastern part of the Roman Empire became Greek, not Latin; and even if 'Vulgar Latin' became the language of the western part of the Empire, it was not because the Roman conquerors forced their language upon the aboriginals, but because participation in the Roman culture was a desired material asset. The same is true of Arabic: Arabic was acquired with Islam and the Islamic culture; the Arab masters taxed their subjects higher if they did not embrace Islam but they never did force Arabic upon Christians, Sabians, or Jews. Note that the number of Arabs who entered Egypt in the 7th century was merely about 12,000, but this did not prevent the Egyptians adopting, with time, the Arabic language while retaining their anthropological type and, to a great extent, their way of life.

A language may spread without appreciable population movement. Thus during the twentieth century the borders of Uzbek speaking territory have constantly spread at the expense of Tajik speaking territory. The reason for the spread of a language may be different: As for instance, the need for wider communications, especially in a multilanguage environment, or at a period of more intensive trade relations in a specific territory; sometimes merely the fact that a language was easy to learn decided which language was to get predominance (as Aramaic in the Near East, or Turkic in Middle East Asia).

However, as a general rule we may state that at least a minority of speakers of the new language *must* arrive in the new territory, in order that a new language should spread to it. Such an infiltration, however, does not necessarily leave any important traces in the racial features, in the archaeology of the region, nor even in official texts which may continue to be couched in the traditional official language (Akkadian, Urartian, Hieroglyphic Luwian, etc.); only catastrophic invasions leave clear archaeological traces, but such invasions, as mentioned above, were not frequent. A slower movement and longer periods of settlement can be traced through onomastics, toponyms and hydronyms.

Language territory cannot in principle be unreservedly identified with the territory of one certain archaeological culture. Especially in the archaic periods, with little communication between tribes, different archaeological cultures can form within one dialect continuum. Such cultures would not perhaps be quite dissimilar. Language being the most important medium for the transfer of cultural features, it stands to reason that inside one major archaeological culture we should expect one language or at least one dialect continuum. However, let us remember that Akkadian and Sumerian cannot, in the absence of written sources, be sorted out from archaeological sources alone; and the same is true of the Hurrians and Semites of Upper Mesopotamia in the second millennium B.C. Thus, the existence, at a certain time and in a certain territory, of a major more or less homogenous archaeological culture may be an approximate indication of a continuum of interrelated dialects, but is not a sure proof of its existence.

Now I turn to how I envisage the spread of the Indo-European dialects in antiquity. This is only a subjective opinion: one *has* to make hypothetic constructions when one thinks, but it is not something I should stake my head on.

The triumphant spread of the Indo-European languages over most of the Eurasian continent is due, no doubt, to the fact that their original speakers had a more viable economy than their neighbours, with relatively low infant mortality. This must have been an economy based on high grade agriculture and animal breeding, which supplied milk and meat food for the population in relative plenty. Let us recall that the mass of Sumerians and Akkadians had no meat or milk in their daily diet. For me, that means that the Indo-European speakers must have been the descendants of the first agriculturists and cattle-breeders in Europe. Were it otherwise, it would be another language which would spread all over these great spaces. This, for me, points to the Balkans and the Danube basin as the *original* home of the Indo-Europeans; only later some of them must have moved into the region between the Elba and the Vistula.

It seems established that grain cultivation and cattle breeding reached Macedonia and Thrace from Asia Minor at some moment in the seventh millennium B.C. It is the palaeobotanists and palaeo-zoologists who have the word here; but if this is actually the case, then the Catal-huyuk proto-urban farmer culture of the eighth-seventh millennia B.C. in Asia Minor might have been the homeland of pre-Proto-Indo-Europeans *et al*. This, of course, is no more than a guess with no necessary validity. The Catal-huyuk culture perished by the sixth millennium with the beginning of a prolonged drought period.

Only in one case is the identification of an Indo-European group with a certain archaeological culture possible with nearly complete probability: The Srubnaya, a

Bronze culture in the steppe and forest-steppe regions of Russia and the Ukraine (second half of the second millennium B.C. - early first millennium), as well as its neighboring and kindred Andronovo culture extending from Southern Siberia to the borders of Iran and Afghanistan. These archaeological cultures can confidently be regarded as Indo-Iranian or, more probably, North-Eastern Iranian. The other archaeological cultures of Eastern Europe between the late fourth millennium and the early first millennium have been variously identified with different early Indo-European speakers. The identification perhaps most popular in the West is that of Marija Gimbutas; it is not so popular in my country, because our archaeologists feel she is not quite *au courant* with the newer Soviet finds. There is a number of other identifications; I shall, at random, stake upon the unpublished identification of a young Ukrainian scholar, Stanislav Kaira; it is quite plausible and in no way inferior to any other suggested identification, and may give a representative view of how the problem stands.

According to Kaira, the Yamnaya, or Kurgan culture of the fourth - early second millennia B.C., situated between the Dniester and the Urals, represents mainly the ancestors of the languages of the eastern Indo-Europeans (Greeks, Phrygians, Thracians, Armenians, and Indo-Iranians); to the North-East of it, the Afanasievo culture represents the Tocharians; the Usatovo, the Middle Dnieper culture, as well as the *Schnur-Keramik* and related cultures of Eastern Europe represent the Balto-Slavic, Germanic, Celtic, and Italic speaking tribes.

Also Ivanov and Gamkrelidze reconstruct the habitat of the early Indo-Europeans more or less in the same way; the difference, however, is that they bring them into Eastern Europe from Eastern Anatolia and Iranian Azerbaijan, and that by different devious routes, and in such a way that linguistically closely related languages are assigned different routes, while linguistically remote languages are supposed to have followed one and the same route.

A long sojourn of speakers of a certain language in a given territory means usually that (a) one can *approximately* identify a certain archaeological culture as created by the speakers of that language, alone or jointly with other ethnic groups; (b) one can identify substratum words borrowed from the language in question into the later language or languages of that area; (c) one can identify toponyms or hydronyms borrowed from the same substratum language; (d) the way of migration can approximately be traced by migration of archaeological artifacts which have a diagnostic value for the archaeological culture in question. On the strength of these indicators, one can confidently say that Indo-European languages have not been spoken in the Near East before the arrival of the Hittito-Luwians (probably in the third millennium B.C.), the Proto-Armenians (late in the second millennium B.C.)^2, and the Indo-Iranians (probably during the second millennium B.C.). Ivanov and Gamkrelidze themselves concede that their hypothetic Indo-Europeans in Eastern Anatolia and Iranian Azerbaijan cannot be identified with any particular archaeological culture, and the tentative identifications with the Tell-Halaf and the Shulaveri-Shomutepe cultures (the latter in Transcaucasia) are by no means convincing. There are no toponyms or hydronyms of early Indo-European origin in Eastern Anatolia; as to the hydronyms quoted by Ivanov and Gamkrelidze for the peninsula of Asia Minor, I cannot see why they could not be early Hittito-Luwian. As to words borrowed from Proto-Indo-

European into Near Eastern languages, the authors quote I.-E. *woi-no- 'wine' and Semitic *wain- do., Kartvelian * wino- do. and also Georgian venaq- 'vineyard' allegedly from an I.-E. *weinag- (p. 881); but on p. 649 the same I.-E. gloss dwindles down to a late Southern Slavic word-compound vinyaga 'wine-berry,' i.e. 'grape' which cannot by any stretch of imagination be responsible for Georgian venaq-. However, *wain- is only Western Semitic, not Common Semitic or Common Afrasian, and hence may have been borrowed from Mycenean Greek; actual Indo-European-Kartvelian isoglosses will be mentioned below.

Furthermore, the authors cite Hattic aia- 'to give' as an allegedly I.-E. borrowing. Since the word belongs to the main semantic nucleus to which foreign words are very seldom borrowed, I prefer to regard the Hattic word as *Sirene des Gleichklangs*, and the same is true of Hattic urai 'well, spring' and Uret 'goddess of water and springs,' allegedly from Indo-European.

Also quite improbable is the suggestion that Elamite borrowed from Proto-Indo-European its anaphoric pronouns and some other words which are, with one or two exceptions, misquotations anyway. Elamite has now been safely classed together with Dravidian by McAlpin, and also the words in question have received satisfactory native etymologies. This is also true of Hurro-Urartian ag- 'to lead,' and ass- 'to be placed, to sit;' both have good Eastern Caucasian etymologies and need not be regarded as borrowings. Moreover, the verb ass-, being Common Hurro-Urartian, i.e. dating back to about the fourth millennium B.C., cannot be borrowed from Indo-Iranian; and if borrowed from Common Indo-European, it would have been represented as *es-, not ass-! Urartian burgana means 'pole,' not 'fortress,' and has a satisfactory Eastern Caucasian etymology. Hurrian kade 'barley' represents the phoneme k, not *q (spelled k or ḫ) and cannot be identified with I.-E. *Hat-, etc., etc.

Ivanov and Gamkrelidze cite also a number of glosses which allegedly are borrowed from Semitic into Proto-Indo-European. I have already analyzed these glosses elsewhere and shown that they (   ) do not satisfy the necessary phonetic and/or semantic requirements; in a few cases they may be wandering *Kulturwörter* having reached *some* Indo-European areas but certainly not Common Indo-European. Still less reliable are the alleged borrowings into Common Indo-European from Sumerian, like Indo-European *gwou- (or, according to the authors, even *k'ou 'cow') from Sumerian *gud 'cattle; bull' and simultaneously from Egyptian ng;.w, i.e. [*naga'-w-], to quote only one example out of six quite impossible etymologies.

Then we come to the question whether there exist archaeological traces of any mass movement from Anatolia and Azerbaijan towards the East and North-East - towards India, Central Asia and Southern Siberia, and thence to Eastern Europe (the Yamnaya, or Kurgan Culture). Such a movement is postulated by Ivanov and Gamkrelidze. Space does not allow me to dwell upon this point in more detail; it is sufficient to state that no such traces going back to the fourth-second millennia B.C. are at all attested; on the contrary, all evidence points to popular movements in the opposite direction, i.e. from Eastern Europe towards the East, from Southern Siberia towards the South, etc., etc.

We must unavoidably come to the conclusion that the Proto-Indo-Europeans did never dwell in Eastern Anatolia and Iranian Azerbaijan, nor anywhere else in the Near East, at least not in the fifth to third millennia B.C.

Now we can turn to the positive evidence that we have at our disposal concerning the linguistic areas in the Ancient Near East.

The oldest linguistic area is that of the so-called 'Banana'-language, also known as Proto-Tigridian. It appears in a few late third millennium B.C. personal names from Gasur at the site of Yorghan-tepe near Kirkuk in Eastern Iraq, east of the Tigris, and in a number of borrowed cultural words in Sumerian, like *urudu* 'metal, copper,' *apin* 'plough,' and others, as well as in a number of names of deities, like Inana, Ishkhara, Kubaba, Zababa, Aia, Bunene, Igigi and others. The language was certainly extinct by 2000 B.C.; its kinship connections are unknown.

Next comes Sumerian. The Sumerian language seems to have been brought to Southern Mesopotamia presumably in the early fourth millennium B.C., and apparently from the East. The pronunciation of Sumerian words is known only from Akkadian transcriptions in Sumero-Akkadian vocabularies and in Sumerian borrowings into Akkadian. However - as I think I was able to prove (work in print) - the current pronunciation of Akkadian is the result of uncritical transposition to it of Hebrew and partly Arabic pronunciations of the Common Semitic phonemes, and the real phonetics of Akkadian was very far from the conventional. This means that also the Akkadian transcriptions of Sumerian words are, as of today, practically worthless until deeper investigations have been made. It is fairly certain that the Sumerian phonetic system was very complicated, reminding one of, *e.g.*, Eastern Caucasian. No kinship connection between Sumerian and any other language in the world has been established.

The Sumerians lived in modern Southern Iraq in a peaceful cohabitation with the Eastern Semites, or Akkadians. No archaeological traces of ethnical conflicts in Southern Mesopotamia between the years 4000 B.C. and 2000 B.C. have been observed, although local wars were of course waged, but regardless of the language spoken by the adversaries. Both peoples shared the common denomination of 'blackheads' (Sumerian *sang-ngiga*, Akkadian *salmat qaqqadi*). The whole population of Southern Mesopotamia, after a prolonged period of bilingualism, changed over to Akkadian at a date which has been variously estimated, from ca. 2500 B.C. to ca. 1500 B.C.

The Semites form a linguistic family inside the Afrasian, or Afro-Asiatic linguistic phylum. The Semites were living in Western Asia south of the Asianic and the Armenian Taurus and west of the Zagros, in a territory probably including the Arabian Peninsula, at least since the fourth or even the fifth millennium B.C. The analysis of the Common Semitic vocabulary by Pelio Fronzaroli has shown that the Proto-Semites were neolithic and chalcolithic agriculturalists and animal breeders.

Since it has been proved that Semitic is related to the African linguistic families Egyptian, Cushitic (and probably Omotic), Berbero-Libyan and Chadic, the question of the original homeland of the whole phylum arises. I had suggested the eastern part of the Republic of Sudan and Western Sahara, but weighty arguments have been brought against this hypothesis. Another such hypothesis is that of Alexander Militarev. According to him, the Proto-Afrasians were very early agriculturalists acquainted with certain metals and living in an environment of half desert and steppe, half Mediterranean maquis and forest-land. On glottochronological grounds he dates Proto-Afrasian to *ca.* ten-eleven thousand B.C. and identifies their original habitat with the area of the Natufian mesolithic culture in Palestine. The Natufians, however, had still no agriculture, and the economic picture drawn by Militarev's proto-language reconstruction points rather to the seventh or eighth, not the eleventh millennium B.C. According to Militarev, the speakers of the 'African' Afrasian languages left Western Asia during the sixth millennium period of drought and passed to Africa partly via Suez, and partly via the Bab al-Mandab. In both cases the groups of migrants could not have been very numerous, although their languages were to be adopted by a great number of people - of the Ethiopian local black race (the Cushites), the Negroid local black race (the Chadians), the Mediterranean local white race (the Egyptians) and the Atlanto-Baltic local white race (the Berbero-Lybians and the Guanche in the Canarians). As an argument in favor of a Western Asiatic origin of all Afrasian speakers Militarev adduces the existence of Berber - East-Caucasian, and Cushitic - West Caucasian specific isoglosses; whether or not the isoglosses in question are of better quality than that postulated by Ivanov and Gamkrelidze for Proto-Indo-Europeans and the languages of Ancient Near East, remains to be seen.[3]

The Elamites, inhabiting the whole southern part of present-day Iran during the third and second millennia B.C. - probably also earlier - seem to be linguistically akin to the Brahui in modern Baluchistan (Afghanistan and Pakistan) and further with the Dravidians of Southern India. The Elamite - and the possibly related Kassite language - gradually gave way during the later second and the first millennia B.C. to the speakers of Western Iranian languages of the Indo-European linguistic family. No archaeological evidence of ethnic conflicts exists.

The next linguistic family to be considered is the Northern Caucasian. Formerly Caucasian was divided into three branches: North-Western with Abkhazian, Adygh, Ubykh, etc., Southern or Kartvelian with Svan, Georgian, Mingrelian and Ch'an and North-Eastern with Chechen, Avaro-Andian, Lezghian etc. After the work done by S.A. Starostin and S.A. Nikolaev it appears evident that North-Caucasian is a superfamily divided into two families, the North-Eastern (or Eastern Caucasian), and the North-Western (or Western Caucasian); while Kartvelian does not belong to the Caucasian superfamily at all but constitutes a separate family of its own. The typology of Proto-Kartvelian word structure is strikingly similar to that of Proto-Indo-European. There exist also a number of Proto-Kartvelian - Proto-Indo-European lexical isoglosses. What is especially important, they do not belong to the cultural vocabulary so often easily borrowed, but to the nuclear vocabulary, as e.g. *dew-: *dw- 'to lie, to put;' *lag-: *lg- 'to lay, to plant;' *gen-: *gn- 'to understand, to hear,' *zisxl 'blood,' *m-k'erd 'breast' *k'rep- 'to pluck, to gather (fruit),' *brg 'strong, sturdy, large' and a number of others which an Indo-European scholar will immediately recognize. Therefore, in spite of the fact that such eminent experts as G.A. Klimov and Th.V. Gamkrelidze regard these isoglosses as borrowings, I am inclined to regard them as evidence of a collateral kinship between Proto-Indo-European and Proto-Kartvelian going back to a common Proto-Kartvelo-Indo-European dialect continuum.

The Georgians themselves, including the Georgian linguists, regard their language as autochtonous. The whole Ivanov-Gamkrelidze theory shows a picture of Indo-European languages moving in a gigantic rotating movement with immovable Georgian as the axis of the giant wheel. But note that also the Armenians and even the Azerbaijanis tend to regard their mother tongue as autochtonous and immovable since early antiquity. If the Georgian language has never budged from its place in Eastern and Central Transcaucasia, then it is truly unique in the world. I think it more probable that the first speakers of Kartvelian arrived from outside, and namely (since no connection between Catal-Huyuk in early Asia Minor and the later archaeological cultures of Georgia can be traced), from the North. As a probable archaeological nucleus one might regard the Maikop culture of the North Caucasus, and the newly found tumuli in Kakhetia, Georgia. The date of the Maikop culture (second half of the third millennium B.C.) fits the glottochronology of Kartvelian. Although formerly the Maikop culture was regarded as isolated, now it can be regarded as having certain features in common not only with the Near Eastern cultures, but also with the Pre-Proto-European cultures of the third millennium B.C. in Southern Europe (Megalithic and others). The Northwest-Caucasian dolmens do not differ from the European Megalithic ones.

The speakers of Northern Caucasian languages inhabit at present a very limited mountain zone in the Greater Caucasus and belong to a specific local European race - the Caucasionic one (also the Ossetes whose language is the descendant of the Scythian dialect of the Alani, *i.e.* North-Eastern Iranian, - belong to the same local race). However, some time ago, conjointly with S.A. Starostin, I seem to have proved that also Hurro-Urartian belonged to the Eastern Caucasian linguistic family, having its place between Chechen, Andian and Lezghian. This does not tell the non-expert very much. But if you put a compass leg, on a map of the Causacus, in Tbilisi, the capital of Georgia, then in about a hundred miles due NE you will find the Kodori pass leading into Chechnia; just west of the Kodori pass are the sources of the Andian-Koisu river, whose valley North of the Greater Caucasus is inhabited by the Andians; and the different Lezghian tribes live on both sides of the Greater Caucasus, south of a line due East of Tbilisi. Supposing the Proto-Chechen, the Proto-Andian and the Proto-Lezghian languages were spoken in about the same region some five or six thousand years ago, this means that the homeland of the Hurro-Urartians would be to the South of the Chechens and the Andians and to the West of the Lezghians, somewhere between modern Tbilisi and the mountains to the east of it. Of course, the suggested homeland may have lain also farther to the northeast, or the southeast, or the southwest.

According to Starostin, the Caucasian languages are related to the Ket on the Yenissey River and to Sino-Tibetan. This seems to be a rather mad statement, but coming from a linguist of the stature of Starostin, cannot be just disregarded. Anyway, it is not improbable that the Caucasian languages, like the other language groups in the region, have been imported from the North or North-East at an early date. They do not belong to the Nostratic phylum (with Indo-European, Kartvelian, Fenno-Ugrian and Elamo-Dravidian). The glottochronological date for Proto-Caucasian is well beyond the 4000 B.C. mark, perhaps 5000 B.C.

Margarita Khachikyan in Erevan has shown that the infiltration of the Hurrian speakers to the foothills and the plains of the Near East went on in several discrete waves during the late third and the first half of the second millennium B.C., coming apparently from the North-East (*hurri-le* seems to have meant 'Easterners' or 'North-Easterners', c.f. Hurrian *hurri* 'morning'). The northern limit of Hurrian is unknown, but it certainly lay far up in eastern Anatolia or even in Transcaucasia. The western limit of the Hurrian language area lay certainly West of the Taurus, the eastern somewhere in the Zagros. The homeland of the Urartian was, in the late second and early first millennia B.C., around Lake Van and east of it in Eastern Anatolia. It is perhaps unavoidable to regard Eastern Anatolia (and Transcaucasia?) as the region of the Hurro-Urartian language before its descent to the foothills and into the plains, i.e., in the third millennium B.C. There is good reason to believe that in the third millennium B.C. the Hurro-Urartian language zone more or less coincided with the area of the Eastern Anatolian Early Bronze culture. The Soviet archaeologists call it the Kur-Araxes culture: its center is thought to have lain in Transcaucasia, and its northern frontier crossed the Greater Caucasus at Kodori and farther to the East.[4] This actually leaves no space here for the Indo-Europeans. Also Iranian Azerbaijan was inhabited at that time (and later) by a people called the Qutians. The term *quti coincides with the name of the little modern Lezghian people Udi (< *qut i) living on the frontier between Georgia and Azerbaijan. We know very little about the Qutian language, but most probably it also was Eastern Caucasian.

Caucasian languages (in the proper sense, i.e. not including the Kartvelian) seem also to have been the substratum for Hittito-Luwian. This is fairly certain for the Hittites (and the Palaians of Paphlagonia). Here the substratum was Hattic which, after the recent work of I.M. Dunajevskaja, V.G. Ardzimba and V.V. Ivanov, we can fairly certainly consider as a Western Caucasian language. The certainty is perhaps not so cast-iron as in the case of the eastern Caucasian origin of Hurro-Urartian, but the evidence is not to be discarded, and anyway, even *a priori* Hattic could hardly be anything else but Western Caucasian.

But the Hattic linguistic area did not stretch beyond the Halys (Kizil-Irmak), and the substratum of the Luwians and the rest of Asia Minor, including Cyprus, Lemnos etc., - was apparently Eastern Caucasian. At the time of working with Starostin on Hurro-Urartian I had a look through the Etruscan material. I was struck by the typological similarity between the Etruscan and the Hurrian grammar structures; it was obvious that the Etruscologists were so long unable to solve the riddle of the Etruscan grammar because they were hampered by their Indo-European background. This fall Starostin and his collaborator V.E. Orel read a paper postulating a material kinship between Etruscan and the Hurro-Urartian branch of the Eastern Caucasian linguistic family, both in vocabulary and in morphology. In their opinion the Etruscan language was one of the languages of the aboriginal population of Asia Minor, its speakers having emigrated to the Central Mediterranean long before the Peoples of the Sea movement in the late second millennium B.C.

While we are speaking about Eastern Caucasian, and Hurrian in particular, it would be appropriate to touch upon the problem of the so-called "Mesopotamian Aryan." Ivanov and Gamkrelidze greatly overrate the value of the existing evidence on "Mesopotamian Aryan;" they even suggest that the Indo-Iranians dwelled in Iranian Azerbaijan as early as the fourth-third millennium. As proof they bring the supposed kinship of Sumerian *si-si* 'horse' with the Indo-Iranian name of the horse in its *sat3m*-form (*asva-* < *ek'uo-*). I just cannot believe in the existence of *sat3m*-forms already in the *Ur-Heimat*, allegedly in Anatolia - Azerbaijan; and anyway the connection of *si-si* even to *asva-* (not *ek'uo-*) is a *Sirene des Gleichklangs*, if ever there was one.

According to the common opinion, there are Indo-Aryan (allegedly "Mesopotamian Aryan") glosses in the handbook of horse-training written by one

Mitannian Kikkuli for the Hittite kings in about the thirteenth century B.C., and there is a list of Indo-Aryan gods: Mitra, Varuna, Indra, and the Nasatyas, invoked as guarantors of a treaty between the Hittite king Suppiluliumas I and the Mitannian pretender Shattiwazza. It has been pointed out as important in this connection that Mitra is a god of treaties.

As to Kikkuli's handbook, the above is substantially correct; whether the glosses are actually Indo-Aryan is, as we shall see, a moot question. As to the Hittite-Mitannian treaty, the statement in the form cited is wrong, as very justly pointed out by Annelies Kammenhuber. She also noted that all extant 'Aryan' glosses in second millennium cuneiform texts are not actually Aryan but manifestly transmitted by Hurrian speakers.

The list of deities in the treaty is very long indeed, and the so-called 'Aryan' gods are enumerated very far down the list (the deities being listed according to their importance, and the list including Hattic, Hittito-Luwian, Sumero-Akkadian and Hurrian gods). The 'Aryan' gods are not listed on a par with the others: their names are included in a Hurrian quotation, as follows: *Mitra-ssi-l urwa-na-ssi-l Ind(a)ra Nasatya-nna*, which means: 'those of the belonging to Mitra, those of the belonging to the *urwa*'s, Indra, (and) the Nasatya's." The variant of the treaty has *aru-na-ssi-l* for *urwa-na-ssi-l*. The place of Mitra far down the long list points to the fact that his function as treaty-god was in this case quite unimportant, and as to *urwa-na* (*aru-na*), it can by no means be a transcription of Varuna, because Hurrian does not know a development of an initial *w-* to zero (neither does Hittite). *Urwa-na* is probably the Hurrian plural of the Indo-Iranian mythological term *urwan* 'soul' (preserved in Old Iranian), and *Mitra-ssi-l urwa-na-ssi-l* means 'Those of the belonging to Mitra, those of the belonging to (the dead) souls', Mitra appearing here in his quality of the deity of light as *opposed* to the dead, or, contrariwise, as *judge* of the dead.

Now *urwa-* cannot be Indo-Aryan, while other glosses, especially *aika* 'one,' seem to point rather to Indo-Aryan than to Iranian. The 'Prakrit' form *satta* for 'seven' is, however, unexpected.

There certainly never was an Aryan language spoken in Mesopotamia. The Mitannian Hurrians belonged to the last wave of Hurrian immigration according to Margaret Khachikyan, coming apparently from modern Iranian Azerbaijan about 1700 B.C. The kingdom was officially called Hanigalbat; *Mittanni* < **Maitani* being apparently the dynastic name; the same name had been preserved as a territorial designation in the first millennium B.C., when the country near lake Urmia in Iranian Azerbaijan was called Matiane. The dynasty was apparently Matianian and originally - but no longer in Mesopotamia - Indo-Iranian-speaking. The Kingdom Hanigalbat itself was Hurrian. Note that the *marianna*-charioteers were *not* an aristocracy and were exclusively recruited from Hurrians, as follows from hundreds of documents. The term has a satisfactory Eastern Caucasian etymology.

However 1700 B.C. is too early for Iranians, and Iranian Azerbaijan is too far West for the Indians. But one is apt to forget that there are three, not two sub-branches in the Indo-Iranian linguistic branch: it was divided into Kafirs, Indo-Aryans and Iranians, and the Kafirs were, according to the authority of Georg Morgenstierne, the first to move south from Middle Asia. Note that Avestan, spoken originally on the main road from Middle Asia to the South, namely in the Marw-rud and Tejen-Harirud valleys, has no non-Indo-Iranian linguistic substratum, and thus must have overlaid another Indo-Iranian language. This, not improbably, could have been the Kafir; later pushed up into the mountains, the Kafirs could have preceded the Iranians on a much greater area, even including Matiane in Azerbaijan (but not Mesopotamia). The glosses *aika, satta*, etc. fit Kafir perfectly, Indra was the chief god of the Kafirs until the beginning of this century; the other great god of the Kafirs, Imro, united in himself the images of Mitra and Yama, the god of the dead.

There is no more space for description of other ancient Near Eastern linguistic contacts in this paper; but since my books referring to Phrygian and Armenian[5] have just appeared in the States I think I can refer the readers to them. One last point: there is a number of Hurro-Urartian substratum words in Armenian, referring to the local plants, animals, and to social institutions in Eastern Anatolia during the first millennium B.C.; also the dramatic change from Proto-Indo-European to Armenian morphology is easily explained by the influence of an Urartian substratum with a fixed stress on the penultimate syllable[6]. But there is no Armenian substratum in either Hattic, Hittite, Hurrian, or Urartian.

END NOTES

[1] As to Eastern Europe, Thrace and Illyria adopted Slavic languages, and Pannonia, Hungarian. But the population of these countries did not change in its physical anthropological features.

[2] Note also the spread of Proto-Balkanic Phrygian and Thracian into Asia Minor during the first millennium B.C., and Celtic, also into Asia Minor, in the third century A.D.

[3] Militarev also points out that nearly a dozen of cultural (agricultural and technological) terms are common to Sumerian and not only Akkadian but actually to Proto-Afrasian.

[4] Certain followers of Ivanov and Gamkrelidze have attempted to prove that the Kur-Araxes culture was Indo-European, basing their conclusions on a supposed Indo-European origin of the myths illustrated in Kur-Araxes artifacts. It goes without saying that the spread of a myth (given that its interpretation is correct) is not necessarily limited to one linguistic area. Cf. the numerous examples in Stith-Thompson's great reference book.

[5] *Pre-History of the Armenian People*, Delmar, N.Y. 1985; *Phrygian* (with V.P. Neroznak), Delmer, N.Y., 1986.

[6] Another feature of the Armenian grammar which is due to the Hurro-Urartian substratum is the loss of genders. It is usually ascribed to Georgian influence, but Georgian was not a substratum language for Armenian.

KARTVELIAN CONTACTS WITH INDO-EUROPEAN[1]
ALICE C. HARRIS
Vanderbilt University

In their work on the Indo-European language family (*Indoevropejskij jazyk i indoevropejcy*, vol. I, 1984), Gamkrelidze and Ivanov have presented arguments for intense contact between the Indo-Europeans and the Kartvelians as early as the fourth or third millenium B.C. This hypothesis has implications for the Indo-European homeland and is an important part of their proposal for locating it in Anatolia. They suggest three types of parallel between Indo-European and Kartvelian: (i) phonological parallels, some of them studied by Gamkrelidze and Machavariani 1965 and reiterated in the more recent work, (ii) syntactic parallels, and (iii) lexical borrowings, set out in the more recent work. The purpose of the present paper is to call attention to some additional facts that need to be taken into account in assessing proposed parallels between Indo-European and Kartvelian, with emphasis on the morphological and syntactic systems of the languages.

In section 1 below, I address some issues concerning the nature of linguistic diffusion and the methods involved in its investigation and assessment. The second section focuses on the proposed syntactic parallels, and the third on some of the proposed phonological(-morphological) parallels. The final section provides an evaluation of proposed linguistic parallels between Indo-European and Kartvelian and their implications for the question of the Indo-European homeland.

---

1. This material is based upon work supported in part by the National Science Foundation under Grant No. BNS-8712111. I am very grateful to Lyle Campbell, John Greppin, and Brent Vine for comments on earlier drafts.

1. The Investigation of Areal Linguistics

The kind of intense, prolonged contact that has been suggested for Indo-European and Kartvelian typically results in a number of shared linguistic traits. In recent years linguists have learned a great deal about the nature of diffusion and the investigation and definition of a linguistic area or *Sprachbund*. Some linguists have considered a single shared feature the minimum for establishing the existence of a *Sprachbund* (Masica 1976), while many others find a linguistic area based on a set of shared features more acceptable (see discussion in Campbell 1985 and Campbell, Kaufman, and Smith-Stark 1986).

In assessing proposed diagnostics of any *Sprachbund*, it is essential first to distinguish diffused areal features from chance correspondence, from shared genetic material, and from correlates of some other feature.

Once we have eliminated the reasonable possibility of a parallel resulting from genetic affiliation or from another parallel, we must evaluate the particular proposed feature from the point of view of ease of diffusion. It is well accepted that lexical borrowing is extremely easy and does not require intense contact. Diffusion of lexical items is expected in a linguistic area but alone is not indicative of one. Borrowing of structural features may be more difficult and, other things being equal, may be indicative of more intense contact.

A further point essential in evaluating a proposed diagnostic of contact is just how common that feature is among languages of the world. Clearly, a highly unusual feature is more valuable as an indicator of contact, for it is less likely that it could have developed independently in the languages concerned. To illustrate the importance of this principle, let us take an extreme example. Nasal consonants are extremely common, being found in all languages of the world apart from a few American Indian languages spoken on the North West coast of the United States and perhaps some languages of New Guinea. Obviously, the presence of nasal consonants in two languages would not be a highly valued diagnostic of contact. As a less extreme example, we might consider word order. The orders VSO, SVO, and SOV are all very common among languages of the world, while

VOS, OVS, and OSV are more rare. While any one of the last three might be indicative of contact, none of the first three would be a convincing diagnostic.

In well-understood linguistic areas, it is possible to show that some of the members of the *Sprachbund* under consideration acquired the defining traits by diffusion from remaining members. For example, some Indo-European languages are part of the South Asian linguistic area, and the roots of these languages are understood in relation to Indo-European languages spoken outside India. For this reason, we can be reasonably clear about which features of the Indo-European languages of India underwent change as a result of contact with Dravidian, Munda, and other languages of India. For example, it can be shown then that the Indo-European languages in India first lacked retroflex consonants, then acquired them over a period of time. Since the Munda and Dravidian languages (and others) have this feature, the historical development of this feature in Indo-Aryan language make it possible to infer that the acquisition was due to contact with languages already having the feature. Hamp 1977, Jacobsen 1980, Campbell 1985, and Campbell, Kaufman, and Smith-Stark 1986, have stressed the importance of this historical dimension in establishing a linguistic area; following these authors, I refer to this as the "historical" approach.

In the absence of this historical dimension, we are left with the problem of evaluating the likelihood that the observed parallels developed independently in the two families or that they are due to mere chance. Following the authors cited in the prededing paragraph, I refer to this as the "circumstantial" approach. For example, the North East Caucasian family and the North West Caucasian family are in close geographical proximity and share the feature of ergative agreement (defined below). However, it cannot be established that this is due to close contact. We cannot establish that one family first lacked this feature then acquired it through contact; we have only circumstantial evidence.

Any evidence that can relate Indo-European to Kartvelian in the fourth or third millenium is necessarily circumstantial, in the sense that it goes well beyond the possibilities of linguistic science to demonstrate that a particular feature first was not to be found in one of these language families and later was present there, or to establish clearly how it got from one to the other. In part this is due to the fact that there are no languages that are related but outside the *Sprachbund* to act as the "control" case.

The fact that the origin of a structural characteristic can be explained on internal grounds does not indicate that it was not diffused from other languages. (This point has been made by Campbell 1985 and, regarding the Balkan linguistic area, by Joseph 1983). The importance of multiple causation in language change is now recognized. It is, in fact, unlikely that syntactic characteristics can diffuse in the way words do, by simple wholesale borrowing. It seems more likely that in all cases diffusion of structural characteristics has internally explicable mechanisms as well, and that when these are not recognized it is only because we have not been able to find them.[2] A further problem that we face in the instance at hand is due to the fact that contact between Indo-European and Kartvelian continued, perhaps for thousands of years without a break, though perhaps somewhat less intensely at some times than at others. Thus we must be careful to disentangle the oldest features from the web of diffused structural characteristics. Similarly we face the difficulty of distinguishing between possible diffusion due to contact at the level of proto-language or subgroup and possible diffusion due to influence from single languages, for example Armenian contact with the individual Kartvelian languages.

A final point that must be emphasized for its relation to the discussion below is the fact that the absence of parallels does not, indeed cannot, establish the absence of contact. Thus, although I will argue below that the syntactic structure of Indo-European may not be as parallel to that of Kartvelian as Gamkrelidze and Ivanov have suggested, it must be remembered that this does not by any means establish that there was no contact, or even that that contact was less intense than

---

2. An example of this is the evidential, seemingly an areal feature; we can, however, show the language internal mechanisms by which it arose in Kartvelian (Harris 1985).

claimed by the authors. It accomplishes no more and no less than calling into question one piece of the evidence they adduce in support of their hypothesis.

2. Proposed Syntactic (Alignment) Parallels

2.1. Case Alignment and the Structure of the Proposal Concerning It

The term *alignment* is not used by Gamkrelidze and Ivanov, but is one introduced by Plank 1979, and one I have used extensively in my own writing on this subject. Gamkrelidze and Ivanov 1984 follow Fillmore (1968: 54) in defining ergative, accusative, and active distributions of cases, all of which together I refer to as "alignment."[3] In a language with ergative case marking, the subject of a transitive ($S^{tr.}$) is marked with one case, while the direct object (O) and the subjects of intransitive verbs ($S^{intr.}$) are marked with another. In the schema, the lines indicate the distributional boundaries of the case.

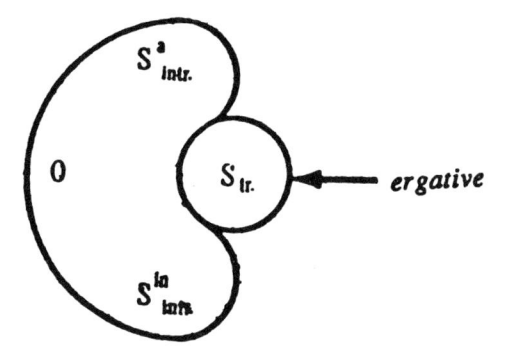

Figure 1: Gamkrelidze and Ivanov (1984:313)

---

3. Rather, it is the general idea of Fillmore's figures that they adopt, changing his constant A (agent) and O (object) to other terms, depending upon which alignment they describe. They also cite Sapir 1917.

In accusative case marking, the direct object (O) is marked with one case, while all subjects (S) are marked with another.

accusative → O, $S^a_{intr.}$, $S_{tr.}$, $S^{in}_{intr.}$

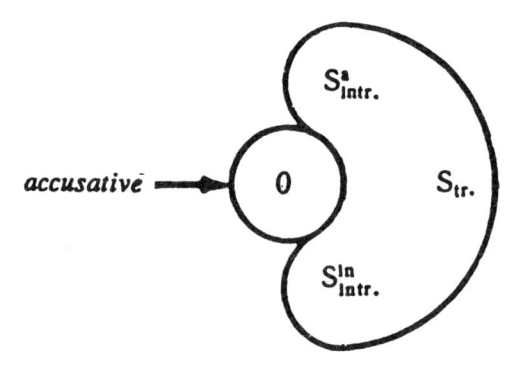

Figure 2: Gamkrelidze and Ivanov (1984:314)

Active case marking systems have one case marking the subject of transitives and of active intransitives (both A), while another case is assigned to the subject of inactive intransitives and to direct objects (both In).

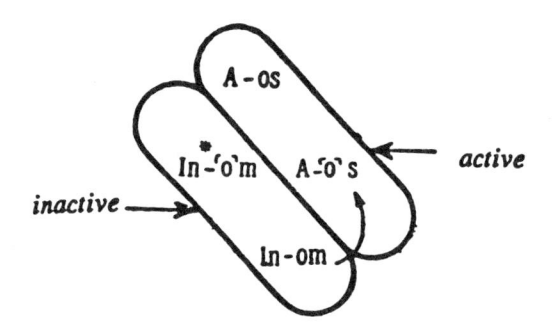

A - os, In -*'o'm, A -'o' s, *active*, *inactive*, In - om

Figure 3: Gamkrelidze and Ivanov (1984:315)

Like a number of other Indoeuropeanists, Gamkrelidze and Ivanov 1984 reconstruct to Proto-Indo-European a binary opposition between animate and inanimate nouns. Gamkrelidze and Ivanov present evidence that both *-*os* and *-*om* can be reconstructed as formants of the genitive case. These authors argue that, although the distribution of these endings was later altered, originally *-*os* was used for inanimates, *-*om* for animates. For them, other facts confirm this binary opposition in other spheres. An evaluation of these arguments within Indo-European is more appropriately undertaken by Indo-Europeanists and lies quite outside the scope of the present paper.

Having accepted an opposition between animate and inanimate nouns in Proto-Indo-European, Gamkrelidze and Ivanov (1984:314) state correlates (or implications) of the several alignment types, following, for the most part, proposals in Klimov 1973, 1977 and the same author's other works. In languages with the ergative and accusative types of case marking, they say, there exists an opposition between transitive and intransitive verbs. In languages with case marking of the active type, they continue, there is no such opposition of transitive to intransitive, but there is instead an opposition of animate to inanimate nouns. On this basis they argue that Proto-Indo-European had case marking of the active type.

The authors continue by citing Klimov's 1973 statements (also in subsequent works) that Common Kartvelian was likewise active. The two language families changed in different directions, they believe, with Indo-European eventually developing case marking of the accusative type, and Kartvelian developing case marking of the ergative type.[4]

---

4. Both their hypothesis for Indo-European and their hypothesis for Kartvelian, following Klimov 1977, are based on the position that either ergative or accusative structures can develop from active, but that the reverse is not possible (Gamkrelidze and Ivanov 1984:318). This idea would not be accepted by most linguists.

2.2. Assessing the Ancestral Active Hypothesis

2.2.1 Problems Relating to Indo-European

As observed above (section 2.1), Gamkrelidze and Ivanov follow Fillmore 1968 in defining specific alignment types in terms of the distribution of cases, citing his schema, in Figures 1-3 (Gamkrelidze and Ivanov's Figures 2-4, 1984:313-315), and his descriptions. However, to Fillmore's definitions they add the claims that there are correlations with transitive/intransitive and animate/inanimate dichotomies, as stated above. A problem then arises in identifying a specific language as belonging to one type or the other; when there is a conflict between the actual distribution of case markers and the two dichotomies named, which of these will be the determining factor? We have already seen that instead of using the distributional definitions they give, in identifying the alignment type of a particular language the authors use the putative correlations between case distribution and the otherwise unrelated phenomenon of an animate/inanimate distinction in nouns. For example, in identifying the original alignment type of Proto-Indo-European, they use the criterion of animate/inanimate as a grammatical category and on this basis conclude that the language had active case marking, without regard to the actual distribution or use of the cases. They might have reconstructed the distribution of cases on the basis of archaic patterns of case distribution preserved in daughter languages and on this basis determined the alignment type for case marking in the proto-language. Instead, they reconstructed an animate/inanimate dichotomy on the basis of archaic morphology preserved in daughter languages and on this basis made claims about the distribution of case in the proto-language.

This reconstruction and the hypotheses upon which it rests pose serious problems from at least two points of view. First, the putative correlations proposed by Klimov 1973 were not based on a systematic investigation according to objective, stated criteria. The supposed correlations have not been widely accepted.[5]

A second problem, related to the first, concerns the methodology used. Even if the correlates proposed by Klimov turn out to be entirely accurate, why should a correlate, rather than the defining feature, be used in identifying the type of an individual language? For most scholars in the West it has been the syntactic distribution of case marking that formed the only diagnostic for identifying an alignment type. Identification of type is meaningless unless there is a clear criterion for the typing, and it is distribution that scholars in the West have relied on. Clearly hypotheses regarding alignment type are untestable or meaningless without a reliable criterion. For several generations, most scholars in the West have rejected the idea of whole-language typologies (ones that would claim a correlation between morphological type and word order type, for example), and for them the grammaticalization of animate/inanimate or transitive/intransitive distinctions must be considered independently of alignment type (see Harris 1986:56-57).

In the typology set up by Gamkrelidze and Ivanov (1983:313-319), distribution of cases (Figures 1-3) has typological correlates in binary divisions between transitive and intransitive (for ergative and nominative alignment) or between animate and inanimate nouns (for active alignment). The structure of their argument is this: if the proto-language had the correlate of active alignment, namely the binary division animate/inanimate, one can infer that it had active alignment. This is a typological argument. This kind of typological approach to historical linguistics has received severe criticism from a number of scholars (e.g., Campbell and Mithun 1980, Jeffers 1976, Watkins 1976) and is not accepted by most linguists.

2.2.2. Problems Relating to the Comparison with Kartvelian

---

5. For example, see Comrie 1976:254-255 on the dubious validity of the correlates.

For the alignment of Kartvelian, Gamkrelidze and Ivanov cite Klimov's statements that the proto-language was active (Gamkrelidze and Ivanov 1984:318); we must therefore examine the basis on which Klimov reached this conclusion. On he whole, Klimov seems to have considered the modern Kartvelian languages to have ergative case marking because this is the traditional view.[6] Klimov (1973:50) cites patterns such as the following as the basis for reconstructing earlier case patterns: e.g., *deda-m it'ira* [mother-Nar she-cry] '(the) mother cried.' Here the so-called narrative (or ergative) case marks the subject of an active intransitive. Klimov concludes that this indicates that case marking in the proto-language was active.

Here Klimov has, in fact, used distributional criteria, finding evidence of the pattern in Figure 3 above, labelled active. The problem with his analysis here is that he has used the regular pattern of the language as evidence of an archaism. It is well-established practice in linguistics that what is regular and productive is the basis for a synchronic analysis, while what is irregular, restricted, and archaic is the basis for reconstruction of earlier stages (Kurylowicz 1964:10, Meillet 1954:27, Watkins 1976). The class of verbs and the case marking pattern cited by Klimov is entirely regular and productive in the language (as established by Holisky 1981). Klimov, in the works cited, offers no evidence as to whether this is an old state of affairs or the result of later innovations; his inference that it is archaic is thus unfounded.

Klimov 1976 examines the case marking patterns of Laz, one of the Kartvelian languages. Here he reports that one case, with a zero-morpheme, marks direct objects, while subjects are marked with the ending -*k* or zero. According to his analysis, one zero morpheme represents one case, while -*k* and zero are alternants (allomorphs) of a second case. Since the zero-marked subject is used just

---

6. Strictly speaking, for Georgian and Svan this statement relates only to a subsystem traditionally termed Series II.

with inactive intransitives, while the *k*-marked subject occurs with active intransitives and with transitives, Klimov concludes that Laz preserves this distribution of a former system. Again he has used productive patterns, rather than relics, as an indicator of earlier patterns; but here he has broken another elementary principle of linguistic analysis. Basic tenets would require the zero-marked forms to be treated as one case, the *k*-marked forms as a second case; they cannot be mixed in an unprincipled way. Analyzing the cases in this way would have resulted in an entirely different analysis.

In spite of the problems outlined above, I have argued that when dealing with the Kartvelian languages, we cannot simply dismiss Klimov's theory out of hand, because of the important contributions he has made to Kartvelian studies in his earlier work (Harris 1985:12, note 2).

An additional problem here is that, whatever our opinion of the criterion used to determine the alignment of Proto-Indo-European, it is not the same criterion as that used to determine the alignment of Common Kartvelian.[7] Results obtained on the basis of the criterion of correlates is not directly comparable with results obtained on the basis of distribution.

2.2.2. A Distributional Approach

My 1985 book (Harris 1985) is devoted entirely to the question of the original case marking type of Kartvelian and the changes that system subsequently underwent. I argued there that the original case system was ergative, not active, in alignment. Because the work by Gamkrelidze and Ivanov 1984 is dated a year earlier, it is worth pointing out that their book was bot actuallly released that year, and my copy did not reach me until after my own book had appeared in print. My book was in no sense an argument against their thesis, and I was quite

---

7. Klimov has also reached the conclusion that Proto-Indo-European had active alignment; for some discussion, see Klimov 1977:209ff.

unaware of the content of their book until much later. My argument was made entirely independently of anything contained in Gamkrelidze and Ivanov 1984; I was, however, aware of Klimov 1973, 1976, 1977, and other works.

How could I have reached conclusions so different from those reached by Klimov and adopted by Gamkrelidze and Ivanov? First, like most other scholars working on alignment, I do not accept the validity of the correlation of case marking alignment with either a transitive-intransitive dichotomy or an animate-inanimate dichotomy. Therefore, in identifying the alignment of case marking in any language, I relied entirely on the distribution of cases. Thus, I use the distributional table from Sapir 1917 or the figures from Fillmore 1968, both cited by Gamkrelidze and Ivanov 1984, as the sole basis for typing. Second, unlike Klimov in the works cited above, I used productive patterns for determining current structure and unproductive relics in internal reconstruction to arrive at older stages, according to accepted practice. I followed other standard procedures of linguistic analysis and described my methods in a separate section (Chapter 2).

The relics used in my reconstruction involve the syntactic patterns governed by specific verbs, such as the verb 'come, go.' Some of these have been regularized in the historical period, while others remain irregular. For example, in Old Georgian we find the sentence in (1) in several different locations.

(1) katam-i q'iva (Mt 26:74; L 22:60, J 18:27)
 chicken-Nom he/crow
 'The cock crowed.'

In Modern Georgian this would be ungrammatical; we find instead (2).

(2) mamal-ma iq'ivla
 cock-Nar he/crow
 'The cock crowed.'

The case traditionally called the narrative (Nar) is used in this subsystem to mark subjects of transitive verbs; at issue is its use in marking subjects of active intransitive verbs, as in (2). The case traditionally called the nominative (Nom) marks direct objects and subjects of inactive intransitives in this subsystem; at issue is its use to mark subjects of active intransitives, as in (1).

Example (1) can be identified as a relic on the grounds that it is both irregular in Old Georgian and is archaic, rather than an innovation. We know that it is irregular in Old Georgian because other verbs of the same morphological type do not occur in this pattern, that is with a subject in the so-called nominative case. We know that the irregularity must be archaic, rather than innovative, because over the course of history it changed to correspond to the productive pattern, illustrated in (2). These procedures are absolutely standard in diachronic linguistics. Principles that were first developed for phonology are here applied to syntax, as has been done in the reconstruction of syntax in other language families.

The significance of the examples above is that they point to a time when the subject of the active intransitive was marked with the so-called nominative case, as the subjects of active intransitives are still. That is, if we assume that lexical relics of this sort preserve an earlier situation, then the system we must reconstruct has the distribution in Figure 4, following the format set up above.

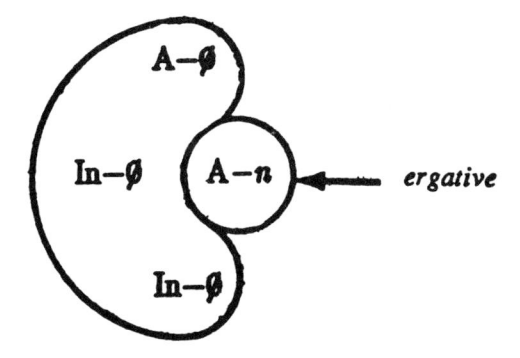

Figure 4: Reconstructed Pattern, Earliest Stage of Common Kartvelian

When the cases are encircled, following Figures 1-3, we see that this is an ergative pattern. The pattern found today in Georgian, however, is shown in Figure 5, which takes into account changes also in the form of the suffixes.

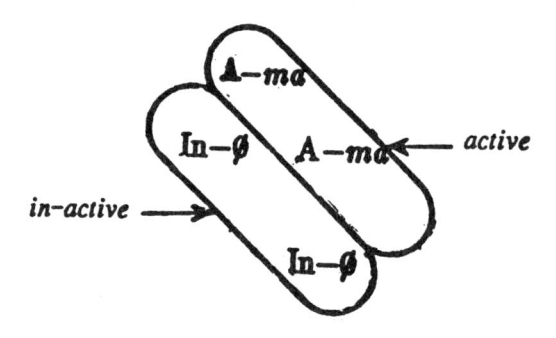

Figure 5: Pattern of Modern Georgian[8]

It may be noted that this trend in the history of Georgian has been previously described, in particular by Shanidze (1973:483-484). Here Shanidze put no labels on the case marking patterns, but observed that the use of the narrative case with active intransitives seems to be secondary.

In Harris (1985:133-141) I explicitly compared my hypothesis, which I referred to as the Ancestral Ergative Hypothesis, with Klimov's proposal, referred to there as the Ancestral Active Hypothesis. I adduced nine arguments against the latter, all of them following established linguistic principles.

Given that there is a difference between the criteria used by Gamkrelidze and Ivanov 1984 and the criterion used in my work (Harris 1985), we may agree that

---

8. In Modern Georgian the pattern in Figure 5 is found only in the set of tense-aspect paradigms known as Series II; for further discussion of the relation of this to other patterns in the language see Harris 1985.

the different labels applied are due to the different diagnostics. Therefore, let us put aside the labels and compare the facts on which they are based.

2.2.3. The Binary Opposition of Animate/Inanimate Nouns

Gamkrelidze and Ivanov's typing of Proto-Indo-European is based on the opposition of animate to inanimate nouns. If Common Kartvelian had the same structure in this regard, we should find there too a binary opposition between nouns.

There is no morphological difference between animate and inanimate in any modern Kartvelian language. Nor do we find any morphological difference between human and non-human, or other categories that might be expected to have evolved out of an earlier dichotomy based on animacy. In all Kartvelian languages there is a single declension used for all nouns, except in Svan. This is a secondary development in Svan (see Harris 1985, Chapter 4, and sources cited there), and no one has suggested that this development in Svan had anything to do with an opposition of animate to inanimate or a related dichotomy.

However, it has, in fact, been suggested that Kartvelian once had an opposition of animate to inanimate (Chikobava 1942). Interestingly, this was proposed as a basis for establishing a genetic relation between Kartvelian and the North Caucasian languages, especially North East Caucasian, for which a gender-class system is reconstructed.[9] Chikobava, in the work cited, reconstructs *m- as the marker of the human (*adamianis*) class in the noun itself and *s-, d-, n-, r-, l-, etc. as markers of the inanimate (*nivtis* 'thing') class in the noun. In the daughter languages, reflexes of *m- are productive in the formation of agentive nouns, such as *me-(u)p-e* 'monarch' from the root *up* 'reign,' thus 'one who reigns.'

---

9. Dzavakishvili 1937 had earlier argued for reconstructing a class system for Common Kartvelian. Because he did not discuss the inanimate class(es), I have omitted his work here.

This is the sort of insight on which Chikobava's argument rests, and we have no difficulty imagining that a marker of the human class might come to be used as a formant of agentives. What is troublesome is that some other prefixes that begin with *m-* or circumfixes that contain *m-* form words that are not animate. While I do not find Chikobava's arguments convincing, we must conclude that a claim that Common Kartvelian made a binary division between animate and inanimate would not be without basis.[10]

2.3. Conclusion Concerning Proposed Syntactic (Alignment) Parallel

The alignment argument made by Gamkrelidze and Ivanov 1984 has two distinct parts. One is the reconstruction of the syntactic distribution of cases; the second is the morphological distinction between animate and inanimate nouns, taken by the authors as their basis for reconstructing the syntactic distribution of cases. I have argued at length (in Harris 1985) that Common Kartvelian did not have active alignment, as claimed by Klimov 1976, and no new evidence has been presented by Gamkrelidze and Ivanov to support their claim. In the present paper, I have summarized the argument that the morphological marking of a distinction between animate and inanimate nouns is not an appropriate basis for reconstructing the distribution of cases. Thus, I find no convincing evidence that Proto-Indo-European and Common Kartvelian had the same case alignment; I find no syntactic parallel.

3. Proposed Phonological (and Morphological) Parallels

---

10. The parallel between the phonetic substance of the two Kartvelian prefixes and that of the two reconstructed Indo-European suffixes has not escaped my notice. A more extensive critique of Chikobava'a reconstruction is given in Deeters 1955.

Gamkrelidze and Ivanov propose five principal parallels involving the phonological system: the inventory of consonants, the sonorant system, the canonical form of root and affix, the rules for combining them, and the ablaut system.

> *Characteristic of the Proto-Indo-European, Kartvelian, and Semitic languages is an isomorphic structure in the consonant system, with three series of stops: glottalized (or pharyngealized), voiced, and voiceless. The Kartvelian and Indo-European languages show an identical system with syllabic and non-syllabic variants depending on the position they occupy in the word. The construction of root and affix morphemes and the rules for combining them into multimorphemic sequences, with a mechanism of alternation of vowels based on ablaut are also identical in the linguistic systems.* (Gamkrelidze and Ivanov 1985:14)

The first of these, the "glottalic theory" has already been the subject of much discussion, and treatment of it falls outside the scope of this paper. The others are each discussed briefly below.

I assume that Gamkrelidze and Ivanov, in the passage quoted, are referring to Kurylowicz's notion of isomorphism, which entails structural similarity (Kurylowicz 1973). They also use the term *identical* twice in that paragraph in characterizing the systems of Indo-European in comparison with those of Kartvelian. The extent to which these are indeed alike is the principal issue addressed in the subsections below.

3.1. The Sonorant System

The sonorant system of Common Kartvelian was studied in detail in Gamkrelidze and Machavariani 1965 and its parallels with Indo-European were likewise discussed there. While the two systems may not be identical, as claimed in the passage quoted above, they do have the kinds of structural parallels that might result from diffusion in a situation of close contact. The Kartvelian system involved the phonemes *w, y, l, r, m, n, each with a syllabic and a non-syllabic allophone. The environments that conditioned the various allophones are similar to those reconstructed for Indo-European (Gamkrelidze and Machavariani 1965). Although the ablaut and sonorant systems in Kartvelian do not interact in as complex a way as in Indo-European, this difference may be natural where the parallels result from diffusion, rather than from inheritance.

3.2. Canonical Form of Root and Affix

In Gamkrelidze and Machavariani (1965:303 ff.) and in Gamkrelidze and Ivanov (1984:253 ff.) the canonical form of roots in Common Kartvelian is given as basically CVC and that of suffixes as basically -VC. This is the basis for the statement that Indo-European and Kartvelian are isomorphic, for the formulae given are identical (Gamkrelidze and Ivanov 1984: 216 ff., Gamkrelidze and Machavariani 1965:377), and in both instances "C" may represent a consonant or sonorant. However, consideration of details shows that the possible realizations in the two families are not *identical*, in the ordinary sense of that word. The discussion below is based on Gamkrelidze and Ivanov's description of the complex issue of root structure in Indo-European.[11] The formula obscures the fact that "C" in the root can also be a decessive harmonic cluster in Common Kartvelian. The points of articulation of the segments composing a decessive cluster progress towards the rear of the oral cavity. The Kartvelian rules of harmonic clusters put restrictions on the types of consonants (with respect to manner of articulation) that can be combined (see Vogt 1958, Machavariani 1965 for details). Only one of the two C's may be a decessive harmonic cluster, either morpheme-initial or morpheme-final (Gamkrelidze and Machavariani 1965:305, Gamkrelidze and Ivanov 1984:255).

Indo-European permitted a morpheme-initial cluster of *s* plus a consonant

---

11. Given the complexity of the problems involved in Indo-European root structure, exceptions to some of my statements will certainly be found. Nevertheless, the generalizations made here hold for the vast majority of roots. My purpose here is to point out some problems with the claimed identicalness of structure.

(Gamkrelidze and Ivanov 1984:217). For Common Kartvelian, the dictionary of roots lists one root in #(s)t and six in #(s^1)t (Klimov 1964:160-179). In each of the six, the provisional reconstruction of *s^1 is based on the presence of a reflex in Svan alone, the other languages having #t (compare Gamkrelidze and Machavariani 1965:130-140). If the reconstruction of s^1t is correct, Kartvelian, unlike Indo-European, permits clusters with s initial to occur elsewhere in the morpheme; e.g., *da(s^1)tw- 'bear,' cf. Georgian datv-i 'bear' (Klimov 1964:70); *-e(s^1)t topographical suffix, cf. Georgian -et (Klimov 1964:80); *a(s^1)t 'ten,' cf. Georgian at-i 'ten' (Klimov 1964:45). In Kartvelian, sibilants could also follow another consonant in a root-initial cluster, *ps 'urinate' (Klimov 1964:191), or occur between a sonorant and another sibilant; *msxal- 'pear,' cf. Georgian msxal-i 'pear' (Klimov 1964:137).

In Indo-European and Kartvelian alike, "C" in the formula may also represent a consonant combined with a sonorant. In root-initial position, this may be a consonant followed by a sonorant, and in root-final position a sonorant followed by a consonant (1985:217, 253). In Kartvelian, but evidently not in Indo-European, the root-initial "C" may consist of a sonorant followed by a consonant or a cluster; for example *msxal- 'pear,' cf. Georgian msxal-i 'pear' (Gamkrelidze and Machavariani 1965:334); *rt'q' 'hit,' cf. Old Georgian art'q'ams 'he/she hits someone with something' (Klimov 1964:157); *wlt' 'flee,' cf. Old Georgian wiwlt'i 'I flee' (Klimov 1964:85). The root-final "C" may consist of a consonant or cluster followed by a sonorant; for example *d^{z1}aɣ [12]'dog,' cf. d^zaɣḷ 'dog' (Klimov 1964:236).

In Kartvelian, "C" may also be realized as a consonant plus w, a combination which Gamkrelidze and Ivanov interpret as a labialized consonant and which they compare with Indo-European labialized consonants (Gamkrelidze and Ivanov 1984:256). This is limited to one per morpheme.

Kartvelian exceptions to the root form CVC include the structure C (eg. *ɣ'receive,' cf. Georgian iɣebs 'he/she receives it'), CV (eg. *da, cf. Georgian da 'sister'), CCV (eg. *gza, cf. Georgian gza 'way, road'), VC (eg. *at, cf. Georgian

---

12. The symbol d^z represents a voiced palatal affricate.

at–i 'ten,' and others (all examples from Gamkrelidze and Machavariani 1965:307 ff.). Of these, CV in Indo-European is limited to pronouns and particles (Gamkrelidze and Ivanov 1984:218), VC occurs more widely (1984:217), and the others are not included in the inventory (1984: 216–219).

Indo-European had other constraints on the canonical form of roots represented by the simple formula CVC, including (in traditional terms) (1) the prohibition against the same stop occurring in the two C positions, and (2) the proscription of a voiceless aspirate occurring with a voiced consonant (Gamkrelidze and Ivanov 1984:18–20). Kartvelian permits the combination described in (1) in roots like **deda* 'mother' (Klimov 1964:71), **dud* 'tip' (Klimov 1964:75), **k'ak'al* 'walnut' (Klimov 1964:105), **t'ot'* 'branch, arm' (Klimov 1964:182), **t'ut'a* 'ashes' (Klimov 1964:183), **ke(n)k* 'rummage' (Klimov 1964:197). Not only may these two consonants be the same in Kartvelian, according to a rule stated by Machavariani (1965:80), if the consonants are both labial or both dental, they are required to be the same in voicing and glottalization; thus **pab*, **pap'* and **p'ap* are ruled out in Kartvelian. There appear to be few Kartvelian roots of the form described in (2), but Klimov (1964:195) lists two: **kab-* 'know' and **kad-* 'err, be mistaken.' An additional constraint on Indo-European roots, expressed by Gamkrelidze and Ivanov in terms of their glottalic theory, is said to be shared, not only with Kartvelian, but with other languages that have glottalic consonants (1984:18).[13]

Because of the large number of possible realizations of C in the CVC root formula, and because of the large number of exceptions to the formula, there is really not a great similarity between the canonical form of roots in Indo-European and Kartvelian. Some of the examples adduced above may turn out to be no more

---

13. As they state the constraint (loc cit), non-identical ejective stops do not cooccur in roots of the structure C^1VC^1. Although "C" is understood to include consonant clusters in the statement of the canonical form of the root (Gamkrelidze and Ivanov 1984:253 ff.), evidently they are using the symbol "C" here to represent a single consonant. The two Common Kartvelian roots **č'q'int'l-* 'unripe, immature' and **č'q'let'-* 'press' (Klimov 1964:256) each have an ejective stop (*q'* and *t'*) included in a consonant cluster in each of the two C positions.

than exceptions to otherwise valid generalizations. Nevertheless, it remains true that Kartvelian roots on the whole are quite different from Indo-European roots. While some Kartvelian roots do share the CVC form, roots like the following do not look like Indo-European: *br̄g-* 'fight,' **rc'q'a-* 'water,' **t'k'wer-* 'crack open,' **rt'q'-* 'gird,' **msxal-* 'pear,' **mq'ar-* 'shoulder,' **mc¹er-* 'insect,' **k'l̥de* 'cliff, boulder,' **t'w'oc-* 'throw, hit' (Klimov 1964:53, 159, 182, 157, 137, 144, 141, 113, 184). Yet roots like these are very common in Kartvelian.

Kartvelian suffixes of the form -V were not unusual at the earliest period (eg. **-a*, marker of third person singular subject agreement in certain tense-aspect categories, **-e*, formant of the optative). Suffixes of the form -C(V) seem also to have existed at the oldest stage reconstructable; for example **-n(a)*, an ancient suffix found in locatives and pronouns, cf. Georgian **me-na* 'I' (see Gamkrelidze 1959:37-38). Thus, if the canonical form of suffixes is presented as -VC, we must at the very least acknowledge the existence of many exceptions.

If we add the forms of prefixes, we find as much variation as in the form of roots and suffixes. The following patterns all date from Common Kartvelian: V-, eg. **a-* transitive formant, **i-* with various meanings, including medio-passive; C-, eg. **m-* first person object, **g-* second person object; CV-, eg. **li-/si-* prefix used in word formation, **la-/sa-* prefix used in word formation (compare Klimov 1964:42, 100, 123, 57, 172, 168).

The description above reveals that the canonical forms of roots and affixes of Indo-European and Kartvelian do not have a great deal in common. The form of roots in Kartvelian is limited primarily by the constraint on decessive harmonic clusters and the proscription against two unlike glottalic stops in the two C positions in roots of the form CVC. Indo-European shares only the last of these, which is claimed to be universal or extremely common (Melikishvili 1970, Gamkrelidze and Ivanov 1984:18) and is thus not relevant to claims of diffusion.

3.3. The Rules for Combining Morphemes

In the quotation at the beginning of section 3 above, the "rules for combining [root and affix morphemes] into multimorphemic sequences" might be understood in a number of different ways. Some of these will be discussed below.

The Kartvelian languages employ prefixes, suffixes, and circumfixes. While the last of these may distinguish this family's morphological rules from those of Indo-European, the circumfixes show evidence of being secondary, the result of combining prefixes and suffixes in a unified function. Prefixes may have been more important than suffixes in inflection and derivation in archaic Common Kartvelian (see Gamkrelidze and Machavariani 1965:373).

In terms of morphological type, the two families are not obviously parallel. The Kartvelian languages are predominantly agglutinating, while the Indo-European languages, in their attested forms, are mostly fusional. This need not be an overwhelming problem, however, as there is evidence for agglutination in Proto-Indo-European as well.

The internal structure of words in the two families, especially finite verbs, does not show a high degree of parallelism. In all Kartvelian languages we find some evidence for at least the following morpheme "slots," in this order: (1) agreement markers, (2) character vowel, (3) root, (4) series marker, (5) stem augment, (6) screeve marker, (7) agreement markers. A preverb is also found in slot (0), but this is generally considered secondary. Agreement markers in slot (1) include at least the first person subject marker and markers of first and second person objects; prefixal agreement markers are not found in Indo-European. Among the functions of character vowels (2) is to serve as a morphological marking of syntactic processes involving benefactives and possessors (Harris 1981, Ch. 6); another is marking medio-passives. Although both of these functions may be secondary, this morphological "slot" appears to be very old; it is doubtful that a parallel exists in Indo-European. Morphemes that follow the root form tense-aspect categories, serve derivational functions such as inchoative and causative, and mark other agreement; many of these are secondary.

To describe the process of combining morphemes, Gamkrelidze and Machavariani (1965:76) propose the Principle of Monovocalicity: "In a polymorphemic form, only one morpheme may occur in the normal grade." As Gamkrelidze and Machavariani note (1965:372), this cannot explain the fact that we find i-grade in some forms with normal grade suffixes, but $\emptyset$-grade in others. A proposal in terms of specific phonological processes which were later morphologized comes closer to accounting for all the facts. These include progressive and regressive syncope and vowel reduction. Two of these rules are stated below; they led to the ablaut system, discussed in the next subsection (see Harris 1985, Ch. 8 for discussion of details).

(3) Vowel Reduction
$e \longrightarrow i \ / \ C \_ C + V(C)$

(4) Regressive Syncope
$\begin{vmatrix} V \\ \text{-high} \end{vmatrix} \longrightarrow \emptyset \ / \ C \_ C + V(C),$

where (4) was a later rule and applied to the output of (3).

Gamkrelidze and Ivanov (1984:257-8) reconstruct an ancient system of reduplication in Kartvelian languages, and this could be included as part of the system of combining morphemes. As they reconstruct it, there was partial reduplication with voicing of the initial segment and sometimes with excrescent *n* at the end of the reduplicated prefix; the vowel may be *i, e, o,* or *a*. In the two examples where the non-reduplicated root survives, reduplication seems to have served to form nouns. The authors compare Kartvelian reduplication with that in Indo-European, citing a nice example where both language groups form 'wheel' by reduplication from the root 'turn.' Here the Indo-European reduplication follows the pattern of a repetition of the first root consonant plus the vowel *e* (*$k^{lh^r}ek^{lh^r}l$-o-*, Gamkrelidze and Ivanov 1984:220), while the Kartvelian example, according to their analysis, involves repetition of the full syllable, but in Ø-grade (*br-bar*, 1984:258); therefore the example cannot be a calque. The rules of reduplication in Kartvelian, as one may infer from the examples presented, would have allowed Kartvelian to follow the same pattern as Indo-European; yet here there is no calquing. The presence of a calque would have more strongly suggested contact.

Reduplication is very common in languages of the world, and the process often involves only partial repetition, as it does here. The authors draw analogy with Shuswap and Squamish, two Salishan languages; one could add examples from many other families: Ewe, Yidin^y, Indonesian, Tagalog, Niuean, etc. The use of voicing in the repeated initial seems to be unusual and is thus the sort of feature that might indicate diffusion in a Kartvelian-Indo-European Sprachbund −if it were present in Indo-European.

3.4. Ablaut

The ablaut system of Common Kartvelian was likewise similar, but not identical, to that of Proto-Indo-European, as suggested in the quotation above. Specifically, the vowel alternations in Common Kartvelian involved $e \sim i \sim \emptyset$ (the best understood), as well as $e \sim e$: (probable), and possibly $a \sim \emptyset$, $e \sim \emptyset$, and $e \sim a \sim \emptyset$. We do not find the vowel o involved in Kartvelian ablaut, as it was in the $e \sim o \sim \emptyset$ pattern of Indo-European, assuming no laryngeals following o at this stage.

While the Kartvelian system became a true ablaut system, that is a system of morphologically conditioned vowel alternation, at least some of the alternations can be seen to have arisen out of originally productive phonological processes, dependent in part on movable accent (see Gamkrelidze and Machavariani 1965:370, Harris 1985:170-176; compare in this regard, Schmidt 1962:41, Schmidt 1971:266). Thus we may assume that the origin of the ablaut systems in the two proto-languages involved similar processes. The fact that an internal cause can be identified for this development in no way suggests that contact was not also responsible for it.

In terms of function, the two ablaut systems are not identical. Within the verb, the functions are difficult to compare because of the different structures of the tense-aspect-mood systems in the two families. One of the clearest functions of ablaut in the attested Kartvelian languages was to distinguish transitive from intransitive forms (see Gamkrelidze and Machavariani 1965: 179ff. and Harris 1985, Ch. 8), and this is almost certainly one of its original functions; compare Old Georgian *v-drik'-e* 'I bent it' with *v-derk'* 'I bent' (intransitive). Ablaut also distinguished among subject persons of the verb. This is a somewhat later development, the result of syncope, (4), which remained a productive rule quite late; compare Old Georgian *v-derk'* 'I bent (intransitive)' with *drk'-a* 'he/she/it bent (intransitive).'

One of the functions of ablaut in Proto-Indo-European was the formation of the aorist, but it would be difficult to say that this was a function of ablaut in Common Kartvelian. In the ancient Kartvelian tense-aspect categories known as Series II, ablaut did not have the function of distinguishing aorist forms from those of the other paradigms, permansive and subjunctive, for transitive verbs; compare Old Georgian aorist *v-drik'-e* 'I bent it' with the permansive *v-drik'-i* 'I bend it" and the subjunctive *v-drik'-o* 'I might, will bend it.' For intransitive verbs, the aorist was distinguished from the other paradigms in part by a contrast of full-grade to zero-grade, although it is not clear that this contrast had been morphologized (been made part of the ablaut system), instead of being subject to the productive rule of syncope, (4) (compare Old Georgian aorist *v-t'ep* 'I warmed up' with permansive *v-t'p-i* 'I warm up' and subjunctive *v-t'p-e* 'I might, will warm up'). As a secondary phenomenon in Kartvelian, ablaut partially distinguished the derived set of tense-aspect categories traditionally referred to as Series I from the archaic set known as Series II, but this was originally based on the syntactic intransitivity of Series I (Harris 1985). Thus, although in both proto-languages ablaut was important in distinguishing between various forms of the verbs, the two systems are not directly parallel in function.

Ablaut was evidently not involved in deriving nouns from verbs in Kartvelian as it was in Indo-European.[14] In the daughter languages other than Svan, the deverbal nouns preserve the reflex of normal-grade (*e*-grade); compare Old Georgian *drek'-a* 'a bending.' There are said to be three deverbal nouns formed from some verbs in Svan. One is cognate with deverbal nouns of the sister languages and, like them, preserves the *e*-grade; *kwec-a* 'breaking, cutting' (Topuria 1968:213). A second, derived from the intransitive, likewise preserves the normal-grade (*e*-grade) that characterizes intransitives (eg., *li-kwec* 'breaking (intransitive).' A third is derived from the transitive, although it preserves not the

---

14. Gamkrelidze and Ivanov (1984:258) describe formation of a noun by reduplication, possibly involving ablaut, but this would not be considered formation of a noun by a change in ablaut grade.

i-grade that characterized transitives, but the ∅-grade that could be derived from *i*- or *e*-grade by rule (4); eg., *li-kwc-e* 'breaking (transitive)' (Gamkrelidze and Machavariani 1965:208). Ablaut does not seem to have played the role that *o*-grade played in the formation of nouns in Indo-European.

The remarks above are intended to provide a better basis for assessing the degree and kind of parallelism found in the systems of ablaut.

3.5. Conclusion Concerning Proposed Phonological (and Morphological) Parallels

There are clearly similarities between Indo-European and Kartvelian in the four areas dealt with in this section: the sonorant system, the canonical form of roots and affixes, the rules for combining morphemes into complex words, and the ablaut system. In the last three categories there are also important differences, including differing interpretations of the CVC formula for root structure, differing constraints on this formula, exceptions to this formula and that for suffixes, use of prefixal "character vowels" in verb forms, use of prefixal agreement markers, different vowel alternations involved in ablaut. Whether or not the structural similarities are great enough to qualify as "isomorphic" in Kurylowicz's sense of this term, these phenomena in these two language families are not *identical* in the ordinary sense of this word.

Wherever possible, I have cited examples from Gamkrelidze and Machavariani 1965 or from Gamkrelidze and Ivanov 1984 in order to make the point that the authors of the latter work are well aware of the phenomena discussed here. This suggests that in the quotation above these authors are using the word *identical* in some special sense. It is important to have these details discussed again here, since many readers of their work will otherwise interpret *identical* as meaning 'exactly alike.' Clearly the sub-systems of these two proto-languages are not alike in their details.

4. Implications for Determining the Indo-European Homeland

A new proposal, locating the Indo-European homeland in eastern Anatolia, has been made by Gamkrelidze and Ivanov 1984 on the basis of very early contacts between Indo-European, Kartvelian, and Semitic families. The argument for very early, intense contact with Kartvelian takes the circumstantialist approach described in section 1 of this paper and in the quotation below.

> *One group's approach [to areal linguistics] has been merely to catalog the similarities found in a particular area -allowing these similarities to suggest diffusion, but without carrying out the research necessary to demonstrate the actual borrowing.* (Campbell, Smith-Stark, and Kaufman 1986:534)

Gamkrelidze and Ivanov have proposed parallels in the areas of (i) phonology (as listed in section 3 of the present paper), (ii) syntax (discussed in section 2 above), and (iii) lexical items (which fall outside the scope of the present paper). They have allowed these similarities to suggest diffusion.[15] Lest it be thought that these amassed parallels uniformly support contact, and hence the proposed homeland, we should consider very carefully the nature of the phenomena suggested as parallels.

As discussed in section 1 above and in works on language contact, in evaluating proposed diffusion of a phenomenon we need to take into account how unusual or common the feature is among languages of the world. A feature that is unusual among languages of the world is more highly valued as a diagnostic of contact than one that is common, since this increases the possibility that it was actually borrowed, rather than developing independently.

Although it was shown in section 2 that no syntactic parallel has been demonstrated to have existed between Indo-European and Kartvelian, section 3 discusses four real, if limited, phonological parallels between these families. Are these parallel features unusual enough to be considered diagnostic of contact? All four of these phenomena are, in fact, very common and could easily have

---

15. After the presentation of this paper at the conference, Gamkrelidze remarked that the syntactic parallels which he and Ivanov had proposed were never intended as evidence of contact, but as facts that could be explained by contact. In the present paper I have argued that in case alignment there is, in fact, no parallel to be explained. The parallels in phonology and morphology require no explanation, for each of them is quite common in languages.

developed independently. The alternations in the sonorant system are due to physical (universal) properties of these sounds; a tendency to make them syllabic in the environment of consonants, and non-syllabic in the environment of vowels, is a natural consequence of these physical properties.

As discussed in section 3.2, there is really very little similarity between the structure of roots in Indo-European and in Kartvelian. In Kartvelian the structure of suffixes is not very tightly constrained (there is no form that is entirely proscribed), and therefore it provides little possibility of being a feature unusual enough to be diagnostic of contact. I see no genuine parallel of canonical form except the proscription of non-idential glottalized stops as the two consonants in the formula C^1VC^1. According to Gamkrelidze and Ivanov (1984:18), this constraint is universal or very common in languages having glottalized consonants. Its very commonness makes it a characteristic incapable of indicating diffusion. There is no aspect of the rules of combining morphemes that is unusual, including the very common processes of vowel reduction and syncope. The single exception that may be unusual is voicing of initials in reduplication; but this characteristic is not found in Indo-European. Ablaut is a very common process among languages of the world, and is thus not diagnostic of diffusion.

In the context of parallels that might suggest contact, what is particularly disturbing is that none of the particular restrictions or other quirks of the system of one language family is found in the other. The case for diffusion would be much stronger, for example, if Kartvelian shared the Indo-European prohibition against identical consonants in a root, or if Indo-European evinced decessive harmonic clusters. Even the most common processes do not share many characteristics in these two families. If we could at least show that ablaut involved alternations of the same vowels in the two families, or that it served the same functions, the evidence would be more convincing. In the absence of any of these tell-tale traces that one of the systems really was borrowed, these parallels remain unconvincing.

In order to make a convincing case for contact one must eliminate all reasonable doubt concerning chance similarities and independent innovations, just as in establishing any other historical fact. The existence of contact-induced change in the phenomena examined in this paper has not been established.

The hypothesis that the Indo-European homeland was located in eastern Anatolia does not rest on these proposed parallels alone and hence cannot be evaluated on these bases alone. In this brief paper I have not discussed the lexical correspondences or the consonant systems proposed as parallels between Kartvelian and Indo-European,[16] nor have I touched on the proposed parallels with Semitic. The problems encountered in the materials that have been discussed here suggest that careful consideration needs to be given to other aspects of this proposal. The hypothesis of the Anatolian homeland is a complex one that must be evaluated at many levels. In the sections above I have discussed only a portion of the facts that must be taken into account.

REFERENCES

Campbell, Lyle.
1985. "Areal Linguistics and Its Implications for Historical Linguistics." *Papers from the 6th International Conference on Historical Linguistics*, ed. by Jacek Fisiak, 25-56, Amsterdam: Benjamins.

Campbell, Lyle, Terrence Kaufman, and Thomas C. Smith-Stark.
1986. "Meso-America as a Linguistic Area." *Language* 62.530-570.

Campbell, Lyle, and Marianne Mithun.
1980. "Syntactic Reconstruction: Priorities and Pitfalls." *Folia Linguistica Historica* 1.19-40.

Charachidzé, Georges.
1986. "Gamq'relid^{z}e/Ivanov, Les indo-européens et le caucase." *Revue des études géorgiennes et caucasiennes* 2.211-222.

---

16. On lexical correspondences, see Diakonoff 1985 and, to some extent, Charachidzé 1986; much more evaluation remains to be done.

Chikobava, Arnold.
1938. *Č'anur-megrul=kartuli šedarebiti leksik'oni.* [Laz-Mingrelian-Georgian Comparative Dictionary.] Tbilisi. Ak'ademia.

1942. *Saxelis pud^{z}is ud^{z}velesi agebuleba kartvelur enebši.* [The Oldest Structure of the Noun Root in the Kartvelian Languages.] Tbilisi: Ak'ademia.

Comrie, Bernard.
1976. Review of G. A. Klimov, Очерк общей теории эргативности, in *Lingua* 39:252-260.

Deeters, Gerhard.
1955. "Gab es Nominalklassen in allen kaukasischen Sprachen?" *Corolla Linguistica (Festschrift Ferdinand Sommer).* Wiesbaden: Harrassowitz.

Diakonoff, I. M.
1985. "On the Original Home of the Speakers of Indo-European." *The Journal of Indo-European Studies* 13.92-174.

Dzavakishvili, I.
1937. *Kartuli da k'avk'asiuri enebis tavdap'irveli buneba da natesaoba.* [The Original Nature and Genetic Relationship of Georgian and the Caucasian Languages.] T'pilisi: Ak'ademia.

Fillmore, Charles J.
1968. "The Case for Case." *Universals in Linguistic Theory.* ed. by Emmon Bach and Robert T. Harms, 1-88. New York. Holt, Rinehart and Winston.

Gamkrelidze, T. V.
1959. *Sibilant'ta šesat'q'visobani da kartvelur enata ud^{z}velesi st'rukt'uris zogi sak'itxi.* [Sibilant Correspondences and Some Questions of the Ancient Structure of Kartvelian Languages.] Tbilisi. Ak'ademia.

Gamkrelidze, T. V., and V. V. Ivanov (Гамкрелидзе, Т. В., В.В. Иванов)
1984. Индоевропейский язык и индоевропейцы. Tbilisi. Universit'et'i.

1985. "The Ancient Near East and the Indo-European Question: Temporal and Territorial Characteristics of Proto-Indo-European Based on Linguistic and Historico-Cultural Data." *The Journal of Indo-European Studies* 13.3-48.

Gamkrelidze, T., and G. Machavariani.
1965. *Sonant'ta sist'ema da ablaut'i kartvelur enebši*. [The System of Sonants and Ablaut in the Kartvelian Languages.] Tbilisi. Universit'et'i.

Hamp, Eric.
1977. "On Some Questions of Areal Linguistics." *BLS* 3.279-282.

Harris, Alice C.
1981. *Georgian Syntax: A Study in Relational Grammar*. Cambridge. Cambridge University Press.

1985. *Diachronic Syntax: The Kartvelian Case. (Syntax and Semantics, 18)*. New York. Academic Press.

1986. "Commensurability of Terms." *Language Typology 1985*. ed. by Winfred P. Lehmann, 55-75. Amsterdam. Benjamins.

Holisky, Dee Ann.
1981. *Aspect and Georgian Medial Verbs*. Delmar, NY. Caravan Books.

Jacobsen, William H.
1980. "Inclusive/Exclusive: A Diffused Pronominal Category in Native Western North America." *Papers from the Parasession on Pronouns and Anaphora*. ed. by Jody Kreiman and Almerindo E. Ojeda, 204-227. Chicage. CLS.

Jeffers, Robert.

1976. Review of W. P. Lehmann, *Proto-Indo-European Syntax* in *Language* 52.982-988.

Joseph, Brian D.
1983. *The Synchrony and Diachrony of the Balkan Infinitive: A Study in Areal, General, and Historical Linguistics*. Cambridge. Cambridge University Press.

Klimov, G. A. (Климов, Г. А.)
1964. Этимологический словарь картвелских языков. Moskva. Akademija.

1973. Очерк общей теории эргативности. Moskva. Akademija.

1976. "Анамолии эргативности в лазском (чанском) языке" *Aγmosavluri Pilologia* 4.150-159.

1977. Типология языков активного строя. Moskva. Akademija.

Kurylowicz, Jerzy.
1964. "On the Methods of Internal Reconstruction." *Proceedings of the Ninth International Congress of Linguists*. ed. by Horace Lunt. 9-29. The Hague. Mouton.

1973. "La notion de l'isomorphisme." *Esquisses linguistiques I*. 16-26. Munich. Fink.

Machavariani, Givi.
1965. *Saerto-kartveluri k'onsonant'uri sist'ema*. [The Common Kartvelian Consonant System.] Tbilisi. Universit'et'i.

Masica, Colin P.
1976. *Defining a Linguistic Area: South Asia*. Chicago. University of Chicago Press.

Meillet, A.

1954. *La méthode comparative en linguistique historique.* Paris. Librairie Ancienne Honoré Champion.

Melikishvili, Irine.
1970. "Mark'irebulobis p'irobebi mżɣerobis, siq'ruis, labialobisa da velarobis nišnebisatvis." *Macne* 5.137-158.

Plank, Frans, ed.
1979. *Ergativity: Towards a Theory of Grammatical Relations.* New York. Academic Press.

Sapir, Edward.
1917. Review of *Het passieve karakter van het verbum transitivum of van het verbum actionis in talen van Noord-Amerika.* by C. C. Uhlenbeck. 1916. *IJAL* 1.82-86.

Shanidze, Akaki.
1973 *Kartuli enis gramat'ik'is sapudᶻvlebi, I.* [Fundamentals of the Grammar of the Georgian Language, I.] Second edition. Tbilisi: Universit'et'i.

Schmidt, Karl Horst.
1962. *Studien zur Rekonstruktion des Lautstandes der südkaukasischen Grundsprache. (Abhandlunger für die Kunde des Morgenlandes, XXXIV, 3).* Wiesbaden. Steiner.

1971. "Sprachstruktur und Sprachbund." *Bedi Kartlisa* 28.262-268.

Vogt, Hans.
1958. "Structure phonémique du géorgien." *Norsk Tidsskrift for Sprogvidenskap* 18.5-90.

Watkins, Calvert.
1976. "Towards Proto-Indo-European Syntax: Problems and Pseudo-Problems."

Papers from the Parasession on Diachronic Syntax. ed. by Sanford B. Steever, Carol A. Walker, and Salikoko S. Mufwene. 305-326. Chicago. CLS.

THE INCEPTION OF FARMING IN THE BRITISH ISLES AND THE EMERGENCE OF INDO-EUROPEAN LANGUAGES IN NW EUROPE

Roger J. Mercer
University of Edinburgh

It is perhaps in the study of the neolithic that, in Europe, most preconceptions, most barriers to understanding and most outright problems have been overcome in the last twenty years. I say this as a researcher intimately involved with some of these problems and it therefore behooves me to say that workers in the neolithic have been at an enormous advantage in their enquiry. We have not been exposed to the seductive *placebo* that tells us that some outline model of basic social complexion is an understood datum against which our archaeological evidence is to be assessed. Within Iron Age studies we still regularly see the use of racial and linguistic terms (Celtic, Illyrian, Thraco-Cimmerian, Scythian, Teutonic, Germanic, etc., etc.) which must imply equation with societies mentioned, often described at second hand, but seldom defined by, classical authors. Such is the degree of material cultural continuity between our Bronze Age societies throughout Europe and these later manifestations that the cultural record of the second millennium BC has inevitably caught up in this web. The Neolithic has perhaps remained largely preserved from these pressures in its chronological isolation and in the occasional unfamiliarity of its material development. It has however, not escaped entirely.

Ever since Vere Gordon Childe proclaimed the quintessential "Europeanness" of his vision of European prehistory while accepting its overall indebtedness to Eastern inspiration (Childe 1929) the pressure has been to amalgamate this vision with that which preceded it and against which to some extent he was reacting - the idea of Indo-European solidarity (Childe 1925). Elegant and persuasive models have been prominently presented drawing our later neolithic into the pattern, seeking to establish the roots of pan-European developments, as observed in the archaeological record, in eastern counterparts (Gimbutas, 1961).

The two most prominent examples are, of course, the so-called Beaker and Corded Ware/Single Grave/Battle Axe traditions. But here "counter-revolution" from the isolated *Alteuropa* of the earlier neolithic, witnessed by the clear continuity between its early cultural expressions in the TRB and the Corded Ware development and thereby to the Beaker development has produced a confrontation between the small Division of the West assessing their new evidence afresh and the mighty divisions of the East couched in the scholarship and ideas of the nineteenth century.

Britain, the *Ultima Thule* of Europe, has perhaps been thought to lie beyond the limits of this debate. Yet its importance as the source for data in the light of which to discuss current ideas (Renfrew 1987) relating to the spread of Indo-European languages in N and W Europe in prehistory is not thereby diminished.

My text therefore is the earliest registered neolithic farming development in Britain and, as in essence our interest, in this forum, is the *arrival* of cultural, ethnic or linguistic traits, perhaps I should focus for a short while on how I visualize this process occurring. Let me say before I begin that this is not a matter upon which there is universal agreement in British or wider archaeological circles.

Our predicament is, and has been for a quarter of a century now, that the vast majority of our radiocarbon assays relating to this period have been obtained from deposits reflecting a fully established neolithic development in Britain and, with notable exceptions, have yielded dates of 3200 bc or later. This chronological threshold coincides neatly with major vegetational changes where attention has focused, perhaps unduly, upon the very general and catastrophic reduction in the frequency of elm trees as witnessed by fossil pollen analysis. In many, but by no means all, instances this decline is accompanied by reductions in other arboreal species and is accompanied by increases in grasses, weeds of cultivation and other species associated with open ground that has undergone agricultural activity. It would be possible to view this relatively cataclysmic vegetational change alongside the "sudden" appearance of a fully established neolithic development as evidence of an abrupt and perhaps violent introduction of a farming economy to Britain. To do so, however, involves the rejection of some relatively slight evidence within Britain itself and the acceptance of major difficulties in so far as the wide-European evidence is concerned.

In the European context two principal objections arise. Perhaps first is the universality of the vegetational phenomena referred to above. From Finland to the Rhineland to Ireland, the decline of the elm tree (which in itself defines the boundary of pollen zone VII/VIII) is broadly synchronous and can be seen over this vast tract of land to bear only an incidental relationship to the widely variant introduction of farming practice which ranges from the later fifth to the early second millennia bc.

Secondly is the lack of a satisfactorily defined antecedent development for the British neolithic in proximate continental Europe. If we are to accept the idea of a neolithic "descent" upon Southern Britain in the latter centuries of the fourth millennium bc then we should logically seek the direct parallelisms that ought to exist between southern Britain and the near continent. These parallels simply do not exist other than in the most generalized terms and the tracing of specific parallels has met with a customary lack of success (Piggott 1954, Whittle 1977). To take an example which we will return to in another context, the whole of British early and middle neolithic archery is dominated by the highly distinctive and ubiquitous bi-facially worked leaf-shaped arrowhead. A few by no means *closely* similar arrowheads are known in Belgium and beyond this we have to look to NE Germany and the Iberian Peninsula. Furthermore, where we have a knowledge of artefact distribution - for example in the instance of stone axes with sources of rock in Brittany and Cornwall, in so far as we can recognise it, we see virtually no counter-supply (four axes of the so-called Group X Breton factory are known from the S coast of Britain). Similarly monumental developments in the early and middle neolithic in Britain are quite distinctive (while eclectically borrowing features) from continental peers and as the neolithic advances even their hazily stated debt to continental prototypes recedes to nothing as we enter the period of stone-circle and "henge" development.

Within Britain itself the evidence exists, furthermore, for the existence of farming economies well prior to the advent of elm decline conditions (Edwards & Ralston 1984). Some, but by no means all, of these dates have been challenged (Kinnes forthcoming), but they cannot all simply be shrugged off. Furthermore, we return to the apparently well-established nature of the British neolithic from dates of at least 3200 bc. Thirdly, we have the difficulty of the mesolithic hiatus- the generally scarce dates for mesolithic occupation *after* 4000 bc especially in S. Britain (Jacobi 1973).

If we are then to eschew a predominately "invasive" farming colonization of Britain, what model can one visualize for the transmission of this new mode of subsistence across the English Channel. For here indeed is the rub. Whereas up to this point the "Wave of Advance" model (Ammerman and Cavalli-Sforza 1971) involving the "budding off" of daughter farming communities maintaining active communication with parent settlements does appear to be the *modus operandi* of the extension of farming across Europe up to 3500 bc. *That* development appears to have taken place against the background of the climatic optimum in N and W Europe in the centuries surrounding 4000 bc when prevailing circumstances may have favored that extension to a degree not hitherto possible. The curtailment of these favorable circumstances after c. 3500 bc may well have blunted the edge of farming expansion but may well also have provoked crises among successful hunting communities on the fringe of the farming advance. We know that the aurochs had been extinguished in parts of Denmark by 4000 bc (Jensen 1982) - presumably by over-hunting and other evidence of declining resources for hunting groups is available from NW Europe at this time. Dennell (1983) has also made the important point that the navigational and marine constructional skills necessary to allow the successful negotiation of the Channel obstacle would be unlikely to reside within the essentially terrestrial tradition of the European Early Neolithic (First Temperate - LBK - Rossen).

Nevertheless, these skills were, as we know, present among coastal gatherer-hunter groups widely dispersed from Portugal to Denmark along the NW facade of Europe. Furthermore the evidence from sites in Britanny and in the Low Countries, as well as further to the N, indicates that such communities were adopting various and selected aspects of the new farming economy that was increasingly dominating the margins of their resource-base. Such adoption would have been natural enough. The procedures of successfully exploiting forest ungulates such as red deer, roe deer, aurochs and pig can have left these "hunters" no strangers to the business of animal husbandry. Indeed the increasing dependence of LBK communities upon cattle as they moved into the NW may reflect *their* adoption and exploitation of this expertise.

That the navagational pretensions of these groups was not merely coastal is witnessed by the deep sea species (hake, mackerel, saithe and cod) located in their midden deposits. In a seminal paper (Clark 1977), Graham Clark draws attention to the importance of fishing grounds to the movement of populations along the NW facade of Europe. He did this in (to the writer's mind) the less apposite context of the "spread" of megalithic construction. The burden of his argument, however, is closely related to our present train of thought. Mesolithic communities operating from bases on both sides of the channel would have inevitably come into contact pursuing the same shoals of fish. Furthermore, the rigors of the marine way of life would have dictated contact between groups in their base location (whether by foundering or misprision). Generations of such contact may well have built relationships of the kind that Caesar was to recognize 4000 years later. The transfer of subsistence innovation along the lines of these linkages within this peri-marine community is easy to imagine - a slow process and one by definition difficult to recognize in the archaeological record.

Within Britain, however, the outcome is clear to see. We see the emergence of neolithic communities, generally speaking in the S of Britain within the very enclaves of country where the evidence indicates mesolithic communities to be most firmly established. Furthermore, the broad regional divisions within the S British neolithic (largely defined on ceramic typological grounds) closely reflect those of the succeeding mesolithic. This is all natural enough as both ways of life would have demanded the resources of light soils on the margins of the forest where hunting would have been richest and farming most easily accomplished.

But what about the internal evidence for continuity within Britain? We have observed the broad continuity of culture provinces. Are there more specific elements of continuity? These are indeed few and far between and it is this element among others that has generated much support for the idea of direct neolithic colonization generally so unsupported in the "neolithic" evidence. In general terms however, the narrow-blade lithic industry of the earlier neolithic is a lineal successor to the mesolithic predecessor, and flint axes and scrapers (*pace* Whittle 1977) would appear to relate closely to mesolithic antecedents. Furthermore, as in N Europe, the exchange of raw materials for edge-tool manufacture seems to have clear origins within the mesolithic with both the specific exploitation of sources (Arran pitchstone, Rhum bloodstone, Portland chert, Group XIX rock in Cornwall) and the general dispersal patterns (Cornish rocks in use in mesolithic contexts in Hampshire and Sussex).

Yet we clearly do see massive distinctions in the assemblages of mesolithic and neolithic communities. The vastly increased importance within assemblages of heavy edge-tools with neolithic is one major input, as well as, the advent, of course, of ceramics. Then, too, there is the abandonment of the whole tradition of microlithic armature manufacture and the substitution for it of bifacially worked single-piece heavyweight arrowhead manufacture. How, in the face of such material cultural disruption, can one argue coherently for continuity and acculturation in the way that I have?

To the writer this problem is not an unduly daunting one. Once the process of husbandry is commenced, then the abandonment of hunting will be rapid and near-total as a less efficient activity *in the context of the farming settlement*. However, hunting may well continue as a specialized or seasonal activity but almost certainly in isolation from a farming context and progressively governed within a farming regime. We know that, in Britain, coppicing of wood (implying the enclosure and deer/pig-proofing of tracts of woodland) and the control of red deer to allow the regulated and large scale supply of antler are both features of our early neolithic. The conception of forest as the foe of the farmer is an extraordinary notion unfamiliar to any farming society and certainly outside the experience of early farmers in Europe for whom woodland would have provided a range of indispensable resources from fuel and construction materials to alternative food resources. The increased dominance of edge tools in farming settlements is the natural *sequitur* of the activity conducted there, the common factor of the scraper is easily understood and the absence of the hunting arrow is absolutely in accord with the near absence of hunted animal bone on these sites where the record survives. The new leaf arrowhead, I shall argue in a short while, indicates yet another total socio-economic change just as the cultural discontinuities already mentioned do.

This very cultural discontinuity, social, economic, psychological and environmental - probably the most demanding ever undertaken by man must have involved colossal conceptual adaptation which, in turn, must have been reflected in the linguistic construction and vocabularistic content of spoken communication. A whole new vocabulary involving hundreds of words would have been necessary - but perhaps more importantly, an apparatus of reasoning and argument would have become necessary to deal with the complexities of longterm investment, genetic management, enclosure measurement, labor quantification, species identification, and calendrical notation. A parallel may perhaps be broadly drawn with the circumstances, nearer our own time, consequent upon the Enlightenment and Industro-Agricultural "Revolution" of the eighteenth century AD which demanded and attained the lexicographical codification without which the precision necessary for the technological and intellectual trajectories that have been maintained ever since could not have been sustained.

Much of this apparatus would have been derived from contexts quite outside the immediate system (like the now universal word *diesel*). Many would be adapted from existing vocabulary. No substantial immigrant population is seen to be necessary to this process and the writer has perhaps taken too long to demonstrate that in the rather dramatic case of Britain (in terms of the spread of farming in Europe) this can be strongly suggested not to have been the case.

The economy established at this point remains essentially similar to that prevailing in Britain and indeed throughout N Europe for the remainder of prehistory. Its organization may have changed and perhaps the degree of its intensity but there is little indication of any substantial change in its technology or content until the eve of the Roman conquest. The ard and traction animals are present by 2800 bc as are all the principal component crops (even oats are present at Bronocice in Poland in LBK contexts and at Balbridie, Grampian, Scotland, in the earlier third millennium bc). The advent of metal would necessarily have involved a number of technical and descriptive terms hitherto not required but the development would have been minimal compared with that we have just described. If a vocabularistic and syntactical "revolution" is *required* in prehistory, then the advent of farming *must* provide a setting. Its implantation by *force majeure* is another matter - but this writer would argue that so subject to political, psychological, institutional and military vagary is this notion that he is not convinced that the apparatus has yet been developed to link the engine of archaeology to the wheels of this argument in the pre-literate context.

Before I move <u>wildly</u> beyond the boundaries of my competence, let me return to the British neolithic. We have seen that a "colonist" model for the inception of farming in Britain is unlikely in both "European" and "British" terms. Acculturation around the shores of a common fishing pond seems a more acceptable notion. How does this insular society of early farmers develop?

We are still at an early stage of understanding these processes. Naturally enough, we have failed, by and large, to recognize and understand those marginally developed incipient farming communities that the proposed model demands. We do, however, through the abraded lens of archaeology see these societies quite clearly once they have become established. It is fascinating to record the phenomena that we observe by this stage.

By 3200 bc we observe the construction of vast monuments to the living within which the remains of the dead are incorporated. The idea proposed by Renfrew (1976) that link these monuments to the idea of "territorial signature" is both elegant and persuasive - and the explicit idea of land pressure that follows from this once again presupposes the long and scarcely recognized neolithic prologue demanded above. One of these great monuments involved an estimated 50,000 man-hours of constructional input at Fussell's Lodge (Ashbee 1966). Both probably at that site and certainly at Kilham in Yorkshire (Manby 1976), long histories of land-use *prior* to barrow erection involving at Kilham two separate phases of arable agriculture with periods of woodland recovery in between all prior to a date *ante quem* for the construction of the barrow of 2880 ± 125 bc (BM-293). By this date other great stone-built chambered tombs were being constructed in geologically suitable areas of S. England - in some instances (West Kennet - Piggott 1963) involving prodigious expenditure of labor. At South Street, near Avebury (Ashbee *et al* 1979) a small, and apparently cenotaphic long barrow is dated *post* 2810 ± 130 bc (BM-356). Its clearly demonstrated lack of any trace of burial rite must add to our conception of the complexity of this monumental tradition probably only incidentally linked with the disposal of human dead. Certainly, both probably in terms of earthen long barrows (East Hesterton, Yorks) (Vatcher 1965), Hambledon Hill, Dorset - (Mercer 1980) and run on of stone-built chambered tombs (Mid-Gleniron Farm, Wigtownshire - (Corcoran 1972, Dyffryn Ardudwy Merioneth - Powell 1973) and between earthen long barrows and stone-built chambered tombs (Waylands Smithy, Berks - Atkinson 1965) long sequences of development are visible on many sites. Recent work on the Cotswold-Severn type tomb at Hazleton Glos (Saville et al. 1987) suggests that bodies were deposited in the two reaccessible chambers at this site over a period of time "perhaps considerably less than 300 years" around 2950-2700 bc when 27-30 individuals in intact condition were cumulatively deposited in the two chambers of the tomb indicating a probable contributory and contemporarily living population of c.5 - a far smaller group than can conceivably have been responsible for the construction of the tomb (estimated time 16,000 man-hours - Startin 1982). Hazleton, like so many other barrows of this class, as well as earthen long barrows as far N as Yorkshire, displays internal "herring bone" subdivision of the mound which it has been suggested, performed the function of subdividing the mound into "bays" for construction purposes - a notion which might support the idea of contributory construction of the monument by a multi-originating local community. Further support to this idea is lent by detailed consideration of the land molluscan content of the long mound (admittedly not a long barrow *sensu stricto* but certainly a ceremonial monument) built over the destroyed causewayed enclosure at Crickley Hill, Glos (Dixon, pers. comm.) Here the profile of the molluscan population on neolithic land surface on this hilltop site is *not* replicated in the content of the mound (the snails within it reflect a range of different microenvironments some of which could only have been found a distance in excess of 3km.). The irresistible conclusion is that the material for the mound was brought in in discrete loads from a series of locations at some distance from the site - hinting again perhaps at contributory construction by a broadly-based population, for a central and commanding location which furthermore appears to have been most carefully sited at this location so as to be invisible to any but those standing closest to the monument with the suggestion even being that a screen was erected to reinforce this esotericism.

Communal construction of monuments to which access was limited is perhaps most strikingly illustrated by the human bone record at the site at Lanhill, (Keiller and Piggott 1938) a chambered tomb in Berkshire of the Cotswold-Severn type where a series of skulls incorporated in the chamber each displayed a genetically transmitted irregularity - Wormian ossicles - that would very strongly suggest that the incumbent remains were members of one family or closely related group.

If we could allow ourselves to amalgamate the evidence from these isolated locations in southern England (that all fall within a statistically indistinguishable radiocarbon bracket 3000-2800 bc) we could then visualise a social structure in competitive crisis expressing territorial and other rights by monumentalization of lineage burial. Renfrew (1973) went so far as to suggest territorially defined chiefdoms on the basis of the subjective division of long barrow distribution in S England into a series of clusters focussing upon causewayed enclosures - the principal enclosure type functioning in Southern Britain. Let us now turn to the evidence that we have from this class of monument that has been subject to an extraordinary period of investigation and elucidation over the last decade or so.

It was, of course Alexander Keiller who carried out the first large-scale scientific investigation of a causewayed enclosure in Britain - at Windmill Hill, N. Wilts. The site was in many ways typical of its class - a series of broadly concentric ditches interrupted by frequent narrow "causeways" at irregular intervals enclosing an eminence. The large quantity of material from the ditch deposits become the type assemblage for the earlier neolithic of S. Britain - the plain bowl neolithic formerly known as the Windmill Hill Culture. Since 1930 we have expanded our understanding of the distribution and nature of these enclosures and others relating to this date. Over fifty causewayed enclosures are now known throughout S. Britain. Many are situated on low eminences on the terraces of river valleys - sometimes the circuits of ditches are not complete but the sites appear to be promontory enclosures with the interrupted ditches cutting off only the aspect of easy approach. Indeed, since 1970 we have become aware of hilltop stone-walled enclosures of this date in Cornwall in areas of granite bedrock where ditch digging would have been quite impossible.

Indeed, the ditch digging appears to have been a quarrying operation to obtain the raw material for the construction of a continuous bank - a fundamental consideration that appears to account for the irregular and "interrupted" nature of these ditches. Nevertheless, having been dug, the ditch very regularly becomes the focus on these sites for deposits of cultural material and bone that can only be considered as deliberate and of a ceremonial nature.

In the early 1930s Dorothy Liddell (1930-35) embarked upon the excavation of a later prehistoric hillfort at Hembury, Devon. She encountered a previously unsuspected causewayed enclosure which was to become the type-site for the SW faces of the British earlier neolithic. Hembury was a promontory enclosure which unlike Windmill Hill produced evidence that its interior had been the focus of intensive occupation linked to radiocarbon dates ranging from 3200 - 3000 bc. Liddell was prevented by ill-health from producing a full report but inspection of her records makes it clear that this settlement was a focus of wide-ranging contacts for exchanges of raw materials and products. Axes of Cornish rock from the St. Ives/Camborne area, chert from Dorset, flint from further E and pottery from Cornwall were being moved along an E-W route astride which Hembury clearly sat. Perhaps more important in the present context is the fact that the obvious prosperity of this site was apparently terminated by widespread burning. The timber- and hurdling-faced rampart was set ablaze and the body of the rampart destabilized by the disruption of its forward revetment which collapsed forward into the ditch - the heat of the burning material scorching the green sand to a wine-red color. In association with this burning, 150 leaf arrowheads were located with a notable concentration around the gateway through the rampart leading to the site.

One swallow does not make a summer, and it was not until the 1970s that we were able to place the Hembury evidence in any wider sort of context. In 1970, the writer commenced excavations at Carn Brea (Mercer 1981) near Redruth in Cornwall - a site that proved to be a one hectare enclosure defined by a stone rampart built of mighty blocks of granite. The enclosure was in turn confined within an outer enceinte of five hectares which comprised a mighty ditched rampart - stone-faced - with complex gateways clearly constructed with a view to defense in depth. The Carn Brea one hectare enclosure was, like Hembury, a settlement site with houses built on terraces within the rocky interior. It too participated in the E-W exchange network to which Hembury subscribed. It apparently commanded the "Group XVI" axe source ("near Camborne") and axe polishers as well as numerous products manufactured from rock from this source were located on the site. Flint and chert from at least five different sources were located which must emanate from distances in excess of 150 kms to the E. Moreover the evidence of petrological analysis would suggest that *all* vessels in use on the site (with over 500 represented in the excavated sample) were imported from a manufactory set 25 kms to the S in the Lizard peninsula. Radiocarbon dates suggest that the site was in use between 3000-2700 bc, but that once again its obvious prosperity was terminated by savage destruction. Evidence for burning is ubiquitous on the site, there is evidence that the great stone wall was deliberately slighted and over 700 leaf-shaped arrowheads were found (again in the excavated sample) with a substantial concentration near the entrance to the site.

While work was in progress at Carn Brea, Philip Dixon, like Liddell, was beginning to explore a hitherto unknown causewayed enclosure sealed beneath a later prehistoric hillfort at Crickley Hill in Gloucestershire. The resulting picture of the development of an enclosure of this type is of enormous complexity that can only briefly be summarized here. Although sited on a most dramatic promontory on the scarp edge of the Cotswolds just above Cheltenham, the site in fact comprises two broadly concentric circuits of ditch forming a sequence of development in which the basic unit would appear to be the causewayed ditch in front of a low platform 8m in breadth at the rear edge of which is a palisade - seemingly a "distancing" exercise to create an effective "killing ground." This scheme of defence is reconstructed on at least five occasions developing progressively in complexity. Probably one of the phases of reconstruction follows an attack in which archers played a prominent role. In the final phase for which, in the nature of things, the clearest picture survives, the site interior is occupied by a planned settlement of rectangular houses (at least fifteen existed on the site) set on either side of cobbled roadways leading into the site from timber-framed entrances. This final enclosure phase was brought to an end in a veritable holocaust of burning and arrowshot with two or three hundred arrowheads found clustered in the entrance and along the palisade line. This destruction phase, as at Hembury and at Carn Brea, sees the end of settlement on the site - only to be followed by the construction of the long mound in its final phases referred to above.

We are of course puzzled by one difficulty in relation to these traces of warfare. At Hembury, Carn Brea and Crickley the subsoil on the sites does not support bone. Evidence of economy is therefore hard to come by and furthermore evidence of death among humans is difficult to demonstrate. To what extend therefore is this "warfare" a ceremonial demonstration - an act of theater. We must be wary of veneering our ethnocentric view of warfare onto past societies the values of which we know next to nothing.

To some extent, in the British context, the answer may lie with the evidence from the last site we shall consider in this context - Hambledon Hill in Dorset (Mercer 1980). This site, excavated by the writer between 1974 and 1986, comprises a causewayed enclosure complex site at least two and probably three integral enclosures set within a massive defensive outwork system. At the focus of the whole system is the 9 hectare single ditched enclosure on the crown of this great island hill set just to the W of Cranborne Chase. Large-scale excavation indicated that this enclosure was a necropolis center for the excarnation of the dead. It seems likely that in some instances deposits of cadaveric material were accompanied by offerings placed in pits, these offerings comprising objects of apparently prestigious nature. Here we meet at the other end of the E-W route running through SW England and, as mentioned earlier, gabbroic pottery 270 kms from its source, axes of N Cornish origin, jadeite axes from Britanny and large quantities of shed red deer antler - positively scarce elsewhere on the site. The dates attached to this enclosure and indeed to the whole complex range from 2900-2600 bc. The evidence for excarnation resides in large quantities of human bone either wholly or partly disarticulated located either deliberately placed or accidentally incorporated in the ditch on the enclosure. Skulls are prominently selected and placed on the ditch floor along with deposits which seem to be the remains of feasting - the conspicuously uneconomic consumption of meat, mostly beef. The recovered human remains represents a minimum of eighty individuals suggesting on the basis of the site sample a total of some 500 parts of individuals either accidentally (or in some cases their skulls) deliberately incorporated within the ditch filling. Of this population, in contradistinction to the long barrow population discussed above, the male/female balance is even and 60% of the individuals recorded are children or early adolescents.

Associated with this extraordinary necropolis site is a smaller enclosure of apparently domestic function - the whole surrounded by a mighty outwork system of triple chalk-built and timber-framed ramparts involving the use of many thousands of timber beams. Eventually, like Carn Brea and Crickley, the site was destroyed in a mighty conflagration but at Hambledon the preservative qualities of the chalk bedrock has led to the preservation of five intact skeletons of individuals apparently killed during this episode - one of whom indeed had one of the distinctive leaf arrowheads embedded in his chest. However ceremonialized the warfare that we are glimpsing, its consequences were unpleasant enough for at least some of its participants - all of them, at Hambledon, robust young males.

As one of a relatively small group of archaeologists present at Bellagio in February of 1988, I was privileged to learn a very great deal about an area of study with which most archaeologists fail to come to terms. Language as the most pervasive and flexible of human artefacts has however the crushing drawback that it cannot survive independently in the archaeological record. Can, however, this sketched account of the early neolithic of Britain and the development of warfare have much to offer by way of understanding for the palaeo-linguist?

I think it may seek to clarify the limitation to any close harnessing of our two disciplines. We have seen that the exigency of fundamental economic change in N and W Europe may well have led to the adoption by degrees of new economic practices without necessarily any major ethnic movement. Certainly there is no evidence for such movement and the clear separation to be noted between the European evidence and that from Britain might hint that the reverse is true. Thus we are faced with the *sui generis* production of a highly organized farming community on the basis of hunting/fishing communities under stress and intercommunicating around the land locked seas of NW Europe. Along these lines of communication moved materials quite foreign to these indigenous communities (cereals, sheep/goats in material terms but, probably, and vastly more significantly, a prodigious array of conceptual innovations which almost certainly would have demanded vocabularistic and syntactical innovation). The precise nature and source of this likely innovation is not, and almost certainly never will be, known to us. From these lowly but complex origins we see the independent, unmatched development in Britain of highly competitive pressurized societies within which (to be highly selective) warfare, fortification, cranial cult, axe-ritual, dairy-oriented economy, ox-traction ploughing and a number of other features that might be expected to be "at home" in an *Urheimat* all played a recognizable role. All this was established here by 3000 bc - and recently the Zvelebils (this volume) have suggested that it may be in concert with *conceptual* changes aligned with Sherratt's Secondary Products Revolution (of which traction and milking are the principal early components) that Indo-European languages were introduced to NW Europe between 4000-3000 bc in a series of radiating "ripples" (Sherratt 1988) though Sherratt would not go so far as to call Britain into that pool at so early a date. Certainly if we reject the period before 3000 bc with its registered innovation, enhanced contact and consequent tension as the period of proto-Indo-European linguistic introduction in N and W Europe, then we have to wait at least another millennium and half until after 2000 bc for far less persuasive archaeological disjunctures to perhaps signal an appropriate period for linguistic introduction.

The writer suspects that the organizers' inclusion of a consideration of prehistoric warfare in the Bellagio symposium may have had little to do with the above comments. The writer also suspects that language is spread by people talking to each other, not fighting each other - all the more so if they had something absolutely new and very exciting to talk about.

BIBLIOGRAPHY

Ammerman A.J. & Cavalli-Sforza L.L. 1971
"Measuring the Rate of Spread of Early Farming in Europe" *Man* VI(1), 674-688

Ashbee P. 1966
"The Fussell's Lodge Long Barrow Excavations 1957" *Archaeologia* C, 1-80

Ashbee P., Smith I.F. & Evans J.G. 1979
"Excavation of Three Long Barrows Near Avebury, Wiltshire" Proc. Prehist. Soc. XLV, 207-300

Atkinson R.J.C. 1965
"Waylands Smithy" *Antiquity* XXXIX, 126-33

Childe V.G. 1929
The Dawn of European Civilisation

Clark J.G.D. 1977
"The Economic Context of Dolmens of Passage Graves in Sweden" *in* Markotic V. ed. *Ancient Europe and the Mediterranean*

Corcoran J.X.W.P. 1972
"Multi-period Construction and the Origins of the Chambered Long Cairn in Western Britain and Ireland" *in* Lynch F. & Burgess C. *Prehistoric Man in Wales and the West* 31-64

Dennell R. 1983
European Economic Prehistory - A New Approach, London

Edwards K. & Ralston I.B.M. 1984
"Post-Glacial Hunter-Gatherers and Vegetational History in Scotland" *Proc. Soc. Antiq. Scot.* CXIV, 15-34

Gimbutas M.J. 1961
"Notes on the Chronology and Expansion of the Pit-Grave Culture" *in* Bohm J. and De Laet S.J. eds. *L'Europe a la fin de l'age de pierre* 193-200 (Prague)

Jacobi R.M. 1973
"Aspects of the Mesolithic Age in Great Britain" *in* Kozlowski S.K. ed. *The Mesolithic in Europe*, Warsaw

Jensen J. 1982	*The Prehistory of Denmark*
Keiller A. & Piggott S. 1938	"Excavation of an Untouched Chamber in Lanhill Long Barrow" *Proc. Prehist. Soc. Soc.* IV 122-150
Kinnes I.J. (forthcoming)	"The Cattleship Potemkin -Reflections on the First Neolithic in Britain"
Liddell D.M. (1930-35)	"1st-5th Reports of Excavations at Hembury Fort" *Devon Archaeol. & Explor. Soc.* I 39-63, 90-119, 162-190; II 135-75
Manby T. 1976	"The Excavation of the Kilham Long Barrow, East Riding of Yorkshire" *Proc. Prehist. Soc.* XLII, 111-159
Mercer R.J. 1980	*Hambledon Hill - A Neolithic Landscape*, Edinburgh
Mercer R.J. 1981	*Excavations at Carn Brea, Illogan, Cornwall 1970-73 A Neolithic Fortified Complex of the Third Millennium BC*, Redruth
Piggott S. 1954	*The Neolithic Cultures of the British Isles*, Cambridge
Piggott S. 1963	*The West Kennet Long Barrow - Excavations 1955-56* HMSO London
Powell T.G.E. 1973	"The Excavation of the Megalithic Chambered Cairn at Dyffryn Ardudwy, Merioneth, Wales" *Archaeologia* CIV 1-49
Renfrew C. 1973	"Social Organisation in Neolithic Wessex" *in* Renfrew A.C. ed. *The Explanation of Culture Change: Models in Prehistory* 539-558
Renfrew A.C. 1976	"Megaliths, Territories and Populations" *in* De Laet S.J. ed. *Acculturation and Continuity in Atlantic Europe* 198-220, Brugge
Renfrew A.C. 1987	*Archaeology and Language: the Puzzle of Indo-European Origins*, London

Saville A., Gowlett, J.A.J. & Hedges R.E.M.	"Radiocarbon Dates from the Chambered Tomb at Hazleton, Glos.: a Chronology for Neolithic Collective Burial" *Antiquity* LXI, 23i, 108-119
Sherratt A. & S.	"The Archaeology of Indo-European: an Alternative View" *Antiquity* LXII, 236, 584-595
Startin D.W.A. 1982	"Prehistoric Earthmoving" *in* Case H.J. & Whittle A.W.R. eds. *Settlement Patterns in the Oxford Region: Excavations at the Abingdon Causewayed Enclosure and Other Sites* CBA Res. Rep. No 44, 153-156
Vatcher F. de M. 1965	"East Heslerton Long Barrow, Yorkshire: the Eastern Half" *Antiquity* XXXIX, 49-52
Whittle A.W.R. 1977	*The Earlier Neolithic of Southern England and its Continental Backgrounds* Brit. Archaeol. Rep. Suppl. Series XXXV, Oxford
Zvelebil M. & K.V.	"Agricultural Transition and Indo-European Dispersals" *Antiquity* LXII, 236 574-583

Astronomical and geometrical influences on monumental design: clues to changing patterns of social tradition?

Clive Ruggles, University of Leicester, U.K.

Abstract

When applied with due caution and with due regard to the archaeological and cultural context, statistical studies of design features of Neolithic field monuments, such as shape and orientation, and of the relationship of such design features to the surrounding landscape and skyscape, can be of considerable interest in shedding light on changing patterns of social tradition. This is especially the case when applied to groups of sites, such as the small rings and alignments of standing stones found in abundance in northern and western parts of the British Isles, which yield little in the way of stratigraphical and artefactual evidence.

This paper attempts a critical overview of some recent results from this type of approach, with particular reference to astronomical and geometrical practices as evidenced by their influence on monumental design. It then sets out to draw some tentative conclusions about changing patterns of social tradition, and their relationship to social structure, during the third and second millennia bc. Particular reference is made to the British Isles, but mention is also made of related work in other parts of western Europe.

1 Introduction

The study of the design of Neolithic field monuments in western Europe has evolved very differently in different contexts. Thus investigations of the architectural design of large megalithic tombs have long been established in the mainstream of western European archaeology; on the other hand studies of the shape and design of smaller megalithic sites, such as the small rings and short alignments of standing stones found in abundance in northern and western parts of the British Isles, were until relatively recently confined to the domain of astronomers, engineers and statisticians, and were confused in the minds of many archaeologists (e.g. Daniel 1980) with the activities of the 'lunatic fringe' who had been much attracted to megalithic monuments in the 1960s and 1970s. A history of lack of communication and understanding across the 'cultural divide' has given rise to some very anomalous attitudes to different studies of monumental design in its cultural context, which obscure much work of interest which has taken place during the last five to ten years.

Prior to the methodological revolutions of the 1970s, investigations of the design of prehistoric monumental sites were epitomised by studies such as those of megalithic chambered tombs in western Europe which concentrated upon the classification of structural elements in the tomb architecture and upon typological sequencing based upon these (e.g. Daniel 1958; Powell 1969). The quest for explanatory models in the 1970s has led to considerations of field monuments in relation to the surrounding landscape, natural and cultural. A recent example of this approach is the work of Fraser (1983) on the chambered cairns of Orkney. The present decade has also seen the emergence of various approaches to explore more direct relationships between monumental design and social practice and structure. Thomas (1988), for example, studies changes in the design of the Cotswold-Severn Tombs in relation to changes in mortuary practice, concluding that the past was manipulated and recreated in order to support social change. In studies of shape and design Hillier & Hanson's (1984) analysis of the relationships between social and spatial order has been influential.

Concurrently with this development, and in relative isolation, investigations have proceeded of the smaller megalithic sites, most of which yield little in the way of stratigraphical and artefactual evidence. Amongst the many possible factors influencing the design and placement of a such a monument, astronomical ones have, it may seem, received far more than their due share of attention. This situation has arisen partly for historical reasons—for two centuries individuals had sporadically become fascinated by the idea that there might have been an astronomical significance in many prehistoric monuments, with eminent astronomers occasionally backing up such speculations with accurate measurements (e.g. Lockyer 1909); partly because of the huge popular interest aroused by Gerald Hawkins' *Stonehenge Decoded* (Hawkins & White 1965); and lastly because of the influence of the work of Alexander Thom

(Thom 1967; 1971; Thom & Thom 1978a). Independently of his mainstream academic career as an engineer, Thom developed a deep and active interest in the prehistoric megalithic sites of Britain and Brittany, surveying many hundreds of them between the 1930s and the 1970s. Astronomy was one of his three areas of interest, the others being mensuration (the possible use of 'standard' units of measurement in setting out megalithic rings and rows), and geometry (the methods used to set out the rings, many of which are markedly non-circular).

These three lines of enquiry—mensuration, geometry and astronomy—form the legacy of so-called 'megalithic science'. The term derives from the title of a book by Heggie (1981). Subtitled 'Ancient mathematics and astronomy in northwest Europe', although confined almost exclusively to the British Isles and Brittany, the book sets out to review, from the point of view of a mathematician and astronomer, the evidence in the three areas. Heggie was perhaps the first person from this side of the 'cultural divide' to cast a critical eye upon the theories generated by his colleagues in the numerate disciplines.

Criticisms had been forthcoming from archaeologists for a good deal longer. Indeed, the term 'megalithic science' is still an immotive one, redolent of scientists and engineers proceeding with considerable but misguided enthusiasm in the pursuit of evidence of prehistoric protoscience while paying rather too little attention to matters of archaeological and social context. For example, almost all the attention was focussed upon spectacular and relatively well-preserved field monuments: alignments along and between standing stones are easily picked out, and can easily be imagined to be 'indicating' something. The idea that such alignments indicated horizon astronomical events has dominated investigations of prehistoric astronomy, almost to the exclusion of any others. As megalithic science rose to become a vigorous field of enquiry as well as one attracting considerable popular interest, there was much talk of a 'megalithic culture' harbouring a hitherto unexpected astronomical and geometrical expertise: 'Megalithic Man', according to Thom (1971: ch. 1), was a competent engineer, had an extensive knowledge of practical geometry, and studied the movements of the sun and moon in great detail. The ethnocentrism inherent in such discussions is manifest. Unfortunately, however, because of this many have simply dismissed all aspects of Thom's work, and that of others in 'megalithic science', without any further consideration of the quantitative arguments and raw field evidence.

Some authors, however, have attempted to bridge the divide. Burl, for example, has considered results from Thom's fieldwork within a range of more conventional archaeological evidence in various publications on megalithic rings (e.g. Burl 1976; 1980; 1981a; 1983; 1987; 1988). The present author has proceeded from critiques of Thom's work (Ruggles 1981a; 1982a; 1983) to the consideration of the astronomical significance of certain groups of monuments within an approach which attempts to combine statistical rigour with less formal reasoning based on the archaeological context (Ruggles 1984a; 1984b; 1985a; Ruggles & Burl 1985; Ruggles 1988b). Factors such as astronomical significance and/or geometrical design are increasingly being considered within more conventional archaeological investigations, Fraser's work (1983) being a case in point.

This paper attempts to review some recent results in areas of investigation deriving from those in 'megalithic science', i.e. regarding astronomical and geometrical practices as evidenced by their influence on monumental design. Most of the work described relates to British sites, although recently some interesting investigations have emerged in other parts of Europe. The final section of this paper attempts to draw some tentative conclusions about changing patterns of social tradition, and their relationship to social structure.

2 Orientation and astronomy in late Neolithic and Bronze Age Britain

2.1 Astronomy and the material record

The claim that astronomical observations, even of some considerable sophistication, might have been made by various groups in prehistoric Europe is scarcely highly controversial in itself. The movements of the heavenly bodies are of almost universal concern, even amongst the most technologically primitive of hunter-gatherer societies (see, e.g., Thorpe 1981; Chamberlain *et al.* 1989). Many instances are known of careful and precise astronomical observations amongst relatively simple societies, such as the much-quoted example of the Hopi Indians, an essentially egalitarian society with no centralised political organisation, yet with an elaborate ceremonial calendar regulated by carefully tracking the horizon rising position of the sun from fixed points on the ground (Renfrew 1973; McCluskey 1977).

The difficulty is in extracting direct evidence for astronomical practice from the material record, and in its interpretation. Many aspects of celestial lore and observations of astronomical bodies, well known from ethnographic examples world-wide, may simply leave no direct trace in the material record. An obvious example is the naming and observations of constellations. Some activities might give rise to particular artefacts (for example, the counting off of months by observing the phases of the moon, a very widespread activity, might leave its trace in the form of tally sticks) but have no direct influence on ceremonial architecture since the observation can be made from any position with a clear view of the sky.

Even where astronomical influences on monumental architecture are demonstrable, interpretations are likely to be complex. With perhaps the Hopi example in mind, calendar regulation is often quoted as a motivation for monumental orientations in the direction of sunrise or sunset at particular times of the year. However, even where sunrise observations are made from particular spots for this purpose, it does not follow that there is a necessity to erect markers of any great permanence at these positions or to orient them towards the horizon in question (indeed, the Hopi do not; and in many cases a natural object such as a boulder or tree suffices as a marker (e.g. Turton & Ruggles 1978)). It is also misleading to imply that a reasonably accurate agricultural or ceremonial calendar can only be regulated by keeping track of the horizon rising or setting position of the sun: it can be done perfectly adequately, as in many other known cases, by means of observations of the heliacal rising or setting of stars (Ruggles 1981b)—observations which do not have to made from particular spots on the ground—as well as by indirect and composite methods, for example combining observations of a variety of astronomical events with observations of a range of other natural phenomena. Such methods, although seeming haphazard to ourselves, may work perfectly adequately within the framework of the society in question (Turton & Ruggles 1978).

Finally we must consider at the outset how, given a set of data such as the orientations of a group of field monuments, one assesses the nature of the astronomical observations (if any) that influenced those orientations. It is clear that any individual alignment of apparent astronomical significance could have arisen through factors quite unrelated to astronomy. There needs to be some attempt to demonstrate the intentionality of putative astronomical alignments.

One way is through the statistical analysis of as large as possible a set of data, whereby it may be demonstrable that certain astronomical alignments are significantly more common than would have been expected by chance. This approach has the advantage that unavoidable errors and uncertainties, such as the difference between the present disposition of the material remains and that intended by the builders, will merely add to the background 'random noise'. Since, however, a large number of factors may have influenced monumental design and orientation, great care is needed in drawing inferences, even when trends of apparent astronomical significance are encountered. One must check whether factors unrelated to astronomy could equally well account for the orientation pattern observed. The present author (Ruggles 1981c; 1982b) has considered this point in some detail, suggesting a methodology for studying orientations which is followed in later work.

One must of course also bear in mind the complexities of the material record and the limitations of a statistical approach of this sort. In particular, one can only hope to isolate general trends at reasonably large groups of sites. For this reason this author feels that statistical rigour must be combined with interpretative reasoning in a well-structured way. Results of some interest have been emerging recently through such an approach (Ruggles 1988b).

2.2 Technical background

The key concept in the consideration of putative astronomical alignments is that of *declination* (Thom 1967: ch. 3; Ruggles 1984a: Appendix I). At each site, any range of horizon 'indicated' by a structure orientation can be defined in terms of declination. Declination is a function of azimuth, horizon altitude, and the latitude of the observer (the effects of astronomical refraction must also be taken into account). From the declination one can deduce the celestial bodies that will rise or set at the point indicated, and those that would have done so at any past era.

We can regard all the heavenly bodies—sun, moon, planets and stars—as positioned on a 'celestial sphere' surrounding the earth. From any position on the earth at a particular time we can observe the half of the celestial sphere which is above our horizon, as in a planetarium. The earth rotates once daily inside the celestial sphere; thus if we regard the earth as fixed, the celestial sphere rotates once daily with all the heavenly bodies affixed to it. On this rotating celestial sphere we can identify a north and south pole (the 'celestial poles'), an equator (the 'celestial equator'), and lines of ('celestial') latitude and longitude. Declination is simply a synonym for celestial latitude. The celestial equator is the line where the declination is 0°. By convention, declinations north of the celestial equator are positive and those to the south negative. All the heavenly bodies move daily around lines of constant declination: thus the Pleiades have a declination of about +24° and Polaris, which is very near to the north celestial pole, has a declination of about +89°. The declinations of stars change gradually on a timescale of centuries owing to a phenomenon known as the precession of the equinoxes.

The sun, moon and planets move slowly about on the celestial sphere as it rotates. The result for the sun is that its declination varies annually between about +23°.5 at the June solstice and -23°.5 at the December solstice, in a sinusoidal manner. The motions of the moon are more complicated. The moon's declination varies rapidly, moving between northerly and southerly limits once a month. These monthly limits themselves vary over a period of 18·6 years. Thus at one point in the 18·6-year cycle the moon's declination will be varying each month between limits of about +18° and -20°; a little over nine years later these monthly limits will have expanded to about +28° and -30°; and after another nine years they will have contracted back to +18° and -20°. The maximum northerly and southerly limits of the moon's monthly motions are sometimes known, following Thom (1971: 18), as the 'major standstill' declinations, and the minimum limits as the 'minor standstill' declinations. This terminology will be used here, although it must be remembered that the declination of the moon itself continues to vary rapidly day by day at all times.

The limits of variation of the sun and moon, the solar solstitial and lunar standstill declinations, are unaffected over the centuries by the precession of the equinoxes, but they do change noticeably over a timescale of millennia. Since 2000 BC they have changed by about 0°.5, an amount roughly equal to the width of the solar or lunar disc.

2.3 The legacy of 'megalithic astronomy'

'Megalithic astronomy', a term much used in the 1960s and 1970s, concerned itself almost exclusively with the possible alignment of structures upon the horizon rising and setting positions of certain celestial bodies. In its heyday the megalithic astronomy debate was dominated by arguments about the interpretation of a few individual sites. There are many pitfalls in lavishing so much attention on so few sites (Ruggles 1984c), especially where independent archaeological evidence relating to the astronomical hypothesis is either absent or ignored.

The passage grave at Newgrange is perhaps the least contentious example of a monument incorporating an astronomical alignment to emerge from these debates. O'Kelly's excavations and restorations (O'Kelly 1971) revealed a mysterious 'roof-box' above the entrance which would have continued to admit light into the interior after the entrance itself was sealed. O'Kelly's own observations, followed up by a survey by Patrick (1974), established that the sun's rays enter the roof-box, penetrate the entire length of the passage and illuminate the central chamber just after sunrise for a few days on either side of the winter solstice, and would have done so since the erection of the tomb somewhat before 3000 BC. Given that south-easterly orientations are quite common amongst passage graves, and may be favoured for other reasons, the probability of a chance solstitial alignment is appreciably high; however the presence of the roof-box (not readily explicable otherwise) in just the right position for the shaft of light to penetrate the entire passage has made its intentionality almost universally accepted. The alignment was clearly not for the use of living astronomers.

The interpretation of most of the other 'classic' sites of megalithic astronomy is much more contentious; indeed, it seems fair to say that they merely illustrate the dangers of attempting an astronomical interpretation of individual sites in isolation from their wider archaeological context. The long debate concerning the three-stone row at Ballochroy in Kintyre, Scotland (MacKie 1974; Bailey *et al.* 1975; Burl 1979: 66; Patrick 1981), hailed as a high-precision solar 'observatory' by Thom (1971: 36), illustrates clearly that such debates can never be satisfactorily resolved on their own merits (Ruggles 1984c). A detailed and balanced appraisal of the various astronomical theories concerning Stonehenge has been given by Heggie (1981); it seems that the only reasonably uncontentious statement that can be made here is that the general orientation of the axis of the monument at various stages in its development is towards midsummer sunrise and midwinter sunset (a precision in azimuth of at best a degree or two of arc is involved), and that this may well have been deliberate. Burl (1987), however, has recently taken the archaeological and astronomical argument further (see below). Even where, as at Kintraw in Argyll, there is an opportunity to test an astronomical hypothesis by archaeological means—an excavation was undertaken by MacKie (1974) to test an astronomical theory of Thom (1969) by determining whether a ledge on a putative astronomical alignment was artificial—the results can be inconclusive, as MacKie himself now concedes they were at this site (MacKie *et al.* 1985). Burl (1981a) has pointed out some poignant examples where seemingly convincing astronomical alignments are present at individual sites, but when these sites are seen as part of an archaeological group the trend is not repeated and the alignment then appears to have come about by chance.

In contrast to these discussions of individual sites, arguably the most important evidence presented over the years by Thom arose from analyses of groups of sites taken together. The evidence is cumulative in nature: four distinct 'Levels' were identified by the present author (Ruggles 1981a). At each Level the evidence consists essentially of one or more analyses of many putative 'indications', and at each Level the degree of precision of indication being tested is greater than at previous Levels. At Level 1 most indications consist simply of a part of the horizon in line with an oriented structure. Some, however, achieve greater precision by making use of natural foresights, such as notches between hills on distant horizons. In the later Levels all indications are of the 'indicated foresight' type.

It is worth commenting on the later Levels first. These concentrate upon lunar sightlines, which Thom claimed were set up to a precision of no more than two or three (Thom 1971), and later no more than one or two (Thom & Thom 1978b; 1980; A.S. Thom 1981) minutes of arc (the diameter of the sun or moon's disc is roughly 30 arc minutes, or half a degree). One is forced to conclude that meticulous observing programmes were carried out lasting up to 180 years (A.S. Thom 1981: 38). A number of authors have challenged these conclusions at their various stages, claiming for example that data selection decisions made by Thom are not justifiable on *a priori* grounds, and that lunar observations of the precision claimed are simply not feasible in practice (Heggie 1972; McCreery 1980; Ellegård 1981). Comprehensive critiques by the present author, based on archaeological reappraisals and remeasurements in the field (Ruggles 1981a; 1982a; 1983; see also Ruggles 1984c for a summary), concluded that the evidence is overwhelmingly against deliberate lunar indications of very high precision.

However such conclusions do not extend to the earlier stages (Level 1) of Thom's work. Here (Thom 1967) he measured 262 putative indications at 145 sites. On the basis of cumulative histograms of the resulting declinations, and associated statistical tests, he suggested the existence of deliberate solar, lunar and stellar alignments set up to a precision of about half a degree. The solar alignments comprise the solstices, equinoxes and intermediate declinations representing equal divisions of the year into eight and possibly 16 parts. The lunar alignments are upon the four major and minor standstill declinations. The latter alignments imply that co-ordinated observing programmes lasted up to 18 years.

These conclusions should not necessarily be taken at face value. Moir *et al.* (1980) and Moir (1981) have drawn attention to the great variety of types of site, geographical location and methods of indication found in Thom's data. Moir has also highlighted several sites where archaeological evidence makes the proposed astronomical interpretation particularly doubtful. The present author has questioned Thom's criteria for selecting candidate indications, and drawn attention to other problems such as the confusion of hypotheses (Ruggles 1984a; 1984c). On the other hand, Thom's conclusions at this level cannot simply be dismissed; it is important to see whether, when the selection criteria are clarified and the other criticisms satisfied, statistical evidence still remains to suuport any of the categories of astronomical alignment claimed by Thom.

An extensive independent survey of megalithic sites in western Scotland was conducted between 1975 and 1981 under severe methodological constraints (Ruggles 1984a). For example, in selecting sites and structures for consideration, rigorous pre-defined criteria were adhered to. No survey data were reduced until the entire sample had been collected, in order to avoid the possibility of the selection strategy being influenced by the results obtained along the way.

Indicated declinations were found to manifest overall trends at three levels of precision.

(1)   At the lowest level, declinations between about -15° and +15° are strongly avoided. This trend reflects an extremely strong preference for structures to be oriented in the N-S, rather than the E-W, quadrants (Patrick & Freeman 1988).

(2)   At the second level, there is a marked preference for southern declinations between
       -31° and -19°. This declination range is of particular interest because it represents, to within a degree or so, the range of possible values of the

southerly limit of the moon's monthly motions at different points in the 18.6-year cycle. A distribution over this range would be expected if sites were oriented upon the most southerly rising or setting position of the moon each month, without recognition of the gradual change of this limit over the longer cycle.

(3) At the most precise level, there is marginal evidence of a preference for six particular declination values to within a precision of one or two degrees: -30°, -25°, -22°.5, +18°, +27° and +33°. Three of them (-30°, +18° and +27°) may indicate a specific interest in the lunar standstills, and would imply that the eighteen-year cycle was recognised. Another (-25°) may indicate an interest in the winter solstice. The others have no particular solar or lunar significance.

Thus although there is clear evidence of lunar orientation, and marginal evidence of orientation upon the winter solstice, there is no evidence whatsoever for an interest in the summer solstice or equinoxes (indeed, declinations in the vicinity of the equinoxes are strongly avoided) and no support for Thom's calendar. Nor is there any evidence of astronomical orientations of a precision greater than about one degree.

Certain coherent groups of sites are found to feature predominantly amongst the indications falling in particular 'preferred' declination intervals. Most interestingly, a well-defined group of sites in Mull and mainland Argyll, consisting of up to five standing stones in a row, are all without exception oriented in the south upon a declination between -31° and -19°.

2.4 'Science or ceremonial?'

A further legacy of the conflict between the 'megalithic science' approach and the mainstream archaeological approach should be mentioned here. This is the protracted discussion as to whether astronomical practice in late Neolithic and Bronze Age Britain was 'scientific' or 'ceremonial' in nature. Strongly on the side of 'scientific' astronomy are, for example, Thom (1967; 1971; Thom & Thom 1978a) and MacKie (1981; MacKie et al. 1985); in the other camp are authors such as Burl (1980; 1981a; 1983), Moir (1981), Ellegård (1981), Barnatt & Pierpoint (1983) and Fraser (1984).

Many of these authors derive support for their view from independent archaeological evidence, but there is a strong tendency to interpret evidence in favour high-precision astronomical observations as evidence in favour of 'scientific' astronomy and evidence in favour of low-precision observations as evidence in favour of 'ceremonial' astronomy. This is not a correlation that can be taken for granted. Indeed, the rigid dichotomy between science and ceremonial is undoubtedly misleading; we need to consider first the existence and precision of intentional orientations, astronomical and otherwise, and then to interpret them using far more than two crude (and actually rather vaguely-defined) categories. As Renfrew (1981) has pointed out, to insist on such a rigid and ultimately subjective dichotomy between science and non-science serves only to obscure the nature of what surely ranks as an interesting development in the evolution of scientific thought.

This author has expressed the view (Ruggles 1984a; 1984c) that we should first examine the dispositional evidence with a view to questions such as (i) how important an influence were astronomical considerations upon the placement and design of a site? and (ii) what was the precision of any astronomical observations made? Then, given conclusions based upon statistical examinations of the evidence, we can consider astronomical observations in their social context alongside the other strands of archaeological evidence at our disposal. The two remaining parts of this section examine recent work, attempting to separate the two stages in this progress.

2.5 Astronomy as a factor in site placement and orientation

In recent years a number of investigations have been undertaken in which astronomy is considered as merely one of a number of possible factors influencing site placement and orientation. They have started to uncover evidence that astronomical considerations were indeed a factor influencing the siting and design of a variety of different types of monument at different times in British prehistory.

Fraser (1983) has attempted to draw together many lines of evidence relating to the people who inhabited Orkney during the third and second millennia bc and the land on which they lived. His main source of data is the Orkney chambered cairns: their architectural form, their relationship to other material evidence (other monuments, artefacts and burial evidence), and their spatial relationships. He concludes that that the Neolithic inhabitants of Orkney situated their chambered cairns in places which were chosen so as to make certain solar observations possible. These observations could have been of importance to a farming people in signalling significant times in the agricultural year.

Barnatt & Pierpoint (1983) have studied the group of stone circles at Machrie Moor on Arran for evidence of astronomical observations using horizon foresights, but without structures on the ground being oriented upon the foresights in question. The area has a large concentration of monuments including six stone circles of various designs, three chambered tombs and over twenty round houses, together with associated clearance cairns and field walls. The authors' approach is to detect those areas on the ground from which certain astronomical events—the solar solstices and lunar standstills—would have been observable in particular horizon notches, and to see whether the placement of sites favours locations where a good many such events would have been visible. They conclude that the stone circles on Machrie Moor were placed at optimally prominent locations, in strong contrast to the other types of site on the moor. Furthermore, five out of the seven circles occupy areas from which at least two astronomical events can be seen, although these areas only make up some 27% of the total. The authors conclude that there is a distinct bias in the siting of stone circles for locations favourable to astronomical observation.

Ruggles (1984b) and Ruggles & Burl (1985) have studied the Recumbent Stone Circles (RSCs) of eastern Scotland. These are a well-defined group of about 100 known sites. They comprise a ring of standing stones including a single recumbent stone flanked by two uprights (Burl 1976). Dating evidence, including radiocarbon dates of around 1400bc from one of the sites, Berrybrae, suggest that the group as a whole belong to the earlier and middle part of the second millennium bc.

Certain general trends are evident in the placement and design of these monuments. They were, for example, always placed in conspicuous settings, often on artifically levelled sites. The direction from the centre of the ring to the centre of the recumbent stone is in every case without exception oriented within the horizon quadrant centred upon SSW. The horizon behind the recumbent stone is, again without exception, non-local. The top of the recumbent appears always to have lain below the horizon, while the flankers usually projected above it, seemingly to demarcate a stretch of horizon.

There was a clear tendency to orient the recumbent stone upon the major or minor standstill moon in the south, although no great precision was involved. However this was not universal: there is evidence of other (possibly conflicting) concerns, such as the presence of conspicuous hilltops within the horizon above the recumbent stone, and placing the recumbent stone due south of the ring centre. There is also evidence that cupmarked stones were placed so as to indicate the major or minor standstill moon as seen from the ring centre. These separate goals would rarely have been achievable simultaneously, and the authors surmise that compromises were reached.

Since they were singled out by the wider-based earlier survey (Ruggles 1984a) described above, further studies have proceeded of the rows of up to five stones found predominatly in two geographical concentrations in western Scotland— Argyll (centring upon the Kilmartin area) and northern Mull. On the basis of new evidence (Ruggles 1985a; 1988b) the southern declinations indicated by the stone rows and aligned pairs seem to fit a clear pattern. Either they are oriented within about a degree of -30°, or else they are oriented within a degree or two of -24° and situated close to another row or pair which does indicate -30°.

The primary orientations around -30° appear to present particularly strong evidence of deliberate orientation upon the southern major standstill moon. It should be noted, however, that because of the low precision of these alignments there is no necessity to postulate (*pace* Thom) strictly regulated nightly observations of the moon at certain critical times in the 18.6-year cycle. Simple observations, e.g. of the rising or setting of the full moon nearest to the summer solstice, would suffice. There is no clear-cut explanation for the secondary orientations: they may have been upon the moon's southerly monthly limit at another point in the 18.6-year cycle, but it is also possible that they were upon the midwinter sun. On the basis of the evidence currently available the two possibilities seem indistinguishable.

A survey and excavation project has been running in northern Mull since 1986 (Ruggles & Martlew, in preparation). The fieldwork has shown that a reconstructed setting of standing stones at Glengorm in the far north of the island was originally a three-stone row oriented in the south upon Ben More, the highest mountain on Mull and a prominent distant horizon feature, and a nearer hill, Beinn na Drise, to its right. The peak of Ben More yields a declination of -29°; that of Beinn na Drise -30°. Thus the site follows the pattern of primary orientation upon the southern standstill moon, with the added feature of two prominent hills on the horizon at this point. There is also evidence from pollen cores of a relatively sudden phase of forest clearance broadly around the time of construction of the site. Further dating evidence is being sought in an attempt to investigate further the closeness of this correlation.

Burl (1987) considers developments in Wessex, and at Stonehenge in particular, emphasizing the role of the latter throughout its long periods of use as a house of the dead, and linking developments in the 'cult of the dead' with changes in the pattern of interest in celestial phenomena. In the early phases, argues Burl, the Neolithic long barrows of Salisbury Plain were oriented between NE and SE on the arc of the horizon where the moon rises (this arc is wider than the corresponding arc for the sun). Later, there was a shift in emphasis towards orientation upon the horizon arc in the south between the moon's extreme rising and setting positions. The original henge entrance at Stonehenge is oriented towards northern limiting moonrise at major standstill (or, equivalently, the northernmost rising of the full moon nearest midwinter). Later again, there was a further shift of emphasis, with the axis of Stonehenge being altered to an imprecise alignment upon the midsummer rising sun. Beaker burials in the Salisbury Plain were also, according to Burl, oriented towards the rising sun. With the Sarsen phase came a final shift from an emphasis upon rising phenomena to one upon setting phenomena. The trilithons offered a range of alignments upon sunsets on dates of calendrical significance.

2.6 Discussion and interpretations

It is well known that orientatation was an important factor in some of the earliest funerary monuments in the British Isles. A great many of the earthen long barrows of Cranbourne Chase are, for example, aligned NW-SE with the larger end at the SE. The orientation of these monuments was largely dictated by the local lie of the land (Ashbee 1970). Entrance graves in the Scilly Isles are generally set on slopes and frequently, though not always, face downhill, which may have been (at least in part) in order to make the monuments conspicuous (Ashbee 1974). Henshall has commented that a north-easterly orientation is favoured for the forecourt of the long axis of the Scottish Clyde cairns (Henshall 1972: 99); that only 12 of the 114 cairns in her Orkney-Cromarty group face the western half of the compass, the normal orientation being between NE and SE (Henshall 1963: 104); and that an easterly direction also seems to have been preferred, although not universally, by the builders of

Maes Howe type cairns (Henshall 1963: 130). Burl (1981a) gives further examples.

It is less clear when astronomical considerations began to influence these orientations. Certainly some of the passage graves and round chambered cairns of the mid-third millennium bc, in areas of increasing social complexity such as the Boyne valley and the Orkney Islands, seem to have incorporated solar alignments. Newgrange (O'Kelly 1971; Patrick 1974) has already been mentioned; the entrance of Maes Howe (Moir 1981; Burl 1981b) roughly faced the midwinter sunset, but the interpretation is more complex (Burl 1981a). Fraser (1983) finds evidence that the Orkney chambered cairns were situated in places which were chosen so as to make certain solar observations possible. These observations could have been of importance to a farming people in signalling significant times in the agricultural year. He suggests that such monuments, situated in the physical centre and social heart of the community, would have been the obvious meeting place to rejoice and celebrate the changing of the seasons. According to Burl (1983), solar alignments such as that at Newgrange expressed a symbolic conjunction between the sun and the dead.

A different picture is emerging in areas of lesser social complexity. Burl (1981a) discusses the Clava cairns of Invernessshire, a group of simple passage graves and ring cairns dating between approximately 3200 and 2300 bc and oriented without exception within a quarter of the compass centred upon SSW. The declinations deduced by Burl (1981a: Table 7.3 & Fig. 7.5) all fall in the range $-30°$ to $-18°$, suggesting that there was a practice of orientation upon the southern monthly limiting moon (at arbitrary points in the 18.6-year cycle). A large cluster of orientations at the $-30°$ end of the range suggests that there was a special interest in the major standstill moon, implying that the builders even at this early stage were aware of the 18.6-year lunar cycle.

The eastern Scottish Recumbent Stone Circles, discussed above, appear to be descendants of the Clava cairns dating to the early and middle second millennium bc (Burl 1976). The pattern of orientation towards the SSW is preserved, as, it seems, is the prepossession with the southern moon (Ruggles & Burl 1985). It is interesting to note that in this part of the country there is no evidence, as in Orkney or Wessex, of earlier Neolithic burial places being gradually replaced by very large monuments reflecting significantly increasing social complexity during the third and second millennia bc. No RSC or other structure in eastern Scotland at around this time seems significantly more grandiose than its fellows. Instead, Ruggles & Burl (1985) argue that the RSCs

> seem to be the elegant but simple ritual centres for small, egalitarian groups of subsistence farmers... Various general features in their placement and design seem to reflect a ritual tradition that was adhered to over a wide area...

The western Scottish short stone rows also belong to a region where there is no evidence of significantly increasing social complexity during the period in question. Here, as we have seen, there is also evidence of a prepossession with the southern moon.

The pattern of orientation in the primary and secondary directions seems universal, but the symbolism by which it is expressed seems to vary from site to site. Thus at some sites the primary and secondary directions are indicated by stone rows placed a few hundred metres apart; at others the rows are only a few tens of metres apart. At the Kilmartin stones we find a long alignment in which both the northernmost and southernmost components, instead of being single stones, have become pairs of slabs oriented across the line. The long alignment indicates the primary direction; the orientation of its components indicates the secondary direction. At Glengorm the alignment upon major standstill moonrise is enhanced by two prominent horizon features.

The overall impression is that both in the east and west of Scotland, in regions where there is no evidence of significantly increasing social complexity during the third and second millennia bc, there is evidence of a widespread interest in the moon and a general tradition of incoporating lunar alignments into monumental architecture. This contrasts with the evidence from regions such as Orkney where the architecture of large-scale 'public' sites seem to have incorporated solar symbolism. The same seems to be true of the great stone rings of Cumbria, dating as early as 2500 bc: according to Burl (1988) they possessed two alignments, one to a cardinal point and one to sunrise or sunset at an important time of year.

Moving to southern England, while the more precise details of the chronological sequence at and around Stonehenge are still uncertain, and Burl's (1987) evidence, outlined above, needs further examination from both an archaeological and a statistical point of view, it is possible to discern a definite shift, with the coming in the bluestone phase of social change and potential competition, from a predominant concern with the moon to a predominant concern with the sun. According to Burl, this is linked to changing developments in the 'cult of the dead'.

3 Design and geometry in Neolithic and Bronze Age Britain

3.1 Geometrical design and the material record

The problems of extracting information on geometrical design from the material record bear some similarity to those of extracting information on astronomical influences. First, a monumental layout which appears to fit a particular geometrical shape may not have been conceived by the builders as doing so. Secondly, a monumental layout may fit several shapes equally well. Thirdly, a proposed construction method may bear no resemblance to that actually used by the builders.

The problem of determining how well the layout of a monument fits a particular geometrical shape or shapes may be approached through the statistical analysis of a large quantity of data. However, many problems beset any such study.

Most work in this area, following Thom (1967), has considered the geometrical design of the British megalithic rings. The fundamental pitfall here is the diversity of types of megalithic ring (Burl 1976). There are regional preferences. Many rings have associated cairns, kerbs, banks and ditches; sometimes they are part of a henge. Incomplete preservation often obscures these elements. Attempts at comprehensive classification (e.g. Lynch 1972; 1979) have only been partially successful. Even the selection of free standing menhirs as the crucial diagnostic of a stone ring does not free one from ambiguity. Some rings, such as Temple Wood in Argyll, contain almost contiguous stones which are clearly not kerbs of cairns; others, such as Grey Hill in Gwent, have very large stones spaced within a kerb; others again, such as Castlehowe Scar in Cumbria, have so few stones that it is uncertain whether the site represents a robbed cairn or barrow. Whatever the classification criteria, the list of exceptions is a long one.

The preservation of stones within the ring is variable due to natural, animal, and human interference. The Rollright Stones in Oxfordshire provide an excellent example of the kinds of alteration which can occur (Lambrick 1983).

Given all these problems, the importance of excavated sites cannot be overestimated in the study of geometry and design. Yet very few have excavated on a large scale and with modern techniques. Those that have have revealed such a number of alterations, both in prehistoric periods and in modern times, that one must question the wisdom of accepting any site plan of extant stones as indicative of single-period, unadulterated activity. Many, if not most, of the sites were multi-period, with the extant plan a result of several phases of growth and alteration. A number of sites, such as Hampton Down (Wainwright 1966), Brandsbutt (Shepherd 1983), Strichen (Hampsher-Monk & Abramson 1982), and Fowlis Wester West (Young 1943), manifested layouts entirely at odds with the shapes extant before excavation.

Any methodology which attempts to analyse the form and pattern of these monuments must take into account the complexity introduced by their likely long period of use, their changes in function, and the deficiency of the surviving evidence. Statistical studies based on extant remains can only hope to isolate general trends at reasonably large groups of sites.

3.2 The evidence on geometrical design

The analysis of the shapes of stone rings is not a new phenomenon. Early observers in general assumed that sites were intended to be circular, although large deviations from circularity were often encountered in the field. Early plans (e.g. Logan 1829) often smoothed out imperfections and imposed symmetry. With the advent of accurate surveying techniques, non-circular sites were recognised and recorded. A fundamental question that arises immediately is whether circularity was intended but missed by the builders, or whether a wider range of shapes were intentionally laid out.

Thom was the first to deal with this problem in depth. In the opening paragraph of his first research paper concerning the geometry of megalithic rings, read to the Royal Statistical Society in 1955, he states (Thom 1955):

> In the past twenty years I have visited some 250 megalithic sites in England and Scotland, and made accurate surveys where there appeared to be anything worthy of survey... This mass of material provides data for a geometrical and statistical survey of the sites.

Thom concluded (1955; 1967) that several different shapes were intended by the builders, laid out to considerable accuracy using techniques of Euclidian geometry. In addition to circles, he argued that the builders of megalithic rings planned ellipses, two forms of flattened circle, 'egg shapes', and several more complex constructions.

A number of criticisms have been raised of these conclusions. Archaeologists were quick to point out the functional diversity of megalithic rings taken as a class (Childe 1955). Others pointed out that Thom had done no more than demonstrate that his range of 'standard shapes' provided reasonable fits to the measured data; he had not demonstrated that other shapes might not fit equally well. Angell (1976; 1977) went so far as to provide several examples of alternative construction techniques leading to shapes which appear to fit certain sites just as well as Thom's ones. This leads on to the question of how one tests which of two different shapes provides a better fit to some measured data. In general this is a difficult problem, although some techniques have been suggested for its solution, for example by Patrick & Wallace (1982). Patrick (1978) applied the technique to groups of stone rings in Ireland, concluding that there was no support for Thom's constructions at these sites. A thorough critique of Thom's geometrical theories has been given by Heggie (1981: 23-31, 60-82).

The criticisms of Thom's conclusions are most difficult to answer in the case of the most complex shapes, for here the present-day interpreter has the greatest freedom of choice in adjusting the (many) parameters of his model to fit the field data. On the other hand the observation that the shapes of megalithic rings fall predominantly into one of a few simple categories has found some archaeological favour and attracted further discussion, most notably by Burl (e.g. 1976).

The least contentious of Thom's geometrical interpretations of non-circular sites are the ellipses. A number of excavated stone rings are elliptical in shape, for example Cultoon in Islay (MacKie 1981). Two excavated Recumbent Stone 'Circles' are in fact elliptical: at one (Strichen) the recumbent stone lies on the major axis of the ellipse, whereas at the other (Berrybrae) it lies on the minor axis (Ruggles & Burl 1985). On the other hand the Thoms' claim that the great trilithons at Stonehenge originally lay on an ellipse (Thom, Thom & Thom 1974) seems ruled out by the archaeological evidence (Burl 1987: 184).

There is some evidence of astronomical orientation being interrelated with the geometrical aspects of design. Burl (1985) has noted that a number of megalithic rings are elliptical with their major axes oriented in a direction of astronomical significance, an example being Cultoon, which is an ellipse with its long axis aligned upon midwinter sunset (MacKie 1981). The timber rings at Woodhenge are also ellipses with their major axes aligned upon midsummer sunrise/midwinter sunset (Thom 1967; Burl 1987). According to Burl (1988), many of the Cumbrian stone rings, the earliest built before 2500 bc, were laid out according to strict rules concerning cardinal points (Burl 1988) and also incorporated calendrical alignments in their designs. From a statistical point of view astronomical orientation and geometrical design are formally independent (Ruggles 1984a: 61), so caution is needed in interpretation.

There is some direct evidence for particular geometrical design and construction methods in the form of peg-holes at critical points such as the foci of ellipses. J.C. Orkney (priv. comm.) has reported that such features were found during excavations at Temple Wood.

Recently, some different perspectives have been brought to bear upon studies of geometry and design. Barnatt and his collaborators (Barnatt & Moir 1984; Barnatt & Herring 1986) argue that although the constructors of the megalithic rings possessed the ability to construct perfect circles if so desired, and in some cases did so, most shapes should be seen as poor attempts at circles resulting from laying them out by eye. Barnatt & Moir (1984) base this conclusion on existing survey data, excluding from consideration sites such as the kerbs of cairns, ring cairns, enclosed cremation cemeteries, chambered tombs, or wooden structures. Primarily this appears to be an attempt to distinguish funerary from non-funerary purpose; yet the authors do admit some sites which had funerary functions (such as Brats Hill), and are often inconsistent in their exclusion of ring cairns (e.g. Tordarroch). Barnatt & Herring (1986) describe an experiment using volunteers to lay out over 100 simulated megalithic circles by eye.

Cowan (1988) suggests that in many cases rings were constructed by two people moving at opposite ends of a piece of rope. This would result in equal-width figures. This idea is intriguing since it does not rule out the possibility that the intention might have been to produce a circle; we usually take it as self-evident that a radius-and-circumference method would be best for the purpose, but this might not be self-evident to the builders.

Rather fewer independent attempts have been made comprehensively to reassess Thom's geometrical claims than has been the case with the astronomical ones. To a certain extent, this is due to the unavailability of site plans. Thom's own plans are available in the National Monuments Record of Scotland (Ferguson 1988), but though they form one of the most comprehensive sources of plans of megalithic rings, they generally only record standing (or fallen) stones, often failing to mark important associated features. They also generally lack contouring which would give some idea of the local topography. For documented changes at sites, one must search the voluminous literature on individual sites, although Burl's remarks in Thom, Thom & Burl (1980) are most helpful.

Ruggles & Kruse (in preparation) have recently attempted a comprehensive re-analysis of the available data from England, Scotland, and Wales. Sites were classified into five catagories, from those which have been excavated in their entirety (22 sites) down to those which are ill-preserved or known from documentary evidence to have been extensively altered. Only the top two or three categories, comprising fewer than 90 sites in all, are considered susceptible to geometrical analysis. The results of this work have yet to be published.

3.3 Mensuration

The third and final strand of 'megalithic science' relates to mensuration. Thom hypothesised that many of the British megalithic rings and other free-standing megalithic sites, such as the long multiple rows in Brittany, were laid out using a precise unit of measurement, the 'megalithic yard' (MY) of 0.829m (e.g. Thom 1967). Later publications postulated the existence of a 'megalithic rod' equal to 2.5 MY, and a 'megalithic inch' (MI) of 1/40 MY (e.g. Thom & Thom 1978a). Thom (1967: 34) suggested a relationship between the MY and the Iberian *vara*, with MacKie (1977: 192) taking the theme much further.

This article will not attempt to discuss megalithic mensuration in any detail: for a full account the reader is referred once again to Heggie (1981). It is fair to note, however, that statistical reassessments of Thom's data both from classical (Kendall 1974) and Bayesian (Freeman 1976) viewpoints reached the conclusion that the evidence in favour of the MY was at best marginal, and that even if it does exist the uncertainty in our knowledge of its value is of the order of centimetres, far greater than the 1mm precision claimed by Thom. In other words, the evidence presented by Thom could be adequately explained by, say, monuments being set out by pacing, with the 'unit' reflecting an average length of pace. It is also fair to point out that not all authors are in agreement with this conclusion (e.g. Davis 1983).

It should be pointed out here that the statisticians only accepted evidence from circular stone rings, thus severely reducing Thom's own (1967) data set. The reason was that Thom linked his arguments about geometrical shapes to the proposed unit of measure. Thus geometrical constructions were fitted to sites by assuming an MY value, while data for the analysis seeking to establish the reality of the MY included the lengths of constructors in these same geometrical models. From a statistical point of view mensuration and geometrical design are formally independent hypotheses, requiring separate testing.

3.4 Discussion and interpretations

The design layout of a site cannot be separated from consideration of its functions. Whatever these were, and they are demonstrably not the same for the entire corpus, stone rings were civic monuments. Rarely are these sites associated with settlements, or is dating evidence available. Generally built during the late Neolithic and early Bronze Ages, their durability ensured a long usage, and often one involving modification in plan and function. A large number of sites, though not all, were designed, or adapted, with a funerary function in mind. The apparent transition from the Clava Cairn tradition to the later Recumbent Stone Circles (Burl 1976), some with internal ring cairns and some without, highlights the difficulties in classification. Sometimes only a token amount of an entire cremation is present at a site (e.g. Lynch 1984: 28-29). Where a burial or cairn was erected at the same time as a stone ring, the emphasis may well have been focussed not upon the ring, but upon the part of the site which would contain the funerary remains. As a result, the shape of the ring would have depended on that of a central monument. Thus phasing information is directly relevant to the consideration of site design.

It is hardly surprising, then, that the statistical evidence for geometrical influences on monumental design is much weaker than that pertaining to astronomical ones. All authors accept that some megalithic rings are more perfectly circular than others. Most would accept that certain other sites were planned as ellipses, although Barnatt & Moir (1984) see all other sites as poor attempts at circles. Beyond circles and ellipses, some tentatively accept that many other sites may be classifiable into a small number of further simple shapes, but others would disagree. The results of the comprehensive analysis by Ruggles & Kruse may bear upon the argument.

The evidence for any exact unit of measurement is extremely weak and rests essentially upon secondary geometrical hypotheses.

Burl (1976: 41) notes that the large open rings of western Britain tend to be circular whereas many of the smaller Scottish and Irish rings with burials are elliptical. However he continues: 'There is... an overlapping of shapes amongst all the smaller sites and it is very doubtful whether any valid geometrical distinction may be made between them'. And indeed, later analyses of the shapes of the large open rings (Burl 1988) seem to indicate a virtually even balance of circular and non-circular shapes.

Barnatt & Moir (1984) claim that in southern England, and perhaps in north-eastern Scotland, there are groups of stone rings which have distinctive architectural traits and appear to have been planned to be circular, i.e. laid out using by peg and rope rather than by eye. These more carefully constructed stone rings, they suggest, may be associated with other phenomena, such as craft specialization, that demonstrate the emergence of a society that could support individuals who concentrated on particular skills.

4 The wider scene

There have been investigations of orientation and astronomy in other parts of Europe right through from the Upper Palaeolithic (Marshack (1972a; 1972b; 1979) provides evidence for astronomical observation and notation in the Ice Age) to the Iron Age. However, they tend to have involved a number of isolated examples and do not yet provide any sort of coherent picture. Thus, for example, Barlai (1980) finds evidence in a selection of prehistoric cemeteries in eastern Europe of grave orientations on sunrise and sunset on each burial day. Ouzounian (1984) describes evidence of a variety of astronomical observations in Bronze Age Armenia. There is possible evidence of lunar orientation amongst the oldest Nuraghic tombs in Sardinia, built in the late second millennium bc (Proverbio *et al.* 1987), and of stellar orientations in the taulas, a group of monuments associated with villages of the talayotic culture (first millennium bc) on the island of Menorca (Hoskin 1985; 1989; Hoskin & Waldren 1988). It would be foolish to attempt to derive any broader hypotheses from such diverse data.

Apart from Thom's investigations in Brittany (see, e.g., Thom & Thom 1978a) there have been few discussions of geometrical aspects of design in prehistoric monuments outside the British Isles. Some aspects of recent work concerning more modern stone circles in the Basque Country are, however, worthy of special comment.

In the Basque country there appears to be evidence of a system of the social organisation of space dating back to at least the early Middle Ages and surviving into the present century. It is reflected in the material record through the physical demarcation of communal space by stone circles and menhirs, as well as in constructs and concepts in the Basque language. Some aspects of the system have been reconstructed by Frank (1980; 1989) through historical texts, ethnolinguistic reconstructions based on terms found in the Basque language and linked to concrete objects used in the pastoral society, particularly those objects used to record and measure, and extensive interviews with Basque speakers.

Communal lands in the Basque Country were laid out in circular configurations marked by stone circles, menhirs and more modern boundary stones. These configurations bore an intimate relationship to the socio-economic and political structures of Basque pastoral society. The stone circle defined the communal space of the basic unit of Basque pastoral society, the *polis*, where a shepherd and his family along with other families lived, cared for their livestock, and conducted their social, religious and economic activities. Space was provided in the circle for judicial proceedings, ritual gaming and dance. Meetings took place here on matters of common concern. Circles are related to transhumance practices, and are found both in areas of summer and winter grazing. They are only found where the pasture is appropriate for grazing, near a water source and sheltered from the winds (Barandiaran 1953; 1973).

The geometrical organisation of this communal space provided the members of the *polis* with significant information, including knowledge of an astronomical and calendrical nature. The circular configuration relates to the structuring of power within the *polis*. The position of 'head' of the circle was constantly rotated around the stones. Similarly, the position of *buru*, or 'head' of the *polis* was rotated around its members. The Basque term *buruzagi* (literally the keeper or guardian of the head) refers to the one whose position places him or her at the head, a concept distinct (unlike in Indo-European languages) from that of the head itself. Power resides in the group, not in the individual; it is positional, but not intrinsic to a fixed position. Power and knowledge are shared amongst, and rotated around, the group.

Historical documents indicate that the stone circles and a geometrical system for their construction was fully developed by the early Middle Ages. Many circles continued to function in this way into the present century, and legal documents abound relating boundary disputes. These documents also give an insight into construction methods. The most commonly described method is first to place a centre stone, then to place four further stones at a specified distance in each of the cardinal directions, then four further stones on the perimeter mid-way between the cardinal stones, the finally to add smaller 'witness' stones on the perimeter. The centre stone and eight boundary stones would typically measure two metres or more in height.

According to Frank, the Basque measuring system was a complex entity growing out of an interlocking set of social, ideologically motivated perceptions and organisational principles. Thus, for example, circles were set out using ropes knotted off in units of seven (smaller knots) and 49 (larger knots) 'feet', a foot being one third of a *vara*, a traditional short yard of 0.836m which is still used in many parts of the Basque Country. The same units of measurement crop up elsewhere, as in the length of the staff or bar used in ritualised jousting (seven feet). Perimeter circles comprise eight or multiples of eight stones. The Basque calendar was conceived of as being divided into chains of eight units each of eight days. On a practical level, tasks such as the making of cheese were passed round the *polis* according to the calendar. There is also a sequence of three days which may be linked to the phases of the moon (Bausani 1982).

The eight larger perimeter stones reflected the total number of sheep allowed in each *polis*, each representing a unit of 56 milking ewes, or eight subunits of seven ewes each. There was a need for precision here: the planet Venus was associated with a belief in a goddess who lives off people alleging that they have too many or too few sheep, taking in either case the number of animals over- or understated and leaving the shepherd with fewer than before.

Frank claims that elements of the geometrical design of the Basque stone circles bear a resemblance to what is found in the prehistoric material record, both locally and further north in north-western Europe. Here the evidence is more circumstantial, but it is supported by consideration of pre-Indo-European cultural artefacts embedded semantically in the Basque language. The argument for continuity is also strengthened by the very survival of a language derived from the pre-Indo-European linguistic substratum.

Whatever the merits or otherwise of these arguments, the Basque stone circles example clearly illustrates the potential of a broader perspective on matters of the incorporation of geometrical features in monumental design. There have, for example, been few attempts to discern how the constructors of megalithic rings might have conceptualised a particular design. Instead, the conventional approach is built upon the fundamental concept of geometrical shape, whether circle, ellipse, egg, or whatever. We might ask why prehistoric communities *should* have been interested in demarcating geometrical shapes, circles or otherwise.

The following passage from Frank (1989) is instructive:

> I had great difficulties getting the Basque speakers to admit that the entities I am discussing were stone circles at all. Since they see them as pasture lands marked off with stones at a certain distance from the centre, evidently they did not fill in the rest of the circumference space to create a circle, rather leaving it as a 'centre' stone and eight 'outer' stones without taking the conceptual leap forward which would have allowed them to see that this done in fact create a 'stone circle'.

The assumption that the constructors of megalithic rings conceptualised shape in the same way as we do moulds our interpretation, for example towards an absolute demarcation between the interior and exterior. It is notable that the assumption is still not openly questioned that *some* shape, even if it be merely a circle (very poorly achieved in some cases), was actually intended. Examples such as the Basque one may help us to devise new approaches through broader understanding.

5 Some conclusions and speculations

Investigations in 'megalithic science' tended until recently to concentrate on large spectacular sites. In fact, groups of simple, architecturally similar sites provide the most promising means of extracting reliable evidence on factors influencing design and orientation where these merge into a discernible common tradition. In studies of such sites—sites yielding little in the way of stratigraphical and artefactual evidence—the approach of the surveyor or engineer, concentrating more on features such as shape, design and orientation, can be of considerable interest in shedding some light on changing patterns of social tradition. Recently we have begun to see the archaeologist and astronomer or engineer working together in order to consider the relationship of sites to the surrounding landscape and skyscape.

Within those areas of investigation deriving from 'megalithic science', the astronomical line of enquiry is at present by far the most promising; there is important evidence of astronomical influences on monumental orientations which may bear upon changing ritual practice in different parts of Britain during the third and second millennia bc. Some new and potentially fruitful lines of enquiry have recently emerged with regard to the geometrical construction of megalithic rings, but the conclusions must be regarded as tentative. Mensuration seems to be a relatively unrewarding topic: there is simply too little evidence in the material record for any convincing conclusions to be drawn.

The general picture which seems to emerge from archaeoastronomical studies is one of low-precision astronomical alignments being incorporated in various ways in monumental architecture in Britain through the third and second millennia bc. There is evidence of a change from a lunar to a solar emphasis, accompanying social change, in areas as widespread as Orkney in the north and Wessex in the south. However in areas such as western and eastern Scotland, where social change was much slower, the lunar tradition seems to have persisted.

The lunar alignments do involve the observation of the extreme positions of the moon in its 18.6-year cycle and thus would have required organised lunar observations over a period of at least twenty years. However the precision of the alignments is sufficiently low that the observations involved are not arduous: occasional observations of the full moon nearest the summer solstice would have sufficed.

This picture is rather different from MacKie's (1977): he argues that a 'two-tier' social system was in operation in some megalith-building societies, the top tier being a élite of astronomer-priests undertaking intricate astronomical observations. He also argues strongly that a precise solar calendar was in use (e.g. MacKie 1988). However, these arguments rest heavily upon Thom's evidence for high-precision alignments, evidence which has been much questioned (see above), and upon his interpretation of the evidence from a new site at Brainport Bay, Argyll (MacKie et al. 1985), which has also been questioned (Ruggles 1985b).

It is of some interest to ask how often an interest in the rising or setting major standstill moon is encountered in the cultural record world-wide. While knowledge of the lunar month is almost universal, and many seasonal calendars are lunar-based, ethnographic instances of horizon lunar observations are unknown, at least to the present author. This must lead us to seek an explanation for their apparent importance in prehistoric Scotland. One such explanation might be the latitude, at which the major standstill moon is seen to scrape along just above the southern horizon—a rare and spectacular event which could perhaps have assumed great importance. Clearly it would be of great interest if any evidence were forthcoming of a similar interest in the rising and setting moon amongst communities in similar latitudes, such as in eastern Europe.

One of the most challenging aspects of investigations in the areas deriving from 'megalthic science' is that they represent areas of enquiry where the physical scientist and the archaeologist or anthropologist have conflicting, but both undeniably relevant, points of view on the nature of admissible evidence, and on the conclusions that can reasonably be drawn from that evidence. Many authors, and particularly those trained in the humanities, would conclude (and have concluded) that any rigorous statistical approach, since it can ultimately only isolate overall trends and necessarily excludes most of the cultural and functional diversity represented in the material record, is of very limited value indeed. Others, however, and particularly those trained in the numerate sciences, would say the same of any investigation which fails, through the *lack* of such an approach, to attempt to distinguish between deliberate design features and chance occurrences. Ironically, both camps end up by arguing that not to accept their viewpoint would be to open the floodgates to unabated speculation.

These problems are of wider relevance than just to the areas of enquiry in question—or indeed to archaeology as a whole. The fundamental problem is that evidence acceptable to a numerate scientist is of a very different nature from that acceptable to his counterpart trained in the humanities. It is the view of this author that much of the controversy stirred up by investigations in 'megalithic science' stems not from sheer prejudice, as is often claimed on both sides, or even from the lack of detailed background knowledge or ability in mathematics, astronomy or archaeology; but merely from this simple fact. In investigating astronomical and geometrical influences on monumental design two very different approaches to the interpretation of the material record meet head-on, and in order for progress to be made they must be reconciled so that the available evidence can be considered in its entirety in a satisfactory way.

The present author (Ruggles 1988b) has suggested ways of bringing about this reconciliation. It is to be hoped that integrated methodological approaches resulting from such suggestions, together with the further accumulation of field evidence, will add substance to the tentative conclusions given here.

Acknowledgements

I am most grateful to Susan Kruse for permission to publish comments from our joint work on stone rings which has yet to be published.

References

Angell, I.O.
   (1976). Stone circles: megalithic mathematics or Neolithic nonsense? *Math. Gazette*, **60**, 189-193.
   (1977). Are stone circles circles? *Sci. Arch.*, **19**, 16-19.
Ashbee, P.
   (1970). *The earthen long barrow in Britain*. London.
   (1974). *Ancient Scilly*. Newton Abbot.
Bailey, M.E., Cooke, J.A., Few, R.W., Morgan, J.G. & Ruggles, C.L.N.
   (1975). Survey of three megalithic sites in Argyllshire. *Nature*, 253, 431-433.

Barandiaran, J.M.
  (1953). Aspectos sociográficos de la población del Pirineo vasco. *Eusko Jakintza*, **7**, 3-26.
  (1973). Vida pastoril vasca—albergues veraniegos, transhumancia intrapirenaica. In *Obras Completas, Tomo V*, Bilbao, 389-398.
Barlai, K.
  (1980). On the orientation of graves in prehistoric cemeteries. *Archaeoastronomy bulletin*, **3**(4), 29-32.
Barnatt, J. & Herring, P.
  (1986). Stone circles and megalithic geometry: an experiment to test alternative design practices. *J. Arch. Sci.*, **13**, 431-449.
Barnatt, J. & Moir, G.
  (1984). Stone circles and megalithic mathematics. *Proc. Prehist. Soc.*, **50**, 197-216.
Barnatt, J. & Pierpoint, S.
  (1983). Stone circles: observatories or ceremonial centres? *Scott. Arch. Review*, **2**, 101-115.
Bausani, A.
  (1982). The prehistoric Basque week of three days. *Archaeoastronomy Bulletin*, **5**(2), 16-22.
Burl, H.A.W.
  (1976). *The stone circles of the British Isles*. New Haven & London.
  (1979). *Rings of Stone*. London.
  (1980). Science or symbolism: problems of archaeo-astronomy. *Antiquity*, **54**, 191-200.
  (1981a). 'By the light of the cinerary moon': chambered tombs and the astronomy of death. *In* Ruggles & Whittle (1981), 243-274.
  (1981b). *Rites of the gods*. London.
  (1983). *Prehistoric astronomy and ritual*. Aylesbury.
  (1985). Stone circles: the Welsh problem. CBA Report 35, 72-82.
  (1987). *The Stonehenge people*. London.
  (1988).'Without sharp north...': Alexander Thom and the great stone circles of Cumbria. *In* Ruggles (1988a), 175-205.
Chamberlain, Von del, Young, J. & Carlson, J.C.
  (1989). *Proceedings of the first World Ethnoastronomy symposium*. Washington, D.C.
Childe, V.G.
  (1955). Comment on Thom (1955). *J. Royal Stat. Soc.*, **A118**, 293-294.
Cowan, T.M.
  (1988). Megalithic compound ring geometry. *In* Ruggles (1988a), 378-391.

Cowgill, G.L., Whallon, R. & Ottoway, B.S.
    (1981) (eds.). *Manejo de datos y Métodos Matemáticos de Arqueología.* Mexico City (UISSP Congress X, Commission IV).
Daniel, G.E.
    (1958). *The megalith builders of western Europe.* London.
    (1980). Megalithic monuments. *Scientific American,* **243**, 64-76.
Davis, A.
    (1983). Pacing and the megalithic yard. *Glasgow Arch. J.,* **10**, 7-11.
Ellegård, A.
    (1981). Stone age science in Britain? *Curr. Anth.,* **22**, 99-125.
Ferguson, L.
    (1988). A catalogue of the Alexander Thom archive held in the National Monuments Record of Scotland. *In* Ruggles (1988a), 31-131.
Frank, R.M.
    (1980). Basque stone circles and geometry. *Archaeoastronomy Bulletin,* **3(1)**, 28-33.
    (1989). *Basque stone circles.* Draft Ph.D. thesis, University of Iowa.
Fraser, D.
    (1983). *Land and society in neolithic Orkney.* Oxford (BAR 117) (2 vols.).
    (1984). In support of festive astronomy. *Scott. Arch. Review,* **3**, 16-18.
Freeman, P.R.
    (1976). A Bayesian analysis of the megalithic yard. *J. Royal Stat. Soc.,* **A139**, 20-55.
Hampsher-Monk, I. & Abramson, P.
    (1982). Strichen. *Curr. Arch.,* **8**, 16-19.
Hawkins, G.S. & White, J.B.
    (1965). *Stonehenge decoded.* London.
Heggie, D.C.
    (1972). Megalithic lunar observatories: an astronomer's view. *Antiquity,* **46**, 43-48.
    (1981). *Megalithic science: ancient mathematics and astronomy in northwest Europe.* London.
    (1982) (ed.). *Archaeoastronomy in the Old World.* Cambridge.
Henshall, A.S.
    (1963). *The chambered tombs of Scotland, 1.* Edinburgh.
    (1972). *The chambered tombs of Scotland, 2.* Edinburgh.
Hillier, W. & Hansen, J.
    (1984). *The social logic of space.* Cambridge.

Hoskin, M.A.
(1985). The talayotic culture of Menorca: a first reconnaissance. *Archaeoastronomy*, **9**, S133-151.
(1989). The orientation of Menorcan taulas. *In* W.H. Waldren (ed.), *Archaeological techniques, technology and theory: Proceedings of the second Deia conference on prehistory*. In press.

Hoskin, M.A. & Waldren, W.H.
(1988). *Taulas and talayots*. Cambridge.

Kendall, D.G.
(1974). Hunting quanta. *Phil. Trans. Royal Soc. Lond.*, **A276**, 231-266.

Lambrick, G.
(1983). *The Rollright Stones*. Oxford.

Lockyer, J.N.
(1909). *Stonehenge and other British stone monuments astronomically considered* (2nd edn.). London.

Logan, J.
(1829). Observations on several circles of stones in Scotland. *Archaeologia*, **22**, 198-203.

Lynch, F.
(1972). Ring cairns and related monuments in Wales. *Scott. Arch. Forum*, **4**, 61-80.
(1979). Ring cairns in Britain and Ireland: their design and purpose. *Ulster J. Arch.*, **42**, 1-19.
(1984). Moel Goedog Circle I: A complete ring cairn near Harlech. *Arch. Camb.*, **133**, 8-50.

McCluskey, S.C.
(1977). The astronomy of the Hopi Indians. *J. Hist. Astron.*, **8**, 174-195.

McCreery, T.
(1980). Megalithic lunar observatories—a critique, Part II. *Kronos*, **5(2)**, 6-26.

MacKie, E.W.
(1974). Archaeological tests on supposed astronomical sites in Scotland. *Phil. Trans. Royal Soc. Lond.*, **A276**, 169-194.
(1977). *Science and society in prehistoric Britain*. London.
(1981). Wise men in antiquity? *In* Ruggles & Whittle (1981), 111-152.
(1988). Investigating the prehistoric solar calendar. *In* Ruggles (1988a), 206-231.

MacKie, E.W., Gladwin, P.F. & Roy, A.E.
(1985). A prehistoric calendrical site in Argyll? *Nature*, **314**, 158-161.

Marshack, A.
  (1972a). *The roots of civilization.* New York.
  (1972b). Cognitive aspects of Upper Paleolithic engraving. *Curr. Anth.*, **13**, 327-332.
  (1979). Upper Paleolithic symbol systems of the Russian plain. *Curr. Anth.*, **20**, 271-311.
Moir, G.
  (1981). Some archaeological and astronomical objections to scientific astronomy in British prehistory. *In* Ruggles & Whittle (1981), 221-241.
Moir, G., Ruggles, C.L.N. & Norris, R.P.
  (1980). Megalithic science and some Scottish site plans. *Antiquity*, **54**, 37-43.
O'Kelly, M.J.
  (1971). *An Illustrated Guide to Newgrange* (2nd. edn.). Wexford.
Ouzounian, J.G.
  (1984). Armenian astronomy in the Bronze Age. *Archaeoastronomy Bulletin*, **7**, 105-109.
Patrick, J.D.
  (1974). Midwinter sunrise at Newgrange. *Nature*, **249**, 517-519.
  (1978). An information measure comparative analysis of megalithic geometries. Ph.D. Thesis, Monash University, Australia.
  (1981). A reassessment of the solstitial observatories at Kintraw and Ballochroy. *In* Ruggles & Whittle (1981), 211-219.
Patrick, J.D. & Freeman, P.R.
  (1988). A cluster analysis of astronomical orientations. *In* Ruggles (1988a), 251-261.
Patrick, J.D. & Wallace, C.S.
  (1982). Stone circle geometries: an information theory approach. *In* Heggie (1982), 231-264.
Powell, T.G.E.
  (1969) (ed.). *Megalithic enquiries in the west of Britain.* Liverpool.
Proverbio, E., Romano, G. & Aveni, A.F.
  (1987). Astronomical orientations of five megalithic tombs at Madau, near Fonni in Sardinia. *Archaeoastronomy*, **11**, S55-66.
Renfrew, A.C.
  (1973). *Before civilization.* London.
  (1981). Comment on Ellegård (1981). *Curr. Anth.*, **22**, 120-121.
Ruggles, C.L.N.
  (1981a). A critical examination of the megalithic lunar observatories. *In* Ruggles & Whittle (1981), 153-209.

(1981b). Prehistoric astronomy: how far did it go? *New Scientist*, **90**, 750-753.
(1981c). Orientation analysis and prehistoric astronomy. *In* Cowgill, Whallon & Ottoway (1981), 228-234.
(1982a). A reassessment of the high precision megalithic lunar sightlines, 1: Backsights, indicators and the archaeological status of the sightlines. *Archaeoastronomy*, **4**, S21-40.
(1982b). Megalithic astronomical sightlines: current reassessment and future directions. *In* Heggie (1982), 83-105.
(1983). A reassessment of the high precision megalithic lunar sightlines, 2: Foresights and the problem of selection. *Archaeoastronomy*, **5**, S1-36.
(1984a) (principal author: contributions by P.N. Appleton, S.F. Burch, J.A. Cooke, R.W. Few, J.G. Morgan & R.P. Norris). *Megalithic astronomy: A new archaeological and statistical study of 300 western Scottish sites*. Oxford (BAR 123).
(1984b). A new study of the Aberdeenshire Recumbent Stone Circles, 1: Site data. *Archaeoastronomy*, **6**, S55-79.
(1984c). Megalithic astronomy: The last five years. *Vistas in Astron.*, **27**, 231-289.
(1985a). The linear settings of Argyll and Mull. *Archaeoastronomy*, **9**, S105-132.
(1985b). Prehistoric astronomy: evidence from a new site. *Nature*, **314**, 134-135.
(1988a) (ed.). *Records in stone: Papers in memory of Alexander Thom*. Cambridge.
(1988b). The stone alignments of Argyll and Mull: A perspective on the statistical approach in archaeoastronomy. *In* Ruggles (1988a), 232-250.

Ruggles, C.L.N. & Burl, H.A.W.
(1985). A new study of the Aberdeenshire Recumbent Stone Circles, 2: Interpretation. *Archaeoastronomy*, **8**, S25-60.

Ruggles, C.L.N. & Whittle, A.W.R.
(1981) (eds.). *Astronomy and society in Britain during the period 4000-1500 BC*. Oxford (BAR 88).

Shepherd, I.A.G.
(1983). A Grampian stone circle confirmed. *PSAS*, **113**, 630-634.

Thom, A.
(1955). A statistical examination of the megalithic sites in Britain. *J. Royal Stat. Soc.*, **A118**, 275-295.
(1967). *Megalithic sites in Britain*. Oxford.

(1969). The lunar observatories of Megalithic Man. *Vistas in Astron.*, **11**, 1-29.

(1971). *Megalithic lunar observatories*. Oxford.

Thom, A. & Thom, A.S.

(1978a). *Megalithic remains in Britain and Brittany*. Oxford.

(1978b). A reconsideration of the lunar sites in Britain. *J. Hist. Astron.*, **9**, 170-179.

(1980). A new study of all megalithic lunar lines. *Archaeoastronomy*, **2**, S78-89.

Thom, A., Thom, A.S., & Burl, H.A.W.

(1980). *Megalithic rings*. Oxford (BAR 81).

Thom, A., Thom, A.S. & Thom, A.S.

(1974). Stonehenge. *J. Hist. Astron.*, **5**, 71-90.

Thom, A.S.

(1981). Megalithic lunar observatories: an assessment of 42 lunar alignments. *In* Ruggles & Whittle (1981), 13-61.

Thomas, J.

(1988). The social significance of Cotswold-Severn burial practices. *Man*, **23**, 540-559.

Thorpe, I.J.

(1981). Ethnoastronomy: its patterns and archaeological implications. *In* Ruggles & Whittle (1981), 275-288.

Turton, D.A. & Ruggles, C.L.N.

(1978). Agreeing to disagree: The measurement of duration in a southwestern Ethiopian community. *Curr. Anth.*, **19**, 585-600.

Wainwright, G.J.

(1966). The excavations of Hampton Down Circle, Portesham, Dorset. *Procs. Dorset Nat. Hist. & Arch. Soc.*, **88**, 122-127.

Young, A.

(1943). Report on standing stones and other remains near Fowlis Wester, Perthshire. *PSAS*, **77**, 174-182.

THE MAFIA HYPOTHESIS

Antonio Gilman
California State University–Northridge

Any analysis of the entry of Indo-European languages into Europe must take into account the subcontinent's social landscape during the period of their diffusion. If, as most Indo-Europeanists seem to believe, the entry took place in the third millennium B.C., then the spread of Indo-European coincides with a major transformation in the social organization of prehistoric European societies. As the authors of the best modern synthesis of the European Bronze Age conclude:

> During the course of the Bronze Age a number of important changes took place—changes that lend the period its characteristic appearance and distinguish it from anything that had gone before ... Perhaps the most obvious of these is the rise of the privileged ... It is hard to think of this process in terms other than those of the aggrandizement of the few, the rise of the elite, and the start of social stratification (Coles & Harding 1979: 535).

In the context of this conference it may be appropriate, therefore, to consider the causal dynamics of the emergence of elites in the later prehistory of Europe.

Anthropological studies over the course of the past century have presented two broad contrasting accounts of the origins of social stratification. The first position, nowadays accepted by the great majority of prehistorians, underlines the functional integration needed for the development of economic and social complexity. In their recent *Evolution of Human Societies*, Allen Johnson and Timothy Earle emphasize the services chiefs render to commoners:

> As population increases, there comes a time when the local group or intergroup collectivity can no longer be relied on to handle these life-and-death matters [risk management, technology, warfare, and trade] (Johnson & Earle 1987: 209).

This is a straightforward echo of Marshall Sahlins' (1972: 140) proposition that:

> The chief creates a collective good beyond the conception and capacity of the society's domestic groups taken separately. He institutes a public

economy greater than the sum of its household parts.

Depending upon the specific setting in which incipient stratification is observed, the public services which the elites would have organized for commoners may be the construction and management of irrigation systems or other public works (e.g., Wittfogel 1957), the organization of systems of exchange (e.g., Rathje 1971), the military leadership required to obtain the *Lebensraum* for a larger population (e.g., Webster 1977), the provision of insurance in the event of subsistence failure (e.g., Halstead & O'Shea 1982), or (more generally) the regulation of the information required to manage large-scale, internally differentiated society (e.g., Flannery 1972).

In a recent review article on chiefdoms Earle (1987: 293-294) points out the central deficiency of the mainstream, managerial account of elite origins:

> Intensification and related changes in the subsistence economy do create problems requiring management, but low-level management would seem in most instances best for the local population. Such management can be expected to be responsive to the needs of the population in contrast to a distant, regional chiefly hierarchy that would be more inaccessible and unaccountable for their actions.

Provision of such low-level administrative services would, of course, be entirely compatible with achieved managerial statuses (of "big men"). The very hallmark of complex societies is that superordinate statuses are ascribed, however.

The second major approach to the origins of social complexity responds to these difficulties. Instead of asking, "What good are elites?" this approach asks, "How do elites maintain their power?" Precisely because both chiefs and big-men at times provide useful managerial services to their subjects and/or followers, what distinguishes chiefs from big-men has nothing to do with management. Tribal leaders had achieved their positions from time immemorial by providing the benefits of leadership to their followers. Thus, when leaders contrived to consolidate their positions on a hereditary basis, that consolidation must have been due to something other than their services. It must be due, rather, to novel opportunities for control absent in simpler economies. In short, circumstances must have arisen that would permit leaders to exploit their followers on a relatively stable, long-term basis. A focus on exploitation involves, of course, a shift from a functionalist orientation to one which stresses the internal conflicts of class societies.

Given such a perspective, one should begin investigation of the development of hereditary inequalities by looking for contrastive relationships of exploitation.[1] A conflict-oriented approach to European prehistory must, then, take up two issues: first, what is the nature of class divisions (if these can be demonstrated to exist at all)? second, what is the dominant form through which exploitation takes place? Any attack on these questions faces daunting problems of evidence, problems due in part to the research orientations which have generated the available archaeological record. European archaeologists have too often regarded economic matters as mundane common denominators of little significance to the prehistory that really mattered, and evidence for them has only been developed on an uneven basis. Likewise, the archaeological measures of stratification and class conflict suggested by Jonathan Haas (1982: 91-123) are difficult to apply to a record recovered by scholars who have adopted a systematic methodological pessimism in order to avoid dealing with such matters. That the social divisions which would have existed in societies on the threshold of complexity would be relatively small in scale only compounds the difficulties.

As a result, it is only by resorting to a kind of trickery that we can advance at all. The ruse, in essence, is to use the idealist predilections of most prehistorians against themselves in order to construct a prehistorical materialism. The archaeological record is largely the unintentional residue of human activities: it consists mostly of garbage. Its students have generally sought to recover from it the same kind of information that is available to students of history, and they have brought to that task the normativist theoretical perspectives of most

---

1. I am mindful here of the famous passage from volume 3 of *Capital*: "The specific economic form in which unpaid surplus-labour is pumped out of direct producers determines the relationship of rulers and ruled ... Upon this ... is founded the entire formation of the economic community ..., thereby simultaneously its specific political form. It is always the relationship of the owners ... to the direct producers ... which reveals the innermost secret, the hidden basis of the entire social structure" (Marx 1967 [orig. 1894]: 791).

historians. Prehistorians have, therefore, primarily sought to recover and study those aspects of the material record most laden with overt human intentions: stylistically distinctive artifacts (especially those of intrinsic value and aesthetic merit), major architectural remains, and burials. These, of course, are the aspects of the material record that are liable to concentrate the greatest amount of value (that require large investments of human labor to gain the intrinsic qualities sought by the prehistorians).

Now, in general, classes should be defined on the basis of an objective relation of exploitation and not on class consciousness. In a class society, however, it is essential that at least one class be a class for itself: to the extent that rulers are deceived about themselves and do not act in their common self-interest, they will be unable to maintain their exploitation in the face of their subordinates' inevitable reluctance to surrender surplus value. The propertied class must devote part of the surplus they control to making their position overt and conspicuous to each other. The material residue of their efforts is precisely what has attracted the interest of normativist prehistorians. Archaeologists are, therefore, in a reasonably good position to reconstruct the early development of ruling-class consciousness.

In the area where I have done most of my work, southeast Spain, the development of fortifications and burial patterns over the course of the Neolithic, Copper and Bronze Ages clearly reflects a progressive strengthening of elite class consciousness.[2] The late Neolithic "Almeria Culture" of the early fourth millennium B.C. is characterized by a collective burial rite in caves, rock-cut tombs, and simple megalithic chambered tombs in which grave goods consist of utilitarian goods, simple ornaments, and ritual fetishes. In the Copper Age "Los Millares Culture" (3500-2250 B.C.) the collective burial rite continues but the chambered tombs are sometimes larger and more complex in their construction and the grave goods are sometimes rendered in exotic or expensive raw materials (ivory imported from North Africa, copper). The Beaker pottery and accompanying trinkets and weapons of the late Copper Age are part of a fancy sumptuary assemblage

---

2. See Gilman & Thornes (1985) for a detailed review of the evidence for the later prehistoric sequence in southeast Spain.

popular throughout the Peninsula. The wealth of the grave goods becomes significantly differentiated both within and between tomb groups. In the early Bronze Age "El Argar Culture" of the late third and early second millennium the burial pattern changes radically. The dead are buried individually under the floors of their houses with grave goods consisting of their personal finery: the weapons, jewelry, and fine pottery interred in the richer burials form part of a more standardized sumptuary assemblage than in the preceding period, and wealth differentials between tombs become larger. The increasing social differentiation in burial rites is accompanied by evidence for increasing social conflict between communities. Open-air settlements of the Neolithic are poorly known but seem to have consisted of short-term unfortified hamlets built of relatively flimsy raw materials. In the Copper Age settlements are often long-term occupations (the stratigraphies may span several centuries) of stone houses, and they are sometimes protected by walls with bastions. These defensive preoccupations become even stronger in the Bronze Age, when settlements typically are acropoles located on high hilltops relatively distant from good arable land and water. In southeast Spain, then, the development of metallurgy, an expensive technology for the production of luxury goods; the wide distribution of particular styles of finery; the increase in military activity, both as a practice and as a value; the shift from collective to individualized burial rituals; all point to the development of an upper class whose rule depended, at least in part, on strong-arm tactics and whose recruitment was stable enough to establish wide-ranging, mutually supportive partnerships.

As Stephen Shennan (1982: 11) notes, "on the whole the Iberian situation fits in very well with the general European trends ... of intensification, growth of ranking and increased emphasis on prestige goods" during the third millennium. The details vary in the sequences of each area of the continent, but whether or not one cares to describe this process as involving a transition from a Lineage to a Germanic Mode of Production (Thomas 1987), it seems clear that "starting in south east Europe in the later fourth millennium and extending to the most western fringes by the mid-second millennium, a series of profound and structurally similar changes occurred" (Rowlands 1984: 150), all involving a shift towards greater, more permanent social inequalities.[3]

It is clear, of course, that the privileged class of third-millennium southeast Spain must have been constrained in its self-aggrandizement by the absence of state institutions permitting indirect, collective exploitation of followers and by the presence of continuing kinship obligations to followers. The class societies of prehistoric Europe would have been based on direct patron-client relations, within which the amount of surplus leaders can take from their followers is limited by the rationale upon which surplus capture is based. What, then, can we say of the sources of upward income flow within these incipiently stratified societies?

Here we are limited, of course, by the nature of the purely archaeological evidence available to us. If we suppose that control over systems of exchange gave leaders the opportunity to extract a surplus from their dealings, we cannot point to records of the transactions to support our views. If we argue that the surplus consisted of rent obtained from a peasantry, we must do so without direct evidence for the arrangements governing land tenure (although field systems, where these survive, may provide interesting insights). We can hope that the scenarios for exploitation which we devise are consistent with available evidence, but inevitably the validity of any line of argument must be based more on the realism than on the empiricism of the claims advanced. Insofar as Europeanist prehistorians have dealt with the problem of the nature of exploitation at all, they have (implicitly for the most part) based their thinking on Engels' treatment of commodity exchange in *The Origins of the Family*. I would like to argue here that this view is less realistic than one which sees the capture of surplus by the privileged as the collection of rent from agricultural producers.

The development of class divisions in later prehistoric Europe is associated with the development of copper and bronze metallurgy, and it is control over the supply of metal that is principally implicated in the commodity-exchange account of Bronze Age exploitation. As this was originally developed by Gordon Childe,

---

3. An important contrast between the Iberian Peninsula and northern and central Europe during the third millennium is the much greater importance of settlement nucleation in the former. The significance of this contrast is discussed below.

the demand of Near Eastern civilizations for metal would have stimulated the genesis of compradore elites in the Near East's European Third World. The development of evidence that metallurgy and attendant class divisions were well under way in Europe before the reach of Near Eastern economies could possibly have extended there makes a core-periphery interpretation of European prehistoric development untenable prior to the Iron Age, however. More recent thinking has concentrated, therefore, on the significance of the local development of metallurgy in stimulating a network of exchange whose control could generate income for the chiefs. For the El Argar culture of southeast Spain, for example, Vicente Lull argues as follows:

> The development of metallurgy ... produced a sharp change in ... production which in turn ... made necessary other changes in social relations. The original self-supporting communities became communities with complementary production requiring trade. This also caused an improvement in communication and routes of transport; an improvement that fostered a managerial hierarchy, most likely for security reasons. The hierarchy formed in this manner from direct production became concerned in the tasks of organization and protection of [their] interests. The division of labor ... produced an emerging trade of products with quite different exchange values. The political classes found in the self-supporting tribal communities were replaced by a new stratification (Lull 1984: 1222-1223).

Positions such as Lull's are more common in various functionalist versions, in which leaders are seen as providing higher-order regulation of exchange systems as a service to their followers, but whether or not the relations are envisaged as exploitative, they face two empirical problems. First, the production of metal was extremely limited during the early Bronze Age: in southeast Spain the type-site of the El Argar culture, the richest and largest site from that time and region yet excavated, with over 1200 burials spanning several hundred years, yielded just over 34 kg of copper, an amount obtainable from about one ton of ore (Chapman 1984: 1150). Second, the metal produced was almost exclusively devoted to weapons and finery; in Spain there are no Bronze Age agricultural tools. Eleanor Leacock (1972: 33) has commented that:

> Despite Marx's important discussion of commodity production in the first

section of *Capital*, there has been little follow-through by marxist scholars on how the acquisition and exchange of a surplus by early states entrapped urban populations as a lower class ...

For the village-sized communities of Copper and Bronze Age southeast Spain it is hard to see how such a follow-through is possible. The metal-working industry could have been operated at the village level by occasional exploitation of nearby ore bodies. Failure to obtain access to metal would have had little effect on basic agricultural production. Thus, in the terms usefully elaborated by Haas (1982: 167-169), both the compliance costs and the refusal costs of participating in the network of metallurgical production and exchange would have been slight.[4]   For this reason I have argued (Gilman 1976, Gilman & Thornes 1985) that the emergent ruling class of the Copper and Bronze Age in southeast Spain derived the bulk of their income by the same means that their successors did until well into the modern period, i.e., by extracting rent from a peasantry (through "staple finance" in the sense developed by Terence D'Altroy & Earle [1985]). The emergence of class stratification in the third millennium B.C. is associated with the introduction of intensified agriculture as the basis of subsistence production: irrigation, exploitation of animals for their secondary products (traction [horses for transport, oxen for the plow], fiber, milk products), and perhaps cultivation of tree crops such as olives and vines. All of these intensifications could be introduced by the primary producers without managerial assistance, but all have the common feature that they increase agricultural yields at the price of raising the fixed costs of production. The accumulation of agricultural investments expected to yield income over a long term would make primary producers vulnerable to the extraction of rent in that it would be wiser to deliver a portion of a surplus to an overlord than to relinquish the income from their investments altogether. The

---

4. It seems unreasonable to suggest, as Childe (1954: 158) did and as Johnson and Earle (1987: 210) do, that possession of metal weapons would provide rulers with control of the "means of destruction" in the sense developed by Goody (1971). A mob of peasants armed with slingshots could overcome the best equipped Bronze Age hero, provided that they were organized to resist. Effective violence is a social, not a technological fact.

sumptuary arrangements of Bronze Age elite burials bear ample witness that, in the absence of state political entities, members of the ruling classes themselves provided the enforcement required to maintain the social asymmetries arising from the extraction of rent. In southeast Spain (and elsewhere in the Iberian Peninsula: Harrison & Moreno López 1985), the development of social stratification attends the development of the Mediterranean polyculture on which all later Mediterranean civilizations rested. On this reading of the evidence, the social formation of Bronze Age southeast Spain would have fallen at the most petty 'feudal' end of the range of "tributary modes of production" (Wolf 1981: 51).

The importance of agricultural intensification in the Millaran/Argaric trajectory can be seen by comparing developments in southeast Spain to those of adjacent regions to the north and west. The southeast is the most arid region, not just of the Iberian Peninsula, but of all Europe, so that irrigation, terracing, tree crops, and so on, would have been particularly useful in stabilizing and increasing production. Better-watered regions adjacent to the southeast (such as the uplands of Andalusia and the Spanish Levant), where capital intensification of agriculture would have been less critical, have archaeological sequences contemporaneous and similar to the Millaran and Argaric, but with markedly smaller concentrations of wealth.

To underline the role of an expanding system of staple finance in the emergence of social complexity in prehistoric southeast Spain is not to suggest that rent extraction was the only source of income for Millaran/Argaric rulers. There is ample evidence for the creation, concentration, and circulation of luxuries (for "wealth finance" in D'Altroy & Earle's terms): ivory, fine pottery (such as Beakers), and of course metal (not just copper and bronze, but gold and silver), among other finery, were increasingly represented in high status burials over the course of the Copper and Bronze Ages. The progressive development of metal working reflects the expanding importance of a material whose durability and fungibility make it an ideal primitive valuable. Two points are clear, however. First, any system of wealth finance presupposes some system of staple finance. To suggest that wealth exchange can lead to the development of complexity without specifying how the surplus concentrated into wealth is obtained in the first instance, that complex societies "emerged *together*, pulling each other up by the bootstraps" (Renfrew

1986a: 11), would be to say that elites "arose by taking in each other's washing" (Carneiro 1977: 222). Second, the scope of wealth finance operations seems quite limited in the Millaran/Argaric world. Very little in the way of materials of specifically southeast Spanish origin is found outside that region (Gilman 1987); only a trickle of exotic valuables made their way into that region (cf. Harrison and Gilman 1977); and within the region valuables seem to have circulated over quite short distances.[5] It seems clear that the main force underlying the increase in social complexity over the course of the third and early second millennium B.C. in southeast Spain was the progressive intensification of agricultural production and the increased possibilities of rent collection this intensification afforded.

A model along these lines has the merit that it specifies a realistic link between class stratification and the intensified systems of subsistence production which universally accompany such stratification (Gilman 1981). In southeast Spain it is the value as capital of fixed assets such as irrigation systems, terraced fields, and so on, that binds primary producers to their masters. It is clear, therefore, that an approach to the origins of stratification that emphasized the viability of non-economic coercion must be modified when it addresses areas where capital assets are not spatially fixed. This is the case for northern and central Europe, where social stratification arises in the context of the secondary products revolution (Sherratt 1981). Thus, Shennan (1986: 132) argues that the widespread use of the plow

> removed the pressure on local resources [of the previous horticultural subsistence system] and resulted in a diminution of warfare. Once this had occurred, the main pressure for defended nucleation was removed, and community fission in response to internal conflict and population increase would have become a possibility; it may also be that in the absence of other constraints, there is a tendency toward dispersed patterns of agricultural settlement for least-effort reasons. This expansion is one of

---

5. Thus, Lull (1983: 439) notes that tin (as opposed to arsenical) bronzes are much more frequent in Argaric burials of the Cartagena/Mazarrón district (where a source of tin exists) than in contemporaneous burials in the Vera basin, 50 km to the southwest.

the main empirical reasons for rejecting Gilman's account of the growth of social stratification in temperate Europe in the Bronze Age since it runs directly counter to the situation he postulates in which people are reluctant to move from existing cleared land because of the investment they have put into it and are therefore potentially open to exploitation.

Now, while clearing fields for the plow is certainly more costly than clearing them for horticulture, the main capital assets in secondary products subsistence systems are the the animals themselves. An agriculturist is vulnerable to the expropriation of his animals wherever he may move.[6] He does not simply consume his animals as they grow to maturity, he retains them so as to produce, and for the privilege of doing so he is vulnerable to extortion. Furthermore, an individual farmer who keeps oxen for his plow will not ordinarily maintain breeding stock for their replacement and will, therefore, be dependent on the larger-scale livestock owners who supply him.[7] In secondary products systems, precisely because livestock function both as productive assets and as transferable wealth, they offer excellent opportunities for elite control. Rather than see the dispersed settlement pattern characteristic of third-millennium temperate Europe as the result of diminished social conflict, one may interpret it as the result of the mode of elite control. Peasants would be subject to threats, not to their persons, but to their animals. The ethnographic record on pastoral societies far more mobile than

---

6. As Julian Thomas (1987) points out, even in Neolithic subsistence systems, where livestock were kept largely for their primary products (meat, hides, etc.), cattle "management" constituted the material base for the social dominance of lineage elders.

7. James Lewthwaite, whose amusing critcal comments to my 1981 article led the organizers of this symposium to suggest "The Mafia hypothesis" as the title of this paper, has latterly changed his views on the realism of my approach. Commenting on the significance of the secondary products revolution, he observes:

"A small group controlling the critical means of production (the herds) would clearly have been in a powerful position to exploit the remainder ... The infrequent renewal of the feudal [landlord] class in Sicily has always taken place from the ranks of the *gabelotti*, the possessors of cattle; in fact, *gabelotto* is practically synonymous with *mafioso* ..." (Lewthwaite 1985: 219).

any which can be supposed to have existed in later prehistoric Europe is replete with examples of the opportunities for control which herds of livestock present to leaders (e.g., Shahrani 1979, Barth 1964).[8]

The temperate European focus on cattle-herding is entirely consonant with a view of the political economy of early stratified societies which underlines non-economic coercion as the basis of elite power.[9] The production and exchange of valuables certainly seems to have been far more active in temperate Europe than in the central and western Mediterranean, but (to use Haas's terminology) the cost for primary producers of refusing participation in that trade cannot have been important. It is difficult to see how the trade in bronze, amber or other preciosities could establish the basis for economic pressure on peasants who would never receive such material. The "monopolistic conditions of exchange" which Shennan (1986: 139) places at the root of "growing social differentiation" would have affected directly the relations of emergent elites with one another, but only indirectly the relations of such elites with the primary producers of the surplus on which they depended. As Colin Renfrew (1986b) points out, valuables do not function as economic commodities until well after the period under consideration here. Johnson and Earle (1987: 249) discuss cogently the similarities between "feudalism" and chiefdoms. One point of similarity is the primacy of non-economic coercion in the process of elite surplus capture. In Europe, of course, chiefdoms

---

8. Thus, in traditional Luristan the pastoralist economy gave rise to stratification (local groups were led by *khavanin* [princes]), but without the stability conferred by state institutions. This gave rise to "congeries of turbulent tribes ever given to plundering or at feud with each other, but rarely controlled by capable chiefs" (Sir Aurel Stein, quoted in Black-Michaud [1986: 83]). Comparable situations are well attested in Europe (proto-historic Ireland is a good example). On the peripheries of state power, such social "orders" (if one may call them that) lasted into modern times (see, for example, George MacDonald Fraser [1972] on the "reiver economy" of the sixteenth century [A.D.] Scots borderlands.)

9. The Apennine Bronze Age of central and southern Italy (Barker 1981: 90-102) and the Cogotas I complex of Late Bronze Age Iberia (Fernández-Posse y de Arnaiz 1986) seem to be Mediterranean variants of the temperate European pattern.

and feudalism are not just structurally similar, but historically sequential.[10]

The simplest link between the social and economic changes which occurred in Europe in the third millennium and the dispersal of Indo-European languages into the continent is that proposed by Marija Gimbutas (1963): the Kurgan people from the north Caucasus Indo-European homeland introduce intensified livestock exploitation, hierarchical social institutions, and their language into eastern, central, and northern Europe. The empirical and methodological difficulties of this model have been exhaustively discussed in the literature and require no repetition here. It is simply unwarranted to postulate a fixed link between particular styles of material culture and particular linguistic groupings. What can be done, however, is to elucidate the correspondences between the social institutions which can be reconstructed in the archaeological record and those which can be reconstructed from the linguistic record. When Thomas Markey (1981: 239) observes that "totemism and its attendant bestial epithets are non-Indo-European, but were later acquired by the Indo-Europeans as they integrated the religions of those they conquered," the prehistorian will note how well this fits with the contrasts in religious behavior observed in the archaeological record of the Neolithic and the Bronze Age, respectively. The "oath/ordeal" orientation, which Markey (1988) notes is characteristic of Indo-European ideology, corresponds to the "individualizing" character of Bronze Age rituals.[11]

In this way, then, without claiming indefensible matches between particular archaeological assemblages and particular linguistic groupings, one may see the

---

10. Shennan (1987: 370) seems to believe that an approach such as mine to the development of social complexity, with its emphasis on the importance of coercive control over subsistence, postulates "a universal urge to dominance in the human (male) psyche." I make no assumptions about human nature except that it is variable. In all societies, *some* individuals (male or female) have such urges. Where appropriate conditions exist (in my model, technological conditions), greed has the opportunity to be translated into effective social action.

11. This is part of a broad evolutionary pattern of changing forms of legitimation according to which, as Earle (in press) notes, tribal leaders claim ancestors who emerge from the earth, while chiefs claim ancestors who descend from the sky.

development of stratified societies in Europe as of the third millennium as providing the structural conditions for linguistic spread through the processes of what Renfrew (1987) calls "elite dominance." Renfrew believes that elite dominance sufficiently effective to impose a new language on a subject population requires either state-level political organization or significant disparities in military technology. Such conditions are certainly not attested to in late Neolithic and early Bronze Age Europe. Accordingly, Renfrew opts for a radical alternative to the conventional wisdom as to the date and source of Indo-European spread into Europe. At the same time, however, he notes several cases where particular linguistic displacements may have taken place through dominance of elites whose bureaucratic and military organization were not much more complex than those attested to in the European Bronze Age.[12] Given the hesitation of so notable a processualist as Renfrew (and given the difficulties of his own "wave of advance" model), it might be well for processualists to develop in greater detail the lessons which might be gained from a comparative sociology of language spread through elite dominance.

---

12. Renfrew (1987: 132) allows that chiefdoms may be sufficiently well organized to give subject populations incentives to change their languages. He cites the spread of Gaelic into Scotland in the Dark Ages (1987: 164) and the introduction of Indo-Iranian languages to India (*ibid.*: 205) as possible examples of pre-state linguistic spread through elite dominance.

BIBLIOGRAPHY

Barker, G.
    1981. *Landscape and Society: Prehistoric Central Italy.* London: Academic Press.

Barth, F.
    1964. *Nomads of South Persia.* London: Allen & Unwin.

Black-Michaud, J.
    1986. *Sheep and Land: The Economics of Power in a Tribal Society.* Cambridge: Cambridge University Press.

Chapman, R.W.
    1984. "Early Metallurgy in Iberia and the Western Mediterranean: Innovation, Adoption, and Production." In W.H. Waldren et al., eds. *The Deya Conference of Prehistory: Early Settlement in the Western Mediterranean Islands and Their Peripheral Areas.* 1139-1165. Oxford: BAR International Series 229.

Childe, G.
    1954. *What Happened in History.* Harmondsworth: Penguin Books.

Coles, J.M., and A.F. Harding.
    1979. *The Bronze Age in Europe.* London: Methuen.

D'Altroy, T., and T.K. Earle.
    1985. "Staple finance, wealth finance, and storage in the Inka political economy." *Current Anthropology* 26. 187-206.

Earle, T.K.
    1987. "Chiefdoms in Archaeological and Ethnohistorical Perspective." *Annual Review of Anthropology* 16. 279-308.
    in press. "Style and Iconography as Legitimation in Complex Chiefdoms." In M. Conkey and C. Hastorf, eds. *The Uses of Style in Archaeology.* Cambridge: Cambridge University Press.

Fernández-Posse y de Arnaiz, M.D.
    1986. "La cultura de Cogotas I." *Homenaje a Luis Siret (1934-1984).* 475-487. Seville: Conserjería de Cultura de la Junta de Andalucía.

Flannery, K.V.
> 1972. "The Cultural Evolution of Civilizations." *Annual Review of Ecology and Systematics* 3. 399-426.

Fraser, G.M.
> 1972. *The Steel Bonnets*. New York: Alfred A. Knopf.

Gilman, A.
> 1976. "Bronze Age Dynamics in Southeast Spain." *Dialectical Anthropology* 1. 307-319.
>
> 1981. "The Development of Social Stratification in Bronze Age Europe." *Current Anthropology* 22. 1-23.
>
> 1987. "Unequal Development in Copper Age Iberia." in E.M. Brumfiel and T.K. Earle, eds. *Specialization, Exchange, and Complex Societies*. 22-29. Cambridge: Cambridge University Press.

Gilman, A. and J.B. Thornes.
> 1985. *Land Use and Prehistory in South-East Spain*. London: George Allen and Unwin.

Gimbutas, M.
> 1963. "The Indo-Europeans: Archaeological Problems." *American Anthropologist*. 65. 815-836.

Goody, J.
> 1971. *Technology, Tradition and the State in Africa*. Oxford: Oxford University Press.

Haas, J.
> 1982. *The Evolution of the Prehistoric State*. New York: Columbia University Press.

Halstead, P. and J. O'Shea.
> 1982. "A Friend in Need is a Friend Indeed: Social Storage and the Origins of Social Ranking." In C. Renfrew and S. Shennan, eds. *Ranking, Resource and Exchange*. 92-99. Cambridge: Cambridge University Press.

Harrison, R.J. and G. Moreno López.
> 1985. "El policultivo ganadero o la revolución de los productos secundarios." *Trabajos de Prehistoria*. 42. 51-82.

Harrison, R.J. and A. Gilman.
- 1977. "Trade in the Second and Third Millennia B.C. Between the Maghreb and Iberia." In V. Markotic, ed. *Ancient Europe and the Mediterranean.* 90-104. Warminster: Aris and Phillips.

Johnson, A.W. and T.K. Earle.
- 1987. *The Evolution of Human Societies: From Foraging Group to Agrarian State.* Stanford: Stanford University Press.

Leacock, E.B.
- 1972. "Introduction." In F. Engels [orig. 1884]. *The Origin of the Family, Private Property and the State.* 7-67. New York: International Publishers.

Lewthwaite, J.
- 1985. "Social Factors and Economic Change in Balearic Prehistory, 3000-1000 B.C." In G. Barker and C. Gamble, eds. *Beyond Domestication in Prehistoric Europe.* 205-231. London: Academic Press.

Lull, V.
- 1983. *La "Cultura" de El Argar.* Madrid: Akal Editor.
- 1984. "A New Assessment of Argaric Society and Culture." In W.H. Waldren et al., eds. *The Deya Conference of Prehistory: Early Settlement in the Western Mediterranean Islands and their Peripheral Areas.* 1197-1238. Oxford: BAR International Series 229.

Markey. T.L.
- 1981. "Indo-European Theophoric Personal Names and Social Structure." *Journal of Indo-European Studies* 9. 227-243.
- 1988. "The Celto-Germanic 'Dog/Wolf'-Champion and the Integration of Pre-/Non-IE Ideals." *Nowele* 11. 3-30.

Marx, K.
- 1967. [orig. 1894]. *Capital: A Critique of Political Economy, Vol. 3: The Process of Capitalist Production as a Whole.* New York: International Publishers.

Rathje, W.L.
- 1971. "The Origin and Development of Lowland Classic Maya Civilization." *American Antiquity* 36. 275-285.

Renfrew, C.
- 1986a. "Introduction: Peer Polity Interaction and Socio-Political Change." In C. Renfrew and J.F. Cherry, eds. *Peer Polity Interaction and Socio-Political Change.* 1-18. Cambridge: Cambridge University Press.
- 1986b. "Varna and the Emergence of Wealth in Prehistoric Europe." In A. Appadurai, ed. *The Social Life of Things.* 141-168. Cambridge: Cambridge University Press.
- 1987. *Archaeology and Language: The Puzzle of Indo-European Origins..* New York: Cambridge University Press.

Rowlands, M.
- 1984. "Conceptualizing European Bronze and Early Iron Ages." In J. Bintliff, ed., *European Social Evolution.* 147-156. Bradford: University of Bradford.

Sahlins, M.
- 1972. *Stone Age Economics.* Chicago: Aldine.

Shahrani, M.
- 1979. *The Kirghiz and Wakhi of Afghanistan.* Seattle: University of Washington Press.

Shennan, S.J.
- 1982. "The Emergence of Hierarchical Structure." In C. Renfrew and S.J. Shennan, eds. *Ranking, Resource and Exchange.* 9-12. Cambridge: Cambridge University Press.
- 1986. "Central Europe in the Third Millennium B.C.: An Evolutionary Trajectory for the Beginning of the European Bronze Age." *Journal of Anthropological Archaeology.* 5. 115-146.
- 1987. "Trends in the Study of Later European Prehistory." *Annual Review of Anthropology.* 16. 365-382.

Sherratt, A.G.
- 1981. "Plough and Pastoralism: Aspects of the Secondary Products Revolution." In I. Hodder et al., eds. *Pattern of the Past.* 261-305. Cambridge: Cambridge University Press.

Thomas, J.
- 1987. "Relations of Production and Social Change in the Neolithic of North-West Europe." *Man.* 22. 405-430.

Webster, D.L.
    1977. "Warfare and the Evolution of Maya Civilization." In R.E.W. Adams, ed. *The Origins of Maya Civilization.* 355-372. Albuquerque: University of New Mexico Press.

Wittfogel, K.
    1957. *Oriental Despotism.* New Haven: Yale University Press.

Wolf, E.R.
    1981. "The Mills of Inequality: A Marxian Approach." In G.D. Berreman, ed. *Social Inequality: Comparative and Developmental Approaches.* 41-57. New York: Academic Press.

THE COLLISION OF TWO IDEOLOGIES

Marija Gimbutas
Professor of European Archaeology
University of California, Los Angeles

The Indo-European culture, with its patriarchal and classed social structure and its religion of warrior gods, was superimposed on Europe in several stages: first in central Europe in 4500-3000 B.C., it spread to the north and south in the first half of the third millennium B.C., coming later to the Aegean and Mediterranean islands. From the third millennium on, *hybridized* cultures and mythologies emerged.

The culture that the Indo-European culture was superimposed on, Old Europe, with its tens of thousands of figurines, beautifully painted pottery, frescoed temples, and conveniently located towns, disappears. It is replaced instead by hillforts and weapons and the emergence of a totally different symbolic system.

The recognition of the collision of two ideologies, Old European and Indo-European, as presented here is based on my research of some thirty years which can be summed up in the following central points: 1) The definition of distinct Neolithic and Copper Age Europe of c. 6500-3500 B.C. as *Old Europe*, opposed to what is known as "Indo-European." 2) The reconstruction of the complex religious and philosophical system of goddess-worship which was central to Old European cultures. 3) The recognition of the clash between Old Europe and the proto-Indo-European Kurgan culture of Volga Neolithic origin and the three successive infiltrations of the Kurgan horse-riding people into east central Europe in the period between 4500 and 3000 B.C. which led to the transformation of Old Europe: the change of the social structure, transition from matrilineal to patrineal order, from learned theocracy to militant patriarchy, from balanced to unbalanced society, from the chthonic goddess religion to the Indo-European male-dominated and sky-oriented pantheon of gods. 4) The formation of the secondary, European, homeland in central Europe, composed of indigenous and Kurgan elements.1

European culture, as well as that of Anatolia and southern Asia, has two main constituent ingredients: substratal (Old European) and superstratal (indo-European), both extant up to the present in language, myth, and symbols. The Old European and Indo-European belief systems are diametrically opposed. This fact alone speaks for the collision, i.e. the intrusive character of the Indo-Europeans in Europe. There is no possibility of the Indo-European belief system having evolved in a straight line from the Old European. There is also no possibility that the Indo-European society -exogamic, patriarchal, patrilineal and patrilocal, with strong clanic organization and social hierarchization which gave prominence to the priestly and warrior classes -developed from Old European kin-group society which focused on the harmonious interaction of humans in nature, and of men and women with each other as complementary.

Old European symbols are intimately related to the moist earth, to her life-giving waters, to female regenerative organs; they are cyclic as the moon and the female body. In no way could the philosophy which produced these images be mistaken for the sky-oriented Indo-European ideology with its horse-riding warrior gods of thundering and shining sky, or of the swampy underworld, its gods equipped with lethal weapons, its polar (day/night, shining/black, male/female) structuring of the world, its ideology in which female goddesses are no longer creatrixes, but reduced to mere beauties -"Venuses," brides of the sky gods.

Summary of functions and images of Old European goddesses and gods

The main theme of Old European goddess symbolism is the mystery of birth

---

1. I have published these theses in a series of articles in the *Journal of Indo-European Studies* and elsewhere; and in books: 1)*The Goddesses and Gods of Old Europe, 6500-3500 B.C.*, London: Thames and Hudson, 1974 and 1982 (second edition), 2) *The Language of the Goddess*, Harper and Row, San Francisco, 1989, and *Goddess' Civilization. Europe before the Patriarchy*. Beacon Press: forthcoming.

and death, and the renewal of life, involving not only human life but all life on earth. Symbols and images cluster around the parthenogenetic (self-generating) Goddess. She was the single source of all life who took her energy from the springs and wells, from the moon, sun and earth, and from the animals and plants. Her basic functions were as Giver-of-Life, Wielder-of-Death, Regeneratrix, and the Earth Fertility Goddess, rising and dying with plant life. Male gods also exist, but not as creators: they are guardians or owners of wild nature, or they are metaphors of life energy and vegetation spirit. Table I.

Summary of functions and images of Indo-European gods and goddesses

The proto-Indo-European pantheon of gods was organized to a socially and economically oriented ideology: the prominent sovereign, priestly, and warrior classes were suited to the predominant role of pastoralism in their mixed farming economy, with the special emphasis on the horse. Their principal male gods rode horses and carried weapons. Life-creating and death-wielding functions belonged to the principal male gods. Female goddesses, like the Dawn and Sun Maiden, are not creatrixes, but are brides or wives of male gods. The religion was oriented toward the rotating sun and other sky phenomena, such as thunder and lightning. Their sky gods shone "bright as the sky." In Bronze Age representations they carried shining weapons -daggers, swords, and shields -and were adorned with copper or gold chest plates, gold or amber discs, and copper-plated belts.

On the other hand, the god of death was a frightening black god of the underworld. The Indo-Europeans glorified the swiftness of arrow and spear and the sharpness of the blade. The touch of the axe blade awakened the powers of nature and transmitted the fecundity of the god (Thunder god); by the touch of his spear tip, the god of death and the underworld marked the hero for glorious death.

Time was conceived as an inexorable onward movement, as a "wheel track." The horse draws the wheel of the four seasons, and of the day, from morning to night. The sky is seen as a hill: the movement of the sun is up the hill and down, as it is drawn in a vehicle (later a chariot), by horses who never tire. The sun in Indo-European languages is called "the runner," "the tireless racer," "the seesaw," or "the horse."

There were three main gods, none subordinated to the others. Each is intimately associated with domesticated animals: horse, bull and he-goat. There was no one Great God as there was one Great Goddess; however, the God of the Shining Sky in some Indo-European mythologies appears as a "summus deus," the most important one. The images associated with this god are the most numerous. Table II.

Summary of beliefs in afterlife

The two systems exhibit two very different sets of beliefs in an afterlife.

Old European

A strong belief in cyclic regeneration is reflected in neolithic burial rites. The pervasive idea in grave architecture is *Tomb is Womb*. Graves are oval, egg-shaped, oven-shaped, uterus-shaped, or anthropomorphic. The latter being conceived as the body of the Goddess. The generative triangle also figures in grave and shrine outlines and architecture. Symbols on stones of megalithic graves are symbols of regeneration, life-giving water, and life energy (cupmarks, concentric circles with central dot, concentric arcs, winding snakes, snake coils, bullheads as uteri, triangles, lozenges, hourglass shapes, zigzags, lunar cycles); or images of the Goddess of Regeneration with labyrinths, vulvas, breasts.

There is a barrier of water between this world and the next, which is crossed by ships, themselves symbols of regeneration. The location of the afterworld is in the West. Life after death is pleasant, enjoyable.

Indo-European

There is a linear continuity from this life to the afterlife. Therefore mortuary houses were built, and the dead take their belongings, tools, weapons, ornaments, according to their rank, to the afterworld. Gifts provide the dead with status. Royal tombs and those of other important members of the society are lavishly equipped. The kings and chieftains are buried with people (wife, servants, children) and animals (horses, teams of oxen, dogs). Death in battle is glorified. Gifts of food continue to be made after the funeral: necessary to the well-being of the shades.

The otherworld is underground, swampy, ruled by the male sovereign god. It is gloomy, chilly, sterile. The journey to the otherworld involves a road or a river, and usually a three day period of walking, riding, or travel in chariots. Souls remain there and drift in a pale and passive manner. There is no belief in rebirth or continuity of life energy in other living beings as in Old Europe. Such different beliefs of the Indo-Europeans could not have developed from the Old Europeans. With the formation of the Baden-Ezero culture in east central Europe and the Globular Amphora in northern central Europe in the second half of the fourth millennium B.C., the Indo-European mode of burial and beliefs in the other world take root in Europe and gradually replace the communal burial of the Old European type.

The contrast between Old European and Indo-European symbols

The analysis of Old European and Indo-European symbols shows that the two religions and mythologies had entirely different sets of symbols. Both sets are still extant today in the mythologies and folklore of Europe. Below, I shall give just a few examples, not the whole glossary of symbols. Examples are taken from the animal world, sky bodies, and colors. Table III.

Conclusion

The above summaries of functions and images of gods, of beliefs in afterlife, and the different sets of symbols prove the existence of two religions and mythologies, the Old European indigenous, inherited from the Paleolithic, the Indo-European intrusive, related to the Near Eastern. Their collision in Europe resulted in the hybridization of two symbol structures. The Indo-European prevailed, but the Old European survived as an undercurrent. Without the insight into the different symbolic structures, the ideologies of the European peoples, and the genesis and meaning of symbols, beliefs, and myths cannot be comprehended.

TABLE I

Functions and images of Old European goddesses and gods, (based on Neolithic and Copper Age materials, 7th-5th millenium B.C.)

Life-Giving and Life-Protecting

Images:

1. Bird/woman, duck, goose, other water birds. Cuckoo, other birds of spring. Vessel. Menhir.
2. Serpent/woman. Harmless snake.
3. Anthropomorphic birth-giver (in birth-giving posture). Zoomorphic: bear, deer.
4. Nurse: bear-masked woman carrying a pouch.
5. Madonna: anthropomorphic or zoomorphic (bird, bear, snake).
6. Mistress of animals and plants. Anthropomorphic flanked by animals and plants.
7. Male guardian/owner of wild animals and forests. Anthropomorhic, bearded. Enthroned holding a hook.

Death-Wielding and Regeneration

Images:

1. Bird of prey/woman, vulture, owl, crow, raven, white dog, boar.
2. Stiff nude ("White Lady") with owl or snake mask.
3. Bone with owl eyes.
4. Regenerative triangle, axe, hourglass.
5. Uterus in zoomorphic shape: fish, toad, hedgehog, turtle, bucranium. Fish/woman, frog/woman, hedgehog/woman.
6. Life column: upward winding snake, tree, water column, phallus.
7. Bee, butterfly. Bee/woman, butterfly/woman.

Fertility

Images:

1. Pregnant woman/earth fertility.
2. Metaphors of pregnant belly: hill, stone, oven, grave (oven shaped, beehive-shaped, round chamber tombs).
3. Sow/woman, sow.
4. Young, rising goddess with upraised arms and Old Hag, dying nature.
5. Rising and dying vegetation god: ithyphallic man, old, sorrowful enthroned.

TABLE II

Functions and images of proto-Indo-European gods and goddesses based on comparative Indo-European mythology and archaeological finds of 4th-2nd millenium B.C.

The God of the Shining Sky

Year god, inseparable from the sun- new, young, mature - and the changing seasons, appearing in different shapes in each season. In spring and summer aspects he is a young and beautiful god dressed as king. Creator of vegetation, birds, and domestic animals. Epiphanies: white horse, birch. Weapons: dagger, sword, halberd. Guardian of contracts. God of peace and friendship.

Satellites:
Moon God
    The night aspect of the God of the Shining Sky. Warrior.
The Twins
    Horses or anthropomorphic.
Sun Maiden
    Daughter of the Sun God, heavenly bride.
Dawn
    Beauty, goddes of love. Epiphanies: mare and cow.
The brother or servant of the Dawn
    Herder of cows.
Heavenly Smith
    Hammers a new sun.

Thunder-god

Inseminator of earth. God of justice. Adversary of the God of Death and the Underworld with whom he fights incessantly with his arrows or axes. Imagined as a middle-aged red-bearded man. Epiphanies: bull and he-goat, oak tree, rowan. Weapons: axe, bow and arrow.

God of Death and Underworld

Cruel and angry god of death imagined as an old man or a black god. Creator of ugly animals and birds of prey, coniferous trees, and roots. Animals: stallion and bear. The usual epiphany in fight with Thunder-god: monstrous serpent hiding in whirl-winds. Weapons: spear, loop of cord for hanging. God of contracts.

TABLE III

Serpent (snake)

Old European

Benevolent snake:
Symbol of life energy in cosmos, and in humans, animals and plants. Stimulating and protecting the life powers of the family and domestic animals. Snake coil is interchangeable with sun, moon, and eye.

Poisonous snake:
Epiphany of Goddess of Death

Indo-European

Symbol of evil, especially lurking in whirlwinds. Epiphany of the God of Death and the Underworld, adversary of the Thunder God.

The Postulated Pre-Indo-European Substrates in Insular Celtic and Tocharian[1]
Karl Horst Schmidt
(Bonn University)

In discussing the causes of linguistic change in the IE languages, two factors are generally mentioned: 1. system conditioned, so-called intralinguistic reasons which are determined by the interdependence between economy and function. This finds expression in phrases like *la loi du moindre effort* and *le besoin de s'exprimer* (Martinet 1955, 21); 2. extralinguistic reasons brought about by *Contact and Interference* (Weinreich 1964, 1). My paper is concerned with the latter.

The interference caused by *Languages in Contact*, Haugen's *replica*[2], can be shown on two levels: a) borrowing and adaptation of concrete linguistic substance from the *model language* by the *replica language: loan words, hybrids, loan translations (calques linguistiques)* or *semantic loans* (cf. Haugen 1972, 165) can result in a restructuring of the inherited vocabulary. Besides, as reliable evidence of language contacts, they are of special importance for the history of a language. b) Structural and typological transformation of the phonological and grammatical sybsystems resulting from the influence of foreign substrates on the expanding IE tribes. The process has been described by Deeters 1958, 155 as follows: "Die zunächst zweisprachige unterworfene Bevölkerung paßt die fremde Sprache dem phonologischen System der eigenen an; Phoneme, die dieser fehlen, werden durch ähnliche ersetzt (Lautsubstitution). Auch der Sprachbau kann umgestaltet werden, indem Kategorien der alten Sprache in die neue hineingetragen werden, ihr fremdartige ausgeschieden werden. Je mehr sich im Laufe der Zeit die unterworfene Bevölkerung numerisch und sozial durchsetzt, desto stärker treten

---

1. I would like to thank K. Hlaváček and A. Ó Corráin for correcting my English.
2. Haugen 1972, 326 ff.; cf. also Boretzky 1973, 139.

diese Züge hervor."³ As examples of IE languages influenced by pre-IE substrates, Deeters, l.c., cites Sanskrit, Armenian and Greek, while my talk, which is restricted to morphology and syntax, deals with Tocharian and Insular Celtic. The paper consists of five parts:

1. On the typology of possibly non-IE features in Tocharian and Insular Celtic morphology and syntax
2. On the problem of identifying non-IE contact languages
3. On the position of Tocharian and Insular Celtic within the IE language family as a criterion for dating possible contacts with non-IE languages
4. On the distribution of archaisms and innovations in Tocharian and Insular Celtic
5. Summary

1. *On the typology of possibly non-IE features in Tocharian and Insular Celtic morphology and syntax*

a) *Tocharian*
As to phonology, the merger of the three IE occlusive series (voiceless, voiced, voiced aspirate) into voiceless consonants may just be mentioned in passing.[4] Van

---

3. Cf. also Lewy (1913) 1961, 4, whose theory, however, is difficult to prove because it is not explicit: "und je inniger die Eingewöhnung wird, d.h. je mehr Zeit vergeht, desto stärker wird sich die alteinheimische geistige Art in der neuen, einst fremden Sprache durchsetzen; desto ähnlicher werden die jüngeren Stufen der Mischsprache der alten, nun längst verklungenen einheimischen Muttersprache werden." Similarly Wagner 1959, 242: "Das Formprinzip der Sprache äußert sich im Kategoriensystem und ist durch die Geistesstruktur des Menschen bestimmt." Schönfelder's argument, 1956, 67: "daß auch im Falle einer Völkermischung und eines daraus resultierenden Sprachwechsels des einen Volkes keine direkte morphologische Beeinflussung der Siegersprache durch die unterliegende Sprache eintritt," is unconvincing.

4. On the problem of the dentals -*dh > t : B *mit* 'honey' < *$medhu$, *d > t/c (before vowels):*käntu*, B *kantwo* 'tongue' < *$dn\hat{g}hu\bar{a}$, A -$(a)c$ (allative) < *$(o)de$: Greek -δε (οἰκόνδε); t > t/c : B*cake* 'river' < *$tek^w os$, A *śtwar* 'four' < *$k^w et\mu ores$ - cf. Anreiter 1984, 33ff.; Thomas 1984, 48ff.

Windekens 1976, 76 calls this process *assourdissement*[5], while Gamkrelidze/Ivanov 1984, 400, on the basis of their different reconstruction of series I (cf. no. 1), evaluate it partly as an archaism: "Jazyki soxranivšie seriju I bez posledujěščego ozvočenija (germanskij, armjanskij, verojatno, anatolijskij i toxarskij), mogut rassmatrivat'sja kak soxranivšie arxaizm sistemy i blizkie v étom otnošenii k isxodnoj indoevropejskoj sisteme":

(1) Classical reconstruction vs. Gamkrelidze/Ivanov:

I [b], d, G vs. [p'], t', G';
II b^h, d^h, G^h vs. $b^{[h]}$, $d^{[h]}$, $G^{[h]}$;
III p, t, K vs. $p^{[h]}$, $t^{[h]}$, $K^{[h]}$

As to morphology, Meillet's principle still holds: "Le verbe est tout indo-européen. La flexion nominale a perdu, il est vrai, presque tous les traits indo-européens' (Meillet 1914, 12). The change from inflecting to agglutinative language type is the most important development in Tocharian nominal morphology[6], although the latter does not extend to the nominative, accusative (oblique) and genitive cases. The agglutinative structure of the so-called *secondary cases*, instrumental (replaced by the perlative in Tocharian B), perlative, comitative, allative, ablative, locative and causalis[7], which developed from postpositions (cf. Krause/Thomas 1960, 78), corresponds to the principle of *orders* established by Gleason 1966, 112: "mutually exclusive classes of morphemes occupying definable places in the sequence of morphemes forming a word":

(2) A *käṣṣi* 'magister,' o^1 : oblique case *käṣṣi-m ~ käṣṣi-n-*, o^2 : perlative *käṣṣi-n-ā*, comitative *käṣṣi-n-aśśäl* etc.; plural: o^1: oblique case *käṣṣi-s*, o^2:

---

5. Cf. the corresponding German term *Tenuisierung* used by Anreiter 1984, 12.
6. On the definition of the *inflective* and *agglutinative* types cf. Sapir (1921) 1949, chapter V and Skalička 1966.
7. On the functional differentiation of these cases cf. Schmidt 1987.

käṣṣi-s-ā, käṣṣ-s-aśśäl etc.[8]

This morphological system with the oblique case as the basis for the secondary cases (no. 2) corresponds typologically to the inflection on the principle of two bases (*po principu dvux osnov*) established for the East Caucasian languages of the Daghestan by Magometov 1965, 97: "ot imenitel'nogo padeža (padeža samogo po sebe neoformlennogo ...) obrazuetsja ėrgativ, a ėrgativ ležit v osnove kosvennyx padežej."

As to syntax, the agglutinative declension of Tocharian exhibits the same correlations as that of Ossetic, which, however, carried out the change from inflective to agglutinative type more completely, i.e. including the grammatical cases:

(3) Ossetic sg. : pl. nom. *sær* 'head' : *sær-t-æ*, gen. *sær-ə* : *sær-t-ə* etc.

In both languages we encounter *Gruppenflexion* ('group inflection')[9] instead of inherited *Autonomie des Wortes* ('word autonomy')[10]:

(4) A *kuklas* (oblique) *yukas* (oblique) *oṅkälmās-yo* (instr.) 'with carriages, horses and elephants,' *āṣānikāṃ* 9oblique) *Metrakn-aśśäl* (comit.) 'together with the venerable Maitreya'[11]

---

8. Cf. Schmidt 1969; 1987, 139.

9. On the term *Gruppenflexion* cf. Finck 1910, 154, who mentions three inflecting types in the strict sense of the word; "den griechischen. . .stammflektierenden," "den arabischen. . .wurzelflektierenden," "den georgischen. . .gruppenflektierenden."

10. Cf. the definition of the term *Autonomie des Wortes* by Deeters 1957, 14: "jedes Wort des Satzes ist selbstaendig und traegt an sich die Formantien, die seine Beziehung zu einem anderen Wort (Kondordanz) oder seine Funktion innerhalb des Satzes (Flexion) kennzeichnen."

11. Examples taken from Krause/Thomas 1960, 91. On the typological comparison between the Tocharian, Modern Armenian and Ossetic noun declensions cf. Schmidt 1975; 1987a.

Postpositions outnumber prepositions[12]. The arrangement of the parts of the sentence in the *Basic Word Order* SOV, however, must possibly be evaluated as an archaism[13]. The tendency to mark the accusative singular of rational beings, which in West Tocharian (B) is restricted to the masculine gender, does not generally apply to kinship terms:

(5) AB *käṣṣi* 'magister,' obl. *-ṃ* vs. B nom. obl. *pikul* 'year'; nom. *pācer* 'father,' obl. *pātär*; A nom. obl. *pats* 'husband,' B obl. *petso*; nom. obl. *soy* 'son,' A *se*; A obl. *ñkät* 'God'; Ossetic *mæ mady ragæj nal fedton* 'I haven't seen my mother (acc. = gen.) for a long time'[14]   The marking of the accusative case of rational beings, which is confirmed by similar developments in Romance, Slavic and Modern East Armenian[15],

(6) Armenian *Es tesnum em sarə* 'I see the mountain,' *Maron verçreç girk'ə* 'Maro took the book' vs. *Maron verçreç erexayin* (acc. = dat.) 'Maro took the child'[16]

fits into the frame of *animata* vs. *inanimata*. As early as 1925, 49, Meillet established the principle of a proto-IE dichotomy of *genus commune*, i.e. the generic term for masculine and feminine, vs. *genus neutrum*: "Le trait essentiel de la distinction de l'animé et de l'inanimé consiste dans la caractéristique de

---

12. Tocharian prepositions are in general followed by the oblique case (B *śle*, A *śla* 'with,' B *snai*, A *sne* 'without') or restricted to inherited syntagms (Krause/Thomas 1960, 171), e.g. B *yśāmna* 'among men,' *yñakteṃ* 'among gods'; postpositions, however, are preceded by nouns in various cases.

13. Cf. on the one hand Zimmer 1976, 101, and on the other hand Schmidt 1972; 1975, 285.

14. Cf. Abaev 1964, 18: genitive used as the "direct object (for definite and personal beings)". As to the etymology of *-ṃ* (in *käṣṣi-m* etc.) cf. Krause/Thomas 1960, 109; Schmidt. 1989, 22ff.

15. As to the Armenian, cf. Abeghian 1936, 63: "Bei Substantiven, die ein vernünftiges Wesen bezeichnen und zugleich auch bestimmt sind, ist der Akkusativ im OA dem Dativ gleich. Im WA ist er immer gleich dem Nominativ."

16. Cf. Garibjan 1958, 59; 57.

l'accusatif animé, au singulier et au pluriel. A systematic approach to this question on the basis of the distinction *animate* vs. *inanimate* was attempted a few years ago by Villar 1983, 181ff.[17]. Accusative marking of animate nouns is also attested in non-IE languages, a fact that caused Comrie to establish the principle "that separate accusative marking and verb object agreement are more likely with noun phrases that are high in animacy or definiteness." When applied to ergative languages, this rule implies Silverstein's hypothesis (1976, 122): "If an ergative system splits simply into two two-way case-marking schemes, then minimally either the [+ ego] or the [+ tu] forms are nominative-accusative, the rest ergative-absolutive."[18]

As to Tocharian word-formation, the most important evidence of non-IE influences appears to be the word *akmal* 'face,' a *twin-compositum* (Bednarczuk 1983,12) 'eye-nose,' whose two parts express a new totality[19]. As early as 1927, Wilhelm Schulze compared the word with non-IE parallels:

(7) Tocharian A *ak-mal* 'face' ('eye-nose') : Ossetic *cæs-gom* 'face' (*cæst* 'eye' - *kom* 'mouth') : Adyghe *na-pe* 'face' (*ne* 'eye' - *pe* 'nose'), Avar *bér-ḳal* 'face" ('eye-mouth') : Hungarian *or-ca* (*orr* 'nose' - *száj* 'mouth'), Estonian *suu-silmad* ('mouth-eyes') etc.[20]

---

17. Cf. the reviews of Villar's book by Ködderitzsch 1985 and Schmidt 1986 and see also Villar 1984.

18. Cf. also McLendon 1978, 6: "that the system splits common nouns and personal nouns for which agent function must be marked, from pronouns, kinship terms and proper names for which patient function must be marked"; Bossong 1980; Mallinson/Blake 1981, 52.

19. Cf. Bouda 1932, 95 referring to Avar *ber-ḳal*: "*ber-ḳal* ist ein Kompositum 'Auge-Mund,' die beiden Teile drücken also das Ganze aus."

20. Cf. Schulze (1927) 1966; Bouda 1932, 95ff.; Krause 1951, 197: "(dafür westtoch, *särwāna* pl. tant.)"; 1955, 37: "daß entweder die finno-ugrischen oder die Kaukasussprachen oder beide in diesen Bildungen sowie in der agglutinierenden Kasusrektion auf eine Vorstufe des Tocharischen eingewirkt haben"; Deeters 1963, 42: "In den WKS ist die Wortbildung im wesentlichen auf die Komposition, d.h. die Zusammensetzung von Wurzeln mit materieller Bedeutung beschränkt"; Thomas

Word-pairs consisting of two substantives are particularly frequent in Tocharian. Very often they are composed of synonyms:

(8) A *mrāc śpalyo* 'with top (and) head' = 'with the head'; A *ñom-klyu*, B *ñem-kälywe* 'name (and) reputation' = 'glory'; A *āriñc pältsäk*, B *aräñc pälsko* (obl. sg.) 'heart (and) mind'; A *tuṅk ynāñmune* 'love (and) worship' etc.[21] The IE parallels quoted by Thomas (1972, 462; 1986, 621) do not exactly correspond to the type *akmal*, even in cases where the two parts of the compound are not connected by a conjunction:

(9) Sanskrit *prajayā paśubhiḥ* 'in offspring and cattle'; *nṛttaṃ gītam*'dance and song'; Greek κραδίην καὶ θυμόν B 171; πλοῦτόν τε καὶ ὄλβιον Hes. O. 637; Latin *mentem atque animum*; English *hearth and home* etc.

Summing up, the following features of Tocharian grammar and word-formation seem to indicate non-IE interference: 1. the typological and functional transformation of the nominal case system demonstrated by *agglutinative technique* (Sapir 1949, 142ff.), 2. the enlargement of the concrete (adverbial. local) cases, 3. group inflection on the syntactic level[22].

These characteristics disprove Winter's opinion: "Thus far, in spite of prolonged efforts especially by Wolfgang Krause, no compelling argument for substratum influence upon Tocharian has been presented, let alone that the specific substratum responsible for the changes in Tocharian would have been identified" (1982,3). 4. The East Tocharian gender differentiation of the personal pronouns in the first person singular:

(10) Nom. obl. sg. A *näṣ* (m.), *ñuk* (f.) vs. B *näś* (*ñiś*) 'I, me'; gen. sg. A *ñi* (m.),

---

1985, 148; 1986, 617.
   21. Thomas 1972, 435; 1986, 621.
   22. Cf. also Schmidt 1969; 1972; 1975; 1987.

ñañi (f.) vs. B ñi²³ and the word-formation type *akmal* 'face.' As to the *basic Word Order* SOV and the frequent use of postpositions, it is rather difficult to decide whether these features are due to IE inheritance or to substrate influence.²⁴

b) *Insular Celtic*

In Insular Celtic, most of the features discussed as pre-IE are of a syntactic nature. There are also morphological features, such as the conjugated prepositions already referred to by Robert Atkinson in 1885²⁵ and John Morris Jones in 1900 (l.c. 620):

(11) Welsh *ar* 'on': Sg. 1 *arnaf (fi)* 'on me,' 2 *arnat (ti)*, 3m. *arno cef)*, f. *arni (hi)*, Pl. 1 *arnom (ni)*, 2 *arnoch (chwi)*, 3 *arnynt (hwy)*

A lexico-syntactical tendency, "die idg. abstrakten Bildungen durch konkrete Ausdrücke zu ersetzen" (Pokorny 1959, 156) is dealt with by Pokorny 1927, 239ff.:

(12) Modern Irish *tá scilling agam ort* 'you owe me a shilling,' lit.: 'there is a shilling at me on you; *mo chuid airgid* 'my (part of) money'

On the other hand, the fact that the individual member of a tribe or family cannot be referred to by the mere singular of the group-name, but needs special marking (Pokorny 1927, 248f.), is a widespread phenomenon based on the opposition of *collective* vs. *singulative*:

---

23. Cf. Bednarczuk 1983, 12, referring to "Tibetan and the related languages."

24. Cf. also Thomas 1986, 622: "Im einzelnen fällt es schwer, bei den zur Diskussion anstehenden sprachlichen Problemen jeweils exakt zu bestimmen, was ausschließlich als indogermanischer ... Anteil zu gelten hat und was allein einem nichtindogermanischen Substrat zuzuschreiben ist."

25. Cf. Greene 1966, 125: "Robert Atkinson, a linguist of very wide range, was discussing the conjugated prepositions when he said, in 1885, "we are involuntarily hurried into a different field of languages: these combinations, one fancies, might be Hebrew or Hungarian, Tibetan or Tamil."

(13) Irish *Érennaig* or *Fir Éirenn* '(the) Irish' vs. *fer d(i) feraib Érenn* 'one Irishman,' lit. 'a man from the men of Ireland,' fear de *mhuinntir Néill* 'one O'Neill'; cf. names of groups used only in the plural: Roman Tribus: *Ramnes, Tities, Luceres*; Greek (Homer) Ἀργεῖοι, Δαναοί, Ἀχαιοί; Russian *litva* 'the Lithuanians' vs. *litvinъ* 'one Lithuanian'; Svan *šwan-är*, 'the Svans': *mu-šwan* 'one Svan'; *wonjāna gwar* '(the) Onian family': *mu-wnjān* 'one (member of the family) Onian' etc. [26]

Moreover, the evidence of a tendency to express abstractions in a concrete manner must also be regarded in the light of Thurneysen's assumption that we have to do with elements of colloquial speech.[27] Some of the syntactical features mentioned by Morris Jones (1900) and Pokorny (passim) may also have been influenced by colloquial speech. e.g.,

a) "The pleonastic use of a pronominal suffix after a preposition governing a relative" (Morris Jones 637):

(14) Irish *An fear a raibh tú ag caint leis* 'the man *whom thou wert talking to him*'

b) "The omission of the copula" (Morris Jones 637f.):

(15) Welsh *Pwy y marchawc* 'who (is) the knight?'

c) "The amplification of the negative by a noun placed after the verb, like the French *pas*" (Morris Jones 638):

(16) Wesh *Ni 'th welais dim*' 'je *ne* t'ai *pas* vu'

---

26. Cf. Wackernagel 1926, 86f.; Bräuer 1969, 119; Topuria 1967, 77; Onian 1917, 2.

27. Cf. Thurneysen 1930, 428: "Ich habe den Eindruck, man würde manches davon in der Umgangssprache des täglichen Lebens (nicht in der Literatursprache) vielerorten wiederfinden."

188 When Worlds Collide

d) Juxtaposition of clauses without subordination (Pokorny 1959, 153):

(17) Welsh *Aeth allan ac hithau yn oer* 'he went out *and* it cold' ('*although* it was cold')

A charcteristic feature of Insular Celtic referred to by Wagner is the increasing tendency in Modern Irish to express stative verbs periphrastically:[28]

(18) Old Irish *ad-águr* 'I fear': Modern Irish *tá eagla orm* 'there is fear on me'

It must be admitted, however, that some comparable examples of periphrasis are already attested in Old Irish:

(19) Old Irish *is gó duit* 'you lie': *Canigóo dúib si anasberid* Wb 5a8 'Is it not a lie of yours what ye say': Modern Irish *is fíor dhuit* 'you are right, you tell the truth'

If such developments have been caused by substrates, the tendency to gradually transform the structure or type of a language over a relatively long period of time would confirm the theory established by Deeters 1958, 155: "Je mehr sich im Laufe der Zeit die unterworfene Bevölkerung numerisch und sozial durchsetzt, desto stärker treten diese Züge hervor."

Concluding the Insular Celtic section of my paper, I would like to refer to two important syntactical features which have been discussed as evidence of a pre-IE substrate: a) the *Basic Word Order VSO* which Morris Jones 1900, 619 considered a clear indication of Hamitic influence. Pokorny 1964, a few years before his

---

28. Cf. Wagner 1959, 127: "daß das Air. zuständliche Bedeutungen noch weitgehend finit-verbal zum Ausdruck bringt, während sie im Neuir, in nominalisierter Form erscheinen."

death, defended the substrate theory against attempts at explaining *VSO* on the basis of an IE development;[29] b) initial mutations such as lenition and nasalization which arise within the context of the phrase. These Morphophonemic changes were originally caused by the final of the preceding word. Modifying typological terms, Pokorny called these changes *Anlautflexion, Gruppenflexion* or *Aufgabe der Autonomie des Einzelwortes* (loss of the autonomy of the individual word).[30] This criterion, however, does not prove very much, as the operation of sandhi within the phrase is a wide-spread linguistic phenomenon.[31] On the other hand, the special manner of expressing 'yes' and 'no' in Insular Celtic has been taken as an indication of a close connection between question and answer:[32]

(20) Welsh *A weli di y ty? Gwelaf* 'Do you see the house?' 'I see' (English 'I do, yes'); Modern Irish *Ar bhuail sé thú?* 'Did he beat you?' *Do bhuail* 'he beat' (='yes'), *Níor bhuail* 'he did not beat' (= 'no')

2. On the problem of identifying non-IE contact languages

The substrate hypothese put forward by scholars such as Morris Jones, Pokorny or Wagner have often met with scepticism[33] both for linguistic and extralinguistic reasons: as to the former, it stands to reason that morphological evidence such as the appearance of agglutinative inflection in Tocharian carries more weight than syntactical and semantic structures. The extralinguistic situation, e.e. the lack of concrete evidence from the postulated substrate languages, has an even more unfavourable effect on the hypotheses. Evans has seen this problem in connection with the unknown date of Celtic immigration to the British Isles: "For the pre-Roman period the question of language contact is exceedingly problematic, having to do with unknown non-Celtic and pre-Celtic substrata as well as the complex and vexed question of the 'coming' of the celts. It relates to the problem

---

29. Cf. especially Watkins 1963.
30. Cf. Pokorny 1927, 231ff; 1959, 154.
31. Cf. e.g., Allen 1972; Oftedal 1985; Andersen 1986.
32. Pokorny 1927, 236f.; 1959, 154.
33. Cf. e.g., Thurneysen 1930; Watkins 1963 Schmidt 1986a, 209.

of the separating out and emergence of Celtic languages at an unknown period in contact with other languages about which we have no direct and secure evidence" (1986, 106).

As to the identification of concrete material, the theory already established by Morris Jones in 1900, 618, "neo-Celtic syntax agrees with Hamitic on almost every point where it differs from Aryan" was initially accepted by Pokorny, but greatly weakened later on by the assumption of further substrates (i.e. West Caucasian and Basque). It must be admitted, however, that comparison with West Caucasian is irrelevant, as none of the various Ibero-Caucasian hypotheses has been substantiated.[34] The Basque theory, which is also difficult to prove, was presented by Pokorny 1949, 245: "Zusammen mit dem Baskischen enthält das Irische zahlreiche deutliche Spuren der längst verschwundenen Sprachen der voridg. Bewohner Westeuropas."

Although no attempt at identifying concrete substrates in Insular Celtic has been successful thus far, two linguistic arguments speak in favor of the existence of pre-IE substrates: a) the opposite direction taken by the transformations in Tocharian and Insular Celtic[35]: it does not seem probable that the typological differences—*SOV* plus agglutinative declension vs. *VSO* plus inflective declension—developed without any influence from contact languages. It may be added that the impact of non-IE (Finno-Ugrian, perhaps also Caucasian and other substrates) on Tocharian is better substantiated[36] than the postulated substrates of Insular Celtic. b) The second argument is the typological difference between Continental Celtic and Insular Celtic manifest in the *Basic Word Order VSO* in Insular Celtic in spite of the very close genetic connection between Gaulish and Brittonic:

(21) Insular Celtic *VSO* : Gaulish *SVO* (and a few instances of *SOV*) : Celtiberian

---

34. C.f Schmidt 1987b = 1987c.
35. Cf. Schmidt 1972; 1975.
36. Cf. Thomas 1985, 149ff.: "Beziehungen des Tocharischen zu den ural-altaischen und paläoasiatischen Sprachen."

(Botorrita, Peñalba de Villastar) *SOV*[37]

3. *On the position of Tocharian and Insular Celtic within the IE language family as a criterion for dating possible contacts with non-IE languages*

This section is based on two considerations: a) Leskien's principle (originally established for genetically related languages) (1876, XIII): "Die Kriterien einer engeren Gemeinschaft können nur in positiven Uebereinstimmungen der betreffenden Sprachen, die zugleich Abweichungen von den übrigen sind, gefunden werden"; b) the extension of this principle to common language contacts which genetically related languages had with foreign substrates or adstrates. To put it the other way round, if one of the genetically related contact languages has an innovation due to substrate influence which the other lacks, this may provide information as to the time of the contacts of each language with the substrate or adstrate. The application of this consideration to Insular Celtic is comparatively simple: Insular Celtic innovations which Continental Celtic lacks may possibly be of pre-Celtic, perhaps pre-IE origin. Continental Celtic cannot be fully compared with Insular Celtic because, notwithstanding the important discoveries of the last 15 years—Botorrita, Chamalières, Larzac (cf. e.g., Schmidt 1986b)–, its state of attestation remains very fragmentary. For the same reason, criteria such as e.g., the inflected prepositions (no. 11) or the periphrastic expression of 'yes' and 'no' (no. 20) carry less weight than the *Basic Word Order* (no. 21) as a typological consideration.

The position of Tocharian is much more difficult to define, since the time and circumstances of its emergence are unknown. Henning's theory, "in spite of its late appearance, Tokharian is a relatively archaic form of Indo-European. This claim

---

37. Cf. Schmidt 1980, 188f. J. Untermann's highly polemic criticism of Ködderitzsch's (1985) interpretation of Peñalba de Villastar, based on my theory of the *Basic Word Order SOV* (Untermann 1987 and 1987a, 189), and of my interpretation of Botorrita (Untermann 1987) introduces irrelevancies but does not even discuss the syntactic criterion *SOV* which (for Botorrita) has now been confirmed by J.F. Eska, "Towards an Interpretation of the Hispano-Celtic Inscription of Botorrita" (PhD thesis, Toronto 1988) 179, "The basic word order of the clause is strictly (Subject) Object Verb. . .There are no exceptions."

implies that the speakers of this group separated from their Indo-European brethren at a comparatively early date" (1978, 217)[38], is shared in principle by Gamkrelidze/Ivanov 1984, 369ff. The two Soviet scholars postulate an Anatolian-Tocharian-Italo-Celtic group, from which first Anatolian and then Tocharian branched off. Nevertheless, the investigation of its position within the IE language family remains a difficult task. The statement made by Meillet in 1914 "on ne se trompera sans doute pas beaucoup en attribuant au tokharien une place intermédiaire entre l'italo-celtique d'une part, le slave et l'arménien d'autre" (cf. Meillet 1914, 17) could not take into account the isoglosses between Tocharian and Hittite which to a certain extent consist of IE archaisms:

(22) A *e-*, B *ai-* 'to give' : Hittite *pāi-* < **pa-ai-*; A *ya-* 'to do' : Hittite *iia-*; A B *yok-* 'to drink' : Hittite *eku-*; A *kaṣt-*, B *kest* 'hunger' : Hittite *kašt-*; cf. also A *por* 'fire' < **paur* : Hittite *paḫḫur*[39] A *tkaṃ*, B *keṃ* 'earth' : Hittite *tekan*[40]

After evaluating the then known evidence from Hittite and Tocharian, Holger Pedersen 1925, 52 arrived at the conclusion "que l'italo-celtique, le phrygien, le tokharien et le hittite ont constitué dans une antiquité reculée un groupe continu de dialectes de la langue-mère."[41] On the other hand, Walter Petersen's far-reaching theory "Hittite and Tocharian must have constituted for some time a dialectic unity" has not been accepted. Benveniste, after stressing the archaic character of Tocharian (1936, 228), establishes the theory "le tokharien est un membre ancien d'un groupe préhistorique (auquel appartenait peut-être aussi le hittite) qui confinait d'une part au baltique et au slave, de l'autre au grec, à l'arménien et au thraco-phrygien" (l.c. 237). In his recent report on the position of Tocharian within the IE language family, Thomas 1985, 128ff. takes into account almost all the IE

---

38. I am grateful to T.V. Gamkrelidze for bringing Henning's article to my attention.
39. Cf. Lindeman 1970, 59f.
40. Cf. Mayrhofer 1982.
41. Cf. also Meid 1968.

languages. As to the Tocharian homeland, he follows (1986, 623) Benveniste 1936, 238 ("en gros, la région des steppes qui s'étend au sud-est de la Russie jusqu'à l'Oural") and Krause 1951, 200: "Es erscheint nach alledem möglich, ... die Urheimat (oder genauer eine Zwischenheimat) der Tocharer in einem Gebiet ungefähr zwischen Dnjepr und Ural, also ostwärts in unmittelbarer Nachbarschaft der Finnogrier zu suchen und anzunehmen, daß die Sprache der nachmaligen Tocharer zu einer gewissen Zeit bei ihrer Wanderung gen Osten nicht allein mit baltisch-slawischen, sondern auch mit finnisch-ugrischen Stämmen und Sprachen mindestens an deren südlichem Saum in Berührung gekommen ist." Thomas 1985, 136f. cites, for instance, the following Baltic and Slavic coincidences with Tocharian:

(23) a) Palatalization; b) $\bar{a}$-preterite: B *tāka* 'became' :
Lithuanian *bùvo* 'was,' *sėjo* 'sowed,' Old Church Slavonic *bъra* 'collected';[42] c) infinitive in AB *-tsi*, Baltic and Slavic *-ti*;[43] d) *l*-suffix: B *yamaṣṣälle* 'faciendus': OCS *neslъ jesmъ* 'I have done,' Armenian *sirel* 'to love,' *sireli* 'lovable'[44] etc.; e) adjectives in *-ṣi* (A), *-ṣṣe* (B) < *-skyos* : *cmol-ṣi, cmel-ṣe* 'referring to birth' : OCS *ište*, Armen. *-ači* : *durk'* 'door' : *dr-ači* 'neighbor.'[45]

The conclusiveness of these and other arguments is, however, limited for at least two reasons: a) the etymology is not always undisputed; b) most of the isoglosses are not limited to Tocharian and Baltic and/or Slavic, but occur in other languages as well. Therefore Bednarczuk 1983, 13 seems to go too far in maintaining "On the Indo-European background the greatest typological similarity to Tokharian is shown by Balto-Slavic, especially Russian and East-Baltic, which have probably been formed also on the Uralic substratum."[46] In this context one might refer to Lewy's *Betrachtung des Russischen* (1925), which results in the statement: "Es scheint mir ... nicht möglich, die Identität einer Anzahl

---

42. Cf. Lane 1970, 79, rejected by Oettinger 1984, 197.
43. Rejected by Anreiter 1984, 151, but accepted by Thomas 1985, 90.
44. Cf. Stempel 1983.
45. Cf. Zimmer 1982/83.
46. Cf. the criticism by Thomas 1986, 624.

charakteristischer Züge des Russischen mit Zügen des Finnisch-Ugrischen zu bestreiten" (Lewy 1961, 344). A comparable typological investigation of Tocharian might perhaps provide addition- al arguments for the existence of Finno-Ugrian substrates.

4. On the distribution of archaisms and innovations in Tocharian and Insular Celtic
The preceding observations have shown that the Tocharian and Insular Celtic innovations are concentrated on different linguistic categories: agglutinative declension with group inflection in Tocharian vs. *Basic Word Order VSO*, inflective declension, conjugated prepositions and a tendency to nominal periphrastic expression of stative verbs in Insular Celtic. Conservative features common to both language groups apply to the finite verb with its categories of person, tense, mood and diathesis. A remarkable similarity is the use of atonic pronouns, infixed and suffixed in Insular Celtic and suffixed in Tocharian:

(24) Old Irish *ro-m'gab* 'he has taken me,' *n-a'gnîu-sa* 'I do it,' *beirth-i* 'he bears it,' *mórth-us* 'he exalts her'; Tocharian B *wināskau-c* = A *winasām-ci* 'I adore you.'[47]

As to the relative chronology of preterite, medium and imperfect, both Tocharian and Celtic no longer correspond to the older IE type represented by Greek or Indo-Iranian. The aorist and the perfect have merged into a preterite[48], the medial functions[49] (with passive function in Tocharian) have been neutralized, and imperfect paradigms have been developed. To what degree these processes took place in the Continental Celtic languages as well is difficult to determine because of our fragmentary evidence.[50] These innovations, like the replacement of the *o*-stem nominative plural ending *-ōs* by the pronominal ending *-oi* (an analogical change which did not take place in Celtiberian), correspond to

---

47. Cf. Schmidt 1972.
48. Cf. Thomas 1957.
49. Cf. Schmidt 1972, 199; Thomas 1985, 97f.
50. Cf. Meid 1963, 79-89; Schmidt 1986b.

developments wide-spread in IE. An archaic feature common to Tocharian and Celtic is the differentiation of masculine and feminine gender of the numbers '3' and '4':

(25) Welsh *tri, tair* '3'; *pedwar, pedair* '4'; Old Irish *tri. teoir* '3'; *ceth(a)ir, cethéoir* '4'; Tocharian B *trai, tarya; śtwer, śtwāra*; A *tre, tri; śtwar* (m., f.)

An archaic feature peculiar to Tocharian is the preservation of present and preterite participles.[51] Insular Celtic, on the other hand, lacks a fully developed infinitive category and a verb 'to have.'[52] Celtic vocabulary displays archaisms in the words for 'king,' 'queen,' 'to believe' and 'to drink' (no. 26), which have been discussed as isoglosses between Italic, Celtic and Indo-Iranian since Kretschmer 1896, 125ff.

(26) IE $*rē\hat{g}$-s, $*rē\hat{g}$-$nī$; $*\hat{k}red$-$dheh^1$; $*pi$-ph^3-e-ti
Within the Tocharian vocabulary, the Hittite-Tocharian isoglosses (no. 22) occupy a special position.

5. Summary

a) The main features caused by substrate influences in Tocharian are agglutinative declension, group inflection and the development of a localistic case system (with locative, ablative, allative, perlative). Its *Basic Word Order SOV* may turn out to be inherited from IE. Insular Celtic features which do not correspond to the IE type are the *Basic Word Order VSO*, conjugated prepositions and an increasing tendency towards periphrasis.

b) Although the identification of non-IE substrate languages is difficult in the case of Tocharian and quite impossible for Insular Celtic, both languages must have had

---

51. Cf. Krause/Thomas 1960, 261: B *-ñca*, A *-nt*, B *-mane*, A *-māṃ*, BA *-u*, B *-au*, A *-o*.
52. Cf. Schmidt 1986a, 200.

contacts with pre-IE substrates. In Celtic, the differences between Continental Celtic, which is attested in antiquity, and Insular Celtic, going back to the early Middle Ages, may be partly explained as the result of a pre-IE influence on Insular Celtic. Moreover, the divergent transformations of Tocharian and Insular Celtic may be plausibly explained as a result of their different substrates.

c) The different *Basic Word Order* of such closely related languages as Gaulish (predominantly SVO) and Brittonnic (VSO) may be an indication of substrate influence on Insular Celtic. As to Tocharian, the question of a Finno-Ugrian substrate needs to be thoroughly investigated.

d) In the development of the verbal systems, both languages generally follow wide-spread IE patterns. Archaisms preserved in both languages are evidence by the differentiation of masculine and feminine gender in the numbers '3' and '4' and by the use of infixed and suffixed pronouns. Celtic and Tocharian differ as to other archaic features, i.e. vocabulary (see no. 26 for Insular Celtic and no. 22 for Tocharian), *Basic Word Order* (SOV in Tocharian vs. VSO in Insular Celtic), the lack of a fully developed infinitive and of a verb 'to have' in Insular Celtic and the preservation of participles in Tocharian.

Bibliography

Abaev, V.I.
  A Grammatical Sketch of Ossetic. The Hague, 1964.
Abeghian, A.
  Neuarmenische Grammatik. Berlin. 1936.
Allen, W.S.
  Sandhi. The Hague. 1962, ^{2}1972.
Andersen, H., ed.
  Sandhi Phenomena in the Languages of Europe. Berlin. 1986.
Anreiter P.P.
  Bemerkungen zu den Reflexen indogermanischer Dentale im Tocharischen.

Innsbruck. 1984.

Bednarczuk, L.

"Non-Indo-European Features of Tocharian." *Studia Indo-Iranica*. Th. Probożniak septuagenaria = PrKJK 52. Wrocław 1983. 11-13.

Benveniste, E.

"Tokharien et Indo-Européen." in Arntz, H., ed. *Germanen und Indogermanen. Fs. H. Hirt II*. Heidelberg. 1936. 227-240.

Boretzky, N.

"Sprachkontakte." in Koch, W.A. *Perspektiven der Linguistik I*. Stuttgart. 1973. 134-158.

Bossong, G.

"Syntax und Semantik der Fundamentalrelation. Das Guaraní als Sprache des aktiven Typs." *Lingua 50*. 1980. 359-379.

Bouda, K.

"Zwei baskische Wörter." *Caucasica 10*. 1932. 95-99.

Bräuer, H.

Slavische Sprachwissenschaft III. Formenlehre. 2. Teil. Berlin. 1969.

Comrie, B.

Language Universals and Linguistic Typology. Oxford. 1981.

Deeters, G.

"Die Stellung der Kharthwelsprachen unter den Kaukasischen Sprachen." *RK Bedi Kartlisa 23*. Paris. 1957. 12-16.

"Sprache und Methoden ihrer Erforschung." in Adam, L. and Trimborn, H. *Lehrbuch der Völkerkunde*. ³Stuttgart. 1958. 139-158.

"Die kaukasischen Sprachen." in *Hdb. d. Orientalistik*. I. Abteil. 7. Bd. Leiden - Köln. 1963. 1-79.

Dillon, M.

"Nominal Predicates in Irish." *ZCP 16*. 1927. 313-356.

Evans, D.E.

"The Celts in Britain (up to the formation of the Brittonic languages)." in Schmidt, K.H. unter Mitwirkung von Ködderitzsch, R. *Geschichte und Kultur der Kelten*. Heidelberg. 1986. 102-115.

Finck, F.N.

Die Haupttypen des Sprachbaus. Leipzig. 1910.

Gamkrelidze, T.V. and Ivanov, V.V. *Indoevropejskij jazyk i indoevropejcy. I, II.* Tbilisi. 1984.

Garibjan, A.S.
Kratkij kurs armjanskogo jazyka. Erevan. 1958.

Gleason Jr., H.A.
An Introduction to Descriptive Linguistics. Rev. Ed. New York. 1966.

Greene, D.
"The Making of Insular Celtic." in *Proceedings of the Second International Congress of Celtic Studies.* Cardiff. 1966. 123-136.

Haugen, E.
Studies by Einar Haugen. The Hague. 1972.

Henning, W.B.
"The First Indo-Europeans in History." in Ulmen, G.L., ed. *Society and History. Essays presented in Honor of K.A. Wittfogel.* The Hague. 1978. 215-230.

Ködderitzsch, R.
Review of Villar 1983. *Kratylos* 30. 1985. 78-83.

"Die große Felsinschrift von Peñalba de Villastar." in Ölberg, H.M. and Schmidt, G., edd. unter Mitarbeit von H. Bothien. *Sprachwissenschaftliche Forschungen. Fs. J. Knobloch.* Innsbruck. 1985a. 211-222.

Krause, W.
"Zur Frage nach dem nichtindogermanischen Substrat des Tocharischen." KZ 69. 1951. 185-203.

Tocharisch: Hdb. d. Orientalistik. IV. Bd. 3. Abschnitt. Leiden. 1955.

, Thomas, W. *Tocharisches Elementarbuch. Band I. Grammatik.* Heidelberg. 1960.

Kretschmer, P.
Einleitung in die Geschichte der griechischen Sprache. Göttingen. 1896.

Lane. G.S.
"Tocharian: Indo-European and Non-Indo-European Relationships." in Cardona, G., Hoenigswald, H.M. and Senn, A., edd. *Indo-European and Indo-Europeans.* Philadelphia.1970. 73-88.

Leskien, A.

Die Declination im Slawisch-Litauischen und Germanischen. Leipzig. 1876. Nachdruck. 1963.

Lewy, E.

"Zur Frage der Sprachmischung." in *Beiträge z. Sprach- und Völkerkunde. Fs. A. Hillebrandt.* 1913. 110-120 = Lewy. 1961. 1-9.

"Betrachtung des Russischen." *ZSlPh* 2. 1925. 415-437. Lewy. 1961. 330-346

Kleine Schriften. Berlin. 1961.

Magometov, A.A.

Tabasaranskij jazyk. Tbilisi. 1965.

Mallinson, G. and Blake, B.J.   *Language Typology: Cross-linguistic Studies in Syntax.* Amsterdam. 1981.

Martinet, A.

Economie des changements phonétiques. Berne. 1955.

McLendon, S.

"Ergativity, Case and Transitivity in Eastern Pomo." *IJAL* 44. 1978-79. 1-9.

Mayrhofer, M.

"Ergebnisse einer Überprüfung des indogermanischen Ansatzes 'Thorn': *Anzeiger phil.-hist. Klasse d. Österr. Akad. d. Wiss.* 119. Jhg. 1982. 237-255.

Meid, W.

Die indogermanischen Grundlagen der altirischen absoluten und konjunkten Verbalflexion. Wiesbaden. 1963.

Indogermanisch und Keltisch. Innsbruck. 1968.

Meillet, A.

"Le tokharien." *Indogermanisches Jahrbuch* 1. 1913. 1-19.

Review of Ἀντίδωρον. *Fs. J. Wackernagel.* in *BSL. Anzeiger.* 25. 1925. 46-49.

Morris Jones, J.

"Pre-Aryan syntax in Insular Celtic." in Rhŷs. J. and Brynmor-Jones, D. *The Welsh People.* London. 1900. [4]1906.

Oettinger, N.

"Zur Diskussion um den lateinischen ā-Konjunktiv." *Glotta.* 62. 1984. 187-201.

Oftedal, M.

Lenition in Celtic and in Insular Spanish. Tromsø. 1985.

Onian, A.

Svanskie teksty na lāšxskom narečii. Petrograd. 1917.

Pedersen, H.

Le groupement des dialectes indoeuropéennes. København. 1925.

Petersen, W.

"Hittite and Tocharian." *Language.* 9. 1933. 12-34.

Pokorny, J.

"Das nicht-indogermanische Substrat im Irischen." *ZCP.* 16. 1927. 95-144; 231-266; 363-394; 17. 1928. 373-388; 18. 1930. 233-248.

"Zum nicht-indogermanischen Substrat im Inselkeltischen." *Die Sprache.* 1. 1949. 235-245.

"Keltische Urgeschichte und Sprachwissenschaft." *Die Sprache.* 5. 1959. 153-164.

"Zur Anfangsstellung des inselkeltischen Verbums." *MSS.* 16. 1964. 75-80.

Sapir, E.

Language. 1921; Harvest Book edition. 1949.

Schmidt, K.H.

"Agglutination und Postposition im Tocharischen." *MSS.* 25. 1969. 105-112.

"Tocharisch und Keltisch, historisch-vergleichend und typologisch betrachtet." in Pilch, H. and Thurow, J. (edd.). *Indo-Celtica. Gedächtnisschrift für A. Sommerfelt.* Munich. 1972. 195-200.

"Das indogermanische Kasusmorphem und seine Substituenten." in Rix, H. (ed.) *Flexion und Wortbildung. Akten d. V. Fachtagung d. Indogerm. Ges.* Wiesbaden. 1975. 268-286.

"Continental Celtic as an Aid to the Reconstruction of Proto-Celtic." *KZ.* 94. 1980. 172-197.

Review of Villar. 1983. *IF.* 91. 1986. 344-347.

"The Celtic Languages in their European Context." in Evans, D.E. (ed.) *Proceedings of the Seventh International Congress of Celtic Studies.* Oxford. 1983. Oxford. 1986a. 199-221.

"Zur Rekonstruktion des Keltischen. Festlandkeltisches und inselkeltisches Verbum." *ZCP.* 41. 1986b. 159-179.

"Zur semantischen Differenzierung des indogermanischen Kasussystems im Tocharischen." *TIES.* 1. 1987. 139-151.

"The Indo-European Background of the Classical Armenian Noun Declension."

AArmL. 8. 1987a. 35-47.

"Die beiden antiken Iberiae, sprachwissenschaftlich gesehen." *KZ.* 100. 1987b. 109-134. (= Schmidt 1987c).

"The Two Ancient Iberias from the Linguistic Point of View." in Gorrochategui, J., Melena, J.L. and Santos, J. (edd.). *Studia Palaeohispanica. Actas del IV coloquio sobre lenguas y culturas paleohispánicas.* Vitoria, Gasteiz. 1987c). 105-121. (= Schmidt. 1987b).

"Probleme der tocharischen Deklination." in *Studia W. Thomas.* Munich. 1988. 215-222.

Schönfelder, K.H.

Probleme der Völker- und Sprachmischung. Halle, S. 1956.

Schulze, W.

"Zum Tocharischen." *Ung. Jbb.* 7. 1927. 168-177. = Schulze. 1966. 248-257.

Kleine Schriften. ²Göttingen. 1966.

Silverstein, M.

"Hierarchy of Features and Ergativity." in Dixon, R.M.W. (ed.) *Grammatical Categories in Australian Languages.* Canberra. 1976. 112-171.

Skalička, V.

"Ein 'typologisches Konstrukt.'" *TLP.* 2. 1966. 157-163.

Stempel, R.

Die infiniten Verbalformen des Armenischen. Frankfurt a.M. 1983.

Thomas, W.

Der Gebrauch der Vergangenheitstempora im Tocharischen. Wiesbaden. 1957.

"Zweigliedrige Wortverbindungen im Tocharischen." *Orbis.* 21. 1972. 429-470.

Die Erforschung des Tocharischen (1960-1984). Stuttgart. 1985.

"Zum Problem der sprachlichen Beziehungen zwischen Tocharisch und Baltoslavisch." in Olesch, R. and Rothe, H. (edd.). *Festschrift für H. Bräuer.* Köln-Wien. 1986. 609-624.

Thurneysen, R.

"Lat. 'I' = Ir. Edón." *ZCP.* 18. 1930. 427-428.

Topuria, V.

"Svanskij jazyk." in *Jazyki narodov SSSR.* 4. Mokva. 1967. 77-94.

Untermann, J.

"Lusitanisch, Keltiberisch, Keltisch." in Gorrochatequi, J. et. al. 1987. [cf. Schmidt, K.H. 1987c]. 57-76.

Review of "Sprachwissenschaftliche Forschungen." [cf. Ködderitzsch 1985a]: *BNF. NF.* 22. 1987a. 188f.

Van Windekens, A.J.

Le tokharien confronté avec les autres langues indo-européennes. I. II, 1. II, 2. Louvain. 1976. 1979. 1982.

Villar, F.V.

Ergatividad, acusatividad y género en la familia lingüistica indoeuropea. Salamanca. 1983.

"Ergativity and animate/inanimate gender in Indo-European." *KZ.* 97. 1984. 167-196.

Wachernagel, J.

Vorlesungen über Syntax. Erste Reihe. Basel. 1926. ^{2}1950.

Wagner, H.

Das Verbum in den Sprachen der britischen Inseln. Tübingen. 1959.

"Near Eastern and African Connections with the Celtic World." in O'Driscoll, R. (ed.) *The Celtic Consciousness.* Portlaoise. 1982. 51-67.

Watkins, C.

Indo-European Origins of the Celtic Verb. 1. The Sigmatic Aorist. Dublin. 1962.

"Preliminaries to a Historical and Comparative Analysis of the Syntax of the Old Irish Verb." *Celtica.* 6. 1963. 1-49.

Weinrich, U.

Languages in Contact. 1953. ^{4}The Hague. 1966.

Winter, W.

"Tocharian and Proto-Indo-Europen." *LPosn.* 25. 1982. 1-11.

Zimmer, St.

Die Satzstellung des finiten Verbs im Tocharischen. The Hague. 1976.

"Die Funktion der tocharischen ṣi/ṣṣe-Adjektive." *KZ.* 96. 1982, 83. 277-289.

THE MAKE-UP OF THE ARMENIAN UNCLASSIFIED SUBSTRATUM

John A. C. Greppin
(Cleveland State University)

The Armenian substratum is a many splendored constellation, made from those languages formerly spoken in easternmost Anatolia. They first entered Armenian during the prehistoric period, certainly by the beginning of the first millennium BC, and continued their impulses up to the present day. The best known early component is the Iranian, a stratum that first appeared during the Parthian period in the mid first millennium and which has been well described since the time of Hübschmann (*Armenisch Grammatik*, 1897), though considerably refined in the etymological works of Hratchia Adjarian (*Hayerēn armatakan baṙaran*, Yerevan 1926-1935). This Iranian infestation has continued throughout the life of the Armenian language and such a word as Arm. *p'law* can be shown to be a medieval intrusion, from Per. پلو *plaw* 'pilaf,' just as such a word as Arm. *astuac* 'god,' apparently intruded during the most early period of Iranian contract (Bailey 1985). Greek and Syriac also had their place in the early Armenian lexicon, stemming from the beginning of the Christian period (405 and following). But this intrusion was, by and large, a literary one, comprising words that appeared in the Armenian translation of Greek and Syriac religious texts. An odd example is Arm. *bosor* 'blood' which is a Hebrew word, בָּצְרָה (*bātsrāh*), mistaken in the Greek writings of St. Cyril of Jerusalem as a word meaning 'red, bloody' and carried over as Arm. *bosor* 'blood' by a bewildered Armenian translator from St. Cyril's βοσόρ. And though some words settled firmly into the common Armenian lexicon (Syr. ܕܪܐ [*dārā*] 'age, century,' Gk. λίτρα 'pound'), most words were not actively used, or were of narrow ecclesiastical function (Gk. καθολικός, Syr. ܫܒܬܐ (*šabbĕθā*) 'sabbath.')

Starting perhaps in the fourteenth century Turkish words made their entrance, but before them, certainly from the ninth century, Arab words came in, many of them part of the vocabulary of the natural sciences that the Armenians were acquiring. There were Caucasian words, too, frequently Georgian, the language of a people who had an energetic intellectual class and a vital literature that began to appear not long after that of the Armenian. Lesser Caucasian languages necessarily made their intrusion, too, words noted in Udi, Lezghian and other of the East Caucasian languages, though their path into Armenian cannot be clearly drawn. The last major intrusion was European, described first as 'Frankish'; those were the words of the Crusaders that had an effect: Arm. *baron* 'sir, mister' is one of the most vigorous of that later infusion.

Altogether, we can account for the origin of about three quarters of the Armenian vocabulary, either from Indo-European or by loan from a known source; the remaining one fourth, though, is a yawning and intriguing void. For the most part it represents vocabulary that existed in Armenian from the earliest fifth century, in the Bible or other primary texts. Some of it has been identified as Hurro-Urartian, and Luwian has been suggested for a smaller part. The Hurro-Urartian part seems clear, and we need only cite Hurr. *hinzuri*, Arm. *xnjor* 'apple,' or Urartian *ult'u*, Arm. *ułt* 'camel.' From Luwian we can suggest *wašu* 'good.' Arm. *vaš* 'bravo'; HL *aparanti* 'future,' Arm. *aṙarni* 'id.' Numerous other words are known from the Hittite lexicon: Hitt. *kurkurāi-* 'maim, mutilate,' Arm. *k'rk'rem* 'destroy.'

But those words that can be cited in Hurro-Urartian and Luwian (or Hittite) are actually few; at best we have diagnosed thirty Luwian and Hittite words, and the Hurro-Urartian component numbers only fifteen. And though the Hurro-Urartian component is not excessively small, recalling the limited corpus of Hurrian and Urartian vocabulary we have, the Hittite and Luwian segments are somewhat limited, bearing in mind the considerable bulk of that vocabulary which we now control. The Hittite and Luwian component, if it is legitimate, must reflect only a trivial contact with the Luwians in Cilician area during the first millennium BC. The Hurro-Urartian component, however, is relatively more vigorous, and is supported by the contact between the early Armenians and the Urartians in early historical times. We should in time be able to expand this lexical component more.

Whatever their source, these words of the unknown substratum have a wide semantic spread. For the purpose of this paper, I have examined all the roots in Armenian beginning with the letter *b-*. That vocabulary can be derived from the same sources —Indo-European, Iranian, Greek, Syriac, Arabic, Caucasian, Turkish and Frankish— as can the whole of the Armenian vocabulary. And for words beginning with *b-* for which there are no etymologies, we also note a wide semantic range. These words, which lack etymologies, are as follows.

բագ (*bag*) 'barnacle, snout.' Mandakuni 1x, 5th C.

բալախ (*balax*) 'vanity.' Ephraim 2x, 5th C.

բածին (*bacin*) 'type of fish.' Mandakuni 2x, 5th C.

բակ (*bak*) 'porch, portico.' Philo and following, 5th C.

բահ (*bah*) 'spade, hoe.' Agathangelos and following, 5th C.

բահդակ (*bahłak*) 'something you carry things in or on or with.' Sebeos 1x, 7th C.

բաղ (*bał*) 'united, joined.' Ephraim and following, 5th C.

բալարջ (*balarj*) 'unleavened.' Bible (31x) and following, 5th C.

բաղբաջ (*bałbaj*) 'senile speech.' Seberianos and following, 5th C.

բաղթ (*bałt'*) 'a type of poison.' Dionysios Thrax 1x, 6th C.

բաղձ (*bałj*) 'desire, longing.' Pseudo Khorenatsi and following, 7th C.

բաղտի (*bałti*) 'something bad.' Hexaemeron 1x, 5th C.

բաճկոն (*bačkon*) 'vest, waistcoat.' Bible 4x and following, 5th C.

բանակ (*banak*) 'encampment.' Bible 100x and following, 5th C.

բանդագուշել (*bandagušel*) 'to rave, be delirious.' Bible 1x and following, 5th C.

բանջար (*banjar*) 'beet root, *Beta vulgaris* L. var *rapa*.' Bible 22x and following, 5th C. Note Arabic بنجر (*banjar*) 'id,' as well as Turk. *bancar, pancar*; Gk. παντζάρι 'id.'

բաջաղեմ (*bajałem*) 'to talk nonsense.' Hexaemeron and following, 5th C.

բառաչ (*baṙač'*) 'bellowing, a roar.' Hexaemeron and following, 5th C.

բարամբունք (*barambunk'*) 'bars of a cage.' Chrysostom 1x, 5th C.

բարաշխ (*barašx*) 'hard, stiff.' Philo 1x, 5th C. Arm. *pind* more common: Bible 10x.

բարբա(ն)ջ (*barba[n]j*) 'idle talk, nonsense.' Hexaemeron and following, 5th C. (Saradjeva 1977:37.)

բարբարել (*barbarel*) 'to hesitate.' Bible 1x and following, 5th C. Arm. *varanel* (Bible 7x) and *tarakusil* (Bible 13) more common.

բարգաւաճ (*bargawač*) 'refined, civilized, superb.' Bible 1x and following, 5th C.

բարդ (*bard*) 'hay rick.' Bible 1x, and following, 5th C.

բարի (*bari*) 'good.' Bible 400x and following, 5th C.

բարկ (*bark*) 'sharp, acrid.' Agathangelos and following, 5th C.

բարունակ (*barunak*) 'vine branch.' Bible 1x and following, 5th C.

բարուրք (*barurkʻ*) 'false accusation.' Chrysostom and following, 5th C.

բարք (*barkʻ*) 'manners, customs.' Bible 7x and following, 5th C.

բաւիղ (*bawił*) 'maze, labyrinth.' Eusebius and following, 5th C.

բբչալ (*bbčʻal*) 'lion's roar.' Chrysostom and following, 5th C.

բեճազն (*benazn*) unknown word but apparently 'a material from which a staircase can be made.' Pseude-Khorenatsi 1x, 7th C.

բեստ (*best*) in the word *hastabest* 'strongly built.' Hexaemeron and following, 5th C. Arm. *urax aṙnel* (Bible 25x) and *urax linel* (Bible 175x) more commone.

բերկրիմ (*berkrim*) 'to rejoice.' Bible 10x and following, 5th C.

բերրի (*berri*) 'fruitful.' Agathangelos and following, 5th C. Arm. *ptułaber* (Bible 5x) more common.

բեւեկն (*bewekn*) 'turpentine.' Bible 1x and following, 5th C.

բեւեռ (*beweṙ*) '(metal) nail.' Bible 9x and following, 5th C.

բզզել (*bzzel*) 'to buzz.' Chrysostom and following, 5th C. Onomatopoetic.

բեճ/բեջ (*běč/běj*) 'the back or shoulders; the handle of a weaver's comb.' Chrysostom and following, 5th C.

բժժանք (*bžžankʻ*) 'talisman.' Bible 1x and following, 5th C.

բիբ (*bib*) 'pupil of the eye.' Bible 6x and following, 5th C.

բիծ (*bic*) 'spot, blemish.' Bible 3x and following, 5th C.

բիտ (*bit*) 'spur of a rooster.' Hexaemeron and following, 5th C.

բիր (*bir*) 'stick, cudgel.' Bible 7x and following, 5th C.

բիրտ (*birt*) 'one who exhibits awkward behavior, a bumpkin.' Eusebius and following, 5th C. Possibly a neologism; cf. Eng. 'twerp, jerk.'

բլիթ (*blitʻ*) 'type of bun.' Bible 5x and following literature, 5th C.

բլշակ (*blšak*) of unknown meaning but perhaps 'something to do with the parts of a dining table, or something that is placed upon that table.' Bible 1x, 5th C.

բլուր (*blur*) 'hill.' Bible 75x and following, 5th C.

բծիծ (*bcic*) 'louse.' Nonnos 1x, 6th C.

բղետ (*błet*) 'speckles.' Philo 1x, 5th C. (Djahukian 1965:252.)

բնիոն (*bnion*) 'a small coin.' Bible 1x, 5th C. The Greek word in the New Testament which Arm. *bnion* replaces is λεπτόν 'a small coin,' and no Greek word approaches in form a hellenophonic *bnion*.

բոլոր (*bolor*) 'all.' Bible 13x and following, 5th C. Arm. *amenayn* considerably more common.

բոկ (*bok*) 'barefoot.' Bible 4x and following, 5th C.

բողբոջ (*botboj*) 'bud, sprout.' Bible 2x and following, 5th C. Arm. *saṙawil* more common; Bible 22x.

բոյթ (*boyt'*) 'thumb.' Bible 1x and following, 5th C. (Djahukian 1965.252)

բոյլ (*boyl*) 'an assemblage.' Parp and following, 5th C.

բոյն (*boyn*) 'a nest.' Bible 12x and following, 5th C.

բոյսբուսիլ (*boysbusil*) 'be troubled.' Zgon and following literature, 5th C.

բով (*bov*) 'forge.' Bible 8x and following, 5th C. (Eichner, 1978.155).

բովիճայք (*bovičayk'*) 'type of spice, incense.' Khorenatsi and following, 5th C.

բոտոտ (*botot*) 'grub, worm.' Bible 1x and following, 5th C.

բոր (*bor*) 'leprosy.' Bible in form *borotut'iwn* 30x and following, 5th C.

բորբ (*borb*) 'brightness.' Shirakuni and following, 7th C.

բորենի (*boreni*) 'hyena.' Bible 1x and following, 5th C.

բոց (*boc'*) 'a flame, a great light.' Bible 30x and following, 5th C.

բուշտ (*bušt*) 'abscess.' Plato and following, 6th C.

բուռն (*buṙn*) 'fist.' Bible 17x and following, 5th C. (Čop, 1973.33)

բուրդ (*burd*) 'wool.' Bible 1x and following, 5th C. Arm. *asr* ('fleece') more common; Bible 10x.

բուք (*buk'*) 'snowstorm.' Chrysostom and following, 5th C. Arm. *jiwnaber* more common; Bible 2x.

բրշոպ (*bršop*) 'tumultuous.' Buzand 1x, 5th C.

բրդել (*brdel*) 'to crumble.' Bible 5x and following, 5th C.

բրուտ (*brut*) 'potter.' Bible 16x and following, 5th C. Taken as a loan from Hittite (?): Hitt. *purut* 'clay,' (Greppin 1982.70).

բօթ (*bōt'*) 'loud lamentations.' Bible 1x and following, 5th C.

These words have a wide semantic spread, and I have grouped them below into five categories. At the end of each category I have put two percentages, the first denoting the frequency those words of that semantic range appear in the whole lexicon, and the second standing for the frequency they appear in that part of the lexicon beginning with *b-* (I have rounded off the the nearest 5%, and for this reason the second column does not equal 100%.)

CLASSIFICATION OF SUBSTRATUM WORDS

1. Verbs:
    rave, babble, hesitate, rejoice, buzz, be troubled, crumble. 10%/10%.
2. Adjectives:
    varied, united, hard, acrid, good, refined, fruitful, all, tumultuous, unleavened, barefoot. 15%/15%.
3. Nouns for living things, or products derived from a living thing, or associated principally with living things:
    barnacle, a type of fish, beet root, vine branch, turpentine, louse, bud, type of spice, grub, hyena, hay rick, a poison, rooster's spur, leprosy, wool, thumb, abcess, pupil of the eye, snout, fist. 20%/25%.
4. Nouns representing tangible things:
    porch, spade/hoe, vest, encampment, cage bars, maze, (metal) nail, handle of a weaver's comb, talisman, spot, stick, bumpkin, type of bun, hill, coin, assemblage, nest, forge, flame, abcess, snowstorm, potter. 40%/30%.
5. Nouns representing intangible things:
    desire, roar, babble, perjury, customs, lion's roar, speckles, din, brightness, lamentations, senile speech. 15%/15%.

With the technology we have had up till now, having exhausted our lexical inventories of Hurro-Urartian and Hittito-Luwian, there has been no way to analyze more fully this unknown bulk of Armenian vocabulary. However, with the development of a comparative phonology for the East Caucasian languages, and an etymological dictionary based on that phonological study though not yet in print, we now have a way potentially to recreate lost Hurro-Urartian vocabulary. This will surely give us insights into this bulk of words beginning with Arm. *b-*.

The process that will reconstruct this new vocabulary is dependent on the theory (Diakonoff and Starostin 1985) that Hurrian and Urartian are ancient members of what is now the East Caucasian (EC) group. We thus can construct a Proto-Hurro-Urartian/Proto-East Caucasian (PHU-PEC) that summarizes both those ancient cuneiform languages as well as those twenty-five living languages of the Eastern Caucasus. These latter are broken down into five groups:

1. Avar

2. Andi (Andi, Botlikh, Godoberi, Karata, Bagval, Tindi, Chamalal)

3. Dido (Dido, Khvarsh, Hinukh, Bezhty, Hunzib)

4. Lak and Dargwa

5. Lezghian (Archi, Tabasaran, Agul, Rutul, Tsakhur, Budukh, Khinalug, Udi, Lezghian, Kryz)

Selecting, from any of the living languages of the East Caucasus, a word that approaches in shape an Armenian word, yet because of the differences in shape cannot be a loan word into Armenian from the EC languages, we would take that word back to its possible Proto-EC form; from there we can recreate a Proto-HU form, and ultimately a theoretical Hurrian or Urartian form. If this reconstructed HU form corresponds to an extant Armenian form, we can argue that this reconstructed term constitutes the form of the HU word that came into Armenian by loan in the first millennium BC or earlier. Thus, though we cannot offer, in this present paper, further solutions to the problems of the Armenian substrat, we can propose a new methodology for seeking it out.

A diagram of that movement is as follows:

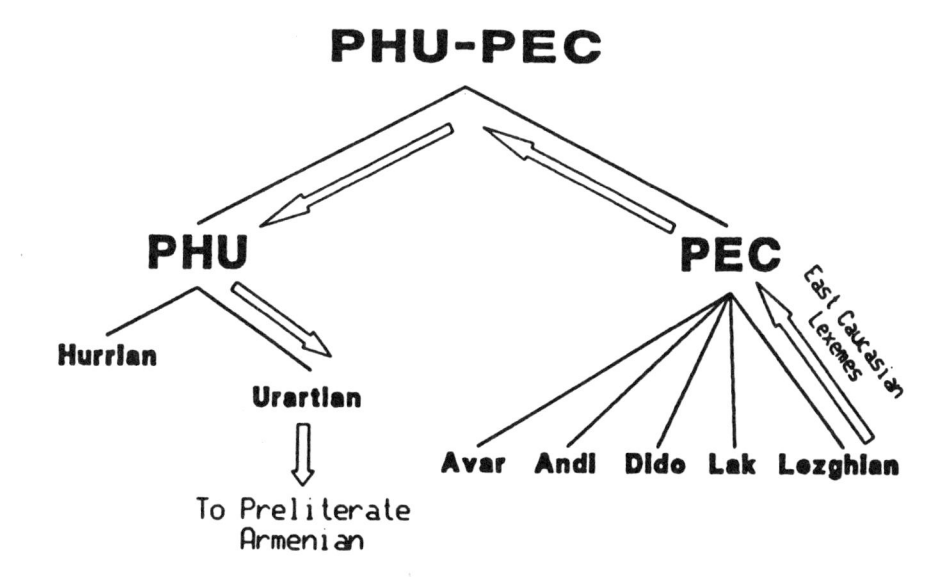

PHU-PEC

PHU **PEC**

Hurrian

Urartian

Avar Andi Dido Lak Lezghian

East Caucasian Lexemes

To Preliterate Armenian

BIBLIOGRAPHY:

Bailey, Harold W.
    1985. "*Astuvāk* 'powerful.'" *South Asian Studies* 2:65-67.

Čop, Bojan.
    1973. "Les isoglosses italo-grecques et la préhistoire des peuples balkaniques." *Godišnjak, kniga X, Centar za balkanološka ispitivanja knjiga* 8, Sarajevo, Akademija nauka i umjetnosti Bosne i Hercegovine.

Diakonoff, Igor M. and Sergei A. Starostin.
    1985. *Hurro-Urartian as an Eastern Caucasian Language*. Kitzinger. Munich.

Djahukian, Gevorg B. (Ջահուկյան, Գևորգ Բ.)
    1965. "Ստուգաբանություններ" ՊԲՀ (1)251-261

Eichner, Heiner.
    1978. "Die urindogermanische Wurzel *H^2reu- 'hell machen.'" *Die Sprache* 24:144-162.

Greppin, John A. C.
    1982. "The Anatolian Substrata in Armenian —An Interim Report." *Annual of Armenian Linguistics* 3:1982.65-72.

Saradjeva, Ludviga A. (Сараджева, Людвига А.)
    1977. "Индоевропейские лексические единицы характеризующие речь, и их отражение в древнеармянском и славянских языках." Вестник общественных наук (10)34-45.

THE INDO-EUROPEAN HORSE

By Eric P. Hamp

Sadly, to the memory of George Walsh

The sheep was in some measure (as was also the goat) domesticated about 11000 years ago.[1] This is a date well before our assured reconstruction of Indo-European, or Indo-Hittite, and almost surely before the earliest level to which our internal reconstructions of PIE, with or without a version of the glottalic theory, would lead us.

The horse belongs to a much later level of domestication, to as early as the sixth millennium B.C. (Bökönyi 1987:136). That date corresponds closely to the time level that we must assume for our classical PIE reconstructions, with or without an Indo-Hittite genetic node or time elapse.

The morphology of our Indo-European reconstructions corresponds well to this archaeological chronology. I have pointed out some time ago (*Science* 179, 30 March 1973, 1279-80)[2] that morphologically $*g^w e^{\gamma}w$-'bovine,' $*^{\gamma}w\acute{e}ui$- 'sheep' (:Arm. *hovi-w* 'shepherd'), **sulH* - 'swine,' and **k̂uon* - 'dog' display old-layer Indo-European configurations, while **ek̂uo* - 'horse' betrays a much more recent morphology in the prehistory of Indo-European; that while the former group (esp. the first two terms) are structurally opaque, the term for the horse is visibly "not a simplex, but a derivative of something else," and as a thematic stem represents a rather recent layer of noun formation; that the structural linguistic chronology strikingly paralleled that indicated by the radiocarbon measurements then available.

At that time I was not prepared to hazard a guess at the source of the derivation which yielded **ek̂uo-*. I believe that I have meantime learned sufficiently more of the grammatical rules of Indo-European noun (and adjective) derivation to make a worthwhile conjecture for this instance. That is to say, I propose a semantically plausible source in the known Indo-European lexicon, an analysis of the structure of that source, a known grammatical rule to operate on that structure (all of these observations respecting known phonological constraints and developments) to yield the observed Indo-European output *eḱuo- (expressed in conventional terms).

We shall start from an adjective meaning 'swift, celer, uelox'; note that our basis of derivation is an adjective, not a verb-base. The phonological shape of this Indo-European adjective is assured by the equation Indic āśú- = Avest, āsu- = Gk ὠκύς . Related forms are Lat. ōcior (comparative), Welsh di-awc > diog 'slow, lazy' (a privative, probably an *s-stem). We may therefore reconstruct an Indo-European adjective *ōḱú-, whose idiosyncrasies have, however, not been sufficient appreciated.

Since a form *ōḱú- cannot be in zero grade of any base, this antonymic adjective fails to conform to the canonical shape of its class; see my study of adjectives of this class (Hamp, 1983). "A morphological law," Lingua 61, 1-8.

It is also a known rule of Indo-European[3] that such adjectives in *-ú- may not be employed as final elements in a compound and that in their stead an *-es- stem appears. Greek conforms to this rule by forming the compound ποδώκης , which is attested in Homer in all case inflexions except the gen. pl.; see the attached tabulation of a computer search, which includes some informative fixed locutions. It is of course also possible that ποδώκης was an innovation in Greek, since this rule was productive at an early stage of that language. However, we must also note the conflicting formation of Indic prāśú- (pra+), which shows a final u-stem.

There can be no doubt that in late Indo-European *ōḱú- was divergent in its structural form and in its grammatical behavior.

We must also ask eventually what the interpretation of the *[ō] is to be. I happen to believe that there was no such thing as Indo-European vṛddhi outside of a few restricted morphological situations. Therefore, if the sequence were simply *oʔ we might expect with insertion of e a resulting *eʔ > *[ē]. A sequence such as *ho is ruled out since e-insertion would yield *he > *[a]. If *fʷ were next to the vowel we might expect *e not to appear under any circumstance. As we shall see, *fʷeʔ at a sufficiently early date offers us a possibility that the foregoing do not.

Let us now turn to the Latin evidence,[4] in some ways surely the most archaic. Here we find the defective comparative ōcior and superlative ōcissimus, with the archaic hapax ōximē; no positive from this base occurs. Remember that in these forms we expect morphologically an e-vocalism; therefore, a stem *fʷeʔḱ-ios- would be quite in order. Alongside these we have the valuable rare compounded forms acupedius[5] and accipiter, the latter supposedly conflated with accipiō. DELL is surely correct in seeing a zero grade acu- < *əḱu- in these forms. The lacking positive to ōcior must, therefore, have dropped out either because of its radically different initial which produced suppletion[6] or because of an unwanted homophony with 'sharp' or because of both.

We see, then, that in late (or earlier?) Indo-European there were two competing forms *ōḱú- and *əḱú-. The latter was certainly the older, and justified by rule; it must have had the earlier, and underlying, shape *fʷʔḱ-ú-. The former was the encroaching form levelled on the distinctive comparative. The presence of both of these made the stem shape uncertain: either *Base-*u*- or *Base (ending in *u*-). Speakers could therefore create well formed grammatical complexes at their option in this respect.

To summarize thus far:

$$*\hat{k}^w e\text{?}k\text{-} (> [\bar{o}\acute{k}\text{-}]) \quad \hat{k}w\text{?}\acute{k}\text{-}u\text{-} \quad \hat{k}we\text{?}\acute{k}(\text{-})\acute{u}\text{-}$$
$$\hat{k}we\text{?}\acute{k}(\text{-})\acute{u}\text{-}$$

Note that Latin seems to have conserved such phonological sequences: *apiō aptus* : -*ēpi* = Hitt. *epzi*

	< *ap-	: *ēp-
	< *ʔʔp-	: *ʔeʔp-
≠	*dent*-'tooth'	: *ed*- 'eat' = Hitt. *ad-anzi* ; *ed*-
	< *ʔd-	:*ʔed-

We must next observe another rule of Indo-European word formation: When a derivative was formed by thematizing a stem other than a verbal base the first vocalism of the resulting stem was an **e* to the exclusion of any other vocalism of the source stem.[7] Thus

Gk-Θήρ, Lith. *žvėris* < **ǵhuēr-* (< old nom.?)
- **ǵhuer-o-* > Lat. *ferus*

So also when a final **u* formed part of the base:
*doru (> δόρυ)- **deru-o-* > Welsh *derw*, OCS *drĕvo*;[8]
*soru - **seru-o-* > Welsh *herw*.[9]

If now we apply this rule to the stem **ḱw?ḱu-* 'swift' we might on the one hand obtain **ḱw?ḱu-o-* > [ō?ḱuo-] or [ōḱuo-], which however would not carry the characteristic contrastive vocalism nor expected e-timbre of such derivatives. Instead, it appears that the stem was vocalized **ḱw?ḱu-o-*. Then either **ḱʷ* was masked by **ʔ* or such initial clusters just simplified. We thus arrive at **ʔeḱuo-*[10] 'the swift one.'[10a]

Is there any memory of this semantic derivation? If a language conserved the derivational process and if the relevant phonological shapes remained intact it is not likely that the tautological sequence "swift horse' = 'the swift swift one' would be current. However, in Helleno-Armenian **ʔeḱuo-* somehow diverged[11] so that such a qualification would no longer produce a simple transparent tautology. When we consult Homer, we find just such a sequence living on as a productive oral formula, in all possible syntactic cases and with interesting variation in diction. This formula is by no means a frozen or fossilized single rote sequence. It furthermore occurs (mainly in the Iliad) at telling points in the epic, and clustered with other locutions of important force; note, e.g.,Π 865 at the end of the episode of Patroclus's death.

The formula 'swift horses' occurs always plural (not, as it happens, dual). This no doubt reflects in part a merger in semantics, which is well known, of the metonymic use of 'horses' for 'chariot' in the epic. What is not so well recognized is the fact that the

214 When Worlds Collide

Indo-European locution(s) for 'cart, chariot' was/were plurale tantum.[12] However, some of the instances certainly represent semantic plurals of 'horse,' e.g., as seen in the important passage (Π 865) at the end of the death of Patroclus, confirmed by the adjective ἄμβροτοι. This ancient passage could be nearly Indo-European verse;[13] a mild inversion, perhaps in the accusative *ń-mṛtóms or *ń-mṛuóms, would restore a regular metrical sequence.

Π 865
ἀντίθεον θεράποντα ποδώκεθς Αἰακίδαο
ἵετο γὰρ βαλέειν· τὸν δ'ἔκφερον ὠκέες ἵπποι
ἄμβροτοι, οὓς Πηλῆϊ θεοὶ δόσαν ἀγλαὰ δῶρα

*e̯i̯i̯H_eto g'r g^{w}lHésen· tom d'éḱs-bheron(t) ōḱéues éḱuoes
ioms ń-mṛtóes Pēléuei dhesóes d$^{?w}$(s)nt "aglaua" dé$^{?w}$rH_a

Note the figura etymologica (cognate accusative). I have here restored as a precaution the "Mycenaean" style dative. The background of ἀγλαός is obscure.

As evidence for the integrity of the locution in Homer, I present here an analysis of the formula "swift horses." Appended is the output of a computer search for all relevant collocations of ἱππ- and ὠκ-. Grammatically and metrically parsed these collocations can then be summarized as follows. The number of occurrences of each sequence is registered; atheized lines have been segregated, and the count for the Odyssey is indicated. The feet of the hexameter are symbolized by number.

Summary of "swift horses" in Homer (Appendix)
Collocations

4) ἵπποι and ὠκύ in Homer, Il 5 295
   ἤριπε δ' ἐξ ὀχέων, ἀράβησε δὲ τεύχε' ἐπ' αὐτῶι
5 295
   αἰόλα παμφανόωντα, παρέτρεσσαν δέ οἱ ἵπποι
   ὠκύποδες· τοῦ δ' αὖθι λύθη ψυχή τε μένος τε.
   Αἰνείας δ' ἀπόρουσε σὺν ἀσπίδι δουρί τε μακρῶι

6) ἵπποι and ὠκύ in Homer, Il 8 122
   υἱὸν ὑπερθύμου Θηβαίου Ἠνιοπῆα
   ἵππων ἡνί' ἔχοντα βάλε στῆθος παρὰ μαζόν.
   ἤριπε δ' ἐξ ὀχέων, ὑπερώησαν δέ οἱ ἵπποι
   ὠκύποδες· τοῦ δ' αὖθι λύθη ψυχή τε μένος τε.
   Ἕκτορα δ' αἰνὸν ἄχος πύκασε φρένας ἡνιόχοιο·

7) ἵπποι and ὠκύ in Homer, Il 8 314
   ἀλλ' Ἀρχεπτόλεμον θρασὺν Ἕκτορος ἡνιοχῆα
   ἱέμενον πόλεμον δὲ βάλε στῆθος παρὰ μαζόν·
   ἤριπε δ' ἐξ ὀχέων, ὑπερώησαν δέ οἱ ἵπποι
8 315
   ὠκύποδες· τοῦ δ' αὖθι λύθη ψυχή τε μένος τε.

8) ἵπποι and ὠκύ in Homer, Il 10 568
   οἳ δ' ὅτε Τυδεΐδεω κλισίην ἐΰτυκτον ἵκοντο,
   ἵππους μὲν κατέδησαν ἐϋτμήτοισιν ἱμᾶσι
   φάτνηι ἐφ' ἱππείηι, ὅθι περ Διομήδεος ἵπποι
   ἕστασαν ὠκύποδες μελιηδέα πυρὸν ἔδοντες·

9) ἵπποι and ὠκύ in Homer, Il 12 50
   ὣς Ἕκτωρ ἀν' ὅμιλον ἰὼν ἐλλίσσεθ' ἑταίρους
12 50
   τάφρον ἐποτρύνων διαβαινέμεν· οὐδέ οἱ ἵπποι
   τόλμων ὠκύποδες, μάλα δὲ χρεμέτιζον ἐπ' ἄκρωι
   χείλει ἐφεσταότες· ἀπὸ γὰρ δειδίσσετο τάφρος

10) ἵπποι and ὠκύ in Homer, Il 16 367
   αἰθέρος ἐκ δίης, ὅτε τε Ζεὺς λαίλαπα τείνηι,
   ὣς τῶν ἐκ νηῶν γένετο ἰαχή τε φόβος τε,
   οὐδὲ κατὰ μοῖραν πέραον πάλιν. Ἕκτορα δ' ἵπποι
   ἔκφερον ὠκύποδες σὺν τεύχεσι, λεῖπε δὲ λαὸν
   Τρωϊκόν, οὓς ἀέκοντας ὀρυκτὴ τάφρος ἔρυκε.

11) ἵπποι and ὠκύ in Homer, il 23 303
   Ἀντίλοχος δὲ τέταρτος ἐΰτριχας ὁπλίσαθ' ἵππους,
   Νέστορος ἀγλαὸς υἱὸς ὑπερθύμοιο ἄνακτος
   τοῦ Νηληϊάδαο· Πυλοιγενέες δέ οἱ ἵπποι
   ὠκύποδες φέρον ἅρμα· πατὴρ δέ οἱ ἄγχι παραστὰς

12) ἵπποιο and ὠκέ in Homer, il 8 87
   ἀλγήσας δ' ἀνέπαλτο, βέλος δ' εἰς ἐγκέφαλον δῦ,
   σὺν δ' ἵππους ἐτάραξε κυλινδόμενος περὶ χαλκῶι.
   ὄφρ' ὁ γέρων ἵπποιο παρηορίας ἀπέταμνε
   φασγάνωι ἀΐσσων, τόφρ' Ἕκτορος ὠκέες ἵπποι
   ἦλθον ἀν' ἰωχμὸν θρασὺν ἡνίοχον φορέοντες

13) ἵπποις and ὠκυ in Homer, il 23 504
   αἰεὶ δ' ἡνίοχον κονίης ῥαθάμιγγες ἔβαλλον,
   ἅρματα δὲ χρυσῶι πεπυκασμένα κασσιτέρωι τε
   ἵπποις ὠκυπόδεσσιν ἐπέτρεχον· οὐδέ τι πολλὴ
23 505
   γίγνετ' ἐπισσώτρων ἁρματροχιὴ κατόπισθεν

14) ἵπποισιν and ὠκυ in Homer, il 2 383
   νῦν δ' ἔρχεσθ' ἐπὶ δεῖπνον ἵνα ξυνάγωμεν Ἄρηα.
   εὖ μέν τις δόρυ θηξάσθω, εὖ δ' ἀσπίδα θέσθω,
   εὖ δέ τις ἵπποισιν δεῖπνον δότω ὠκυπόδεσσιν,
   εὖ δέ τις ἅρματος ἀμφὶς ἰδὼν πολέμοιο μεδέσθω,

18) ἵππους and ὠκύ in Homer, il 5 732
   δῆσε χρύσειον καλὸν ζυγόν, ἐν δὲ λέπαδνα
   κάλ' ἔβαλε χρύσει'· ὑπὸ δὲ ζυγὸν ἤγαγεν Ἥρη
   ἵππους ὠκύποδας, μεμαυῖ' ἔριδος καὶ ἀϋτῆς.
   Αὐτὰρ Ἀθηναίη κούρη Διὸς αἰγιόχοιο
   πέπλον μὲν κατέχευεν ἑανὸν πατρὸς ἐπ' οὔδει

22) ἵππους and ὠκέ in Homer, il 13 535
   αὐτοκασίγνητος περὶ μέσσωι χεῖρε τιτήνας
13 535
   ἐξῆγεν πολέμοιο δυσηχέος, ὄφρ' ἵκεθ' ἵππους
   ὠκέας, οἵ οἱ ὄπισθε μάχης ἠδὲ πτολέμοιο
   ἕστασαν ἡνίοχόν τε καὶ ἅρματα ποικίλ' ἔχοντες·

23) ἵππους and ὠκέ in Homer, il 14 429
   τῶν δ' ἄλλων οὔ τίς εὖ ἀκήδεσεν, ἀλλὰ πάροιθεν
   ἀσπίδας εὐκύκλους σχέθον αὐτοῦ. τὸν δ' ἄρ' ἑταῖροι
   χερσὶν ἀείραντες φέρον ἐκ πόνου, ὄφρ' ἵκεθ' ἵππους
14 430
   ὠκέας, οἵ οἱ ὄπισθε μάχης ἠδὲ πτολέμοιο

30) ἵππων and ὠκυ in Homer, od 18 263
καὶ γὰρ Τρῶάς φασι μαχητὰς ἔμμεναι ἄνδρας,
ἠμὲν ἀκοντιστὰς ἠδὲ ῥυτῆρας ὀϊστῶν
ἵππων τ' ὠκυπόδων ἐπιβήτορας, οἵ τε τάχιστα
ἔκριναν μέγα νεῖκος ὁμοιΐου πτολέμοιο.
18 265

---

31) ἵππων and ὠκε in Homer, il 4 500
ἀλλ' υἱὸν Πριάμοιο νόθον βάλε Δημοκόωντα
4 500
ὅς οἱ Ἀβυδόθεν ἦλθε παρ' ἵππων ὠκειάων.
τὸν ῥ' Ὀδυσεὺς ἑτάροιο χολωσάμενος βάλε δουρὶ
κόρσην· ἣ δ' ἑτέροιο διὰ κροτάφοιο πέρησεν

---

33) ἵππων and ὠκε in Homer, il 7 15
Ἰφίνοον βάλε δουρὶ κατὰ κρατερὴν ὑσμίνην
7 15
Δεξιάδην ἵππων ἐπιάλμενον ὠκειάων
ὦμον· ὃ δ' ἐξ ἵππων χαμάδις πέσε, λύντο δὲ γυῖα.
Τοὺς δ' ὡς οὖν ἐνόησε θεὰ γλαυκῶπις Ἀθήνη

---

34) ἵππων and ὠκε in Homer, il 7 240
ἀζαλέην, τό μοι ἔστι ταλαύρινον πολεμίζειν·
7 240
οἶδα δ' ἐπαΐξαι μόθον ἵππων ὠκειάων·
οἶδα δ' ἐνὶ σταδίηι δηΐωι μέλπεσθαι Ἄρηϊ.
ἀλλ' οὐ γὰρ σ' ἐθέλω βαλέειν τοιοῦτον ἐόντα

---

35) ἵππων and ὠκυ in Homer, il 8 128
κεῖσθαι, ὃ δ' ἡνίοχον μέθεπε θρασύν· οὐδ' ἄρ' ἔτι δὴν
ἵππω δευέσθην σημάντορος· αἶψα γὰρ εὗρεν
Ἰφιτίδην Ἀρχεπτόλεμον θρασύν, ὅν ῥα τόθ' ἵππων
ὠκυπόδων ἐπέβησε, δίδου δέ οἱ ἡνία χερσίν.
8 130

---

36) ἵππων and ὠκυ in Homer, il 10 535
ψεύσομαι, ἦ ἔτυμον ἐρέω; κέλεται δέ με θυμός.
10 535
ἵππων μ' ὠκυπόδων ἀμφὶ κτύπος οὔατα βάλλει.
αἲ γὰρ δὴ Ὀδυσεύς τε καὶ ὃ κρατερὸς Διομήδης
ὧδ' ἄφαρ ἐκ Τρώων ἐλασαίατο μώνυχας ἵππους·

---

39) ὠκέ and ἵππους in Homer, od 4 28
"ξείνω δή τινε τώδε, διοτρεφὲς ὦ Μενέλαε,
ἄνδρε δύω, γενεῆι δὲ Διὸς μεγάλοιο ἔϊκτον.
ἀλλ' εἴπ', ἦ σφῶϊν καταλύσομεν ὠκέας ἵππους,
ἦ ἄλλον πέμπωμεν ἱκανέμεν, ὅς κε φιλήσηι."

4 30

---

40) ὠκέ and ἵππους in Homer, il 3 263
    ἂν δ' ἄρ' ἔβη Πρίαμος, κατὰ δ' ἡνία τεῖνεν ὀπίσσω·
    πὰρ δέ οἱ Ἀντήνωρ περικαλλέα βήσετο δίφρον·
    τὼ δὲ διὰ Σκαιῶν πεδίον δ' ἔχον ὠκέας ἵππους.
    Ἀλλ' ὅτε δή ῥ' ἵκοντο μετὰ Τρῶας καὶ Ἀχαιούς,

41) ὠκέ and ἵππους in Homer, il 5 240
    Ὣς ἄρα φωνήσαντες ἐς ἅρματα ποικίλα βάντες
5 240
    ἐμμεμαῶτ' ἐπὶ Τυδεΐδηι ἔχον ὠκέας ἵππους.
    τοὺς δὲ ἴδε Σθένελος Καπανήϊος ἀγλαὸς υἱός,
    αἶψα δὲ Τυδεΐδην ἔπεα πτερόεντα προσηύδα·

---

42) ὠκέ and ἵπποι in Homer, il 5 257
    ὀκνείω δ' ἵππων ἐπιβαινέμεν, ἀλλὰ καὶ αὔτως
    ἀντίον εἶμ' αὐτῶν· τρεῖν μ' οὐκ ἐᾶι Παλλὰς Ἀθήνη.
    τούτω δ' οὐ πάλιν αὖτις ἀποίσετον ὠκέες ἵπποι
    ἄμφω ἀφ' ἡμείων, εἴ γ' οὖν ἕτερός γε φύγηισιν.
    ἄλλο δέ τοι ἐρέω, σὺ δ' ἐνὶ φρεσὶ βάλλεο σῆισιν·

---

43) ὠκέ and ἵππους in Homer, il 5 261
5 260
    αἴ κέν μοι πολύβουλος Ἀθήνη κῦδος ὀρέξηι
    ἀμφοτέρω κτεῖναι, σὺ δὲ τούσδε μὲν ὠκέας ἵππους
    αὐτοῦ ἐρυκακέειν ἐξ ἄντυγος ἡνία τείνας,
    Αἰνείαο δ' ἐπαΐξαι μεμνημένος ἵππων,

---

45) ὠκέ and ἵππους in Homer, il 5 275
    Ὣς οἱ μὲν τοιαῦτα πρὸς ἀλλήλους ἀγόρευον,
5 275
    τὼ δὲ τάχ' ἐγγύθεν ἦλθον ἐλαύνοντ' ὠκέας ἵππους.
    τὸν πρότερος προσέειπε Λυκάονος ἀγλαὸς υἱός·
    καρτερόθυμε δαΐφρον ἀγαυοῦ Τυδέος υἱὲ

---

47) ὠκέ and ἵππους in Homer, il 8 254
    μᾶλλον ἐπὶ Τρώεσσι θόρον, μνήσαντο δὲ χάρμης.
    Ἔνθ' οὔ τις πρότερος Δαναῶν πολλῶν περ ἐόντων
    εὔξατο Τυδεΐδαο πάρος σχέμεν ὠκέας ἵππους
8 255
    τάφρου τ' ἐξελάσαι καὶ ἐναντίβιον μαχέσασθαι,

---

48) ὠκέ and ἵππους in Homer, il 8 402
    ἔρχεσθ'· οὐ γὰρ καλὰ συνοισόμεθα πτόλεμον δέ.
    ὧδε γὰρ ἐξερέω, τὸ δὲ καὶ τετελεσμένον ἔσται·
    γυιώσω μέν σφωϊν ὑφ' ἅρμασιν ὠκέας ἵππους,
    αὐτὰς δ' ἐκ δίφρου βαλέω κατὰ θ' ἅρματα ἄξω·
    οὐδέ κεν ἐς δεκάτους περιτελλομένους ἐνιαυτοὺς

49) ὠκέ and ἵππους in Homer, Il 8 416
8 415
ὧδε γὰρ ἠπείλησε Κρόνου πάϊς, ἧι τελέει περ,
γυιώσειν μὲν σφῶϊν ὑφ' ἅρμασιν ὠκέας ἵππους,
αὐτὰς δ' ἐκ δίφρου βαλέειν κατὰ θ' ἅρματα ἄξειν·
οὐδέ κεν ἐς δεκάτους περιτελλομένους ἐνιαυτοὺς

50) ὠκέ and ἵπποι in Homer, Il 10 474
καλὰ παρ' αὐτοῖσι χθονὶ κέκλιτο εὖ κατὰ κόσμον
τριστοιχί· παρὰ δέ σφιν ἑκάστωι δίζυγες ἵπποι.
ἡΡῆσος δ' ἐν μέσωι εὗδε, παρ' αὐτῶι δ' ὠκέες ἵπποι
10 475
ἐξ ἐπιδιφριάδος πυμάτης ἱμᾶσι δέδεντο.

51) ὠκέ and ἵπποι in Homer, Il 10 520
ἡΡήσου ἀνεψιὸν ἐσθλόν· ὃ δ' ἐξ ὕπνου ἀνορούσας
10 520
ὡς ἴδε χῶρον ἐρῆμον, ὅθ' ἕστασαν ὠκέες ἵπποι,
ἄνδράς τ' ἀσπαίροντας ἐν ἀργαλέηισι φονῆισιν,
ὤιμωξέν τ' ἄρ' ἔπειτα φίλον τ' ὀνόμηνεν ἑταῖρον.

52) ὠκέ and ἵππους in Homer, Il 10 527
ὅσσ' ἄνδρες ῥέξαντες ἔβαν κοίλας ἐπὶ νῆας.
Οἳ δ' ὅτε δή ῥ' ἵκανον ὅθι σκοπὸν Ἕκτορος ἔκταν,
ἔνθ' Ὀδυσεὺς μὲν ἔρυξε Διὶ φίλος ὠκέας ἵππους,
Τυδεΐδης δὲ χαμᾶζε θορὼν ἔναρα βροτόεντα
ἐν χείρεσσ' Ὀδυσῆϊ τίθει, ἐπεβήσετο δ' ἵππων·

54) ὠκέ and ἵππους in Homer, Il 11 127
οὐκ εἴασχ' Ἑλένην δόμεναι ξανθῶι Μενελάωι,
τοῦ περ δὴ δύο παῖδε λάβε κρείων Ἀγαμέμνων
εἰν ἑνὶ δίφρωι ἐόντας, ὁμοῦ δ' ἔχον ὠκέας ἵππους·
ἐκ γάρ σφεας χειρῶν φύγον ἡνία σιγαλόεντα,
τὼ δὲ κυκηθήτην· ὃ δ' ἐναντίον ὦρτο λέων ὣς

55) ὠκέ and ἵππους in Homer, Il 11 760
ἔνθ' ἄνδρα κτείνας πύματον λίπον· αὐτὰρ Ἀχαιοὶ
11 760
ἂψ ἀπὸ Βουπρασίοιο Πύλονδ' ἔχον ὠκέας ἵππους,
πάντες δ' εὐχετόωντο θεῶν Διὶ Νέστορί τ' ἀνδρῶν.
ὣς ἔον, εἴ ποτ' ἔον γε, μετ' ἀνδράσιν. αὐτὰρ Ἀχιλλεὺς

56) ὠκέ and ἵππους in Homer, Il 12 62
δὴ τότε Πουλυδάμας θρασὺν Ἕκτορα εἶπε παραστάς·
Ἕκτορ τ' ἠδ' ἄλλοι Τρώων ἀγοὶ ἠδ' ἐπικούρων
ἀφραδέως διὰ τάφρον ἐλαύνομεν ὠκέας ἵππους·
ἡ δὲ μάλ' ἀργαλέη περάαν· σκόλοπες γὰρ ἐν αὐτῆι
ὀξέες ἑστᾶσιν, ποτὶ δ' αὐτοὺς τεῖχος Ἀχαιῶν,

57) ὠκέ and ἵππους in Homer, il 15 259
ῥύομ', ὁμῶς αὐτόν τε καὶ αἰπεινὸν πτολίεθρον.
ἀλλ' ἄγε νῦν ἱππεῦσιν ἐπότρυνον πολέεσσι
νηυσὶν ἔπι γλαφυρῆισιν ἐλαυνέμεν ὠκέας ἵππους·
15 260
αὐτὰρ ἐγὼ προπάροιθε κιὼν ἵπποισι κέλευθον

58) ὠκέ and ἵππους in Homer, il 16 148
τὸν μετ' Ἀχιλλῆα ῥηξήνορα τῖε μάλιστα,
πιστότατος δέ οἱ ἔσκε μάχηι ἔνι μεῖναι ὁμοκλήν.
τῶι δὲ καὶ Αὐτομέδων ὕπαγε ζυγὸν ὠκέας ἵππους
Ξάνθον καὶ Βαλίαν, τὼ ἅμα πνοιῆισι πετέσθην,

59) ὠκέ and ἵπποι in Homer, il 16 370
Τρωϊκόν, οὓς ἀέκοντας ὀρυκτὴ τάφρος ἔρυκε.
16 370
πολλοὶ δ' ἐν τάφρωι ἐρυσάρματες ὠκέες ἵπποι
ἄξαντ' ἐν πρώτωι ῥυμῶι λίπον ἅρματ' ἀνάκτων,
Πάτροκλος δ' ἕπετο σφεδανὸν Δαναοῖσι κελεύων

60) ὠκέ and ἵπποι in Homer, il 16 380
πρηνέες ἐξ ὀχέων, δίφροι δ' ἀνακυμβαλίαζον.
16 380
ἀντικρὺ δ' ἄρα τάφρον ὑπέρθορον ὠκέες ἵπποι
ἄμβροτοι, οὓς Πηλῆϊ θεοὶ δόσαν ἀγλαὰ δῶρα,
πρόσσω ἱέμενοι, ἐπὶ δ' Ἕκτορι κέκλετο θυμός·

61) ὠκέ and ἵπποι in Homer, il 16 383
ἄμβροτοι, οὓς Πηλῆϊ θεοὶ δόσαν ἀγλαὰ δῶρα,
πρόσσω ἱέμενοι, ἐπὶ δ' Ἕκτορι κέκλετο θυμός·
ἵετο γὰρ βαλέειν· τὸν δ' ἔκφερον ὠκέες ἵπποι.
ὡς δ' ὑπὸ λαίλαπι πᾶσα κελαινὴ βέβριθε χθὼν
16 385

62) ὠκέ and ἵπποι in Homer, il 16 833
Τρωϊάδας δὲ γυναῖκας ἐλεύθερον ἦμαρ ἀπούρας
ἄξειν ἐν νήεσσι φίλην ἐς πατρίδα γαῖαν
νήπιε· τάων δὲ πρόσθ' Ἕκτορος ὠκέες ἵπποι
ποσσὶν ὀρωρέχαται πολεμίζειν· ἔγχεϊ δ' αὐτὸς
16 835

63) ὠκέ and ἵπποι in Homer, il 16 866
16 865
ἀντίθεον θεράποντα ποδώκεος Αἰακίδαο·
ἵετο γὰρ βαλέειν· τὸν δ' ἔκφερον ὠκέες ἵπποι
ἄμβροτοι, οὓς Πηλῆϊ θεοὶ δόσαν ἀγλαὰ δῶρα.

64) ὠκέ and ἵππους in Homer, Il 17 465
οὐ γάρ πως ἦν οἶον ἐόνθ' ἱερῶι ἐνὶ δίφρωι
17 465
ἔγχει ἐφορμᾶσθαι καὶ ἐπίσχειν ὠκέας ἵππους.
ὀψὲ δὲ δή μιν ἑταῖρος ἀνὴρ ἴδεν ὀφθαλμοῖσιν
Ἀλκιμέδων υἱὸς Λαέρκεος Αἱμονίδαο·

65) ὠκέ and ἵππους in Homer, Il 18 244
φυλόπιδος κρατερῆς καὶ ὁμοιΐου πολέμοιο.
Τρῶες δ' αὖθ' ἑτέρωθεν ἀπὸ κρατερῆς ὑσμίνης
χωρήσαντες ἔλυσαν ὑφ' ἅρμασιν ὠκέας ἵππους,
18 245
ἐς δ' ἀγορὴν ἀγέροντο πάρος δόρποιο μέδεσθαι.

66) ὠκέ and ἵππους in Homer, Il 23 294
Αἰνείαν, ἀτὰρ αὐτὸν ὑπεξεσάωσεν Ἀπόλλων.
τῶι δ' ἄρ' ἐπ' Ἀτρεΐδης ὦρτο ξανθὸς Μενέλαος
διογενής, ὑπὸ δὲ ζυγὸν ἤγαγεν ὠκέας ἵππους
23 295
Αἴθην τὴν Ἀγαμεμνονέην τὸν ἑόν τε Πόδαργον·

67) ὠκέ and ἵπποι in Homer, Il 23 373
νίκης ἱεμένων· κέκλοντο δὲ οἷσιν ἕκαστος
ἵπποις, οἱ δ' ἐπέτοντο κονίοντες πεδίοιο.
Ἀλλ' ὅτε δὴ πύματον τέλεον δρόμον ὠκέες ἵπποι
ἂψ ἐφ' ἁλὸς πολιῆς, τότε δὴ ἀρετή γε ἑκάστου
23 375

69) ὠκέ and ἵππους in Homer, Il 23 516
23 515
κέρδεσιν, οὔ τι τάχεϊ γε, παραφθάμενος Μενέλαον·
ἀλλὰ καὶ ὣς Μενέλαος ἔχ' ἐγγύθεν ὠκέας ἵππους.
ὅσσον δὲ τροχοῦ ἵππος ἀφίσταται, ὅς ῥα ἄνακτα
ἕλκηισιν πεδίοιο τιταινόμενος σὺν ὄχεσφι·

70) ὠκέ and ἵππους in Homer, Il 24 14
δινεύεσκ' ἀλύων παρὰ θῖν' ἁλός· οὐδέ μιν ἠὼς
φαινομένη λήθεσκεν ὑπεὶρ ἅλα τ' ἠϊόνας τε.
ἀλλ' ὅ γ' ἐπεὶ ζεύξειεν ὑφ' ἅρμασιν ὠκέας ἵππους,
24 15
Ἕκτορα δ' ἕλκεσθαι δησάσκετο δίφρου ὄπισθεν,

71) ὠκέ and ἵππους in Homer, Od 3 478
ζεύξαθ' ὑφ' ἅρματ' ἄγοντες, ἵνα πρήσσηισιν ὁδοῖο."
ὣς ἔφαθ', οἱ δ' ἄρα τοῦ μάλα μὲν κλύον ἠδ' ἐπίθοντο,
καρπαλίμως δ' ἔζευξαν ὑφ' ἅρμασιν ὠκέας ἵππους.
ἐν δὲ γυνὴ ταμίη σῖτον καὶ οἶνον ἔθηκεν

72) ὠκέ and ἵπποι in Homer, od 3 496
3 495
ἷξον δ' ἐς πεδίον πυρηφόρον, ἔνθα δ' ἔπειτα
ἦνον ὁδόν· τοῖον γὰρ ὑπέκφερον ὠκέες ἵπποι.
δύσετό τ' ἠέλιος σκιόωντό τε πᾶσαι ἀγυιαί.

73) ὠκυ and ἵπποι in Homer, od 4 708
ὀψὲ δὲ δή μιν ἔπεσσιν ἀμειβομένη προσέειπε·
"κῆρυξ, τίπτε δέ μοι πάϊς οἴχεται; οὐδέ τί μιν χρεώ
νηῶν ὠκυπόρων ἐπιβαινέμεν, αἵ θ' ἁλὸς ἵπποι
ἀνδράσι γίνονται, περόωσι δὲ πουλὺν ἐφ' ὑγρήν.

75) ὠκε and ἵππους in Homer, il 17 614
πεζὸς γὰρ τὰ πρῶτα λιπὼν νέας ἀμφιελίσσας
ἤλυθε, καί κε Τρωσὶ μέγα κράτος ἐγγυάλιξεν,
εἰ μὴ Κοίρανος ὦκα ποδώκεας ἤλασεν ἵππους·
καὶ τῶι μὲν φάος ἦλθεν, ἄμυνε δὲ νηλεὲς ἦμαρ,

76) ὠκε and ἵπποι in Homer, il 23 376

φαίνετ', ἄφαρ δ' ἵπποισι τάθη δρόμος· ὦκα δ' ἔπειτα
αἳ Φηρητιάδαο ποδώκεες ἔκφερον ἵπποι.
τὰς δὲ μετ' ἐξέφερον Διομήδεος ἄρσενες ἵπποι
Τρώϊοι, οὐδέ τι πολλὸν ἄνευθ' ἔσαν, ἀλλὰ μάλ' ἐγγύς·

84) ωκε and ἵππους in Homer, od 23 244
εἰ μὴ ἄρ' ἄλλ' ἐνόησε θεὰ γλαυκῶπις Ἀθήνη.
νύκτα μὲν ἐν περάτηι δολιχὴν σχέθεν, Ἠῶ δ' αὖτε
ῥύσατ' ἐπ' Ὠκεανῶι χρυσόθρονον οὐδ' ἔα ἵππους
23 245
ζεύγνυσθ' ὠκύποδας φάος ἀνθρώποισι φέροντας,

GRAMMATICAL AND METRICAL SUMMARY
"swift horses" in Homer

			Verse Feet
nom.	ὠκέες ἵπποι #	11x	5+6
acc.	ὠκέας ἵππους #	20x	
gen.	ἵππων (⏑⏑ — ⏑⏑) ὠκειάων #	3x	2-3+5+6
	# " " μ'/τ' ὠκυπόδων	2x	1+2
dat.	#ἵπποις ὠκυπόδεσσιν		1+2+3
	ἵπποισιν — — ⏑⏑ " #		2+5+6
acc.	#ἵππους ὠκύποδας	2x	1+2
	ἵππους # ὠκέας	2x	
	" " # — ⏑⏑ ὠκύποδας	(Od.)	
nom.	ἵπποι # (— ⏑⏑) ὠκύποδες	5x + 22θ.	6+1/2
gen.	ἵππων # ὠκυπόδων		
nom.	ποδώκεες — ⏑⏑ ἵπποι #		4+6
acc.	ποδώκεας — ⏑⏑ ἵππους #		

Total: 53x (5 Od.)

νηῶν ὠκυπόρων ... (=) ἵπποι #   Od. 4.708

224 When Worlds Collide

We may now write a rule which will insert the variants of the formula contextually in the observed positions:

A BARDIC RULE

HORSES (incl. CHARIOT) - $hik^w k^w o-$ > ἱππο + PL.

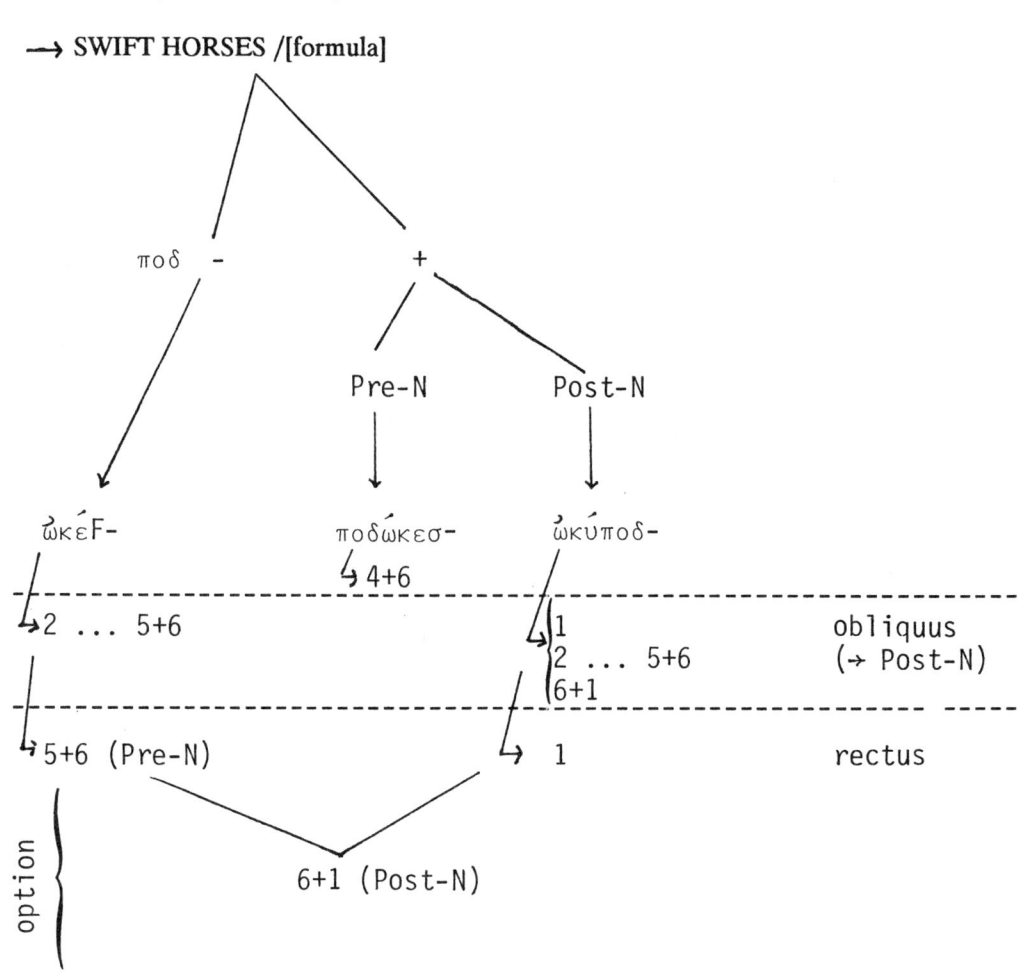

⟶ SWIFT HORSES /[formula]

```
                πoδ  -              +
                 /              /        \
                /             Pre-N     Post-N
               ↓                ↓          ↓
             ὠκέF-          ποδώκεσ-    ὠκύποδ-
                               ↳ 4+6
       ─ ─ ─ ─ ─ ─ ─ ─ ─ ─ ─ ─ ─ ─ ─ ─ ─ ─ ─ ─ ─ ─ ─ ─
       ↳ 2 ... 5+6                ↳ 1                   obliquus
                                    2 ... 5+6           (→ Post-N)
                                    6+1
       ─ ─ ─ ─ ─ ─ ─ ─ ─ ─ ─ ─ ─ ─ ─ ─ ─ ─ ─ ─ ─ ─ ─ ─
       ↳ 5+6 (Pre-N)              ↳ 1                   rectus
           \                       /
            \                     /
  option {           6+1 (Post-N)
```

Note that we have here redefined "formula" to embrace all contextual variants, which are rule-governed.

NOTES

[1] Michael L. Ryder, "The Evolution of the Fleece," *Scientific American*, January 1987, 112-9, esp. 112; Sándor Bökönyi, "Horses and Sheep in East Europe in the Copper and Bronze Ages," *Proto-Indo-European: The Archaeology of a Linguistic Problem. Studies in Honor of Marija Gimbutas* (ed. S.N. Skomal and E.C. Polomé), Washington DC, 1987, 136-44, esp. 136.

[2] I would now make the following revisions of detail to that set of remarks. The term for the swine *suH-appears to me now to be a descriptive appellative within IE; that is, I claim we have here a "root-noun" nomen actoris in the correct zero grade 'breeder (par excellence),' identical with Vedic *sū-*'father, mother,' from the base *sū-* 'beget, bear' (*sū́te - → sū́yate*), disambiguated in Indic from *sū-kará-* 'boar, hog.' I thus agree with the deficiently formulated suggestion reproduced by Pokorny IEW 1039, while rejecting his onomatopoetic alternative, always a last refuge if not a specimen of unprincipled nonsense.

My remarks in *Science* did not take up the goat specifically. I now consider that we can in fact recover the correct IE term for 'goat,' seen in Indic *ajá-* and Lith. *ožỹs*; the pre-form must be *ǵog-o-*. I have argued the dialectology of 'goat' in a paper before the International Congress of Linguists, Berlin, August 1987. However, this etymon leads us to another appellative *fogo- > *fago- > *(H)ago- (Lat. *ago*, Gk ἄγω) 'what is driven.' There must have been constant (local) renewal of this lexeme in IE.

On 'dog' see my article "IE *()ḱuon-'dog,'" *IF* 85, 1980, 35-42; 87, 1982, 74-5; and also *Folia Linguistica Historica* 4, 1983, 137-8. The form of the lexeme must have been *p(V)ḱuon-.

[3] See my exploration of the Greek and Indic fates of this rule, "φοῖβοϛ, αφικσόϛ," *IF* 81, 1976, 41-2; ατρεκήϛ," *Ziva Antika* 29, 1979, 72.

[4] The best, if not quite conclusive, discussions of the Latin forms are to be found under the various entries in Ernout and Meillet *DELL*.

[5] While this is a gloss it can scarcely have been modeled on an imagined or mistaken form that failed actually to occur.

[6] Suppletion by *celer* or *uēlox* is then no more expensive as a grammatical rule.

[7] I have formulated this rule in *Studia Celtica* 18-19, 1983-4, 128-32, and references therein.

[8] CLS *Parasession on the Lexicon* 1978, 186, 191.

[9] *Zeitschrift für celtische Philologie* 40, 1984, 276.

[10] Pokorny *IEW* 301 supports the etymon well, but requires updating. Good support comes from Vedic *áśva-*, Avestan *aspa-*, Lat. *equus*, OIr. *ech*, Welsh *ebol* < *epālo- < *-o-Hal-* (Hamp, *Revue roumaine de linguistique* 21, 1976, 49 and S. Zimmer, *Cambridge Medieval Celtic Studies* 14, 1987, 63-4) Gaulish *Epona*, OE *eoh*, Toch.B *yakwe*, OLith. *ašvà*, OPruss. *aswinan* 'horse milk,' and the river name *Ašvà*. To these should now be added evidence from Latvian names (K. Karulis, *Lingua Posnaniensis* 27, 1985, 19-21) *Asūne, Asugals, Asva, Ese*, and OLatv. dial. *ôssa* equa, Hieroglyphic Luwian *a-zu-wa-* (with Laroche's 3rd *su* sign 448; see now H. Craig Melchert, "PIE velars in Luvian," *Studies in Memory*

of *Warren Cowgill (1929-1985)*, ed. Calvert Watkins, Berlin 1987, 182-204, esp. 202, 203), and Venetic *ekvo*.

Meillet correctly observes (*DELL*, s.v.) that the etymon still lives on in Iranian languages, from which we may instance thanks to recent reports (of Buddruss Hunza Wakhi *yaš*); however, Meillet errs in declaring the etymon is completely replaced in Europe, since it remains very much alive in Scottish Gaelic *ech*, pl. *eich*.

[10a] Cf. the Germanic etymon of OE *hengest* to Lith. *Šankùs* 'nimble' (:*šañkiai*); and Eng. *horse* to Lat. *currō* 'run.'

[11] With Armenian *ēš* 'donkey' < *$eik\!ˬuo$- apparently a derivative by the rule just invoked from the stem represented by Gk.

[12] See E.P. Hamp, *Zeitschrift für Balkanslogie* 19, 1983, 14-5. Note the interesting explicit collocation Il.5.107.

[13] It was by the chance observation and rereading of this passage that my attention was first directed to the Homeric formula here analyzed and to its bearing on our problem. I cordially thank my colleague and friend George Walsh for doing so ably with the computer what I cannot do.

ARMÉNIEN ET IRANIEN
UNE THÉORIE LINGUISTIQUE PASSÉE INAPERÇUE

Giancarlo Bolognesi

1.   J'avais tout d'abord pensé de parler, dans ce Symposium "When Worlds Collide", de l'impact du grec et de l'iranien sur l'arménien prélittéraire, mais je me suis enfin décidé à traiter une question que je considère préalable, c'est-à-dire le problème de la place que l'arménien occupe dans l'ensemble des langues indo-européennes, eu égard surtout aux solutions qu'on a donné à ce problème au cours des siècles.

Il est bon de remarquer à ce propos que dans l'histoire de la linguistique arménienne la question la plus importante et la plus difficile à résoudre ne fut pas celle de reconnaitre le caractère indo-européen de la langue, mais celle de préciser les repports préhistoriques de l'arménien avec les autres langues indo-européennes.

En effet, dans son ouvrage *Ueber die Sprache und Weisheit der Indier* qui - comme on a dit - " appartient encore à la préhistoire de la linguistique ", Friedrich Schlegel avait, déjà avant Franz Bopp, bien clairement relevé des affinités lexicales entre l'arménien et plusieurs autres langues (à savoir l'indien, l'iranien, le grec, le latin, les langues germaniques et les langues slaves), parmi lesquelles on peut mentionner:

arm. *k'an*   lat. *quam*

arm. *mi* "eins"   gr. μία

arm. *hing*   lat. *quinque*

arm. *mi* 'die negative   gr. μή
      Partikel'

arm. *an*-   gr. ἀ- all. *un*-

arm. *lowsaworem*   lat. *luceo*

arm. *lowcem*   gr. λύω

arm. *owranam*   gr. ἀρνέομαι

arm. *arnowm*	gr. ἄρνυμαι
arm. *dnem*	gr. θεῖναι
arm. *atem*	lat. *odium*
arm. *owtem*	lat. *edo*
arm. *lnowm*	lat. *plenus*
arm. *tam*	lat. *do*
arm. *em*	angl. *I am*
arm. *berem*	lat. *fero*, persan *burdan*

"und viele andre".

Il convient encore de remarquer que Friedrich Schlegel avait déjà exactement relevé des affinités non seulement lexicales, mais aussi - ce qui importe le plus - morphologiques entre l'arménien et d'autres langues; en effet il dit explicitement: "Wichtiger noch aber sind die Uebereinstimmungen in der Struktur; zum Beispiel *luanam - lavo, luanas - lavas, luanan - lavant* ... Einige Participia in *al* stimmen dagegen mehr mit den slavischen Sprachen ueberein" (1).

Mais après Friedrich Schlegel les linguistes ont échoué sur la question cruciale de définir la position dialectale de l'arménien. Tout le monde sait bien comment les choses se sont passées. Encore en 1857, dans la préface de la seconde édition de sa *Vergleichende Grammatik*, Franz Bopp soutenait: "das Armenische gehört dem iranischen Zweige unserer Sprachfamilie an" (2).

À ce propos je pense qu'il vaut la peine de reprendre et de développer une recherche précédente (3), pour attirer l'attention sur une théorie linguistique passée inaperçue, dans le but de faire ainsi justice d'un lieu commun bien enraciné et répandu. Concernant le problème des rapports entre l'arménien et les autres langues indo-européennes, et tout spécialement entre l'arménien et l'iranien, on continue encore a dire, et on lit encore d'ordinaire dans les traités, dans les manuels même les plus influents et dans les articles des savants même les plus renommés, que les premiers orientalistes, linguistes et comparatistes avaient été trompés aux siècles précédents par la grande quantité des emprunts à l'iranien, et qu'ils avaient par conséquent considéré l'arménien comme un dialecte iranien, et que ce ne fut qu'en 1875 que Hübschmann rétablit, par son "epochemachender Beitrag" (4), la veritable perspective dialectale en démontrant l'autonomie originale de l'arménien, qui constitue donc un "selbständiger sprachzweig" de la famille linguistique indo-européenne.

Cette opinion commune, selon laquelle la reconnaissance de l'arménien comme indépendant de l'iranien serait une découverte de la seconde moitié du XIXe siècle, se révèle indubitablement fausse à la lumière d'irréfutables documents historiques qu'on a laissès de côté avec désinvolture ou qu'on n'a pas lus avec une attention suffisante.

2. Le fait est que dès le début du XVIIIe siècle l'orientaliste allemand Johann Joachim Schroder, dans son *Aramean lezowin ganj.Hoc est: Thesaurus linguae Armenicae, antiquae et hodiernae* ..., avait clairement et exactement considéré l'arménien comme une langue autonome et indépendante de l'iranien, comme une langue qui a sa propre individualité consistant "ex vocibus ejus propriis", à laquelle furent seulement ensuite ajoutés et/ou superposés pas mal de mots issus de l'iranien, et d'autres langues aussi.

Sur les causes historiques qui ont determiné l'introduction en arménien de mots étrangers, surtout iraniens, Schröder écrit:

> " Cum autem, teste Chorenensi (*scil.* Moyse) nostro, variis aetatibus variae Armeniam ingressae sint illustres familiae, ipsa quoque Haicana natio bella cum vicinis & e longinquo irruentibus populis gravissima gesserit, nec non commercia cum alienigenis coluerit; nequaquam dubitandum, quin tot seculorum lapsu peregrina quaedam vocabula in Haicanam Linguam irrepserint, quae ex frequenti usu postmodum Armenica facta, ab Auctoribus Armenis etiam optimis adhibita, adhuc Libros eorum inspicienti occurrant, uti Capite sequenti monstrabimus" (5).

Et parmi les "illustres familiae . . . quae diversis seculis in Armeniam venerunt", auxquelles on doit la pénétration en arménien de mots étrangers (*peregrina quaedam vocabula*), Schröder mentionne explicitement les *Aršakownik'* ou "Arsacidae", c'est-à-dire les Arsacides (6).

Et de fait, au chapitre suivant (*Capite sequenti*), Schröder se réfère explicitement au discours amorce auparavant:

> "Sed quoniam, uti ex Moyse Chorenensi ostendimus, variae nationes Armeniam ingressae, & exteri bello eam aggressi sunt, quos vocabula aliqua in Haicana lingua reliquisse monuimus, hinc non sine jucunditate eorum vestigia legemus"(7).

Parmi les traces, les vestiges (*vestigia*) que les autres peuples (*variae nationes*) et les étrangers (*exteri*) ont laissés dans la langue arménienne (*quos vocabula aliqua in Haicana lingua reliquisse monuimus*) Schröder indique surtout les mots d'origine iranienne.

C'est précisément en cela que résident la nouveauté et le grand mérite de Schröder, d'avoir bien compris plus d'un siècle et demi avant Hübschmann qu'en arménien les iranismes étaient tout simplement des emprunts, et non des termes originaux. C'est ce qui ressort incontestablement du *Thesaurus* de Schröder où on lit:

> *Antiqua Parthica ab Arsacidis in Armeniam introducta vocabula ... sunt* (8).

Il est bon de remarquer que Schröder ne parle pas génériquement de mots iraniens introduits en arménien, mais qu'il indique avec une grande précision la langue iranienne d'où l'arménien a tiré ses emprunts, et même l'époque historique des emprunts. Il s'agit d'emprunts "parthes", c'est-à-dire issus de l'aire dialectale moyen-iranienne du Nord-Ouest, et de la période arsacide; ces deux délimitations, spatiale et chronolgique, ont été bien appuyées et confirmées, comme chacun sait, par les récentes études linguistiques iraniennes qui ont démontré par des preuves indiscutables qu'effectivement la plus grande partie des emprunts iraniens est d'origine parthe et date de la période òu la branche cadette de la dynastie arsacide gerait le pays d'Arménie. L'indication de l'origine parthe des emprunts arméniens est d'autant plus intéressante qu'au temps où Schröder écrivait (1711) on ne connaissait encore aucun document de la langue parthe.

Il vaut la peine de rappeler qu'exactement deux siècles après Schröder, en 1911, Meillet s'exprimait en des termes semblables quand il parlait des

> " emprunts de l'arménien à l'iranien de l'époque arsacide, à la langue des Parthes " (9).

C'est une ressemblance, même formelle, vraiment frappante, entre deux textes a deux siècles de distance.

Remarquons encore que Schröder a exactement relevé que ces emprunts à la langue parthe sont en arménien des mots d'un emploi courant (*ex frequenti usu*), et également des mots bien employés par les meilleurs auteurs classiques (*ab Auctoribus Armenis etiam optimis adhibita*).

Parmi les mots arméniens, dont Schröder a reconnu avec finesse l'origine iranienne en s'appuyant sur le rapprochement du persan, il suffit de mentionner:

arm. *angam* " vice "	persan *hangām*
arm. *baxt* " fortuna "	persan *baxt*
arm. *brinj* " oryza "	persan *birinǰ*
arm. *dahlic* "vestibulum "	persan *dahlīz, dihlīz*
arm. *dašt* " planities	persan *dašt*
arm. *dipak* " vestis serica "	persan *dēbāh*
arm. *draxt* " hortus "	persan *diraxt*
arm. *kowž* " urceus "	persan *kūz-a*

arm. *vat* " malus "   persan *bad*

arm. *vatt'ar* " pejus "   persan *badtar.*

À propos de l'arm. *dram* " nummus, drachma, pondus " il est intéressant de relever que Schröder avait déjà bien compris que ce mot, d'une évidente origine grecque, pénétra en arménien par l'intermediare de l'iranien (10).

3. La grande finesse d'esprit de Schröder ressort encore mieux du fait qu'il a exactement reconnu en arménien la présence non seulement de plusieurs emprunts iraniens, mais aussi d'emprunts syriaques, grecs, arabes qui, sous l'influence de " parastrats " et de " superstrats ", ont enrichi remarquablement le fonds original du vocabulaire arménien.

Parmi les mots arméniens, que Schröder a exactement reconnus comme emprunts syriaques, on peut mentionner:

arm. *dar* " seculum "   syr. *dārā*

arm. *t'argmanel* "interpretari"   syr. *targmānā*

arm. *mak's* " vectigal "   syr. *maxsā*

arm. *k'ahanay* " sacerdos "   syr. *kāhnā*

arm. *k'aroz* " praeco, concionator,
                    & concio "   syr. *kārōzā*. (II).

4. Schröder a même identifié et exactement indiqué dans le vocabulaire arménien la présence d'emprunts grecs:

> *Graeca* (scil. *vocabula*) *per bella, scientiarum studium, & per Christianam religionem Armenis innotuerunt* (12).

D'où il ressort que Schröder a de fait également découvert les deux causes principales de l'influence lexicale grecque sur l'arménien: le christianisme (*per Christianam religionem*) qui favorisa sans doute la pénétration culturelle grecque en Arménie, et un vif intérêt pour la civilisation grecque qui porta à l'étude et à la traduction de textes non seulement des *nerk'in owsmownk'* ou " sciences intérieures " (ayant rapport à l'étude des Saintes Ecritures et aux dissertations theologiques), mais aussi des *artak'in owsmownk'* ou " sciences extérieures ", à savoir la grammaire, la rhétorique, la philosophie, l'arithmétique et la géométrie, l'astronomie, la médecine, etc. (<*per*> *scientiarum studium*).

En effet, Schröder a bien reconnu en arménien non seulement des emprunts grecs typiques de la terminologie religieuse chrétienne, comme:

arm. *episkopos*	gr. ἐπίσκοπος
arm. *kat'owlikos*	gr. καθολικός
arm. *kiraki*	gr. κυριακή
arm. *het'anos*	gr. ἔθνος
arm. *patriark'*	gr. πατριάρχης
arm. *saɫmos*	gr. ψαλμός,

mais aussi bien d'autres emprunts grecs de la langue profane et laïque, a savoir:

arm. *brabion*	gr. βραβεῖον
arm. *klimay*	gr. κλίμα
arm. *hiwlē*	gr. ὕλη
arm. *moros*	gr. μωρός
arm. *pnak*	gr. πίναξ
arm. *tokos*	gr. τόκος
arm. *p'alang*	gr. φάλαγξ

5. Schröder a également compris que même l'arabe a influencé, bien que plus récemment, le vocabulaire arménien, et il a exactement reconnu, par exemple, que arm. *mkrat* " forfex " est sans doute emprunté à l'arabe *miqrāḍ* (14).

6. De toute facon Schröder ne s'est pas borné à identifier les emprunts iraniens, syriaques, grecs, arabes qui ont remarquablement enrichi le fonds original du vocabulaire arménien, mais il a aussi indiqué clairement les mots qui constituent ce meme fonds lexical originel, c'est-à-dire les mots que l'arménien au cours de son histoire n'a pas empruntés à d'autres langues, mais qu'il a hérité directement de l'indo-européen, comme on dirait en termes modernes. Schröder appelle ces mots arméniens originels *voces ejus* (scil. *Haicanae Linguae*) *propriae* : ce sont les mots qui désignent les réalités primordiales et qui sont en effet les éléments lexicaux les plus anciens de l'arménien, et en général de toutes les langues (*vocabula res naturales primum cognitas & in oculum incurrentes significantia, ceu omnium antiquissima* (15).

Par conséquent les mots originels du vocabulaire arménien, selon Schröder, sont exactement ceux qui désignent en particulier les parties du corps, les éléments fondamentaux de la nature, les noms de parenté tels que: *ayr* " vir ", *ač'k* " oculi ", *atamn* " dens ", *atel* " odisse", *get* " fluvius ", *etbayr* " frater ", *cownr* " genu ", *kin* " uxor ", *hayr* " pater ", *howr* " ignis ", *jeṁ* " manus ", *ji* " equus ", *jowkn* "piscis ", *mayr* " mater ", *mec* " magnus ", *mit* " mens ", *otn* " pes ", *jowr* " aqua ", *sirt* " cor ", *ter* " dominus ", *town* " domus ", *k'oyr* " soror ", etc.

Au fonds original du vocabulaire arménien Schröder attribue encore les noms de nombre *mi* "unus ", *erkow* " duo ", *erek'* " tres ", *č'ork'* " quatuor ", *hing* " quinque ", etc.; les trois séries des démonstratifs (et articles) *-s -d -n, sa da na, ays ayd ayn* " hic, iste, ille "; le pronom réfléchi *iwr* " suus "; le pronom reciproque *mimeans* " invicem " (16).

Et même ces remarques concernant le fonds original du vocabulaire arménien se révèlent fort correctes encore aujourd'hui. C'est en se fondant justement sur ces mots originels que Schröder proclame catégoriquement l'autonomie et l'indépendance de la langue arménienne: " Haicana Lingua summo jure Cardinalis dicenda est " (17). Le sens particulier que le terme *Cardinalis* a dans ce contexte, ressort bien d'un passage précédent qui explique:

" Cardinalem esse Haicanam Linguam probatur ex Vocibus ejus propriis " (18).

À Schröder revient donc le grand mérite d'avoir su distinguer dans le vocabulaire arménien son noyau original et primitif des emprunts secondaires que les rapports historiques et culturels y ont ensuite introduits. C'est une question qui revêt une grande importance, eu égard à l'époque à laquelle Schröder vivait. Une opinion tout à fait différente l'emportait alors, c'est-à-dire que le vocabulaire arménien était fondamentalement dépourvu d'emprunts!

Le jésuite francais Jacques Villotte, missionnaire en Arménie pendant 25 ans et auteur de plusieurs ouvrages en arménien, composa, trois ans après le *Thesaurus* de Schröder, un *Dictionarium novum Latino-Armenium* qui a été même considéré " le meilleur de tous ceux qui avaient été publiés auparavant " (19). Eh bien, dans la *Dissertatio in linguam Armeniam* qui précède son *Dictionarium* Villotte, après avoir exaltè la richesse et la variété du vocabulaire arménien, dit explicitement:

" Hoc deinde Haykanae linguae proprium est, & singulare, quod vocum copiam illam, de suo totam habet, nihil de alieno ",
tandis, qu'au contraire de l'arménien,

" Omnes fere Europae populos videmus, propriarum linguarum immensae molis Vocabularia texere; e quibus ea si detraxeris, quae a peregrinis linguis mutuata sunt, ingentem illum acervum continuo videbis ruere, & in minimam molem redigi. Locupletem illum minime dixerim, qui, quod habet, illud adsciscit aliunde " (20).

Surle fond foncé de telles idées de ses contemporains, se détache encore davantage la théorie vraiment pénétrante et innovatrice de Schröder, qui a bien su distinguer en arménien ce qui est emprunté de ce qui est originel.

Il ressort donc de notre exposé que Schröder parvint à esquisser, avec une clarté suffisante et une surprenante exactitude, l'histoire du vocabulaire arménien et sa stratification complexe. De ce point de vue, même à presque trois siècles de distance, l'ouvrage de Schroder presente les caracteres d'une frappante modernite et actualite.

Je veux enfin relever un autre detail interessant: l'etonnante analogie entre l'ouvrage de Schröder et celui de Hübschmann, non seulement sur le plan du contenu, mais aussi sur le plan de la forme. On sait que *l'Armenische Grammatik* de Hübschmann est structurée en quatre sections fondamentales (abstraction faite de la Section très brève " Armenische Lehnwörter unsicherer Herkunft "), qui traitent respectivement des emprunts iraniens, des emprunts syriaques, des emprunts grecs et des mots arméniens indigènes.

Eh bien, la disposition de la matière est la même dans le *Thesaurus* de Schröder, dont les paragraphes font parfaitement pendant aux grandes sections de l'ouvrage de Hübschmann. À tout cela il faut encore ajouter le parfait parallélisme des titres mêmes chez Schröder et chez Hübschmann:

" vocabula Parthica "	*Persische Wörter*
" (vocabula) Chaldeo-Syriaca	*Syrische Wörter*
" (vocabula) Graeca) "	*Griechische Wörter*
range "voces	range *Echtarmenische*
under "(vocabula	under *Griechische Worter*

"voces ejus (*scil.* Haicanae Linguae) propriae ".

Une analogie si évidente doit vraiment faire réfléchir.

Ce que nous venons de dire donne davantage envie de savoir si Hübschmann connaissait l'ouvrage de Schröder. La réponse à cette question est positive: en effet, Hübschmann cite explicitement le *Thesaurus linguae Armenicae* , pourtant sans dire que son auteur avait déjà clairement et exactement considéré l'arménien comme une langue qui a sa propre individualité consistant " ex vocibus ejus propriis ", dans laquelle furent seulement ensuite introduits des emprunts secondaires iraniens, syriaques, grecs, arabes en conséquence des rapports historiques avec d'autres traditions culturelles.

> Voici tout ce que Hübschmann s'est borné à dire de Schröder: "Einige richtige Etymologien hatte schon (im J. 1711) Schröder in seinem Thesaurus linguae Armenicae p. 45-47 gegeben " (21).

Bien sûr, Hübschmann a eu la possibilité de faire ce que Schröder ne pouvait pas faire, c'est-à-dire il a démontré scientifiquement, surtout par des preuves phonétiques, que l'arménien était effectivement une langue autonome et indépendante de l'iranien, et cette démonstration lui aurait valu l'estime universelle et le titre de fondateur des études scientifiques arméniennes, même s'il avait reconnu la finesse d'esprit et l'étonnante intuition de son devancier.

Nous pouvons, finalement, aboutir à la conclusion qu'il est bon de ne pas négliger *a priori* la lecture de livres appartenant à la ' prehistoire ' de la linguistique, celle-ci pouvant nous réserver la belle surprise de découvrir qu'en réalité des vérités scientifiques, considérées comme des acquisition récentes, ont depuis longtemps été énoncées.

NOTES

1. F. Schlegel, *Ueber die Sprache und Weisheit der Indier. Ein Beitrag zur Begruendung der Alterthumskunde*, Heidelberg 1808, pp. 77-78. Je cite les mots arméniens en *grabar* et dans la transcription scientifique moderne.
2. F. Bopp, *Vergleichende Grammatik des Sanskrit, Send, Armenischen, Griechischen, Lateinischen, Litauischen, Altslavischen, Gothischen und Deutschen*, II éd., vol. I, Berlin 1857, p. XVIII.
3. Cf. G. Bolognesi, " La stratificazione del lessico armeno nell'opera di J.J. Schröder ", dans *Energeia und Ergon. Festschrift for E. Coseriu*, ed. by J. Albrecht - J. Lüdtke - H. Thun, sous presse.
4. H. Hübschmann, " Ueber die stellung des armenischen im kreise der indogermanischen sprachen ", *KZ* 23 (1875), pp. 5-49.
5. J.J. Schröder, *Aramean lezowin ganj. Hoc est: Thesaurus linguae Armenicae, antiquae et hodiernae, cum varia Praxios materia, cujus elenchum sequens pagella exhibet*, Amstelodami MDCCXI, p. 23.
6. J.J. Schröder, ibidem.
7. J.J. Schröder, op. cit., pp. 44-45.
8. J.J. Schröder, op. cit., p. 46.
9. A. Meillet, " Sur les mots iraniens empruntés par l'arménien ", *MSL* 17 (1911), p. 249.
10. J.J. Schröder, op. cit., pp. 46-47. Concernant l'intermédiaire iranien supposé par l'emprunt arménien, cf. G. Bolognesi, *Le fonti dialettali degli imprestiti iranici in armeno*, Milano 1960, pp. 37, 68; R. Schmitt, " Iranisches Lehngut im Armenischen ", *Rearm N.S.* 17 (1983), p. 86.
11. J.J. Schröder, op. cit., pp. 45-46.
12. J.J. Schröder, op. cit., p. 47.
13. J.J. Schröder, op. cit., p. 47.
14. J.J. Schröder, op. cit., p. 46
15. J.J. Schröder, op. cit., p. 43.
16. J.J. Schröder, op. cit., p. 44.
17. J.J. Schröder, op. cit., p. 48.
18. J.J. Schröder, op. cit., p. 43.
19. P.S. Somal, *Quadro della storia letteraria di Armenia*, Venezia 1829, p. 206.
20. J. Villotte, *Dictionarium / novum / Latino-Armenium / ex / praecipuis Armeniae linguae / Scriptoribus concinnatum. / In quo, praeter adjunctos singularum vocum sensus / multiplices, multa etiam Theologica, Physica, / Moralia, Historica, Mathematica, Geographica, / Chronologica, suis quaeque locis / passim explicantur. / Accessit / Tabula Chronologica Regum et Patriarcharum / utriusque Armeniae / Auctore / P. Jacobo Villotte, Soc. Jesu / Apud Armenios per annos XXV. Missionario. / Romae. Typis Sac. Congreg. de Propaganda Fide: / Anno MDCCXIV*. La citation est à p. 2 de la " Dissertatio in linguam Armeniam " qui précède le <u>Dictionarium</u>.
21. H. Hübschmann, *Armenische Grammatik. Erster Teil: Armenische Etymologie*, Leipzig 1897 (réimpr. Hildesheim 1962, 1972), p. XIII.

AGRICULTURAL TRANSITION, "INDO-EUROPEAN ORIGINS" AND THE SPREAD OF FARMING

Marek Zvelebil and Kamil V. Zvelebil

Indo-European origins and the spread of IE languages to the West and towards the East represent one of the greatest puzzles of prehistory, archaeology and linguistics. In this contribution we examine the unconventional hypothesis recently advanced by Colin Renfrew in his book *Archaeology and Language. The Puzzle of Indo-European Origins* (1987), evaluate its validity from both the archaeological and linguistic perspectives, and offer an alternative model with significant modifications of Renfrew's "language-farming hypothesis".

Renfrew's book provoked reaction in both the popular press and in scientific journals (Baldi 1988, Mallory 1988, Ehret 1988, Sherratt 1988) including our own views expressed in the recent issue of Antiquity (Zvelebil and Zvelebil 1988). Renfrew's new model also played a prominent part in the contributions to and the discussions at the Bellagio conference. The present contribution is an elaborated version of our earlier paper on the subject (Zvelebil and Zvelebil 1988), incorporating some of the views raised at Bellagio and taking into the account the current discussion generated by Renfrew's book.

In the following pages, we shall first offer a few critical remarks of general nature concerning both the linguistic and archaeological aspects of Renfrew's hypothesis; then we shall address the issue of the hypothetical westward movement of the IE speakers into Europe, this will be followed by a discussion of the spread of IE peoples towards the East, to India; in conclusion, we shall suggest an alternative model for the IE presence in India and Europe, and its possible ties with the spread of agro-pastoral farmers.

GENERAL CONSIDERATIONS

Renfrew's hypothesis appears relatively straightfoward. Indo-European languages have become widely distributed in Europe:

"If we look at the distribution of Indo-European languages of Europe when we first see them in the centuries shortly before or after the beginning of the Christian era (or, in the case of Grece, a thousand years earlier), virtually the whole of Europe seems to have been Indo-European-speaking... This is a vast area for such a degree of uniformity." (1987:145).

How can one explain such uniform distribution? After considering a number of models which can account for dispersals of language, and after considering the viability of the currently favoured explanation, that of the Indo-European dispersal from the south Russian steppes in the 3rd millenium BC, Renfrew concludes:

"In proposing a specific solution I found it difficult to accept the arguments put foward for profound population and language changes across the whole of Europe at the beginning of the bronze age, somewhere in the third millennium B.C. The main objection to this solution was archaeological: that there does not seem to be any sufficiently profound and widespread shift in the archaeological record at that time to justify such a conclusion.

In surveying European prehistory I do not believe that we can see any one process, nor any series of processes at once sufficiently profound in social and demographic consequences and so widespread geographically as to suggest a viable background for such radical linguistic changes, until we go right back to the time of the spread of farming."(1987: 265)

This passage encapsulates all the assumptions on which Renfrew's hypothesis can be questioned. Renfrew argues that farming was introduced to Europe from Anatolia by immigrant farmers some 8000 years ago (6500 - 6000 BC), that these farmers colonised most of Europe through small-scale migration and occupation of hitherto unfarmed areas over the generations; and that these farmers were the original Indo-European speakers who introduced the language to Europe. He further assumes that by the beginning of the Classical period at the latest, and perhaps as early as 3000 B.C. (by the time the farming colonisation of Europe was completed), Indo-European languages were uniformly distributed over the European continent, save for a few marginal areas such as the Basque country. A final major assumption is that the spread of Indo-European languages in Europe was a single event, and that archaeologically, only the spread of farming can explain such geographically widespread phenomenon.

Suggestions that Indo-European origins extend back to the Stone Age in time and/or to the general area of the Near East in space have recently been made by several authors (Clarke 1968, Gamkrelidze and Ivanov 1984, Dolukhanov 1986c). In the first comprehensive treatment of this hypothesis, Renfrew suggests demographic and economic rationales for the process of the Indo-European dispersals. Transition from foraging to farming engenders an increase in food production and population growth, which in turn fuel the need for the colonisation of unfarmed habitats.

In this way Renfrew provides a socio-economic explanation for the diffusion of farmers to Europe, and for the dispersal of Indo-European languages: a clear advance on previous models.

There are, however, assumptions in Renfrew's line of reasoning, which look distinctly less convincing after a closer examination of the data ordered by Renfrew's clear presentation. At the most general level, there is the whole question of a relationship between language, culture and population. Despite the warning delivered by Renfrew (1987:75-77, see also this volume), the language-farming hypothesis equates, in effect, the IE language group with people (the first farmers) and further, with the archaeological cultures of the Neolithic. This comes at a time when the normative view of culture has finally been recognised as inadequate and oversimplified in archaeology (Clarke 1968, Binford 1962, 1972, Shiffer 1972, 1976,) while in linguistics, already Edward Sapir warned in 1921 against equating language, race and culture. The burden of proof, then, must fall on Renfrew, to demonstrate beyond reasonable doubt, that in this case such normative view holds. As we shall try to show, Renfrew falls short of this requirement.

When it comes to the hypothetical IE protolanguage, we should never forget that Indo-European is a construct, not a demonstrable reality. As A. Meillet put it in 1922, "on ne restitue pas par la comparaison une langue disparue... on ne restitue donc pas l'indo-europeen" (1964:41). We should always bear in mind that not a single sentence, not a single work, not even a single sound of an Indo-European tongue, before its differentiation and dispersal, has been preserved. This makes it even more difficult to equate an archaeological culture – a construct in its own right – with a hypothetical Indo-European speaking people.

Moreover, if there ever was a single Indo-European protolanguage, most linguists are convinced that at that stage it must have been differentiated into several dialects territorially, and perhaps even socioliguistically, since it was a language spoken obviously without any centre of prestige, without any central authority, and since the unifying and standardizing effect of literacy and all that goes with it was totally absent. Thus, when speaking of the spread of Indo-European, one should rather speak of the spread of Indo-European dialects than about the spread of a single homogenous Indo-European speech.

WESTERN MOVEMENTS

Renfrew's model for the westward spread of the Indo-European speaking farmers from their original homeland in Anatolia is based on two key assumptions, which we now wish to question: the notion of a widespread distribution of Indo-European languages in neolithic Europe, and that of Indo-European dispersals as a single, continuous process. To address the first assumption, our reconstruction of the possible distribution of identified non-Indo-European languages (figure 1) shows that virtually the whole of the Iberian peninsula, the whole of Italy, Mediterranean islands, southern France, large parts of the Atlantic coast and large parts of Britain were probably non-Indo-European during most of the prehistoric period. There are at least six identifiable non-Indo-European speeches known to us (Etruscan, Basque, Ligurian, Iberian, Tartessian, Pictish), plus five possible non-Indo-European tongues (Sicel, Rhaetic, Messapic, East Italic, pre-Indo-European Illyrian) (Pulgram 1978, 1958, Jackson 1955, Krahe 1936, Meillet 1964, Stevenson 1983). Hydronyms and other topographic items as well as a number of common words indicate the presence of these, and other non-Indo-European languages which have left no trace, in many parts of Europe, later covered by Indo-European. As a few more or less randon samples we may quote from Occitan (southern France) cf.clap stone<*clapp-, garric var. of oak<*garr-/*carr-, serra mountain-crest<serr-, truc hillock; summit, suc mountain-summit<*cuc-; (Alibert 1977), and from Slavonic cf. les wood, forest; krosna pannier, kuna marten, kolpík var of wading bird, ald'bji/lad'ji (czech loď) ship, vessel. Hence it would seem that Indo-European languages were far more restricted than historical sources would suggest. It may well have been the case that non-Indo-European languages were spoken in large territories, particularly in areas outside the European continental core; and that the initial agricultural colonisation did not reach these areas.

These observations do not necessarily negate Renfrew's model, but they can be accommodated within its framework only if we allow for two distinct areas in the dynamism of a gradual, intermittent spread of Indo-European dialects: one, the area of "primary dispersal" another, the area of "secondary dispersal". Within the area of primary dispersal – south-east and central Europe – Indo-European languages may have been adopted relatively rapidly and on a more massive scale; within the secondary areas – Eastern and Northern Europe, Italy, Iberia, southern and central France, Atlantic coast, British Isles – the dialects of Indo-European were adopted at a later date through cultural diffusion, small-scale population shifts and elite dominance. The primary dispersal may have well involved colonisation in the way envisaged by Renfrew, in the secondary areas, the indigenous pre-Indo-European populations must have played an important role in the process of Indo-Europeanisation.

Ehret (1988) noted different ways in which Indo-European languages may have been adopted by the indigenous populations through contact, trade and elite dominance. We have a recent small-scale model of such developments, historically attested, in the Nilgiri Hills area of Southern India before the time of British colonisation. This analogy shows how the Badaga language (originally a dialect of Kannada spoken by refugees from Karnataka) spread in the 16th and subsequent centuries throughout the Nilgiri area. Thanks to their more complex and productive socio-economic structures (advanced agriculture, market-oriented food production) the Badagas became the dominant people, and their language was adopted as the lingua franca among some sixteen tribal groups, whose languages were fully or partly mutually unintelligible. Badaga is today totally dominant in the areas of their primary colonisation - fertile valleys- and the tongue of common intercourse in the areas originally inhabited by the indigenous tribes which have now become the territory of peripheral, secondary Badaga colonisation. The tribal languages are on the decline, while Badaga speakers grow in number, from some 500 in 1603 to 120 000 today, partly a result of acculturation of indigenous groups (Hockings 1980, K.V. Zvelebil 1980, 1981, Emeneau n.d.).

During the agricultural transition in the Neolithic, the situation was certainly different. As Dennell pointed out (Dennell 1985), social, technological and economic differences between hunter-gatherer and neolithic farming societies were bound to be much smaller than among any recent ethnographic examples, reducing the socio-economic and demographic advantages which the farmers might possess (see also below). But we think the Nilgiri analogy is valid in so far as it underlines the possibility of an Indo-European lingua franca being adopted from a small group of agricultural colonists by the indigenous hunting and gathering population.

The second major assumption in Renfrew's model goes to the heart of the matter. This is whether the Indo-European dispersals were a single process, caused by a single factor - the agricultural transition, and fuelled by a single mechanism - the farmer colonisation. We have tried to show that linguistic paleogeography of Europe does not support this view. We think that archaeological evidence as well casts serious doubt on the suitability of Renfrew's model in most parts of Europe.

While the introduction of agro-pastoral farming to south-east Europe around 6500 BC and its subsequent spread to the rest of Europe can hardly be doubted, profound differences exist about the rate, the direction and method of its dispersal. Are we talking about an indigenous development of farming in Europe based on local and imported cultigens and domesticates (Dennell 1983, Barker 1985), a farmer colonisation involving small-scale migrations (Ammermann and Cavalli-Sforza 1984), or a mixture of the two processes (Zvelebil,M 1986a)? This question concerns the contribution of the local, possibly non-IE mesolithic populations in the subsequent cultural development of Europe. If the farming economies were developed locally, the genetic contribution of intrusive populations was negligible, and Renfrew's hypothesis, in its present form, does not hold. If, on the other hand, farmer immigration from Anatolia was primarily responsible for the introduction of farming to Europe, the language-farming hypothesis cannot be excluded. In the intermediate case, language farming hypothesis may apply in certain parts of Europe, but would not account for the uniform distribution of IE languages one can see in Europe today.

Renfrew opts for the Ammermann-Cavalli-Sforza's "Wave of Advance" model of demic diffusion of farming into Europe, which best suits his case (1987: 124-133). From the archaeological perspective, however, this model has serious shortcomings (Zvelebil,M. 1986a, 1986b), and Renfrew, although he ackowledges some of the problems involved (1987: 149, 151, 266, 268,), is nevertheless tempted to equate the introduction of farming with diffusion of new people regardless of the regional context (1987:148-149,159-161,190, 242,). In our view, the "Wave of Advance" model, based on demic diffusion of farming does not apply in most areas of Europe on following grounds.

Mesolithic–Neolithic continuity.

In most areas of Europe there is no archaeological evidence of immigration or colonisation by new people of areas hitherto occupied by indigenous hunter-gatherers. Migrations are notoriously difficult to identify in archaeological contexts, but most people would not rule out the possibility of immigration occurring where there is a radical break in settlement pattern, material culture, and ideology compared to the previous culture of an area. With the possible exception of the LBK culture in Central Europe, and some areas of south-east Europe, this is not the case at the Mesolithic–Neolithic transition. On the contrary, in most areas, there is continuity of settlement, continuity of some aspects of material culture (such as lithics) and retention of symbols (bear, waterbirds, fish) across the mesolithic-neolithic transition (Dennell 1983, Zvelebil 1986a, etc). It would seem that in most parts of Europe, agro-pastoral farming was added to the existing patterns of resource use by the indigenous populations (generating, naturally, some changes in the material culture), rather than being the "fossil directeur" of immigrant farmer colonisation.

Evidence from physical anthropology.

According to the traditional diffusionist view, the farmer colonisation of Europe can be also detected by the presence of new physical traits in the European populations, particularly the "round-headed" groups who progressively replaced the indigenous "long-headed" types. This argument has been recently used by Vencl, for example (1986). However, the use of the cephalic index to distinguish between round and long-headedness has been criticised on methodological grounds (i.e. Gould 1981), while it remains to be seen to what extent the changes in the shape of the face and the cranium are due to environmental (including nutritional) as opposed to genetic factors (y'Edynak 1978, Gould 1981). As Gould reminded us (Gould 1981), already in 1912 Franz Boas established that significant changes in the shape of the cranium can develop among immigrants to the United States in the course of a few generations. If such changes can occur as a result of dietary changes (Boas 1912, y'Edynak 1978), the cranial differences among European Neolithic population could reflect the shift from hunting-gathering to farming, rather than the arrival of genetically distinct populations.

More recently, Ammerman and Cavalli-Sforza (1984) have employed blood group and other genetic differences within European populations to support their hypothesis of a farmer colonisation. As one of us has argued elsewhere, distribution patterns arising from these differences could result from other, historically documented migrations in Europe, and not necessarily from the neolithic farmer colonisation (Zvelebil, M. 1986b). A latest extensive study of genetic variability among modern populations of Europe and of its relationship to language families by Sokal et.al. (1989) shows just how complex the problem is, and, if anything argues for genetic differentiation resulting from several sources. Although, wisely, Renfrew does not embrace these arguments, they form an integral part of the justification for the "Wave of Advance" model (Ammermann and Cavalli-Sforza 1984), and as such had to be treated here at some length. Our conclusion is that on the present evidence, physical anthropology or genetic patterning do not lend support to the colonisation model of the transition to farming in Europe.

Rate of transition to farming economies.

Despite Renfrew's assertion to the contrary (1987:190), the adoption of farming in Europe was a slow process, which took at least 3000 years to complete and probably much longer. In some areas of Europe, such as peninsular Scandinavia or the temperate zone of eastern Europe, farming was not adopted until the 2nd. Millenium B.C., some 4000-5000 years after its introduction in Greece. The transition to farming was in fact slower than could be expected under the "Wave of Advance" model (Zvelebil,M. 1986a).

Further evidence supporting our case for of a complex nature of agricultural transition in Europe, in which the indigenous groups played a significant part, arises from a paper given at this (Bellagio) conference by Dr. Zohary. Zohary traced the spread of the neolithic Near Eastern crop assemblage to Europe, West Asia and the Nile Valley. If this is compared to the spread of domestic animals, we can see that in some parts of Europe the two events are not contemporary. In parts of Italy, France, in the Iberian peninsula, and generally along the Atlantic seabord of Europe, domesticates were adopted earlier than cultigens. The same is in fact true for the vast areas of Eastern Europe where domesticates often appear a thousand years or more before the first evidence for cultigens. On the present evidence, this may mean that agro-pastoral farming was not introduced as a uniform package to Europe as a whole, merely to its central and south-eastern parts. Some of the delay and variation in the pattern of the spread of farming in Europe can be explained by the local ecological factors and by the colonisation of secondary habitats. But above these local situations a broader pattern is emerging: while in south-eastern and central Europe farming already appears as a well-developed package, in the west, north and east it is adopted selectively, with domesticates often preceeding cultigens. These areas correspond to the "culturally indigenous Europe" where the continuity in material culture between the local hunting-gathering and the first farming societies is apparent. We suggest, therefore, that in these areas, local groups selected from the agro-pastoral package those elements which fit their existing economies and social organisation, while ignoring others. The selective, rather than inclusive adoption of farming in such areas would then argue in favour of demographic and cultural continuity from the mesolithic into the neolithic, and against the colonisation of these areas by immigrant farmers.

Our understanding of the spread of farming economy, and its contribution to the overall diet, is prejudiced by the biases which operate against the preservation and recovery of wild faunal remains on archaeological sites dating to the period of agricultural transition. Wild animals are often butchered away from the main settlements: they often rank among smaller species whose bones do not preserve as well as those of main domesticates, and moreover, other wild resources consist of fish, water fowl and wild plants, all of which stand much smaller chance of preservation than products of farming. In a recent publication Greenfield, for instance, noted differential recovery techniques at Balkan neolithic sites, which discriminated against the retrieval of wild faunal samples (Greenfield 1986). Bearing these points in mind, it may well be the case that the contribution of hunting and gathering in transitional farming-foraging communities has been routinely underestimated, and that the transition to farming has been a much more gradual process than hitherto acknowledged.

DEMOGRAPHIC PATTERNS:

Renfrew adopts Ammermann and Cavalli-Sforza's demographic argument that far greater population growth among immigrant neolithic farmers was bound to displace or absorb the indigenous hunter-gatherer populations, or make their role otherwise insignificant (1987: 124-131, 147, 150, etc.) In this way even a small initial population of farmers, moving into a new niche could rapidly become a decisive cultural and demographic force within a region. While it is undeniably true that the potential for population growth is far greater among farmers than hunter-gatherers, it cannot be automatically assumed such potential had a profound impact in the Neolithic. As Dennell argued (1985), neolithic farmers faced many social technological and environmental handicaps in Europe, which might have reduced their reproduction capability. Palaeopathology of neolithic populations, especially in western Europe, shows that their health status was no better and probably worse than that of the mesolithic populations (Cohen and Armelagos 1984). On the other hand, the viability and population density of the indigenous hunter-gatherers in Europe seems to have been underestimated by both, Ammermann and Cavalli-Sforza (1984) and Renfrew (1987:130). We suggest, therefore, that the demographic differences between the neolithic farmers and mesolithic indigens, were not, in general, as great as Renfrew maintains.

A second serious problem with this view arises from the dichotomy itself. First, if the indigenous hunter-gatherers adopted farming as we suggest was the case in most areas of Europe, then their demographic potential would approach the level of the neolithic agro-pastoral farmers. Second, if the colonising farmers (whether immigrant or indigenous) used wild resources to a greater extent than hitherto recognised (as we argue above), then we are effectively talking about mixed foraging-farming economies in both cases and the productivity levels on either side of the agricultual frontier should not have been that far apart. The difference in reproductive potential, therefore, could not have been so great, although some difference probably did exist. This argument serves to reinforce the view that where Mesolithic-Neolithic transition is concerned the agricultural frontier is a construct as artificial and inappropriate as the Berlin Wall. Instead of a line, it can best be regarded as a broad transitional zone where the process of replacement of foraging by farming is going on. To what extent this process is accomplished by the adoption of farming among local population, and to what extent by the secondary colonisation from earlier farming centres , is regionally variable and, for many regions, still unresolved (Zvelebil,M. 1986a).

In summary then, the "wave of advance" agricultural colonisation of Europe remains an unprobable hypothesis for most parts of the continent. The possible exceptions are certain areas of south-east and central Europe, where a radical break in settlement pattern and cultural traditions are associated with the spread of farming economy (figure 2). In view of this conclusion, one must question the language-farming hypothesis of Indo-European origins as presented by Renfrew. On archaeological grounds, first farmers may or may not have been Indo-European. Archaeologically, there are no compelling reasons to believe that they were.

EASTERN MOVEMENTS

We wish to offer the following critical remarks on Renfrew's treatment of the spread of Indo-European towards the east, particularly to India. When discussing the civilisation of the Indus Valley cities and the arrival of Indo-European speakers in northwestern India, Renfrew apparently ignores the presence of Dravidian in the whole of India including its northwest, north and northeast at a date at least as early as the Rgvedic hymns. This Dravidian presence is not a hypothesis but a fact attested by obvious loanwords in the Rgveda and in later Vedic texts, e.g., mayúra- peacock, phála- fruit, khála-threshing floor, ulúkhala-mortar for grinding, káṭuka-pungent, bitter; etc. T. Burrow (1945, 1946, 1948) finds twenty undisputed Dravidian loans in the early hymns of the Rgveda. If the Rgvedic examples, or any of them, are accepted, this is the evidence for the presence of Dravidian speakers as far toward the northwest as the Punjab, i.e. the upper Indus Valley, during the first centuries of the presence of Indo-European speakers in India. It is not a clear evidence for the Dravidian nature of the Harappan civilisation or language (or one of the Harappan languages) but it does lead toward that hypothesis. Additional support is lent to this hypothesis by the existence of isolated Dravidian "pockets" (Brahui, Kurux, Malto, Dhangar in Nepal) far in the northwest and northeast of the subcontinent even today.

Renfrew appears to favour Indo-European origins of the civilisation of the Indus Valley cities, and refers to several scholars who failed to decipher Harappan as Dravidian, ignoring, unfortunatelly, the more serious and convincing attempts (Mahadevan 1977, 1980, Fairservis 1983). However, the attempts to "read" Harappan as an early form of Indo-European have proved to be a total failure (a typical case being that of B. Hrozný, 1943), and are not even taken seriously today. Although nothing has been proved so far, there is a number of sound reasons to tentatively regard Harappan script/language as Dravidian since certain features revealed by positional statistics and structural patterns of the Indus script/language show convincingly that it is not related to Indo-European, since many cultural features appear to be completely indigenous to India, and since the most probable candidate appears to be Dravidian (K.V. Zvelebil 1985b).

In our view, the Rgvedic Aryas presumably lived in Upper Punjab, roughly to the north and northeast of the Harappan territory proper, while the most important sites of the Harappan civilisation were situated along the Indus, roughly to the south of Upper Punjab, as well as to the east and south-east of the river. Thus the northern fringes of the Harappan territory bordered on the southern fringes of the Rgvedic Indo-European areas, and that is where presumably the contacts, the clashes, even the battles between the Indo-European Aryas and the Dāsyus (Dravidians?) might indeed have taken place, although Renfrew does not give credence to such view and prefers to regard the Dāsyus/Dāsas as demons, ghosts and other evil supernatural beings (1987:182 ff). However, the references to the Dāsas in the Aryan texts, to their forts and the battles with them are completely realistic: they are described as dark-skinned, bull-lipped, snub-nosed or "noseless" worshippers of the phallus, and of hostile speech which was unintelligible. In short, this fits very well with the image the Aryas must have had of the Dravidian (?) speaking "barbaroi" - the Harappans.

We do not have to posit a wholesale destruction of the Harappan civilisation by Indo-European Aryas; in this point we certainly agree with Renfrew. There apparently were complex causes of its decline, a type of system-collapse, with the invasions of Aryan bands as one of the catalysts of that process. Chronologically it fits well: battles between Dāsyus and Aryas date to 2000-1800 BC, composition of Rgvedic hymns to 1600-1200 BC.

AN ALTERNATIVE MODEL

Most of our critical comment, especially where the westward spread of Indo-European is concerned, has been directed at the wave of advance model of agricultural transition (Ammermann and Cavalli-Sforza 1984), rather than at the language-farming hypothesis itself. In trying to locate the socio-economic underpinnings of the Indo-European dispersal, Renfrew has over-emphasised the application of the wave of advance model to the prehistoric situation in Europe. In this context, Ehret's cautious remark is appropriate:

"The previous communities do not disappear, but become the majority demographic component in the new ethnicity. The critical point is that language and ethnic shift can take place without radical change in the material particulars of life and with an amount of change in the human gene pool so small as to be for all purposes undetectable" (Ehret 1988:571).

Although Renfrew considered alternative means of language dispersal to demic diffusion, (systems collapse, elite dominance, "pidgin", etc) he does not integrate them in his model (1987, this volume). Ehret considers other situations of language dispersal which may apply to the Indo-European case (1988), while Dolukhanov (1986c), Sherratt and Sherratt (1988) and Zvelebil and Zvelebil (1988) have developed alternative models for the dispersal of Indo-European language which try to combine socio-economic change at the agricultural transition with other pertinent forms of language dispersal.

In our view, an elaboration of Renfrew's language-farming hypothesis which does not require widespread colonisation of Europe by initial farming populations would be more convincingly supported by the archaeological data. This alternative model, based on the same hypothesis, makes the assumptions that (1) Indo-European language dispersals were not a uniform and continuous process, but a punctuated, multi-stage and repetitive one, (2) that no widespread population displacements took place in most of Europe during the agricultural transition, and that (3) the Indo-European languages spread at different times and due to different causes, resulting in the distributional palimpsest we are seeing today.

Our model envisages three stages of dispersal in Europe: (figure 2):

(1) Introduction of agro-pastoral farming to Europe from the Near East via Anatolia, 6500 - 5000 BC (6000 - 4500 bc).

This is basically the same as the model proposed by Renfrew for the whole of Europe; here, however, we restrict the geographical scope to those areas where ag/ricultural colonisation can be actually postulated: the LBK province in Central

Europe, the Tripolye culture in the Ukraine, the area of the early Balkan Neolithic and some areas of southern Italy. Language dispersal during this stage would take place due to the same socio-economic causes as those advanced by Renfrew in his language-farming hypothesis. In departure from Renfrew's views, however, we view this as an exceptional situation.

(2) Consolidation of farming and "Secondary products revolution" 4800-2500 BC (4000-2000 b.c.)

This period encompasses the middle and late Neolithic in Europe. The period is geographically diachronic, occurring earlier in southern parts of Europe than in the north. Although their timing and contemporaniety are a matter of debate (Sherratt 1981,1983, Barker 1985, Bogucki 1987, Greenfield 1988, Chapman 1988), the significant developments during this period are the development of agriculture in sub-optimal and marginal habitats and agricultural intensification brought about by the development of diary farming, ard plough, animal traction and other aspects of the secondary products revolution (Sherratt 1981).

When regarded at a pan-European scale, only a very broad picture can emerge. But this is the time when agro-pastoral farming was adopted in the "secondary dispersal" areas, referred to earlier. Many of these areas show cultural continuity with the mesolithic hunter-gatherer culture. At a regional scale, farming extends from the best lowland soils into sub-optimal upland areas, some of which have hitherto been occupied by hunting and gathering communities (Barker 1985, Zvelebil 1986a, Bogucki 1987, etc).

We propose that within this framework of secondary dispersals and regional in-filling, two processes aided the diffusion of IE languages from central and south-eastern Europe: adoption of farming by indigenous mesolithic populations and the adoption of Indo-European as a language of exchange, new technology and inter-group communication by non-IE speakers in western, northern and eastern Europe, who were settled in zones then transitional to farming.

The second suggestion needs perhaps some elaboration. The great fragmentation and small-scale diversity of languages among hunter-gatherer societies is well documented. On the assumption that a similar situation existed among the prehistoric hunter-gatherers in Europe, the existence of "lingua franca" for inter-tribal communication would have been of advantage. More often than not, such languages derive from the context outside the societies indigenous to the area (eg. the Badaga example, Ehret 1988). The status of IE as a common language of communication would be further enhanced if innovative technological and economic practices were associated with it – as may have been the case if the first farmers of south-east and central Europe were Indo-European. In time, over many generations, IE would come to replace the original language of the indigenous inhabitants as their mother tongue.

In a recent paper in Antiquity, Ehret argued that "the overall implications of glottochronology (are) that Indo-European divergence and spread was a process beginning, at the earliest, roughly in the range of the second half of the 5th millennium BC, give or take several centuries, and that the early stages of the process continued through the 4th and perhaps 3rd millennia" (1988:572). Without wishing to get involved in the debate surrounding the value of glottochronology (e.g., Renfrew, 1987 and his volume), it is worth noting that this view is in accord with our model, if the initial spread of proto-Indo-European into Europe during the earlier phase (6000-4500 BC) can be regarded as one of a closely related group of dialects before divergence actually began (see also Sherratt and Sherratt 1988 for alternative explanation).

(3) Elite dominance stage, 3800-ca.1000 BC (3000-1000 b.c.)

Renfrew considers this model and does not find it applicable to the European situation prior to the 1st millennium B.C. (1987:163, but see Sherratt 1981, Sherratt and Sherratt 1988). This is in keeping with his rejection of the Gimbutas' "Kurgan" theory (Gimbutas 1970), envisaging the spread of Indo-European languages with nomadic pastoralists from the south Russian steppes. At one point, in fact,

Renfrew suggests that nomadic pastoralism diffused eastwards from an early centre of cultivation in western Ukraine. (1987:208 ,271).There is, however, recent new evidence for the domestication of the horse as early as 6000 BC (Matyushin 1986, Telegin 1986) in the area of south Urals. If this admittedly circumstantial evidence will be borne out by further discoveries, the north central Asian and east European steppes, about which very little is known at present, may yet emerge as the original centers of horse domestication and the development of pastoral economies associated with it.

The area between the Dnieper and the Urals, the northern shores of the Black and Caspian Seas, may have been an early and active centre of Indo-European speaking communities. The early development of the pastoral economy would provide an economic rationale for dispersal, especially within the context of Eastern Europe (Sherratt 1981, Sherratt and Sherratt 1988, Anthony 1986, Telegin 1986, Dolukhanov 1986a) and Central Asia (Zvelebil,M. 1980, Matyushin 1986, Dolukhanov 1986b). There is nothing which would deny such nomadic pastoralist access to sedentary agriculturists, so necessary for their survival (cf. Renfrew 1987: 197-205). On the contrary, nomadic pastoralists often assume the role of social elite in such situations (Irons and Dyson-Hudson 1972, Dahl and Hjort 1976, Khazanov 1984) We suggest that this may have provided a third mode of dispersal of Indo-European languages, especially in marginal zones of Eastern Europe and Central Asia, where the transition to agro-pastoral farming occured late (i.e. 2nd millennium, and therefore would not be covered by stage 2), or did not occur at all, hunting-gathering being directly replaced by nomadic pastoralism. Sherratt and Sherratt (1988) have come to similar conclusions.

Later population shifts had, of course, an effect on the distribution of Indo-European languages. These include the events around 1000 BC and again during the Migration Period, both of which Renfrew subsumes under his system collapse model. They also include the tenure of the Roman Empire, responsible for the diffusion of Romance languages. These repeated demographic and liguistic changes reveal the multi-stage nature of linguistic dispersals. They also suggest that the present picture is radically different from that prevalent in antiquity, and that the initial area of Indo-European settlement in Europe may have been quite small.

(4). The East

As far as the spread of Indo-European towards the east is concerned, we believe we can accept the major premise that greater Anatolia was the key area where early forms of Indo-European might have been spoken even before 6000 BC. We concur with Sheratt and Sheratt (1988) in regarding the larger Zagros area of southern Iran and adjacent territories as one which also had non-Indo-European populations: the Summerians, Elamites, Ḫattics and the (hypothetic) Elamo-Dravidians (McAlpin 1981). The reconstruction of an Elamo-Dravidian linguistic entity may be, after the necessary modifications (K.V. Zvelebil 1985a), accepted, and if so, we could posit a dispersal of Elamo-Dravidian languages to the south and east of the Zagros mountains loop, towards India, where this population established the Harappan civilisation, ethnically possibly rather composite but with its elite speaking the Elamo-Dravidian language developing there into proto-Dravidian (see also Sheratt and Sheratt 1988). From the Indus valley area, proto-Dravidian extended in space to the west and northwest (witness Brahui), northeast (Kurux, Malto, Dhangar) and to central and southern India (today's solid belt of Dravidian languages, both pre-literate and literate).

Thus it would seem that "greater" Anatolia was a tremendously "productive" area with the successive populations of Summerians, Elamo-Dravidians, Elamites, Ḫattic people and Indo-European Hittites. As Renfrew admits (albeit in what sounds like an understatement), "not all the early farmers in the nuclear zone of domestication spoke an early Indo-European language." Nagging questions remain, of course: Can the development of agro-pastoral farming in this area really account for such demographic growth and ethno-linguistic diversity?

While the non-Indo-European, and possibly predominantly proto-Dravidian

Harappan civilisation was still flourishing in the Indus valley and adjacent territories, before and around 2000 B.C., the Indo-European speakers in the steppes of southern Russia developed nomadic pastoralism. Subsequently, Indo-European speaking Aryas entered north-west India in a series of raids sometime after 2000 B.C., and struggled with the (Dravidian?) Harappans, a people of different civilisation, different ethnos, different culture and different language(s). The non-Indo-European Harappan civilisation ended through complex processes which we do not quite understand, its script and language remaining to date an undeciphered enigma; but one of the causes of its decline were the invasions of Indo-European speaking Aryas ca. 2000 BC.

The result of these processes in India was the Aryan "conquest" of much of the peninsula in a typical situation of elite dominance over the Dāsas or Dāsyus, between 2000 -1500 BC, although very strong residues of pre-Aryan languages and cultures remained in the Indic linguistic, social and religious structures until today.

CONCLUSION

Renfrew speaks of a new solution of the Indo-European problem (1987:7). What he has in fact done is to resuscitate an Indo-European Urvolk in an unexpected Urheimat (Anatolia), pushed it back to seventh millennium BC, made them first farmers and proposed successive displacements over the generations of Indo-European peasant farmers who populated Europe and introduced one undifferentiated Indo-European protolanguage. Presented like this, and particularly with its consequences for the east (i.e. India, both Harappan and Vedic), we could not accept it without strong reservations, although we admit its courageous originality.

Presented with certain modifications, it becomes an attractive alternative model to the traditional view of the spread of Indo-European languages by war-like pastoral nomads from south Russian steppes much later, in the 3rd millennium BC.

What are the modifications we would propose?

(1) Renfrew's model is not a solution to the IE problem, but an alternative hypothesis of the emergence of IE languages in Europe and in Iran-India, provided with a plausible socio-economic reasons for their initial spread East and West.

(2) We can accept the region of "greater" Anatolia as one from which the IE speaking farmers began their colonisation.

(3) The language they spoke was not one single homogenous IE protolanguage, but a cluster of very closely related dialects of Indo-European.

(4) The spread occurred as a series of intermittent, successive moves of these closely connected IE dialects, introduced by relatively small bands of farmers to parts of south-east and central Europe.

(5) A great role was played in the subsequent development of IE dialects by non-IE languages spoken in various parts of Europe in quite large territories, particularly in areas outside the European continental core. The initial agricultural colonisation probably did not reach these areas. It is more likely that agro-pastoral farming, and IE languages were adopted in these areas towards the end of the Neolithic and during the Bronze Age through cultural diffusion, small-scale population shifts and elite dominance along the lines suggested in our alternative model. The indigenous population played a decisive role in these later processes.

(6) The spread of Indo-European towards the east, particularly in India: If at all we have to posit, at an early date, a diffusion of people or languages from the larger Anatolia/Iran region to the east, as well as a non-indigenous origin of the Indus Valley Civilisation, then we prefer the spread, between 4000-3000 BC, of non-Indo-European agro-pastoralist farmers from the Anatolian-Iranian plateau eastwards to any other hypothesis (or, alternatively, local farming origins in western India itself, under the ecologically favourable conditions prevalent in the

Indus valley); the origin and development of Harappan Civilisation due to non-Indo-European speakers, possibly the descendants of Elamo-Dravidians; development of Indo-European nomadic pastoralism in the steppes of Russia and the arrival of Indo-European in India associated with the incursions of mounted Aryan warriors about 2000-1800 BC; subsequent process of elite dominance and linguistic Aryanisation of two thirds of the Indian peninsula.

If indeed local farming origins in western India are accepted rather than the introduction by non-indigenous immigrants of an agro-pastoralist farming technology, our model does not at all require large-scale movements of people. The hypothetic Elamo-Dravidian of the Harappan elite might have been imposed on the local population by relatively small groups in successive waves just as, almost 2000 years later, the Aryan of Indo-European mounted raiders was successively and gradually imposed on the indigenous Dāsyus population of India. Just as in the case of the western spread, one of the significant developments in the Indus Valley area might have been the agricultural intensification caused by the development of the plough (there is a striking linguistic evidence in favour of this notion), diary farming, etc., as well as trade, connected with the arrival of the Elamo-Dravidian speaking elite in the Indus Valley area – not, obviously, with any Indo-Europeans.

REFERENCES

Alibert, L. 1977: Dictionaire Occitan-Français. Inst. d'Etudes Occitanes, Toulouse.

Ammerman, A.J. and Cavalli-Sforza, L.L. 1984: The Neolithic Transition and the Genetics of Population in Europe, Princeton Univ. Press, Princeton.

Anthony, D.W. 1986: The "Kurgan culture", Indo-European origins and the domestication of the horse: a reconsideration. Current Anthropology 27: 291-313.

Baldi, P. 1988: Book review of Archaeology and Language by C. Renfrew, Current Anthropology 29,447.

Barker, G. 1985: Prehistoric Farming in Europe. Cambridge University Press. Cambridge.

Binford, L. 1962: Archaeology as Anthropology. American Antiquity 28, 2:217-235

Binford, L. 1972: Archaeological Perspectives. In New Perspectives in Archaeology. Ed. Binford, L. and Binford, S.; 5-33.Aldine, Chicago.

Boas, F. 1912: Changes in the bodily form of descendants of immigrants. American Anthropologist 14, no.3.

Bogucki, P. 1987: The establishment of agrarian communities on the North European Plain. Current Anthropology 28, 1-24.

Burrow, T. 1945: Some Dravidian words in Sanskrit. Transactions of the Philological Society, 79-120.

Burrow, T. 1946: Loanwords in Sanskrit. Transactions of the Philological Society 1-30.

Burrow, T. 1948: Dravidian studies VII: Further Dravidian words in Sanskrit. Bulletin of the School of Oriental and African Studies 12: 365-96.

Chapman, R. 1988: Comment on The origins of wool and milk production in the Old World, by H.J. Greenfield. Current Anthropology 29, 587-588.

Clarke, D. 1968: Analytical Archaeology. Methuen, London.

Cohen, M. and Armelagos, G. eds. 1984: Paleopathology at the Origins of Agriculture. Academic Press, New York.

Dahl, G. and Hjort, A. 1976: Having Herds. Stockholm

Dennell, R. 1983: European Economic Prehistory. Academic Press. London.

Dennell, R. 1985: The hunter-gatherer/agricultural frontier in prehistoric temperate Europe. In S. Green and S.Perlman eds.: The Archaeology of Frontiers and Boundaries, 113-40.

Dolukhanov, P. 1986a: The late Mesolithic and the transition to food production in Eastern Europe. In Zvelebil, M. ed.: Hunters in Transition, 109-120. Cambridge Univ. Press, Cambridge.

Dolukhanov, P. 1986b: Foragers and Farmers in West Central Asia. In Zvelebil, M. ed.: Hunters in Transition, 121-133. Cambridge Univ. Press, Cambridge.

Dolukhanov, P. 1986c: Natural Environment and the Holocene settlement pattern in the north-western part of the USSR. Fennoscandia Archaeologica 3: 3-15.

Ehret, C. 1988: Language change and the material correlates of language and ethnic shift. Antiquity 62,no. 236, 564-574.

Emeneau, M.B. n.d.: The Languages of the Nilgiris. Pre-publication copy, courtesy of the author.

Fairservis, W.A. 1983: The script of the Indus Valley civilisation. Scientific American, March 1983:44-52.

Gamkrelidze, T.V. and Ivanov, V.V. 1984: Indoevropeiskii Yazyk i Indoevropeitsy. Tbilisi State Univ. Publishing House, Tbilisi.

Gimbutas, M. 1970: Proto-Indo-European culture: The Kurgan culture during the 5th to the 3rd millennia B.C. In G. Cardona, H.M. Koenigsvald and A. Senn, eds.: Indo-European and Indo-Europeans, 155-198. Univ. of Pennsylvania Press, Philadelphia.

Gould, S.J. 1981: The Mismeasure of Man. Penguin.

Greenfield, H.J. 1986: Palaeoeconomy of the Central Balkans (Serbia). British Archaeological Reports, Int. Ser.

Greenfield, H.J. 1988: The origins of milk and wool production in the Old World. Current Anthropology 29,4:573-593.

Hockings, P. 1980: Ancient Hindu Refugees. Badaga Social History 1550-1975. Mouton, The Hague.

Hrozný, B. 1943: Die älteste Geschichte Vorderasiens und Indiens, 2nd. ed. Prag.

Irons, W. and Dyson-Hudson, N., eds. 1972: Perspectives in Nomadism. Leiden, Brill.

Jackson, K.H. 1955: The Pictish Language. In F.T.Wainwright, ed.:The Problem of the Picts, 126-66. Nelson, Edinburgh.

Mahadevan, I. 1977: The Indus Script: Text, Concordance and Tables. Memoirs of the Archaeological Survey of India 77. Delhi.

Mahadevan, I. 1980: Dravidian Models of Decipherment of the Indus Script: A Case Study. 10nth Annual Conference of Dravidian Linguistic Association. Delhi.

Mallory, J. 1988: Book Review of Archaeology and Language by C. Renfrew. Antiquity 62, no.236, 607-609.

McAlpin, D.W. 1981: Proto-Elamo-Dravidian: The Evidence and its Implications. The American Philosophical Society, Philadelphia.

Khazanov, A.M. 1984: Nomads and the Outside World. CambridgeUniversity Press, Cambridge.

Krahe, H. 1936: Ligurish und Indogermanish. Festschrift für H.Hirt 2, 241-255. Heidelberg.

Matyushin, G. 1986: The Mesolithic and Neolithic in southern Urals and Central Asia. In Zvelebil, M. ed.: Hunters in Transition, 151-166. Cambridge University Press, Cambridge.

Meillet, A. 1964: Introduction a l'Etude Comparative des Langues Indo-Européennes. University of Alabama Press.

Pulgram, E. 1978: Italic, Latin, Italian. Winter, Heidelberg.

Pulgram, E. 1958: The Tongues of Italy. Harvard Univ. Press, Cambridge, Mass.

Renfrew, C. 1987: Archaeology and Language. The Puzzle of Indo-European Origins. J. Cape. London.

Sapir, E. 1921: Language. Harcourt, Brace and Co. New York.

Sherratt, A. 1981: Plough and pastoralism: aspects of the secondary products revolution. In I. Hodder, G. Isaac and N. Hammond, eds: Pattern of the Past: Studies in Honour of David Clarke, Cambridge Univ. Press, Cambridge.

Sherratt, A. 1983: The secondary exploitation of animals in the Old World. World Archaeology 15:90-104.

Sherratt A. and Sherratt S. 1988: The archaeology of Indo-European: an alternative view. Antiquity 62, no. 236, 584-595.

Shiffer, M.B. 1972: Archaeological context and systemic context. American Anthropology 37: 156-165

Shiffer, M.B. 1976: Behavioural Archaeology. Academic Press, New York.

Sokal, R.R, Oden, N.L., Legendre, P., Fortin, M.J., Kim, J. and Vaudor, A. 1989: Genetic Differences Among Language Families of Europe. American Journal of Physical Anthropology 79: 489-502.

Stevenson, V. 1983: Words. Eddison-Sadd. Harrow.

Telegin, D.Y. 1986: Dereivka: a Settlement and Cemetery of Copper Age Horse-Breeders on the Middle Dniepr. Oxford: British Archaeological Reports, World Series, S 331.

Vencl, S. 1986: The role of hunting-gathering populations in the transition to farming: a central European perspective. In M. Zvelebil, ed.: Hunters in Transition, 43-51. Cambridge University Press.

y'Edynak, G. 1978: Culture, diet and dental reduction in mesolithic forager-fishers of Yugoslavia. Current Anthropology 19, 616-617.

Zvelebil, K.V. 1980: A plea for Nilgiri areal studies. International Journal of Dravidian Linguistics 9,1:1-22.

Zvelebil, K.V. 1981: Problems of identification and classification of some Nilgiri tribes. Anthropos 76: 467-528.

Zvelebil, K.V. 1985a: Review of Prot-Elamo-Dravidian: The Evidence and its Implications by D.W. McAlpin. Journal of the American Oriental Society 105,2: 364-372.

Zvelebil, K.V. 1985b: Recent attempts at the Decipherment of the Indus Valley script and language (1965-1980). A critique. In Karashima, N.: Indus Valley to Mekong Delta. Explorations in Epigraphy. New Era publications, Madras 151-87.

Zvelebil, M. 1980: The rise of nomads in Central Asia. In Sherratt, A. ed.: The Cambridge Encyclopedia of Archaeology. Cambridge University Press.

Zvelebil, M., ed. 1986a: Hunters in Transition. Cambridge University Press.

Zvelebil, M. 1986b: Review of Ammermann, A. and Cavalli-Sforza, L. 1984: The Neolithic Transition and the Genetics of Population in Europe. Journal of Archaeological Science, 13,1.

Zvelebil, M. and Zvelebil, K.V. 1988: Agricultural transition and Indo-European dispersals. Antiquity 62,236:574-583.

Figure 1

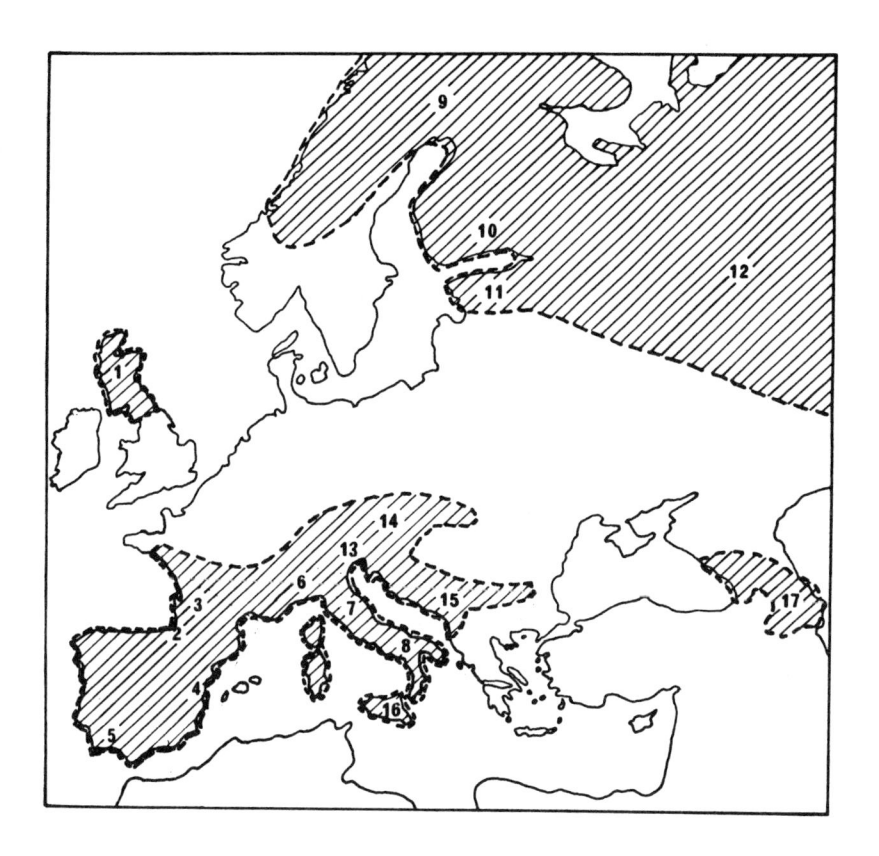

Figure 1: Possible ditribution of identified ancient non-Indo-European languages of Europe (based on the earliest classical sources and related archaeological and linguistic evidence).

1. Pictish
2. Basque
3. Aquitani
4. Iberian
5. Tartessian
6. Ligurian
7. Etruscan
8. Messapic
9. Lappish (Saame)
10. Finnish
11. Estonian
12. Ugro-Finnic
13. East Italic
14. Rhaetic
15. Pre-IE Illyrian
16. Sicel
17. Causasian languages

266 When Worlds Collide

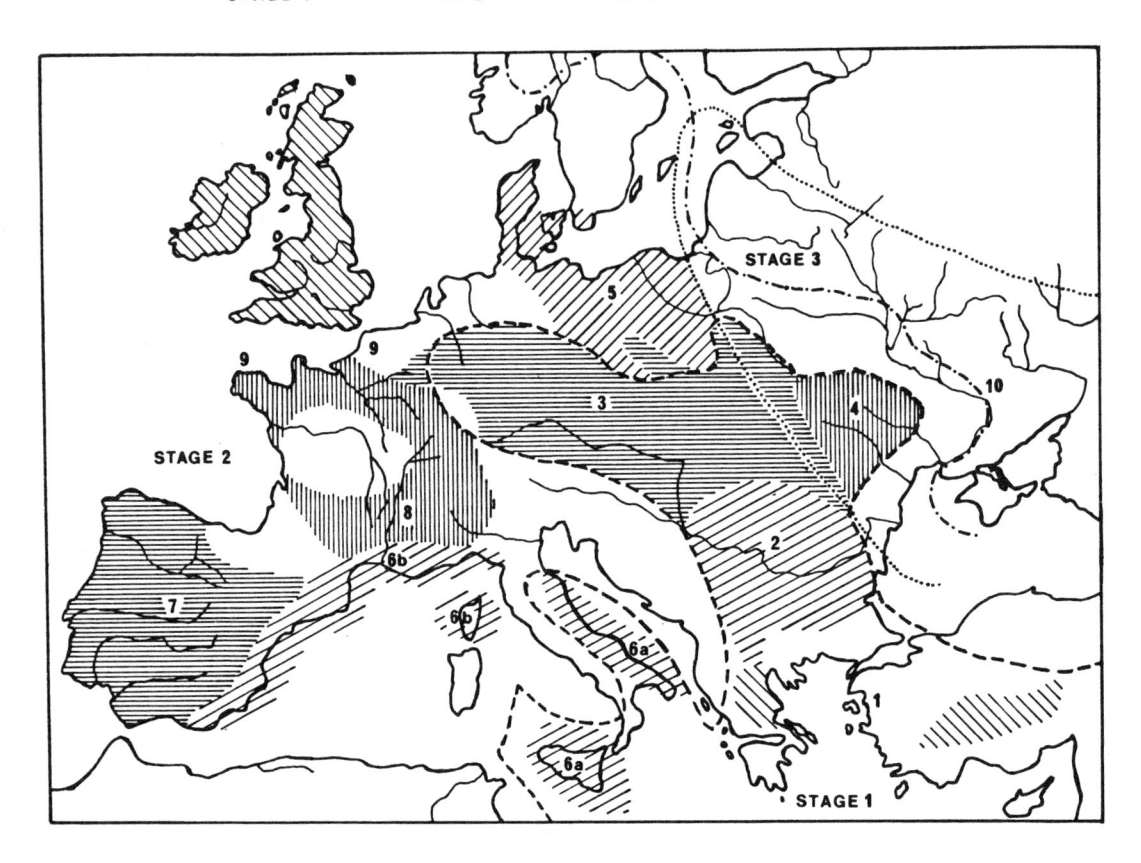

STAGE 1 — — —   STAGE 2 —·—·—   STAGE 3 ········   Figure 2

Figure 2. Spread of Indo-European languages as presented in our model. Stippled areas denote prehistoric cultures in Europe as drawn by Renfrew (1987:160, fig. 7.7). The three stages of dispersal, postulated by us in this paper are superimposed on this pattern. Stage 1: Introduction of agro-pastoral farming: 6500-5000 BC; Stage 2: Consolidation of farming and "secondary products revolution": 4800-2500 BC; Stage 3: Elite dominance: 3800-1000 BC.

1. Early Greek Neolithic
2. Starcevo/Koros/Karanovo
3. Linear Pottery Culture
4. Proto-Cucuneti and Proto-Tripolye
5. TRB cultures
6. Impressed Ware cultures, a: east Mediterranean, b: west Mediterranean
7. Iberian Neolithic
8. Middle Neolithic in France
9. Neolithic of Britain and north-west European littoral

TYPES OF LINGUISTIC EVIDENCE FOR EARLY CONTACT: INDO-EUROPEANS AND NON-INDO-EUROPEANS

Edgar C. Polomé
University of Texas at Austin

Ever since the seminal work of Uriel Weinrich on *Languages in Contact* (1953), which put the achievements of prior generations into perspective and provided a model for the analysis and interpretation of the phonological, grammatical and lexical interferences resulting from contacts between languages, a whole array of extensive studies in various fields have broadened and deepened our knowledge of the subject. It would indeed be fastidious to enumerate here the multiple American and European publications dealing with languages in contact or in conflict, with *Sprachbünde*, with the issues raised by pidginization and creolization, plurilingualism, language death, the ethnography of communication and so many other relevant topics. What concerns us most is what additional insight these works have given us into the problems pertaining to the early linguistic contact between Indo-Europeans and non-Indo-Europeans.

It is obvious that we should not readily project into prehistoric Indo-European times our findings on phenomena that we can document in historical periods and sometimes even test in the field, and that the many factors that condition the linguistic effects of socio-cultural interaction should be carefully weighed before jumping to any conclusion from rash comparisons. My favorite example of this kind of methodological error is the assumption by Sigmund Feist in the late twenties (1928) and early thirties (1932) that the Germanic languages resulted from the pidginization of the Indo-European language of Illyro-Venetic traders by the non-Indo-European population of the Baltic area, allegedly submitted to the cultural domination of the entrepreneurial group carrying on direct commercial relations with the Mediterranean. As proof of this hypothesis he adduced the fact that the Germanic consonant shift reflected the spirantization of the Indo-European stops which was then believed to be documented by the Venetic inscriptions, but it was soon established that the Venetic characters had been misinterpreted by Sommer (1924) and that they actually represented stops. Moreover, the Venetic language was dissociated from the "Illyrian," as originally conceived by Hans Krahe, to be treated either as an independent Indo-European language or as a separate branch of the Italic family. Assuming "pidginization" in Proto-Germanic on account of the alleged "loss" of a number of features reconstructed by the Neogrammarians as part of the verbal system of Proto-Indo-European, mainly on the basis of Sanskrit and Greek, is also a rather specious argument, as the very same reconstruction is open for serious revision on the basis of the later discovery of ancient Indo-European languages like Anatolian. The fairly striking structural resemblance between the verbal system of Germanic and that of Hittite rather makes one wonder whether these languages do not actually represent a more archaic structural model than the further elaborated inflectional pattern of Old Indic and Hellenic. Besides, neither Sigmund Feist nor Giuliano Bonfante who espoused his views, did actually ever bother to back up their hypothesis with a detailed examination of the non-linguistic evidence for the presence of the alleged "Veneto-Illyrians" in the Baltic area. To be sure, Venetic roads across the Alps have been found, and trade routes between the Baltic and the Mediterranean crossed Central Europe in the Bronze Age, but that does not by far make the endeavoring people of the Este culture the linguistic "colonizers" of the Germanic north—the more so as the lexical and other correspondences between Venetic and Germanic are precious few and not very significant (Polomé 1957)!

The idea that Germanic resulted from a *"Sprachmischung"* is not new: it was already advanced by Sir William Jones in his famous discourse to the Royal Asiatic Society in Calcutta in 1786. In 1934 Hermann Güntert still defended the same view: the Germanic people resulted from the mixture of the megalithic agriculturists with the Battle-Ax/Corded-Ware culture, and the neolithic peasantry constituted the "substrate" responsible for the Germanic consonant shift (Güntert 1934: 72). Unfortunately, widely exaggerated claims on the impact and the extent of the alleged "substrate" such as Giovanni Alessio's assumption of a "filone mediterraneo" up to the Baltic contributed to discrediting hypotheses of this kind.

When the views of Hans Krahe on the prominent role of the "(Proto-)Illyrians" of the Lusatian civilization, backed up archeologically by Richard Pittioni and linguistically by Julius Pokorny gave way in the middle fifties to the concept of an initially linguistically coherent Indo-European "Old Europe" on the basis of striking correspondences in the etyma and derivation of the hydronyms, the differentiation of the Indo-European languages of the continent became a process of internal evolution, reminiscent of the development of "northwestern Indo-European," as sketched by Antoine Meillet half a century earlier.

Was there a linguistic continuum in northwestern Europe that reflected the civilization shared by the ancestors of the Celtic, Italic, Germanic, Baltic (and perhaps also Slavic) peoples? To back up this view a set of lexical correspondences have been adduced: terms relevant to the ecology, i.e. names of trees such as the willow or the elm, or animals such as the blackbird or the water-snake; words relating to the cultivation of the land (*$s\bar{e}$-* 'sow,' *$b^h abo$-* 'bean,' *$\hat{g}r̥ə no$-* 'grain,' *sek-* 'cut, mow,' etc.); institutional vocabulary, e.g., *wad^h-/* 'pledge, security,' *$\hat{g}^h osti$-* 'stranger' > 'guest' (Go. *gasts*) or 'foe' (Lat. *hostis*), *$\hat{k}ey\text{-}wo\text{-}/\text{-}mo$-* 'homestead, family,' etc.; terms denoting human activities such as "striking" in the specialized meaning of 'forge' (Lat. *cūdō*, Lith. *káuju*) or taking, buying" (Lat. *emō*, Lith. *imù*); miscellaneous words such as *$wr̥ud^h om$* 'word,' *$\hat{g}^h ə mó'n$-* 'earthling' (= 'man'), *$nizdos$* 'nest,' etc. This view has, however, been strongly criticized by L.R. Palmer (1954: 17-23), as he pointed out that many of these "occidental" words reflect "nothing more than elaborate *argumenta ex silentio* resting on accidental loss by Greek" of the same terms after their entry into the Balkan peninsula. Each word has its own history, and its loss in a language may be due to a lot of different motivations, so that the pattern of correspondence from language to language depends essentially on the complex interplay of largely unpredictable factors: as Palmer notices, why is "fire" indicated exclusively by *ignis* in Latin and by *pir* in Umbrian? Or, why is the common term for "water" (IE *$wédōr$, gen. *udnés* > Goth. *watō*, Umbr. *utur*) only represented by *unda* 'wave' in Latin? Similarly, *ner-* '(strong) man' survives only in the Sabine proper names *Nero*, *Nerio*, besides *wiro-*, in Latin, whereas it appears commonly in Oscan (*niír*), Umbrian (*nerf*), Old Irish (*nert*).

The Italian "Neolinguistica" accounted for this by applying the criteria of linguistic geography to the geographical distribution of the Indo-European dialects. According to this view, the languages originally located at the confines of northwestern Europe were "peripheral" to the core of the Indo-European speech community, and innovations affecting the central part of their vast linguistic territory might therefore not reach its "marginal" areas, which would therefore appear to be more conservative. Thus, for Matteo Bartoli (1945: 2-3), Lat. *ignis* is more archaic than Umbr. *pir*, which, together with Greek πῦρ and Hitt. *pahhur*, belongs to the central part of the Indo-European territory, whereas *ignis* is "peripheral" like Old Indic *agniḥ*. But, as Palmer (1951:28) rightly points out, as a heteroclitic *-r-/-n-*stem, also found in such "peripheral" languages as Tocharian (B *puwar* 'fire') and Germanic (Goth. *fon* [gen. *funins*], ON *fýrr*), PIE *peAur* [gen. *peAwen-*; cf. Hitt. *pahhwenaš*] belongs definitely to the oldest lexical stock of Indo-European. The fragility of the criterion of *Marginalitá* is also illustrated by the case of Lat. *aqua* versus Umbr. *utur*: obviously, here again, the Umbrian word reflects a term belonging to the oldest IE vocabulary, as its heteroclitic flection indicates: Hitt. *watar* (= OS *watar*), gen. *wetenaš* (cf. Goth. [gen.] *watins*). *Aqua* is presumably related to the verb represented in Hittite by *aku-*, *eku-* and Tocharian *yok-* 'drink' (in spite of Puhvel 1984: 268; cf. Tischler 1983: 104). Moreover, these speculations on the distribution of the reflexes of such Indo-European terms as "water" or "fire" fail to take into account such basic facts as the possibility that several designations for them may have coexisted, differentiated by the context in which they appeared and the people who used them: as Benjamin Lee Whorf (1956: 210) showed (and it has been abundantly illustrated by anthropologists), "languages classify items of experience differently," and the Hopi, for example, have two words for "water" − (a) running, in nature (*pāhe*); (b) in various containers (*pēhi*). Obviously, the Indo-Europeans must have distinguished water in nature from drinking water − or perhaps, taking into account the importance of the association of water and fire in their ideology, as Bernfried Schlerath (1973: 28-34) stressed it, the sacrality of water might account for the coexistence of a ritual term versus an everyday term, as the "animate" *egnis versus the "inanimate" *peAur suggests it in the parallel case of the fire.

With the new perception of different registers and social stratification, gained in the study of sociolinguistics, came a growing awareness among Indo-Europeanists that contrasts between two levels of language such as a specific set of terms belonging to "sacred" vocabulary, pertaining to the usually more conservative priesthood, and their "profane" correspondents, used by the rest of the community, could be preserved, not only in such writings as the religious texts opposing the language of the gods to that of the mortals, upon which Hermann Güntert had already drawn the attention in the twenties, but also in the coexistence of different terms for the same entity, surviving with an often unpredictable distribution in the various dialects. Examined in the light of the Dumézilian functional tripartition of Indo-European society, the contrast between *ner- and *u̯iro- to denote a male human being (as opposed to a female), took on a new significance as the former appeared to be linked with the two upper levels of society—brahmins and kṣatriyas in the Veda—and the latter with the third or lower level. Thus, a rationale is also given for the occurrence of *u̯iro- in the name of the third function god *Quirinus* and the derivation of the name of the ancient cult-partner of Mars, *Nerio*, from *ner- (Dumézil 1969: 225-241).

In many cases also, some of these "synonyms" attributed to various orders of beings have no clear Indo-European etymology, while others are clear reflexes of PIE roots, e.g., in the 34th stanza of the Scandinavian *Alvíssmál*, "beer" is called ǫl "among men" — a term with undeniable magico-religious connotations, as Runic *alu* shows, but with IE cognates, perhaps even in Hittite — *bjǫrr* "among the Æsir -a term which has been connected with *bygg* (from Gmc. *bewwu-), but which may rather belong to the monachal vocabulary and be linked with the introduction of hopped beer (< Vulgar Lat. *biber* 'draught') — and *veig* among the *Vanir*: no convincing etymology has been given for this term, which survives in Norwegian *veie* 'fluid, juice.' It has been compared rather unconvincingly with such sets as (a) Old Indic *vésanta-* 'pond,' Latv. *wiekts* 'rapids'; (b) Old Indic *vīcī* 'wave,' MHG *weigen* 'sway, totter'; (c) ON *veig* 'strength,' Goth.

waihjo 'battle,' OCS *věkŭ*, Lith. *vieká* 'strength'—in the meaning of "strong drink"! In the aberrant overstating of his concepts of *Zaun und Mannring* ('fence and circle of men'), Jost Trier has even assumed a semantic development from "circle of men" to "communal banquet" to "festive drink," which would allow the derivation of the term from the same root **wey-* as ON *veggr* 'wall (originally, of wickerwork),' Latv. *vija* 'fence,' etc.! Instead of looking so far, would it not be possible to assume that this isolated term reflects an old inherited name for a local brew of the original agricultural population of the north? A mixture of fermented wheat grains, cranberries, bog-myrtle, linden pollen and honeywater has been found in Egtved (Jutland) as early as 1500 B.C. in a birch-bark container in a woman's grave. It is, however, probable that such beverages were used for ritual purposes long before the Bronze Age, and therefore quite plausible that the name of one such "liquor" could have been taken over from the language of the pre-Indo-European inhabitants of the area.

When dealing with pre-Indo-European "substrate" in northern Europe, the major problem is that there absolutely no direct evidence of the language of the populations that the speakers of Indo-European dialects encountered upon their penetration into the area. It is therefore poor methodology to assume that the idiosyncracies of the Indo-European languages that developed later on the same territory are ascribable to the influence of the linguistic patterns proper to the non-Indo-European languages spoken by the local people who merged with the immigrants to constitute the new Indo-European dialectal entities. So many different things can happen when "cultures collide": at a certain stage, a certain amount of bilingualism is to be expected in which both languages are functional at different levels, e.g., the language of the dominant group being originally restricted to use within this group by its own members and to direct communication with the overlords by the subordinate group, which would continue to use their own tongue among themselves. The Hittites apparently maintained their language in a vast empire in which the majority of their subjects spoke unrelated languages; after more than four centuries of Roman occupation, the parents of the Latin poet Ausonius still spoke Gaulish at home. The form of the ruler's language used by the subdued is however likely to be pidginized: the phonology of the target language will be adapted to the basic sound system of the native tongue of the speakers — as is indeed argued by those who ascribe the Germanic consonant shift to the takeover of an Indo-European dialect by an originally non-Indo-European population; the morphology will be "simplified"–as F. Sommer claimed the Anatolian verb system was under the influence of the surrounding Semitic and other non-Indo-European languages; syntactic patterns will be calqued on those of the speaker's mother tongue; the lexicon will be pervaded with loanwords and loan-translations. The popular Gallo-Latin inscriptions on spindle whorls and the like attest to the kind of *Mischsprache* that could develop under those circumstances (Meid 1980).

It is well-known that in such cases of unstable bilingualism where one language of higher prestige tends to prevail, and where both languages L^1 and L^2 can be acquired in childhood by younger generations, language shift is to be expected. The question is: how much is the "new" language of those who shifted affected by their linguistic background? When dealing with languages attested at a fairly recent date, after the impact of Christianization and of the translation of religious texts as well as the influence of foreign models had affected their syntax, it is rather unwise to try to ascribe to an unknown substrate some phenomena characterizing their syntactic patterns typologically when they are documented only many centuries and sometimes millennia later. Similarly, there are no morphological features that can be referred without hesitation to a remodeling of the PIE pattern triggered by the underlying influence of a lost substrate language. Most of the major divergences between the so-called "peripheral" languages like Germanic and the core languages with highly developed nominal and verbal morphology like Greek and Indo-Iranian can adequately be explained as the result of a diachronic development and diversification within Indo-European. If the ancestors of the Germanic tribes separated from the Indo-European community early enough, the absence of such tenses and moods as the aorist or the subjunctive (the Germanic subjunctive being formally an IE optative) would be due to the fact that these grammatical categories had not yet become operative in the proto-language by that time and would account for the close resemblance of the structural pattern of the Germanic verbal system with that of Anatolian. This implies, however, a staggered emigration of Indo-European groups out of the core territory and their moving towards the northwest at a rather early date—the ancestors of the Germanic people leaving before those of the Celts and the Latins, for example. Unfortunately, all this relative chronology remains based on an *argumentum ex silentio*, and the fact that some linguistic feature is not present in a language can always be explained in two ways:

(a) it was not there to start with (which is the assumption this chronology is based on);

(b) it has been lost somewhere along the way (which is what more traditional scholars assume).

In the latter case, the loss may be due either to internal development or to the action of outside causes – in the case of Germanic, perhaps, the influence of "substrate" language? In the absence of any evidence of the morphological structure of this substrate language, this remains, however, a moot question.

As regards phonology, again, the failure of the efforts to account for the consonant shifts in Germanic or Armenian through the influence of the languages of the original inhabitants of their present territories indicates the difficulty of assessing any undisputable impact of a phonological system of which one has actually no direct evidence on another which is derived from a reconstructed language. The recent presentation of the "glottalic" theory has indeed indicated that a typologically justified revision of the Brugmannian pattern of the Proto-Indo-European consonant system may provide a very elegant solution to the Germanic consonant shift, which makes Proto-Germanic an archaic language and reduces the so-called consonant shift to very simple processes of spirantization and deglottalization: the feature [-continuant] of the simple/aspirate stops becomes [+continuant], and the feature [+glottalic] of the "glottalized" stops become [-glottalic] – a change that certainly does not require an outside influence!

Different is the case when new phonemes are introduced in the language of the invaders from that of the subdued: a typical example is that of the Nguni tribes moving south of the Limpopo and conquering vast territories occupied by the Khoi in southern Africa. While most men were exterminated and women taken in as concubines, a situation developed in which part of the phonology of the defeated people survived in the language of the new masters of the land, namely the characteristic click sounds, which are even more numerous in the *hlonipha* or "respect" forms of language used essentially by women. There is, however, no clear evidence of such an influence of the substrate in northern Europe, though it has sometimes been assumed to account for features in the vocalism of Germanic and Baltic. Actually, when one analyzes the phonology of Germanic, it is obvious that it derives directly from the same Indo-European pattern as Latin or Greek, though it has definitely been less conservative than the latter in the maintenance and treatment of "laryngeals." Whatever the ancestors of the Germanic people may have taken over from the "substrate" language(s) has been thoroughly adapted to their phonological system – in the way loanwords from a "superstratum" can be integrated into a language. In this case, indeed, two solutions are possible: (a) the borrowing language ADDS "foreign" phonemes to its system as it borrows heavily from a language with a different phonological system, e.g., the Bantus of the East Coast of Africa whose language became Swahili added dental spirants like [θ] and [ð] to their phonemic inventory to take care of terms like *thelathini* '30' or *dhamana* 'guarantee,' but when the language spread inland, up-country Bantus replaced [θ] by /s/, e.g., in *selasini* '30' or resorted to other terms (Shaba Swahili: *makumi tatu*/*Roman*/) – which brings us to the second solution:

(b) the borrowing language SUBSTITUTES whichever of its own phonemes appears to be closest to the foreign sound, e.g., /t/ or /z/ for [ð].

This apparently accounts for the fact that non-Indo-European elements in Germanic can only be traced etymologically, and NOT through their aberrant phonological pattern.

Because the "substrate" terms in the Germanic North have obviously been so completely integrated into the language, they will fall essentially into three categories:

(a) those found only in ONE language where they reflect the local ecological and economical conditions, while they are not etymologizable in Indo-European;

(b) isoglosses limited to the Northwest Indo-European languages, indicating the geographical, climatic, botanical, zoological and other typical features of the area;

(c) cultural terms, among which onomastics take a special place.

It stands to reason that if we examine the lexicon of any of the Germanic languages, we will find a considerable number of terms without known etymology. Among these, such terms as names of plants or animals proper to the geographical area in which the languages are used, are fairly numerous. Thus, in Dutch, for instance, we could mention such words as *gaal* 'restbarrow,' or *magge* '(eel)pout' — but could it be legitimate to project terms attested only in post-medieval sources into the pre-Germanic times? To be sure, the older school of etymologists hardly hesitated to do so, but after the severe, but fully justified criticism of de Vries' speculations about prehistoric society in connections with the views of Jost Trier on early forestry, wattling techniques and the like, one is rightly rather reluctant to extrapolate from relatively recent data to archaic ecology. However, when a lexical item like dialectal Germanic **waip-* 'sweetbrier' occurs in Middle Dutch (*wepdoorn*; XVIth c. [Kiliaen] *wepe, weype* "Sicambr." [= dialect of Kleve]), Middle Low German (*wēpe, wepdorn, wēpendorn*) and early New High German (*wipken*), one really wonders whether this does not reflect an old inherited term, possibly from the "substrate" language, though such an assumption remains obviously purely conjectural!

Perhaps the name of the "eel" provides a better case? Here, we deal with a term documented in most of the older Germanic dialects: ON *áll*, OE *ǽl*, OS *āl*,

OHG āl, MDu. ael, for which a number of equally unconvincing explanations have been proposed:

(a) it has been compared with ON áll 'gutter, drain; strip on the back of an animal' under the assumption of a basic meaning "long thin thing," but Old Indic álī- 'line, stroke' which is supposed to confirm this hypothesis, is probably a non-Aryan word!

(b) it has been connected with Old Indic alam 'roe,' to which Norw. ulke 'old tar, sticky slime' is perhaps related, so that it would be the "slimy fish"?

(c) it has been derived from the root *ed- 'eat' as a reflex of *ēdlo- 'eater'!

As Rolf Hiersche (1986:1) indicates, none of these explanations is satisfactory, and in view of the fact that the other western Indo-European languages commonly derive the term for "eel" (Lat. anguilla; OPruss. angurgis, Lith. ungurỹs, Polish węgorz, etc.) from the word for "snake," it is quite plausible that Germanic *ēla- 'eel' reflects a "substrate" term, as Jan de Vries (1971:1) suggested.

Sometimes phonology creates problems in connection with such assumptions: thus, de Vries (1971: 518) intimates that Du. pier '(earth)worm' might be a "substrate" word because of its geographical spread limited to the Low Countries and the neighboring Low German territories (its occurrence in Brandenburg is ascribable to medieval immigration from the Low Countries). Its vocalism suggests, however, an underlying form with Gmc. $*\bar{e}^2$, but as this vowel reflects an internal development in continental Germanic during the later Roman imperial period, a difficult problem of chronology might be involved, though the $\bar{e}^2$ before /r/ might also be of secondary origin.

In other cases, phonological features constitute the main argument for postulating the "substrate" origin of a term: thus, Gmc. *paþa- 'path' (OE pæð, paδ, OFri. *path*, OHG *pfad*, etc.) occurs only in the Ingweonic and Continental dialects of Germanic and therefore is considered as originating in a pre-Germanic language of the area rather than as a loanword from Iranian, where *pa-θ* 'way, road' occurs. The "unshifted" Germanic initial *p- excludes the possiblity of their being direct cognates!.

Such a reference to the "absence of the consonant shift" in a considerable number of Germanic terms has been the source of far-reaching assumptions in recent years: Hans Kuhn worked out an extensive theory on the presence of an "unknown Indo-European people" in the northwestern corner of Europe on the basis of the occurrence of a sizable number of terms with "unshifted" IE *p, *t and *k. Toponymists had already pointed out that numerous place- and river-names of the area appeared with -*apa* as a second component, and Maurits Gijsseling had posited the existence of a pre-Celtic "Belgian" in the Low Countries, but it was not clear whether some of these aberrant *p*-forms might not represent "labialized" IE labiovelars, e.g., in *$ak^w\bar{a}$* 'water.' By positing the existence of an original non-Celtic/non-Germanic "Northwest block", H. Kuhn opened new perspectives, and some archeologists backed up his findings by indicating how the corresponding areas were also distinct in their prehistoric cultural heritage. Closer analysis showed, however, that a large part of Kuhn's material was unreliable and based on recent developments, but quite a few terms listed by him were still wanting for a satisfactory explanation. To try to respond to this need, Maurits Gijsseling collected in a recent article on "substrate terms in Germanic" (1987) all the terms he deemed adequate to illustrate the importance of such a substrate in the Ingweonic and northern continental Germanic languages (i.e., English, Frisian, Dutch and Low German). What is the validity of this material? Is the methodology applied to its examination and interpretation adequate? What positive results have been attained?

There is a basic difference between the alleged "substrate" material gathered by Kuhn and Gijsseling and what other scholars describe as the "substrate" of the northwestern Indo-European languages: in the latter case, we deal with terms that are believed to have been taken over from the tongues spoken by the pre-Indo-European populations of the area; in the former, we assume the presence of an earlier Indo-European substrate which does not shift the voiceless stops /p t k/ into the Germanic fricatives f þ x (with the application of Verner's Law: v ð γ). Thus, when Jan de Vries (1971: 634) doubts that it is legitimate to reconstruct an IE root *(s)kut- to account for OFri. *skedda*, OS *skuddian*, OLFrancon. *scuddan* (Du. *schudden*), OHD *scutilōn* (G *schütteln*) 'shake': OCS *skytati sę* 'vagari'—without initial *s-:* OE *hūdenian* 'excutere,' LG *hūdern* 'tremble': Lith. *kutù, kutéti* 'shake up,' as Julius Pokorny (1959: 957-958) does, it is indeed plausible to assume that this set of terms occurring only in continental Germanic, Baltic and Slavic might belong to the language of the original inhabitants of the southern Baltic area and have possibly been taken over on account of some "expressive" connotation.

I have listed elsewhere (Polomé 1986) a number of such terms designating animals such as the barrow, animal products such as the spawn of a fish, simple implements (e.g., a vessel, a beaker), features of the environment such as a watery deep, human feelings and perceptions (e.g., the word for "sour"), human activities such "sweeping, scraping" or "digging" which Baltic and/or Slavic shares with Germanic, and which have no Indo-European cognates, and could therefore well reflect part of the vocabulary of the "substrate." The same goes for several Germanic words which are totally isolated in Indo-European and denote animals and plants and the products derived from them, e.g., the "gale" or "bog-myrtle" (Gmc. **gagl-* and **pursa-*), the "mew" and "the dove," "tallow" and "roe," etc. Further work is certainly needed in that direction to identify which lexical items relevant to the ecology of northern Europe, but without acceptable Indo-European etymology, may be derived from a substrate language.

The work done recently by W.P. Schmid and J. Udolph on the hydronymy of ancient Europe, as follow-up to the research initiated by Hans Krahe around 1950, but focusing more specifically on the Baltic and Slavic areas, has tended to show that the oldest river-names throughout this northern territory would be derived by typically Indo-European processes from recognizable Indo-European roots, and if a similar conclusion were to be derived from the hydronymy of the oldest southern Germanic territory which Udolph is presently working on, the whole problem of the "unshifted" p/t/k- terms in Germanic would have to be reexamined in a new light. But before jumping to the conclusion that there might have been an unknown Indo-European group preceding the coming of the ancestors of the Germanic people or not participating in the ethnogenesis of the latter, if it coincides with the Jastorf culture as a number of archeologists want us to believe, let us examine the material adduced to back up such a claim.

According to Gijsseling the alleged substrate "roots" fall into four semantic categories: (1) "desire" (Begierde); (2) "vital force" (*Lebenskraft*); (3) "communication"; (4) "apathy." For the *t*-terms, he however substitutes "energetic, strong, excellent" for "vital force." This categorization then allows him to posit an astounding number of homonymous "roots" with initial preconsonantal **(a)-* or with **s-* "mobile," e.g., **(a)per-*:

(1) "desire, love, be happy" — expanded form **peret-*, documented by Du. *pret* 'fun.'

(2) "strive for" — expanded forms **perei-gh-* (MDu. *prīgen*) and **perei-k-* (MDu. *priën* 'strive for').

(3) "perceive, realize" — expanded form **perat-* (OE *prætt* 'trick, skill').

(4) "press together" — expanded forms **perap-* (MDu. *proppe* 'plug, wad'), **per-egh* (with nasal infix: Goth. *anapraggan* 'trouble, oppress'), **per-al-* (in OFri. *pralling* 'testicle'?), **per-em-* (Du. *pramen* 'compel').

(5) "stick out" — expanded forms **per-egh-* (OE *preg* 'pointed stick'), **per-eg* (ON *forkr* 'bar, stick'), **prej-* > **prei-k-* (OE *prica, pricel* 'prickle'), **prew-* > **preun-* (OE *preon* 'awl, prick'). There is even a tentatively assumed expanded form **par-es-* allegedly documented by Flemish *porre* 'wart.'

(6) "announce, say" — expanded forms **prebh-* (Du. *prevelen* 'mumble').

*per-at- (Du. *praten* 'chat').

With *s-* "mobile" the same root means "foam" and is alledly documented by Du. *proesten* 'wheeze and splutter.'

Similarly, a "root" **(a)pew-* occurs with the meanings: (a) "strive for"; (b) "fence in"; (c) "surround" > "skin"; (d) "take"; (e) "hit'; (f) "breathe"; (g) "give birth" > "born, child, young"; (h) "swell"; (i) "stick out" — several of them synonymous with those of **(a)per-*. With *s-* "mobile" it means (a) "mud"; (b) "crush"; (c) "pull off"; (d) "hollow."

It stands to reason that such a polysemy of the "substrate" roots is implausible, as too reminiscent of the same multiplicity of meanings ascribed to Proto-Indo-European roots by Pokorny. Moreover, the listings of Gijsseling give too often the impression that he has gone through the Dutch etymological dictionary of Jan de Vries (1971) and the older concise Old English one of F. Holthausen, pulling out all the terms with initial *p-*, *t-* and *k-* of unknown or doubtful origin and lumping them together under assumed PIE roots by extrapolating their meaning or a kind of common denominator of the attested meanings to their alleged original prototype. It hardly needs to be pointed out how erratic and utterly subjective such an approach is, and classifying under "apathy" such lemmas as **(s)pal-* 'swamp' (OE *pōl* 'pool'), or **(s)pal-* 'stripe' in its expanded form **plōgh-*(ON *plōgr* 'plow'), while deriving **pal-at-* > **plat-*, **palt-* in OE *plot* 'piece of land' from **(s)pel-* 'pull off,' verges on the frivolous!

While it hardly makes sense to project into a pre-Germanic "substrate" a late Middle Dutch maritime term like **pīe* (Du. *pijjekker* = E *pea jacket*—a pilot's coat, presumably borrowed from Dutch into English), we should not reject the whole set of alleged "substrate" terms lock, stock and barrel. However, several methological conditions should be met before considering them further:

(a) no capricious ad hoc reconstructions should be tolerated;

(b) a careful distinction should be made between alleged substrate terms which are recently documented and those for which there is evidence at an early date; in the first case, the sociolinguistic and psychological reasons for its late emergence need to be investigated; in both cases, the motivation for the preservation of the substrate terms must be thoroughly examined;

(c) the geographical spread of the alleged substrate forms needs to be mapped and analyzed;

(d) affective vocabulary of recent origin should not be projected into the proto-language; the existence of combinations of sounds with specific symbolic value in a language should be taken into consideration, e.g., in Dutch, the sequence /pru-/ occurs in a number of derogatory terms applying to something of little value, e.g., *prul* 'trash, junk,' *prut* 'mud, sludge,' [adj.] 'crummy, lousy,' *prutsen* 'mess around,' *pruttelen* 'grumble, grouse' (the latter also, an "onomatopoeic" frequentative in the meaning "simmer, perk"). It stands to reason that such terms, as well as those which fall under the heading of "sound symbolism" (*Lautsymbolik*), e.g., Dutch terms beginning with *pr-*: *prakken* 'mash,' *pramen* 'prod,' *prangen* 'press'—or *pl-*: *plodderen, pledderen, ploeteren* 'plod away, slog, plug,' should not be extrapolated into ill-defined substrate languages.

(e) the terms should not be pressed into vague general semantic categories, as it is more plausible that specific words with well-defined meaning were taken over from the underlying "substrate" language, e.g., designations of characteristic features of the local culture. This applies to the case of OE *pūca* 'evil spirit,' from which ON *púki* 'devil,' which appears only late, essentially in the Christian literature, presumably derives. OE *pūca* is probably also the source of the Celtic terms: W *pwca, pwci*, Ir. *púca*, which Gijsseling leaves out when he claims that the Old English term is related to Lith. *pūkšti* 'snort, puff' under the root *$(a)pew-$ 'breathe' and assumes a further connection with Du. *spook* 'ghost.' In doing so, he neglects to account for the phonological discrepancy between the Old English form with [u:] and the Dutch with an underlying [au]

(Gmc. *spauka-) and to look into the socio-cultural background of the terms. Jan de Vries (1961: 429), however, points out that there are a number of Scandinavian words reflecting an alternation *piuka~pauka~pūka*, e.g., Swed.dial. *pjuk* 'height, hill,' *puk* 'lump, bulb,' *puken* 'swollen,' Norw. *pauk* 'whippersnapper,' which he derives from a root meaning "blow, blow up," also attested by MDu. *pōke* 'bag' (de Vries 1971: 539), but he rejects (1971: 682) its relationship with Du. *spook*, which has cognates in East Frisian (*spōk*) and Low German (*spōk*) in the meaning 'ghost' and in Scandinavian in divergent meanings: Swed. *spok* 'scarecrow,'Dan. *spøg* 'joke, fun,' Norw. *spjok* 'ghost' (Kluge 1975: 733). Gmc. *spōk- has been compared to Latv. *spīgana* 'apparition in the air, dragon, witch,' but as the related Baltic terms: Lith. *spingiù, spingěti* 'gleam, glitter,' OPruss. *spanxti* 'spark,' Latv. *spīganis* 'will-o'-the-wisp,' indicate, there are serious phonological problems involved in this connection. Perhaps this is the very reason why we might assume a non-Indo-European background for this set of terms designating phantomlike apparitions: we would then deal with a reflex of animistic beliefs of the megalithic agriculturists or an even older culture of the Baltic area!

Though it is not possible to survey all the adduced examples within the scope of this presentation, a few samples may further illustrate the various aspects of the question:

(a) the dictionary of Kiliaen (1596) lists as VETUS a Dutch term *poest* glossed as *bubile*, i.e. 'cowshed,' which survives dialectally in Flemish as *poester*: its <oe> [u] represents the normal development of the Ingweonic [o:] resulting from the raising and compensatory lengthening of Gmc. /a/ in the sequence *-ans-, as in dialectal Dutch (S. Holland) *boes* 'part of the cowshed' versus LG *banse* 'granary' (van Loey 1970: 27); it is derived with the same suffix -st- as Goth. *bansts* 'barn,' and its "root" *pan- can also be found in E *pen* which has been recorded only as 'enclosure for domestic animals' since the XIVth c., but appears as OE *penn* with an ill defined meaning (possibly 'hurdle'?). The antiquity of the Gmc. stem is evidenced by OE *onpennad* 'unpenned, opened' from a verb *pennian 'enclose, confine.' A direct connection with E *pin* on the basis of the LG verb *pennen* 'bolt' remains unconvincing, though the Germanic terms borrowed from Latin *pinna* or Vulgar Latin **penna* (Frings) with the original meaning of "pointed object, peg, pin" have partly overlapped semantically with the derivations from Gmc. **pan-*, which could very well come from a substrate language in view of its limited distribution in the Ingweonic area.

(b) the same geographical argument could be used to account for Du. *pees* 'tendon, sinew; string,' and the related *pezerik* 'pizzle,' as well as this English term itself, if E *pizzle* which is documented only since the XVIth c. as *peezel, pysell*, is not borrowed from Flemish *pēzel* (= LG *pēsel, peisel*), diminutive of MDu. *pēze* (= MLG *pēse*). Du. *pees* has been compared with OInd. *bísam* 'shoot or stalk of the lotus,' but this term is presumably of non-Aryan origin (Mayrhofer 1963: 433). It is therefore plausible to consider the Middle Dutch/Middle Low German word as a reflex of a substrate word, but not necessarily belonging, as Hans Kuhn (1969: 364) postulates, as **pes-* 'penis,' to his alleged "Northwest block." Though the Dutch derivative *pezerik* designates the penis of such animals as the bull or the pig, this meaning is only secondary, so that a direct connection with Greek πέος, OInd. *pásaḥ*, etc. is less than obvious. Actually, it is not necessary that the Germanic terms with initial *p-, k-, t-* be borrowed from a substrate pre-Germanic northwestern European Indo-European language which does not shift the voiceless stops to voiceless aspirates. Taking into account the "glottalic" theory, it would be perfectly plausible to have a substrate language with voiceless glottalized stops: these would be taken over as such in early Proto-Germanic and be "deglottalized" together with the inherited PIE glottalic stops, when IE **p' t' k'* went to Gmc. *p t k*. If one does not accept the glottalic theory, the alternative solution would be that the substrate languages would not have a system without initial **b-* as PIE is assumed to have had, so that the Germanic **p-* forms which are by far the most numerous would reflect "substrate" terms with initial **b-*.

Actually, the evidence for allegedly "unshifted" initial **t-* and **k-* is not very strong. One of de Vries and Gijsseling's examples is the word for "nipple": Du. *tit* (Kiliaen [1596] mentions *titte* as Saxon, Frisian and "Sicambrian" [=Kleve dialect]), MLG *titte*, Late MHG *zitze*, OE *titt*, Norw.dial. *titta* – a term which is also widely attested in the Romance languages and is generally associated with "baby talk." On account of Greek τιτθός 'mother's breast,' it is assumed that these words have been borrowed from a pre-Germanic "substrate" language, but τιτθός is closely linked with τίτθη '(wet-)nurse,' a hypocoristic form with "expressive gemination" of τιτθήνη '(wet-)nurse,' a reduplicated form of the root of θῆσθαι 'suck; nurse' (Chantraine 1977: 1118). Accordingly, it should not be taken into consideration when discussing the Germanic words: the parallel Du. *tepel* 'nipple,' whose cognates (LG *tippel* [= Kiliaen *tippel*], MHG *zipfel*) mean "tip, point," suggests "sound symbolism," the initial syllable *ti-* indicating something pointed. It is therefore unwise to look for a "substrate" origin in a case like this.

In other cases, the "substrate" hypothesis will have to be rejected for chronological reasons as a result of an examination of the history of the relevant term, e.g., MDu. *plunderen*, Fri. *plunderje, plonderje*, MLG *plunderen* 'loot, rob forcibly,' a typical "coastal term" which spread inland (into late MHG [*plündern*]) and appeared in England (E *plunder*) only in the XVIIth c., first with reference to the Thirty Years War (ca. 1630), and then, to the Civil War (in 1642). It actually means 'to rob of household effects' (= MDu. *plunder*, MLG *plunder[ware]*, late MHG *plunder* 'bedclothes, clothing, household stuff'). It is apparently originally restricted to a limited territory, but there is no clue that authorizes us to derive it from an older non-Germanic source!

In conclusion, in many cases the evidence remains inconclusive, and only when extralinguistic evidence can be coordinated with the lexical data can we posit a "substrate" origin of the terms. Only along such lines will etymological study contribute to a better understanding of the cultural and ecological situations hinted at by archeology and other methods of reconstructing the prehistorical past!

BIBLIOGRAPHY

Bartoli, Matteo
    1945 *Saggi di Linguistica Spaziale*
    Torino: Vincenzo Bona.

Dumézil, Georges
    1969 *Idées romaines.*
    Paris, N.R.F./Gallimard

Feist, Sigmund
    1928 "Die Ausbreitung des indogermanischen Sprachstammes über Nordeuropa in vorgeschichtlicher Zeit."
    In: *Wörter und Sachen*, vol. 11, pp. 29-53.
    1932 "The origin of the Germanic languages and the Indo-Europeanizing of north Europa."
    In: *Language*, vol. 8, pp. 245-254.

Gijsseling, Maurits
    1987 "Substratwörter in den germanischen Sprachen."
    In: *NOWELE*, vol. 10, pp. 47-62.

Güntert, Hermann
    1921 *Von der Sprache der Götter und Geister. Bedeutungsgeschichtliche Untersuchungen zur homerischen und eddischen Göttersprache.*
    Halle/Saale: Max Niemeyer.
    1934 *Der Ursprung der Germanen.*
    (Kultur und Sprache, vol. 9). Heidelberg: Carl Winter.

Hiersche, Rolf
    1986 *Deutsches etymologisches Wörterbuch* (Lief. 1-2)
    Heidelberg: Carl Winter.

Holthausen, F.
  1934 *Altenglisches etymologisches Wörterbuch.*
    Heidelberg: Carl Winter.

Kiliaen, Cornelis (Cornelius Klianus Dufflaeus)
  1596 (1777) *Etymologicum Teutonicae linguae; sive dictionarium Teutonico-Latinum* (1777 reprint of the 1596 [Antwerp: Plantijn] edition by Gerard Hasselt of Arnhem). 2 volumes.
    Utrecht: Roeland de Meyere.

Kluge, Friedrich
  1975 *Etymologisches Wörterbuch der deutschen Sprache.*
    21st edition (reprint of 20th ed. [1967], revised by Walther Mitzka).
    Berlin/New York: Walter de Gruyter.

Krahe, Hans
  1950 *Sprache und Vorzeit. Europäische Vorgeschichte nach dem Zeugnis der Sprache.*
    Heidelberg: Quelle & Meyer.

Kuhn, Hans
  1969 (1961) "Anlautend P- im Germanischen."
    In: *Zeitschrift für Mundartforschung,* vol. 28 (1961), pp. 1-31 [cited from *Kleine Schriften,* vol. 1 (1969), pp. 361-389].

Loey, Adolf van
  1970 *Schönfelds Historische Grammatica van het Nederlands. Klankleer - Vormleer - Woordvorming.* 8th edition.
    Zutphen: W.J. Thieme & Cie.

Meid, Wolfgang
  1980 *Gallisch und Lateinisch? Soziolinguistische und andere*

Bemerkungen zu populären gallo-lateinischen Inschriften.
(Innsbrucker Beiträge zur Sprachwissenschaft—Vorträge 24)
Innsbruck: Institut für Sprachwissenschaft der Universität.

Meillet, Antoine
  1908 (1922) *Les dialectes indo-européens.*
    (Collection Linguistique, vol. 1)
    Paris: Edouard Champion.

Palmer, R. L.
  1954 *The Latin Language*
    London: Faber & Faber.

Pokorny, Julius
  1959 *Indogermanisches etymologisches Wörterbuch.*
    Berne/Munich: A. Francke.

Polomé, Edgar
  1957 "Germanisch und Venetisch."
    In: ΜΝΗΜΗΣ ΧΑΡΙΝ, vol. 2, pp. 86-98.
    Vienna: Wiener Sprachgesellschaft/Wiesbaden: Otto Harrassowitz.
  1986 "The non-Indo-European component of the Germanic lexicon."
    In: Annemarie Etter (ed.), *o-o-pe-ro-si. Festschrift für*
    Ernst Risch zum 75. Geburtstag, pp. 661-672.
    Berlin/New York: Walter de Gruyter.

Puhvel, Jaan
  1984 *Hittite Etymological Dictionary*
    1. *Words beginning with A*
    2. *Words beginning with E and I*
    (Trends in Linguistics—Documentation, vol. 1)
    Berlin/New York: Mouton.

Schlerath, Bernfried
    1973 *Die Indogermanen. Das Problem der Expansion eines Volkes im Lichte seiner sozialen Struktur,*
    (Innsbrucker Beiträge zur Sprachwissenschaft, Vorträge 8)
    Innsbruck: Institut für Sprachwissenschaft der Universität.

Sommer, F.
    1924 "Zur venetischen Schrift und Sprache."
    In: *Indogermanische Forschungen,* vol. 42, pp. 90-132.
    1947 *Hethiter und Hethitisch.*
    Stuttgart: W. Kohlhammer.

Tischler, Johann
    1983 *Hethitisches etymologisches Glossar. 1. A - K.*
    (Innsbrucker Beiträge zur Sprachwissenschaft, vol. 20:1)
    Innsbruck: Institut für Sprachwissenschaft der Universität.

Vries, Jan de
    1961 *Altnordisches etymologisches Wörterbuch.*
    Leyden: E.J. Brill.
    1971 *Nederlands etymologisch woordenboek.*
    Leyden: E.J. Brill.

Weinreich, Uriel
    1953 *Languages in Contact. Findings and Problems.*
    New York: Linguistics Circle of New York.

Whorf, Benjamin Lee
    1956 *Language, Thought and Reality.*
    Selected Writings edited, with an introduction by John B. Carroll
    Cambridge: Massachusetts Institute of Technology Press.

THE PRE-INDO-EUROPEAN LANGUAGE OF NORTHERN (CENTRAL) EUROPE

Eric P. Hamp

(University of Chicago)

1. On Indo-European Dialectology

First, some preliminaries, which I compress greatly. For any family of languages of an interesting diversification over an interesting amount of time, for which in light of our experience of about two centuries a spread of five or six millennia is certainly sufficient, there will be a diaclectology represented in the branches that have diversified. I personally take it as axiomatic for linguistic comparison not merely that a dialectology is possible but that in fact no comparative problem should be addressed without taking overt account of the implied dialectology in every solution. Diagram One can be regarded, if you will, as a Schleicherian stemma and as a provisional answer to the question: "What did the Indo-European family look like at some time?" But, more importantly, we may use this diagram as an ongoing worksheet to apply to any problem. Every solution must either conform to our proposed dialectology, or it must contribute to a set of answers which are sufficiently serious to force us to alter our diaclectology. Therefore, every time we compare it is no longer sufficient simply to state an equivalence; we must plot the facts on our provisional diversification tree so that, if anything violates an assumed branching, it must either be discarded, and the hypothesis rejected as unacceptable, or it must alter our tree. It is not our task just now in the present paper to consider the genetic dialectology of Indo-European, but we can remember such items as 'barley' (Hamp 1985a) as a handy illustration of what could be considered shared archaisms, and also of what must be innovation. You must rank these. Shared innovations, which are diagnostic, will then show the proper criteria for sub-grouping. I have discussed (Hamp 1985b) the question of innovations at some length in a treatment of a long-debated etymological syndrome in connection with the Greek lexeme ἵημι. See also Hamp 1977a on OE *lēod* and related forms and on the West IE suffix *-n-* for chiefs of social units.

2. Argumenta ex silentio

There is the problem of *argumenta ex silentio* which we must always bear carefully in mind; those false scents have unfortunately confused our deliberations in the past—almost in a traditional fashion. Certain of these have been paraded constantly: the Latin thematic genitive singular, for example. People have even tried to squash the phonology to get four segments of vowels and consonants to squeeze down into a single "i." And there have been quite extensive arguments based on the apparent absence of *-osio* in Latin, as contrasted with Faliscan. Now, we have since found that the *suodales Valesiosio*, that is, *Popliosio*, or *Pobliosio* (if that's the way he called himself) show us that just within the precincts of Latium itself at Satricum we had a perfectly acceptable Indo-European formation, and that the genitive singular of *Valerī* just does not enter into the question (Hamp 1984a:185).

Another example is the supposed absence of the word for daughter in Celtic. Some years ago, Enrico Campanile pointed out that Bonfante had earlier ignored what Michael O'Brien some thirty years ago now had shown: that early Irish attests this word in a frozen form in its onomastics, i.e. in women's names, gynonyms, I guess we should call them. The fact is now, of course, that on the beautiful new Gaulish inscription from Le Larzoc we have the word itself, and in exactly the same form, I am pleased to say, that I predicted ten years ago (Hamp 1975a), i.e. with only two syllables in the stem: *duxtir*, as we now read it. Therefore, this means that, in problems of sub-grouping and genetics, we should by now have learned our lesson. One would hope we had, so that we would not need preparatory remarks every time we turn around; more and more in Indo-European studies we find the need to make prefatory remarks that should have been covered in any beginning course, not just in linguistics, but in some elementary course in logic.

3. On Substrata

Having got these general questions out of the way, we now turn to certain shared traits which raise the problem of substrata. Substrata have been understood in at least two ways. As we know, some people immediately shy away from substrata and condemn everything that mentions the name as something to be automatically rejected; one presumably rejects the notion on grounds of not using loose arguments anchored only in thin air. On the other hand, one also disassociates oneself from the supposed other group that invokes substrata for every set of facts or for even a single fact which cannot be substantiated anywhere else. I take substrata in an entirely different sense: briefly put, evidence of substrata, by definition, will be traces of material that fail to find a correlation in any large body of full language documentation. When we possess such documentation we just call it by name: we say, for example, that something in English or in French has been borrowed from e.g., German or learned Latin or even British Celtic or Gaulish because we have a body of known linguistic material called German or Latin or Gaulish. But when we possess no body of data such as that, yet find traits which cannot by a set of orderly reasoning be assigned within a stemma such as we have just discussed, which thus cannot be fitted into a genetic dialectology, but which yield subgroups in effect cross-cutting established branchings, then we are talking about material which is susceptible of being assigned to substrata.

My further requirement, one which rules out a good many claims, even some that have been tabled at this meeting, is that we cannot fasten upon single facts. This means that we cannot seize upon a single isolated personal name. So, for instance, if we find something like *Venet(o)i* in Europe that can of itself never be conclusive because it depends on only one chain of elements in an equivalence. We must insist on multiple sets of equivalencies between different terms. In other words, we require $n^1 + n^2 = n^3 \ldots - n^q$, and then additionally homomorphous distributions of the form $m^1 = m^2 \ldots m^q$ and so forth, $1^1 = 1^2 \ldots 1^q$. Note that we must have homomorphous distributions of multiple sets of equivalencies. It is the same formal requirement, of course, that we insist on for demonstration of genetic *Lautgesetze*. Finally, for acceptable substrata, when we finish stating these quivalencies, we must make a cohesive statement of structural features which are to be assigned to those summaries of homomorphous equivalent sets. Only then can we say we have a substratum worth talking about. Until those requirements have been fulfilled you may have an interesting breakfast observation, but you do not have an argument.

4. "North Europe" and Its Periphery

Now, where do we find configurations of this sort? Gradually, it has seemed to me more and more as I look at these data, albeit not as a determined object of inquiry—I did not set out personally to explore Northern Europe, but as a repeated set of observations while I worked through things, that items keep dropping out into patterns that I have just alluded to, giving us an entity which we might call "North Europe." It has, so to speak, a heartland, and it has a periphery; therefore, we find that for North Europe the material is to be seen underneath the Indo-European branches known as Germanic, Balto-Slavic (I use the hyphen advisedly), and Albanian; I also believe that Albanian belongs to the last with a hyphen, too, but with a less close binding hyphen: Albanian plus Balto-Slavic. Unfortunately, scholars don't think of Albanian as often as they should, and so it is not so obvious a connection as Balto-Slavic with a hyphen. Note that I now see the genetic connection of Albanian to Balto-Slavic much more clearly and positively, on the basis of work that I have published in the meantime, than I did in Hamp (1966:117-9, especially arts. 15-16). Then there is Celic, less closely bound to these. I also find that the Prehellenic element that is disclosed underneath Greek, and which was called *Pelasgisch* or *Pélasgique* by Georgiev and van Windekens and some others (but in certain details with different rules from those which I use in my interpretation), also belongs in this North Europe aggregate for substratal evidence; I have discussed Prehellenic questions over the past decade in the pages of *Živa Antika*, e.g., in Hamp 1983a.

This must be differentiated from what we would call "Western Indo-European," on which see Hamp (in press a), (1976), and later issues of *Indogermanische Forschungen* and which might be regarded loosely as a candidate, but not yet well substantiated, genetic grouping and which covers over Meillet's

Northwest.[1] The last is not very well developed formally, as we all know, in his own elaboration of it, but the makings of some things are clear there (see also Hamp 1961, 1988), and in some other aspects of Hans Kuhn's *Nordwestblock*. In those arguments we have, if you like, mostly the makings of some type of genetic possibility for Indo-European.

I explicitly leave out of account here Hans Kuhn's presumably Indo-European *Nordwestblock*, on which see most recently and searchingly Meid (1986). I likewise pass over the elusive purely Indo-European problem of "Alteuropäisch," on which see W.P. Schmid (1986).

In this Northern European group, however, we are speaking of an areal grouping that reflects, if viewed descriptively and contemporaneously, a *Sprachbund* relation, but if viewed diachronically, the result of contact with a substratum. There is also a periphery to this area, you might say, less well naturalized by its substratal linguistic influence. In this respect, I speak now as a linguist, and I would like to encourage the entry of other cultural dimensions into the computus. I refer here to a linguistic fringe area, most readily perceived on the western edge, namely the Celtic fringe. We call this periphery "western" mainly because of its modern position. By modern, I refer to the last two and a half or three millennia. When we speak of Northern Europe, not as a genetic subgroup but as a *Sprachbund*, the fringe (Celtic) area may geographically more properly be called something like "central." Perhaps we are talking about facts relating roughly to territory between the Schwarzwald and Hallstatt, or maybe extending even so far over and down as Pannonia or the Vojvodina. We are not, I would submit, talking about Šumadija and certainly not about Paeonia or the Vardar basin. We are not speaking about the Cisalpine areas of northern Italy; we are also not speaking about the uplands south of Hamburg.

The Celtic fringe is less integrated into our *Sprachbund* in the sense that certain facts, for instance the vocalism, depart from the typifying *Sprachbund* characteristics; this fringe was never naturalized so completely, it did not diverge so fully or in the same way from its Indo-European background.

---

1. On this matter, see further Hamp 1974a.

There were other features about Celtic besides the vocalism that class it, if you like, as mor Brugmannian than Germanic and Balto-Slavic, e.g., the less sweeping merger in Celtic of the aorist and perfect.

5. The Phonology of "North Europe"

Now let us look at some of these features which we can assign to this North European substratum. I would submit that we find a syndrome of phonological features which have been stronger in convincing me of the integrity of this set of facts than almost anything else. They persuade me more strongly than the lexicon simply because lexicon, which is usually the favorite object in such discussions, though highly persuasive in its individual items, is much more difficult to allot to the necessary syndromes of homomorphous distributions. It is harder to find a structural cohesion within lexicon, as we all know, than a cohesion in phonology.

The first phonological fact is one which I have discussed in Hamp 1979a and can be illustrated briefly, simply by picking out the Celtic and Latin reflexes of some well known entities. If we take the word for 'sea,' for which we would not be surprised to find a loan since the Indo-Europeans were not a maritime folk, Old Irish $muir^n$ (which is a neuter, as the nasalization shows, even though there was not etymologically a nasal at the end of that particular word) is by common consent equated with Latin *mare*. Yet $muir^n$ has a vocalism which must be credited to *o* descriptively within Proto-Celtic, and we know that Celtic **o* does not formally match Latin *a*. Similarly, Old Irish and Modern Scottish Gaelic *loch* and Latin *lacus* 'lake' fail to give a canonical equation. We see the same correspondence more elaborately in the words for 'apple' and 'apple tree,' which give us a semantic set matching very well also in its morphology.

OIr. *ubull* n.　　Welsh *afal* m.　　Lith. *óbuolas*　　OCS *jablъko* < *əblu
　　aball f.　　　*afall* f.　　　　*obelìs*　　　　*jablanь* < *əbəl-n-*

For these we then reconstruct an initial vowel which must be different from both an Indo-European **o* and an **a* in conventional terms. Note that we have fixed upon Latin and Irish, both of which maintain distinct reflexes of IE **o* and **a*. This leads us to the observation that we reach a reconstructed state of affairs with only four distinctive vocalisms: [i e u ə], as I have argued in Hamp 1979a. In turn, we may now understand how it is that North European Indo-European genetic branches underwent regular Brugmannian mergers of IE *o and *a. Such an *a - *o merger precisely fits within this substratal correspondence. In other words, it seems as if the northern genetic branches of Indo-European within Europe were spoken by people applying the native phonology of their language which lacked a low back distinction in vocalism that economical Brugmannian phonology analytically requires.

Then let us look at certain Germanic terms most elaborately displayed, it just happens, in Old English:

OE mág < *mēgaz 'kinsman' < *mēkó-
OE mága < *mēgan- 'son' < *mēkón-
OE magu < *maguz 'son' → *magwī > Goth. mawi
    *mək-ú- → *mageþ- 'girl' > OE maeg(e)þ < *mək-ét-
    *magu- 'servant' = OIr. mug, W meu-dwy < *məghu-
    (*mək-ú- > meək-ó- = mēkó-)

We see here a word with an apparent Germanic long *ē for 'kinsman' for which I give a hypothetical pre-Verner reconstruction, and a word for 'son' which is an n-stem individuated noun formed on the same stem. Another word for 'son,' a u-stem with a short vowel, also gives some feminizations; in its pre-Verner form this stem looks as if it were a correctly formed zero-grade participle for a very early stage of Indo-European. Feminized, we arrive perfectly at a form for 'girl.' For clarity I then note a fact which I think all the handbooks merged with some of the above forms of Germanic; this is shown by the apparently cognate matching Celtic forms to have the same *ə vocalism that we have already disclosed above. Therefore 'servant' originally had a first syllable different from what we must in 'son' call a *schwa: I call it a *schwa because it has the property whereby in a derivative with thematizing Brugmannian short a the obligatory e-insertion links with the schwa element (as though an inherited laryngeal in Indo-European phonology) to give a long *ē. In other words, all of these forms show perfectly good grammatical formation rules that we know from Indo-European.

We can now write a derivation for the Celtic words for 'son':

*mək-ú- → *məkw-o- > *mak^{w}o > mapo- > W mab
    → Ogam MAQQA- > Oir. macc

Therefore, this recovers for us an etymon with *schwa in the first syllable contrasting with what we are writing with "turned c." I have written about this in Hamp (1979:166, footnote 10) and (in press b). Thus, for this language of North Europe we recover a five-vowel system which we can label using our customary symbols [i e u ə] and a central schwa vocalism to be distributed amongst these.

This language also shows violations of Indo-European phonotactic rules or Indo-European inventory. For instance, the famous Indo-European gap that our colleague Thomas Gamkrelidze has discussed in such elaboration in his glottalic theory, the rare Brugmannian *b, appears in the 'apple' word. In fact, Germanic is rather well supplied with *p from apparent *b (e.g. Eng. *play, spell, ship*, etc.). We also have the violation of media plus media, which is virtually excluded in Indo-European root forms. This sequence shows up in a number of Germanic bases, where it can be seen very easily: e.g. Engl. *cut*, ON *kvett* 'meat,' *kjǫt* n. < *ketu < *gedu (Hamp 1975b). It is easy, we now know, in Balto-Slavic and also, incidentally, in Albanian (when these show the desired etymon) to see the difference between an aspirata and a media; but in Celtic, unfortunately, we cannot so readily see this; therefore, our evidence sometimes is hobbled by a dearth of criterial evidential materials. These phonological violations of Brugmannian Indo-European again show us a set of properties which occur in syndromes.

It is not necessary for us in our present context to discuss Wagner 1964, which, interesting though it is and revised by more recent fieldwork, is occupied rather with the typology of phonetics, allophonics, and phonology (esp. of word accent and consonants) found in the northernmost zone or Eurasia. This by definition would be areal, and not a prehistoric language.

6. Morphology

Instances of morphology are much harder to find; after all, we are dealing with a pitifully small corpus. Even so, I have been struck repeatedly by the fact that items put into this category display an unusual affinity for *u at the end of their stem, not a very ordinary thing in Indo-European forms. I list here certain of them that I have discussed under this rubric in one place or another: *əblu, maghu-, məku-, gedu, linghu* 'heather,' *salu* 'a seaweed,' *məekku-* 'swine,' *suku-* → *sukko-* 'swine,' *b(h)ənu-* or *gʷənu-* 'piglet.'

Also, with Celtic again somewhat on the edge and less integrated with the other branches, there is a strong fusion of what, from an Indo-Europeanist point of view, we call the aorist and perfect systems of the verb. However, we do not have the proper leisure here to discuss this at all satisfactorily in view of the vexed Anatolian question. I simply point out the possible correlation we could see for assignment of tense/aspect functions in this putative substratal language.

There is, thirdly, the linkage of relative and definite forms. Celtic shows this in the complementarity of *-io and *-to in the relative forms of the verb, as I see them. Germanic shows it in what has the appearance of a relative function for 'definite' or deictic or anaphoric shapes, in other words *•þ-, *s-, or *ei. Prokosch (1939:277) must be essentially correct; Germanic would have exploited the inherited forms from correlative constructions such as we see in Skt. *yad ... tad*. Balto-Slavic shows it in the elements suffixed to modifiers in the noun phrase, the so-called definite forms of adjectives, beside the OCS relative *i-že*. Albanian shows it in the conflation of form found in the postposed definite marker (masc. sg: *-y, pl. -të, for example) with the attributive prefix of concord (*i, të*, etc.) < the Indo-European relative pronoun which associates definite marking with relative marking in the noun phrase construction.

It is possible that the animate suffix in *-g- which I have reconstructed (Hamp 1983b, 1987a) for Balto-Slavic and Germanic also rests on a "North Europe" substratum.

7. Grammatical Lexicon

To begin with, I suggest we abandon the search for isolated lexemes. It is not profitable to ponder whether to adopt an item or to reject it without some constraining principle that helps to eliminate chance and the sheer possibility of oversight or undue emphasis through whimsical choice. Rather let us take items in the context of linkages with other grammatical facts that impart a finite scope.

We may consider the word for 'fist' (Baltic *kúmpsti- < punksti- , Slavic *pęsti, Germanic *funhsti- < *pnk^{w}sti-) in relation to the Germanic ordinal < IE *pnk^w-to- 'fifth' and its integration into the ordinal systems (Hamp 1970). On the other hand, the form for 'thousand' (Lith. *túkstant-* OCS *tysǫšti*, Goth. *þūsundi* < *tuH-sk̂-(o)nt-*) looks like a participle of some type of inceptive or continuative verb, for details see Hamp 1973b.

8. Cultural Lexicon

Here we seek syndromes of forms from a *Bedeutungsfeld*, e.g. terms for the pig and swine, on which see in extenso Hamp 1986a, 1986b, 1987b, in press c, d. There is also a finely structured lexical set which I shall discuss in detail elsewhere comprising terms for the bee (Hamp 1971), wax (Hamp 1974b:36), and the bear as man's greatest and tabued competitor for honey. These related terms all congruently cover precisely our area, showing attestations in Balto-Slavic, Germanic, and Celtic; however, the last group is again peripheral since the tabu in Celtic was weaker and failed to oust *artos*, the old Indo-European reflex.

Another semantic syndrome of interlocking terms comprises 'bones,' 'legs,' 'ribs,' and 'branches' in Baltic, Slavic, Germanic and Celtic (Hamp 1985c).

Silver (Hamp 1973c) is obviously of cultural interest for the possible question of control of knowledge, advent, and flow of metals.

The careful sifting of "Indo-European" roots is certain to disclose more candidates for the North Europe lexicon, e.g., Hamp 1985d.

9. Uncertain Areas

There are certain limited areas for which we do not yet know the extent or true affiliation; these involve incomplete congruencies. For example, we observe (Hamp 1967) a word for 'blackberry' in Celtic ($smi^y ar0$) which turns up for 'raspberry' in Romanian (*zmeură*). We may speculate that we see here the presence of Celts in the Carpathian area responsible for this. But just where the source is to be placed and what type of fruit with small seeds this really denoted are questions we cannot yet answer. There is a seaweed $*^w is$-mon- in the northwest attested in Celtic and paralleled in Germanic (Hamp 1979b); merely, you might say, an item of the landscape along the North Sea Coast. In other words, this could be a question of pragmatics and situational semantics as opposed to anything structured in the grammar of the substratum. Again, we find a different dialectological range for OS, OHG, and MLG *horst/hurst*, OE *hyrst*; OIr. *crann* vs. British and Gaulish *prenno-* 'tree, wood,' Welsh *prys* 'brushwood,' which might point to a source in Central Europe in common with Rom. *zmeură* (Hamp 1979c).

We must be prepared to see an untidy set of intruding elements which can not be claimed every time to be a fragment of evidence for our major subject, but it may simply be an intrusion from some other set of phenomena. The important thing is to see the structure of our main object of investigation rather than to argue about the possible relevance or dispensibility of causal intrusions. We can actually recover from these later Indo-European branches a substantial number of characterizing traits to attribute to the pre-Indo-European "North Europe" language.

302 When Worlds Collide

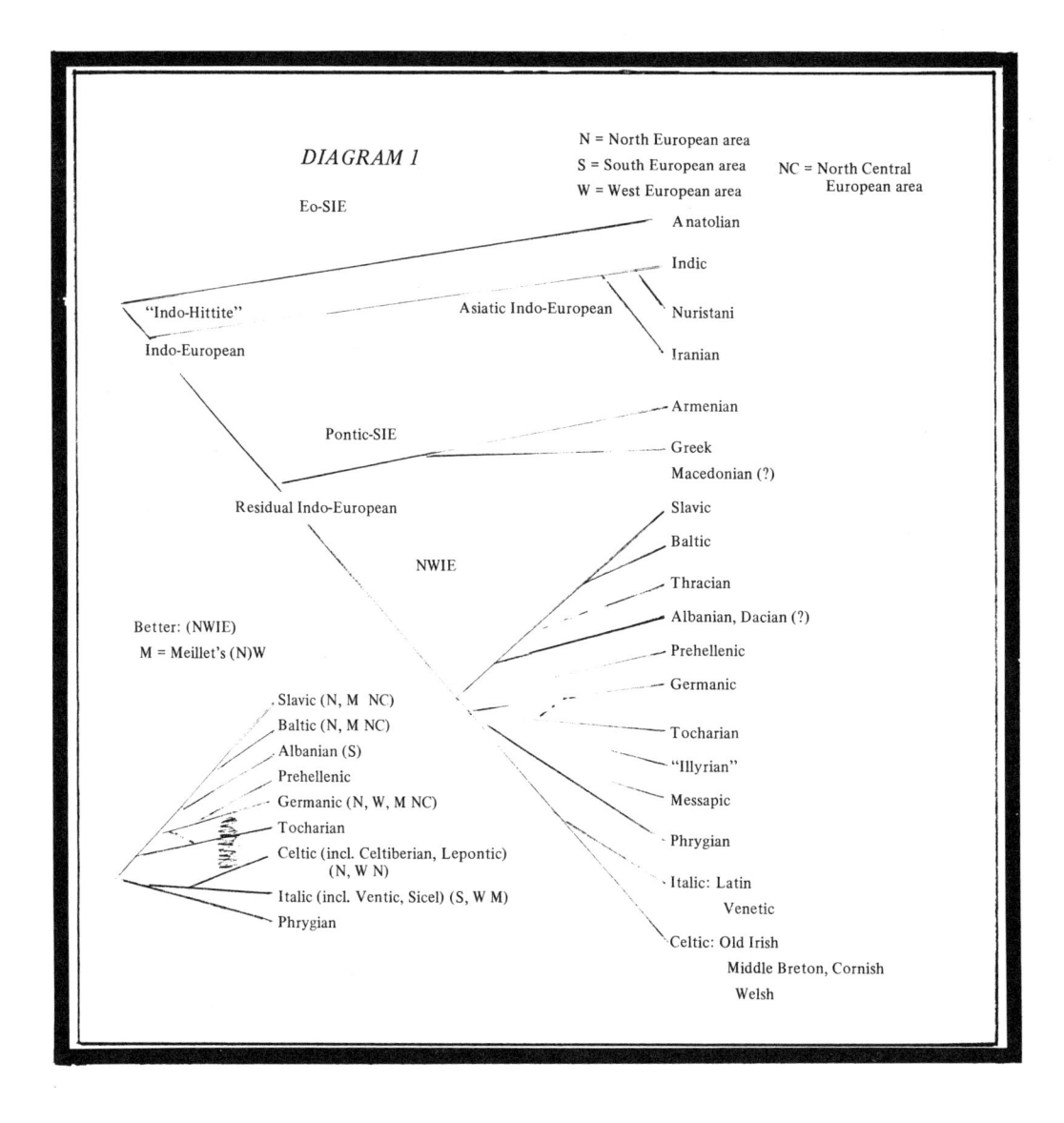

DIAGRAM 1

N = North European area
S = South European area
W = West European area
NC = North Central European area

Eo-SIE

"Indo-Hittite"

Indo-European

Asiatic Indo-European
— Anatolian
— Indic
— Nuristani
— Iranian

Pontic-SIE
— Armenian
— Greek
  Macedonian (?)

Residual Indo-European

NWIE
— Slavic
— Baltic
— Thracian
— Albanian, Dacian (?)
— Prehellenic
— Germanic
— Tocharian
— "Illyrian"
— Messapic
— Phrygian
— Italic: Latin
    Venetic
— Celtic: Old Irish
    Middle Breton, Cornish
    Welsh

Better: (NWIE)
M = Meillet's (N)W

- Slavic (N, M NC)
- Baltic (N, M NC)
- Albanian (S)
- Prehellenic
- Germanic (N, W, M NC)
- Tocharian
- Celtic (incl. Celtiberian, Lepontic) (N, W N)
- Italic (incl. Ventic, Sicel) (S, W M)
- Phrygian

References

Hamp, Eric P.

1961. "Albanian *Pishk* 'Fish.'" *KZ* 77.256. See also 1973a.

1966. "The Position of Albanian." In *Ancient Indo-European Dialects*. edd. Henrik Birnbaum and Jaan Puhvel. Berkeley and Los Angeles: University of California Press. 97-121. See also 1977b, 1980a, 1980b, 1981, 1984b for later work.

1967. *Zmeură*. *Revue roumaine de linguistique*. 12.523-4; 13 (1968) 367.

1970. *pęstĭ*. *Zbornik za filologiju i lingvistiku* (Novi Sad) 13. 292-3.

1971. Varia III (2). "The 'Bee' in Irish, IE, and Uralic." *Ériu*. 22.185-7.

1973a. "Fish." *JIES* 1.507-11.

1973b. "North European '1000.'" *Proceedings from the Ninth Regional Meeting of the Chicago Linguistics Society*. 172-8.

1973c. "Lith. *sidäbras*, OCS *srěbro*." *Baltistica*. 9.57-8.

1974a. "Welsh *achan* and Related Words." *Norwegian Journal of Linguistics/Norsk Tidskrift for Sprogvidenskap*. 28.1-7.

1974b. "Sources of *šk* in Baltic." *Archivio Glottologico Italiano*. 59.31-6.

1975a. "*dhugHtēr* in Irish." *Münchener Studien zur Sprachwissenschaft*. 33.39-40.

1975b. "'Cut' and 'Meat' in Germanic." *Acta Philologica Scandinavica*. 30.49-51.

1976. "Western Indo-European Notes." *Indogermanische Forschungen*. 81.36-40.

1977a. "Old English *lēod-*." *English Studies*. 58.97-100.

1977b. "*Strunga*." *Linguistique Balkanique*.20.113-7.

1979a. "The North European Word for 'Apple.'" *Zeitschrift für celtische Philologie*. 37.158-66.

1979b. "Notulae Etymologicae Cymricae." *Bulletin of the Board of Celtic Studies*. 28.213-7 (esp. *gwymon*).

1979c. "*Horst* and Method." In *Linguistic Method: Essays in Honor of Herbert Penzl*, edd. I. Rauch and G.E. Carr. The Hague: Mouton. 175-81. Correction: Miscellaneous Nots. *Bulletin of the Board of Celtic Studies*. 29 (1980) 86 (*prys*).

1980a. "IE *$k^w eh^a s$*- 'cough.'" Езиковедски проучвания в чест на Акад В. И.

Георгиев. Sofia: БАН Pp. 130-4.

    1980b. "*burtă.*" *Revue roumaine de linguistique.* 25.335.

    1981. "On the Distribution and Origin of *(h)urda.*" *Linguistique balkanique.* 24.47-50.

    1983a. "Prehellenica 3. στιφρός, στῖφος, 4. σμίλη, σμινύη. σμίνθος. *Živa Antika.* 33.147-8.

    1983b. "Animates in *-g-.*" *Baltistica.* 19.175.

    1984a. "Über das Deklinationssystem." *General Linguistics.* 24.179-86.

    1984b."On Myths and Accuracy." *General Linguistics.* 24.238-9.

    1985a. "Indo-European 'Gerste, Orge, Barley.'" *KZ* 98.11-2.

    1985b. "Two Etymological Remarks." *Eirene* 22.35-8.

    1985c. "German *Bein,* Old English *bān,* Slavic *kostĭ.*" *NOWELE* 6.67-70.

    1985d. "From the North European IE Lexicon." *Lingua Posnaniensis* 28.77. (1. **treuk-* 'tug, hack'; 2. **tengh-* 'heavy').

    1986a. "*Culhwch,* the Swine." *Zeitschrift für celtische Philologie* 41.257-8.

    1986b. "Varia XXV. 4 *orc* in Irish." *Études celtiques* 23.49-50.

    1987a. "Малъжена и мажъ". Български език 37.305-7.

    1987b. "The Pig in Ancient Northern Europe." In *Proto-Indo-European: The Archaeology of a Linguistic Problem. Studies in Honor of Marija Gimbutas.* Washington, DC: Institute for the Study of Man. 185-90.

    1988. "Northwest Indo-European 'spoon.'" In *A Linguistic Happening in Memory of Ben Schwartz.* Ed. Yoël L. Arbeitman. Louvain-la-Neuve: Peeters. 501-4.

    in press a. "On Some Celtic Bird-Terms. 1. Welsh *mwyalch,* etc." *Zeitschrift für celtische Philologie* 43.

    in press b. "Language Contact in the Pre-History of English." In *Festschrift for Rudolf Filipovic.*

    in press c. "North European Pigs and Phonology." *Zeitschrift für celtische Philologie* 43.

    in press d. "**orko-, *erko-,* IE **porko-.*" *Zeitschrift für celtische Philologie* 43.

Meid, Wolfgang.

    1986. "Hans Kuhns 'Nordwestblock' Hypothese: zur Problematik der Völker zwischen Germanen und Kelten." In *Germanenprobleme in heutiger Sicht*. Ed. Heinrich Beck. Berlin and New York: Walter de Gruyter. 183-212. (With fine bibliography of Kuhn's work).

Prokosch, Eduard.
1939. *A Comparative Germanic Grammar*. (William Dwight Whitney Linguistic Series). Philadelphia: Linguistic Society of America.

Schmid, Wolfgang P.
1986. "Alteuropa und das Germanische." In *Germanenprobleme in heutiger Sicht*. Ed. Heinrich Beck. Berlin and New York: Walter de Gruyter. 155-67.

Wagner, Heinrich.
1964. "Nordeuropäische Lautgeographie." *Zeitschrift für celtische Philologie* 29.225-98. (Einleitung; I Lappische Phonesis; II Nordgermanische Phonesis; III Irische und schottisch-gälische Phonesis; IV Phonesis des Manxischen; V Eine östliche Fortsetzung?).

Discussion

Tom Markey: This paper is now open for discussion.

Karl Horst Schmidt: I think that this paper presents so many problems that it is difficult to concentrate on just one of them. I will restrict my comments to the position of Celtic within Indo-European. Do you really think that, and I am very interested in this, that Celtic is one of the North European languages and has connections with Germanic, Balto-Slavic, Albanian, and Pelasgian (Prehellenic)? Is that correct?

Eric P. Hamp: Yes, and incidentally, this is coded on Diagram One.

Karl Horst Schmidt: As a connection you have the medio-passive in Germanic, Celtic, Balto-Slavic, and in Albanian, but most restricted there. I certainly see that Celtic has some patterns that are shared. Then, there is a second general problem. I think the more Celtic inscriptions one finds and decodes, and you gave the example of *duxtir*, and there are other examples in other inscriptions, then the more Brugmannian Celtic becomes. There is also the question of the $s^y o$- future. So, I have the impression, on the basis of new discoveries, that Celtic is becoming more and more Brugmannian, particularly so the deeper and older the inscriptions are that we discover.

Tom Markey: Is there a reply to this?

Eric P. Hamp: Very briefly. Thank you, Karl. I agree almost completely with everything that you have said. I agree that the more we find of Continental Celtic, which is priceless and often crucial, the more our picture fills out. I agree with your remarks, for instance, on the $s^y o$- future. I would call it the irrealis, which has become dialectally both future and subjunctive. On the other hand, when I say that Celtic is peripheral, we then envision a European Indo-European dialect just as Brugmannian as you can make it.

Colin Renfrew: What does Brugmannian mean?

Eric P. Hamp: It is an adjective based on the name of Karl Brugmann, the author of the *Grundriss der vergleichenden Grammatik der indogermanischen Sprachen*.

Colin Renfrew: That I know, but specifically?

Eric P. Hamp: Yes. This means that it has a certain set of features of grammatical description, which, for example, include certain traits that were for a long time viewed as the obvious characteristics that every respectable ancient Indo-European language had. In other words, a kind of grammar that looks like a crossbreed, you might say, between McDonell's Vedic grammar, as opposed to Whitney's, which was classical Sanskrit, and your old school classical Greek grammar when filled out with the introductory grammatical notes to your handbook of Homer; if you add to that Old Irish grammar, which people generally don't learn in the same way, then this is Brugmannian grammar.

Colin Renfrew: Thank you.

Eric P. Hamp: But I would say that Celtic is very Brugmannian. However, by moving into this substratum area of North Europe and taking up residence there, their interbreeding with the natives brought in some intrusions into the Brugmannian structure; however, their intrusions were fewer that those of their Germanic and Balto-Slavic neighbors. That is the sense in which I say I agree.

Colin Renfrew: Could you possibly say something more about how we identify Prehellenic and/or Pelasgian and, secondly, about how we assign it such a classification, which I think presents difficulties historically? I am not especially familiar with the literature so as to be entirely confident as to how we distinguish between Hellenic and Prehellenic.

Eric P. Hamp: Very simple. In order to distinguish them you test everything just as you do anywhere else with a comparative problem in a genetic group. In Indo-European, for instance, we take a set of forms and test them with a provisional set of rules. Now, certain words won't yield to the Greek set of rules.

But if you change the set of rules, which is what Georgiev and some others then did, and adopt a different set of rules, and apply them in the correct order, this then produces a result. Once you have analyzed a few such cases to fine a provisional set of rules, you choose fresh words and keep trying them, and find that the rules keep working. The answer, then, is the set of descent rules that will account for a so-called "Pelasgian," or Prehellenic form; simply a different set of descent rules from those that yield normal Honeric or Greek forms.

Colin Renfrew: Thank you. May I take one final position? I find this very illuminating, but I'm always a little skeptical of taxonomical morphological distinctions which then proceed to inject a concept of chronological priority: I don't see where, from the observations you've made, we can assign a chronological priority to one or another set of rules.

Eric P. Hamp: If you assume that Prehellenic came to Greece first with an Indo-European language and that then Greek came in, borrowed a certain number of forms, such as *pýrgos*. That is, the locals say "*pýgos*," so we keep on calling this a *pýrgos*. In other respects, the newcomers bring their Greek, with its different set of rules, and settle on top of these earlier people. That is one assumed train of events. The other assumption is to say exactly the reverse. You arrive with a set of Hellenic rule, and then a group of Prehellenics come in, and settle down on top of the Greeks; they borrow from the Greeks, for example, "pólis." If you make the second assumption, you will then discover that you have no coherent grammar at all; you don't have a total grammar that will work using these rules: you cannot conjugate a Homeric verb while using these rules. If you make this assumption, with an explanation of the descent of twelve or twenty eight or whatever Homeric words, some of them nouns like *agostos*, you will also explain *ageírō*, I think. You will explain a few forms, but almost every other line of Homer will be opaque to you. If you make the first assumption, however, as we always have, with a Homeric grammar, for which Brugmann then provided a background, then these deviant words turn up as small monadnocks, to use a geological metaphor, in an otherwise Homeric peneplane.

Colin Renfrew: But why are these rules North European and not something else?

Eric P. Hamp: Because we find our best matches for Prehellenic in that area. The rules themselves are largely separate from those of every other branch, just as those of Celtic and Germanic are. But we keep finding matches in the forms. Our best matches are found in Baltic.

THE INVESTIGATION OF PROTO-INDO-EUROPEAN HISTORY: METHODS, PROBLEMS, LIMITATIONS

Stefan Zimmer
Freie Universität Berlin

*For Bernfried Schlerath
on the occasion of his sixty-fifth birthday*

I. Methods

The subject of Indo-European Linguistics is languages, viz. those languages found in antiquity from India to Europe which can be shown to be genetically related and belonging to one family, the Indo-European language family. Their relation to each other can only be clarified by historical investigations: therefore the oldest attested documents of the respective languages are of utmost importance. This also holds true for the two other parts of Indo-European Studies, viz. Indo-European Literary and Cultural Studies, on which see further below.

There is one methodological principle governing the whole development of linguistics. It had already been discussed by the Greeks, and received its classical formulation by de Saussure: it is "l'arbitraire du signe". This means that the words men use in referring to things have no natural connection to these things, but are ultimately chosen arbitrarily. Only by social conventions do they become general. It follows from this principle, which is self-evident to anyone comparing a large number of languages, that systematic correspondences between grammatical systems of different languages are the results of genetic relations between the languages in question.

In trying to order the information gained by studying the history and mutual interdependence of genetically related languages and their grammatical systems and sub-systems, the laws of historical phonology have been established. The Lautgesetze allow only merging or splitting of a given phoneme under certain conditions, and nothing else. The method of going backwards from attested word-forms to their unattested pre-forms by using the sound laws is called reconstruction. Every reconstructed language can therefore have only one phonological system. It follows from these principles that the well-known Stammbaum model is the only adequate form of summing up the reconstructed history of a language family. It is possible, and often necessary, to reconstruct (fragments of) unattested languages on various levels: so, we have within the Indo-European language family not only the reconstructed ancestor, Proto-Indo-European, but also regional proto-languages between the attested languages and this ancestor, e.g. Proto-Indo-Iranian, Proto-Germanic, Proto-Celtic, and so on. The great difference between 'reconstruction' in history or archaeology on the one hand and in historical linguistics on the other is that the archaeologist is able to date the strata in which his finds are located with relative confidence, and therefore to situate his reconstructed objects in space and time, whereas the linguist has nothing like a datable stratum: his reconstructions are pure abstracts incapable of being located or dated.[1] He can only be sure that his reconstructed forms are older than the attested ones. Furthermore, it is even impossible to calculate how much older (the proposed theories of 'glottochronology' and 'lexicostatistics' have failed to gain any credit); the speed of change varies enormously among Indo-European languages (probably within all languges of the

---

[1] For similar formulations and more methodological details, see Schlerath 1982, Untermann 1985, W.P. Schmidt 1987.- There has been much discussion on the archaeologists' *absolute* chronology vs. the linguists' *relative* chronology. To my mind, these terms are less than useful for the present discussion: there have been enough cases of archaeological chronology drastically changed and linguistic chronology reversed to be sceptical about "absolute" and "relative" in this field.

world): think e.g. of the Latin verbal categories[2] or the Baltic nominal declension. Therefore, the reconstructed (note the fundamental difference between 'reconstructed' and 'postulated'!) Ursprache cannot be regarded in the same way as a natural language: no philological interpretation of the reconstructed items is possible, and any inference drawn from reconstructions (e.g. words for animals and plants) can never obtain the level of reliability archaeological hypotheses are able to reach. This is due to the incoherence of the reconstructible vocabulary relevant to historical questions; therefore, any systematic reconstruction of extralinguistic features, such as religion, and social structure[3], is excluded beforehand. All we can find are disconnected fragments.[4]

The first aim of Indo-European linguistics is therefore not the reconstruction of the Indo-European Ursprache as one of the languages spoken in an unknown antiquity by unidentified people but as a reference tool in discussing the history and development of the different Indo-European languages. In other words, it is not Proto-Indo-European as spoken in a dark past that we want to know, but how our living languages developed from their common ancestor down to the time of their earliest attestation. In studying this, we further hope to learn something about human languages in general, and about the functioning of the human brain

---

[2] The discussion on the prehistory of the Anatolian verbal system continues. For its relevance to the reconstruction of Proto-Indo-European, see e.g. Neu 1985.

[3] The "quatre cercles de l'appartenance sociale" and the "tripartion des fonctions" proposed by É. Benveniste can no longer be claimed for Proto-Indo-European: they are late and regional developments, and not at all Indo-European, as close philological control and linguistic methodology have shown (Zimmer 1987, with references). Therefore, all theories based on Benveniste's hypotheses are to be discarded.

[4] Even É. Benveniste had to agree on that, cf. his statement: "La grammaire comparée, de par sa méthode même, conduit à éliminer les développements particuliers pour reconstituer le fonds commun. Cette démarche (i.e. linguistic reconstruction) ne laisse substister qu'un très petit nombre de mots indo-européens (1969, II 180)."

vis-à-vis the world.

The methodology of Indo-European Cultural Studies is quite different: starting from the natural assumption that every language – attested or reconstructed – was spoken by people and that the way of life of these people is reflected by their language, the *reconstructed* items of Proto-Indo-European are taken for specimens of the *postulated* Ursprache. This is a further hypothesis, of higher degree and *a priori* weaker than all assumptions made in linguistic reconstruction. Nevertheless, investigations of lost civilizations based on linguistic reconstructions are possible and legitimate if, and only if, they are closely controlled by strict methods: these are, of course, the methods of linguistic reconstruction, so that not only comparable things and institutions are required but also comparable (i.e. etymologically related) words for them. The comparison of alleged structures alone is very weak being dependent on much interpretation; it can never be forcibly convincing. Further evidence (which can only be linguistic) is necessary to support the postulated facts of Proto-Indo-European culture.

As far as I can see, only the study of Indo-European literature can adduce the moment of proof which reconstruction alone is unable to produce. There are two layers of literature which may be named 'Indo-European': one is formed by the traditional literatures in the different old Indo-European languages and one by the remains of Proto-Indo-European poetical language as collected first by Adalbert Kuhn, and in our period in the famous book by R. Schmitt. It has to be kept in mind, however, that the fragments of common poetical language are representative only of a very restricted part of society, viz. the richer adult (and perhaps partly also juvenile) males.[5]

---

[5] The comparative study of the literature of old Indo-European languages for the purpose of gaining insight into the minds of people living in undocumented periods has received an enormous impetus in recent decades through the works of the late Georges Dumézil (for some of the many objections which could be raised to Dumézil's "idéologie tripartie", see Zimmer 1978 and Schmitt 1985, both with further references). Unfortunately, older works as e.g. the publications of Burkard Wilhelm Leist (Leist 1884, 1889, 1892) seem widely forgotten today.

In the absence of a specifically historical (as opposed to linguistic) methodology of its own, Indo-European Cultural Studies therefore rely heavily on neighbouring sciences, viz. Prehistory, Archaeology, Ethnology and Anthropology. Any model or scenario proposed should take into account their respective results and must be typologically supported by historically attested developments.

Much attention has been paid to the question of the original homeland of the Proto-Indo-Europeans. Several arguments with names of plants and animals (e.g. beech and salmon) have been put forward[6], but in the final analysis, nothing decisive remains because the original identity of the the reconstructed meaning of the reconstructed word and the real object cannot be proven, as Jürgen Untermann has again underlined recently.[7] Furthermore, most archaeologists today have become very sceptical about the possibilities of identifying a given archaeological culture with a linguistically reconstructed or historically postulated ethnic group.[8] Nevertheless, many Indo-Europeanists have made their own proposals about Proto-Indo-European civilization on the basis of the sources mentioned above. Every serious description of this kind is bound to be more a sketch than a painting and cannot be more than an intelligent guess at the very best. The most recently published theories may be commented upon briefly.

Marija Gimbutas' Kurgan theory of Indo-European origins has earned widespread

---

[6] A masterpiece of its kind is Thieme 1954.

[7] Studien zur Ethnogenese, p. 148-9.

[8] In any event, it makes no sense to use the name of a language to characterize material things, technical products, and methods of work. It should be kept in mind that peoples with close cultural relations or even identical cultures and very similar ethnic components can speak different languages (as English and French, e.g.), and that linguistic unity does not necessarily mean cultural or racial similarity (cf. the Palestinians speaking Arabic like the Arab nomads!). There are peoples like the Bulgarians who are ethnic Turkish, Slavic-speaking, and professing the Greek form of Christianity.

attention in recent years, mostly in the USA. She has conveniently summarized her own view as follows: "The Indo-European speakers ... introduced hard metal ... for the production of daggers, flat and shaft-hole axes, and [were] fighting on horse-back with dagger, spear, shield, bow and arrows."(1986, 5). They were "patriarchal, horse-riding steppe pastoralists", had a "patrilocal and patrilinear social structure, hillforts and small villages, semi-subterranean houses, the domesticated horse and horse-riding, thrusting weapons and hard metal, and a patriarchal sky-oriented pantheon of gods", whereas the "Old Europeans" (as she calls the non-Indo-European peoples who are covered by the three Kurgan migration waves) "were sedentary, matrifocal, peaceful, art-loving, and possessed of(!) a matriarchal earth- and water-bound pantheon of goddesses". (1980, 1). This is a very neat contrast, and one wonders what the reasons for such a clear-cut distinction could have been. As a linguist I am cautious of discussing archaeological facts, and I will only put forward some points of criticism:

a) The use of 'Indo-European', i.e. the name of a language family, is of doubtful sense if we speak of a period more than two thousand years before the first attestation of any language belonging to that family.

b) A central point in Professor Gimbutas' theory, and crucial for the explanation of the three waves, is the fighting on horseback. This has been disputed[9] by archaeologists for the Kurgan people, and is excluded for Indo-Europeans before the first millennium BC, because of the following facts: The horse was well known by the Proto-Indo-Europeans, as best proven by several poetic formulas mentioning the "swift horse", the "horses of the sun", and using the adjectives "characterized by good horses" and "having horses which are cared for". The formulas tell us nothing specific about the use of horses, but archaeology and history supply the necessary information.

There are two standard works on the matter: one is Joseph Wiesner, Fahren und Reiten (Archaeologia Homerica I, F), Göttingen 1968, the other is M.A. Littauer and J.H. Crouwel, Wheeled Vehicles and Ridden Animals in the Ancient Near East

---

[9] E.g., Renfrew p. 137f.

(Handbuch der Orientalistik 7.1.2.B.1), Leiden 1979.[10] Both agree on the following facts: Riding for military purposes is an Assyrian invention, first attested in the 9th c. BC. The first Indo-European warriors to appear on horseback were Greeks in the late 8th c., and shortly afterwards the Achaemenid cavalry.[11] Hunting on horseback occurs slightly earlier, but still in the first millennium BC. Before that period, horse riding is exceptional, and never occurs in fighting.[12]

c) The region in which the Kurgan culture has been defined is in the given period (4500-2800 BC) in no way in advance of other cultures. On the contrary, archaeologist like Xirotiris underline the fact that the region was "spät neolithisiert und rückständig" (1986, 41). It is difficult to see by what means the Kurgan Proto-Indo-Europeans of Professor Gimbutas could have reached the economic and military superiority necessary for their 'three mighty waves'.

d) There are no forcibly convincing arguments for the existence of most of the characterististics ascribed to the 'Old-Europeans'. It is not certain that matriarchy can been claimed as a typical non-Indo-European feature. The problem is complicated by ethnological theories postulating a regular development of primitive society through matriarchy to patriarchy. If this is assumed, no early contacts between patriarchial Proto-Indo-Europeans and matriarchial non-Indo-Europeans need be suggested in order to explain the fact that Proto-Indo-European society (which was undoubtedly, as well as all Indo-European societies, patriarchal), attributed a special rank to the maternal

---

[10] Cf. further Stuart Piggot, The Earliest Wheeled Transport from the Atlantic Coast to the Caspian Sea. London 1983.

[11] One could of course argue that the Proto-Indo-Europeans had forgotten their horse riding by the time they first came into contact with Near Eastern civilizations - but this cannot be a very serious argument: under such restrictions, everything would be possible.

[12] It is worth noting that so excellent an Iranian scholar as Mary Boyce holds (History of Zoroastrianism vol. I, 1975, p. 151) that "the horse was domesticated among the Indians and Iranians (probably after 2000 B.C.)".- But cf. Bökönyi 1987.

318 When Worlds Collide

uncle, especially the mother's eldest brother (attested in several Indo-European societies including Germanic, Latin, Greek and Indian, and usually understood as a remnant of an older matriarchy).[13]

e) The special use of the term 'pastoralist' in the Kurgan theory seems not to take into account modern ethnological findings, viz. that pastoralism is not an intermediate stage between the hunter-and-gatherer state of civilization and that of agriculture, but always a secondary feature in relation to settled and perhaps even urban populations.[14] Pastoralists depend on agricultural products not produced by themselves.

Recently, another theory has been proposed by Colin Renfrew (1987). According to his proposal, Anatolia was the Urheimat of the Proto-Indo-Europeans, somewhere in the 10th to 8th millenium B.C. This scenario is even more unlikely and far from convincing. His linking of Indo-Europeanization with the spread of agriculture sounds strange enough to the historical linguist, no really specific Proto-Indo-European words for wheat and barley, his basic crops, being attested[15],

---

[13] For Celtic, see e.g. Weisweiler 1939.

[14] Cf. W. Mühlmann's "limitic structures" and his statement: "Nach unsern heutigen Kenntnissen sind die nomadischen Viehzüchter aus seßhaften Bauernkulturen herausgesiebt worden, mit denen sie aber in vielfältigsten Austauschbeziehungen (vor allem auf ökonomischem Gebiet) stehen." (1985, 22).

[15] There are only two words words used in two or more Indo-European languages to designate different kinds of corn, esp. barley and spelt. For none of them, however, can a specific common original meaning be assured. The Greek, Latin, Germanic and Albanian words for barley (Gr κρῖ, κριθή, L $hordeum$, OHG $gërsta$, Alb. $dri\theta$, $dri\theta\varepsilon$) are independent formations; a common meaning could have been 'awny, pointed', cf. OE $gorst$ 'furze'. The Latin word is clearly an adjective in substantival use, and there are ablaut diffences between OHG and OE. The relation of Arm. $gari$ to Georgian $keri$ is unclear, cf. Basque $gari$ 'wheat', $garagar$ 'barley'. The Aryan, Greek, Baltic and Celtic words for different kinds of corn (mostly 'barley'and 'spelt') point to an Indo-European *$ieu̯o$ - with an unspecified meaning 'corn' or perhaps even only 'edible kind of grass'. - Paleobotanists have shown, that emmer, einkorn and barley (in this order) were the prominent crops in the Ancient Near East and in the band ceramics

and his proposed Anatolian Urheimat is excluded by the unanimous conviction of Indo-Europeanists.[16] His proposed chronology moves still further away from the first historical attestations of Indo-Europeans (around 2000 B.C.). Renfrew himself has to admit that his proposal is nothing other than a "sheer hypothesis"[17]; this does not affect, of course, the archaeological parts of his book.

Tamaz Gamkrelidze and Vjačeslav Ivanov, in their monumental study (1984), propose the Caucasus region (including Azerbaijan) as the original homeland of the Proto-Indo-Europeans and explain the ethnogenesis of the different Indo-European peoples by various migrations. This is not the right place for entering a discussion of this important contribution with all its weighty linguistic and historical arguments which deserve further study. At least in its present form, their theory implies a number of assumptions which are difficult to accept, e.g. the crossing of the Caspian Sea by ship, or migrations crossing the Caucasus from South to North.[18] Among the multitude of earlier publications on the subject, Schlerath 1973 is still, to my mind, the most attractive extant proposal.

---

civilizations of paleolithic Europe as well, and not "wheat and barley" (see Körber-Grohne 1987 and Zohary-Hopf 1988, passim).

[16] It is not excluded by the famous passage in the Sun Prayer of Mutawallis (Kl 1, 390), reporting the sun rising out of the sea. F. Sommer (1947, 1-10) took this as a reflex of earlier settlements outside Anatolia.

[17] Archaeology and Language, p. 152.

[18] See Diakonoff's contribution in this volume. - Gamkrelidze seems to take seriously Henning's hazardous idea about the prehistory of the Tocharians (Henning 1978 - he never dared to publish it during his lifetime!). The span of nearly 3000 years between the Akkadian records of *Guti* and the first Tocharian texts should be enough to minimize the probability of Henning's equation. Furthermore, there is another, much more attractive explanation of the *Guti* ("the inital is also spelt with *q*", Henning 1978, 217), cited by Diakonoff (in this volume), viz. to identify it "with the name of the little modern Lezghian people Udi (< *$qut\cdot i$) living on the frontier between Georgia and Azerbaijan".

II. Problems

A number of important problems have to be brought nearer to solution before any reliable picture of Proto-Indo-European history and culture could come into reach. Many of them can only be adequately dealt with by other sciences, and so, my following choice is but a specimen of unequally treated subjects.

Anthropology has put forward two important questions in recent years: the difference between sedentary and pastoralist lifestyle, and the way of emergence of a ruling class or élite. The first is crucial for the problem of Indo-Europeanization, and much can be gained by studying the concepts of *colluvies gentium* and 'snowball system' as developed by Mühlmann (cf. Mühlmann 1962, 1964, 1985): pastoralists are basically "sieved out" of existing sedentary populations, and attract permanently all kinds of uprooted people. 'Snowball system' points to the well-known fact that every new adherent to a new structure (language and/or religion) immediately starts to agitate for its further spread, winning himself new adherents and causing them to multiply in the same way.[19] For the emergence of an élite, Gilman's 'Mafia hypothesis' (cf. Gilman 1981, and his contribution in this volume) seems to offer a path to better understanding of this complicated process.

---

[19] History offers a large choice of examples for such processes: the "Children of Israel", a *colluvies gentium* composed of Habiru ('robbers' for the Egyptians, of unknown descent) and different Semitic (perhaps also non-Semitic families) attracting all kind of other people during "the forty years in the desert"; the Franks who started their existence as Germanic raiders in Roman Gaul, but attracted growing numbers of members from all races and languages (this holds true for many other Germanic tribes, too); the Huns of Attila, with their various Germanic components; the Arabization which resulted from the spread of Islam (Mohammad and his first followers were only a handful of people, but already 100 years after the prophet's death, hundreds of millions of square kilometers were ruled by his successors, and millions of people were to change – voluntarily! – their local language for the sacred standard one); the rise of the Mongol empire; the spread of the Turks (on which see Diakonoff, in this volume). Even the history of the USA could be mentioned here.

An important item of material culture, often referred to as typically Indo-European, is the use of the chariot. One should not overlook the fact, however, that chariots, i.e. "light, fast, two-wheeled, usually horse-drawn, vehicle(s) with spoked wheels; used for warfare, hunting, racing and ceremonial purposes" (Littauer-Crouwel, 1979, 4f.) had been invented in the Near East during the 3rd millennium. In the 2nd millennium, the first Indo-Europeans to learn these techniques were the Hittites and Aryans coming into contact with Mesopotamian civilizations. From the same source, the Greeks of the Mycenean epoch adopted the use of the chariot in the early 16th c. at the latest (Wiesner 1968, 135). Earlier, Indo-European tribes or the Proto-Indo-Europeans themselves had only carts and wagons, exclusively for carrying purposes. This agrees exactly with the results of linguistic reconstruction. As Edgar Polomé has stated (1982, 158), there is no Indo-European etymon for "riding a horse"; "driving a vehicle" is $*u̯eĝ^h$, and there are two words for "wheel", viz. $*k^u̯ek^u̯lo$- and $*ratH$-, as well as words for "axle" and "yoke"[20], but none for typical riding equipments as e.g. cheek pieces or bridle.

If we turn to non-material cultural items, the situation is still very dark, and even if the comparative study of religions may provide a better understanding of many points, their relevance for Proto-Indo-European history will always be limited, due to the fundamental methodological problems explained above. Nevertheless, a brief survey of some concepts may be useful:

Traces of totemism, the belief in an animal ancestor, are found mostly in Western Europe, cf. such tribal names as *Picentes* (: *picus* "woodpecker", also name of a mythical king)[21] and *Hirpini* (: Saminitic *hirpus* = Latin *lupus* "wolf") in Italy, *Cherusci* (:*herut*- "hart, stag") in Germany, and Celtic personal names like Gaulish

---

[20] Cf. further the words for "driving" and "hub". Thieme 1954, 66f. has stressed the antiquity of these items.

[21] Cf. Szemerényi 1971.

Branogenius "born from the raven" and *Matugenos* "born from the bear", etc. (though other interpretations of theses names are possible!). There might have been zoomorphic deities, too (=the totem itself?), cf. the Gaulish Horse Goddess *Epona*, the Indian divine Twins *Aśvinau*, the Anglo-Saxon heroes *Hengest* and *Horsa*, and the Greek goddesses *Athena* and *Hera* who, by their eponyms γλαυκ-ῶπις and βο-ῶπις point to their possibly original owlish and bovine nature. All this could result from early contacts, and be regarded as originally non-Indo-European.[22]

Noteworthy in this context may be the fact that remarkable traces of shamanism, which is usually combined with totemism, are found in Iran (as recently shown by Ph. Gignoux)[23]; elsewhere, only sparse elements survive[24], e.g. in the story of the two billy-goats drawing Thor's chariot: the god eats their flesh every day, but avoids breaking any bones. Afterwards, they are brought back to full life again. The interdiction against breaking bones occurs also in India in the *aśvamedha* ritual. The figure of Odhinn displays many shamanistic traits, too: his change of appearance, his mantic practices, his hanging himself etc.[25]

The belief in metempsychosis, known today from India alone in the Indo-European world, is known from the Greek philosopher Pythagoras and his followers and was current in Gaul according to the Classical authors who however seem to have

---

[22] There seems to be no trace of totemism in Vedic literature which is a strong argument for the non-Indo-European origin of contingent totemism features in Western Indo-European literatures. Markey 1985 tries to establish a dichotomy of 'totem and tabu' vs. 'oath and ordeal', the first being characteristic for non-IE, the second for IE societies.

[23] See Gignoux 1979, 1981, 1984, and cf. further C. Colpe's interpretation of Avestan *astvat-* "physically existing", lit. "bony" (1974-82, 299-300).

[24] On traces of shamanism in Skandinavian literature, see Buchholz 1968 (with references).

[25] It should be kept in mind, however, that some scholars regard shamanism as a relative recent development, grown out of contacts between agrarian and hunter societies during the Bronze Age (e.g. Vajda 1959).

misunderstood or overemphasized their sources.[26] In India, this belief is not yet found in the Veda, but emerges later in a vigorous form. It is safe to infer from that situation that contacts on Indian soil with non-Aryan peoples caused this development.[27] On Western European peoples and their beliefs, we have no information before the first Greek ethnographers. Consequently, we do not know where and when such creeds were first adopted by Indo-European populations. A small hint of substratum people and their religions could be given by a possible trace of similiar concepts in Germanic, cf. the OHG word *anchilo* "grandson", lit. "little grandfather". But all this is insufficient for building far-reaching theories upon it.

Still darker is the case of fertility cults. The type of religion practising vegetation cults and fertility rites is found all over the world and cannot be regarded as a special characteristic of any civilization. Well-known in the history of religions of Indo-European peoples, it is rather absent in the remains of Proto-Indo-European poetical language. This may be due to the fact that these remains reflect the life of the Proto-Indo-European upper class. The rich are always less concerned with subsistence than with luxury; furthermore, this poetry is made for and by men, not women, and vegetation cults are characterized by a prominent number of female deities, priestresses and woman worshippers. Of course, the importance of fertility and vegetation cults grew with the adoption of regular agriculture by the already separated sedentary Indo-European tribes and was strengthend by foreign influences (cf. Greek myths).

I do not know if female soothsayers, famous from e.g. Italy (*Sibylla*), Germany

---

[26] The matter has caused much discussion, see de Vries 1961, 248ff. Roider 1979, 62-78 equates OIrish *cophur* and OIndian *saṃsāra-* as expressing the concept of "zyklische Wiedergeburt". This is disputed by Dröge 1982. Recently, F. Le Roux and Chr.-J. Guyonvarc'h (1986, 271) reject a Celtic belief in metempsychosis altogether (according to a personal communication from E. Polomé - the 1986 ed. of the book cited is not yet available to me).

[27] Similarily Dröge 1982.

(*Veleda*) and Greece (*Pythia*), belong to the same complex. They may simply reflect a commonly held and persistent notion of closer affinities to the irrational on the side of the fairer sex.

As far as Greek culture is concerned, it seems unnecessary in general to postulate early contacts between Proto-Indo-Europeans and non-Indo-Europeans to explain the lower layer of non-Indo-European religion found there; historical and archaeological evidence confirm intensive contacts with local pre-Greek populations and borrowings from non-Indo-European Anatolia during the 2nd millennium BC on Greek soil, thus explaining the strange aspects of many elements of classical Greek religion.

A basic question with far-reaching consequences for any assumption in the field of Indo-European Cultural studies is the concept of Indo-Europeanization.

There are basically two possibilities from which all explanations for the historical facts of cultural change (incl. language change) begin: autochthonous evolution or migration. Whereas in the last century cultural changes, especially in protohistorical periods, have been understood as effects of massive movements of large ethnic units (on the model of the historically attested migration of the Germanic peoples during the transition period between Antiquity and Middle Ages), archaeology and prehistory today tend more to the evolutionary model. The truth may safely be supposed to lie in the middle, as ever. One should not forget, however, that there are undeniable linguistic arguments for migrations[28]; and the historical texts from Mesopotamia, Greece and Rome telling of migrations cannot be all pure fiction. But in fact we do not have precise notions about the nature of these alleged migrations (cf. the contribution of Igor Diakonoff in this volume), and we are still in need of more information on historically attested (and linguistically documented) language change: the study of pidgins and creoles will

---

[28] E.g. Ossetic, today the westernmost group of the Iranian languages, is linguistically an Eastern Iranian dialect, closely related to Pashto, whereas Baloči, spoken in Afghanistan, is Western Iranian and related nearer to Parthian than to Middle Persian (cf. Elfenbein 1974- 82, 492 and 494).

no doubt be of utmost importance insofar as we can find there (or not find!) typological parallels for proposed models of Indo-Europeanization.[29]

For the time being, the term Indo-Europeanization can be used only as a short way of referring to the process which led whole ethnic groups to adopt a certain Indo-European language (and not civilization, religion, or the like). Indo-Europeanization is first and foremost a linguistic i.e. a mental, and therefore social process. Military operations and changes in economy may have played a role in preparing Indo-Europeanization, but are in no way a necessary assumption. In considering the prehistory of different Indo-European peoples we see a variety of possibilities.

The Hittite language shows deep marks of non-Indo-European substratum influences and Hittite religion and literature displays only faint traits of Indo-European character. There was probably no more than a thin layer of Indo-European speakers, a superstratum above (or adstratum to) Anatolian populations who largely managed to retain their own culture. We do not know who really spoke the different Indo-European languages we are accustomed to calling Anatolian in and around the Hittite empire, and for how long. Probably, no more than a very small group was involved whose forefathers had once replaced, perhaps by force, the political and military rulers of Hattusa. We are less well informed on the history of the smaller Indo-European groups in Anatolia, where similar processes may be supposed. On the whole, the Indo-Europeanization of Anatolia failed.

The spread of the Aryans is different. Whereas the first attestations of Aryan elements in the Near East are probably the effects of small-scale raids, e.g. the

---

[29] Typology is of course always secondary to reconstruction (see Dunkel 1982). Gamkrelidze-Ivanov widely neglected this principle.

supposedly Aryan rulers of the Mitanni[30], the later history of Iranian and Indo-Aryan peoples are that of wanderings and invasions by greater ethnic units (cf. from the Iranian side, the Mesopotamian historical sources, and the Avesta; from the Indian side, the Ṛgveda is our only source for this early period). The striking difference to the European branches can be explained only by hypotheses on the period between the separation of Aryan tribes (the future Iranians, Indo-Aryans, and those called Nuristani tribes today) from the other Indo-Europeans and their first arrivals in their later settlement areas. This is a dark period whithout any historical sources, and so we have to construct our hypotheses on typological parallels from better documented periods. We have to reckon with the effects of the snowball system (referred to above) having taken place somewhere between the Urheimat and Middle Asia in the second millennium or earlier: originally relative small groups of wandering pastoralists gradually acquired riches and influence, using power in raids (the formula of "driving off cattle" is well attested) or simply attracting other smaller units by their power offering security and the possibility of gaining riches in sharing cattle raids or other military adventures. After a certain time (impossible to calculate!) they had become strong and numerous enough to invade Iran or the Indus valley. It seems that the Persians incorporated with relative ease the people of Elam of which nothing remained after the fall of the Achaemenid empire. Unlike them, the Indo-Aryans of the Ṛgveda felt a strong difference between themselves and the inhabitants of the countries they were to invade. In the Ṛgveda, no trace of an incorporation of local population exists. Nevertheless, such incorporation must have started rather quickly, probably with the adoption of sedentary life and regular agriculture. Roughly one thousand years later, we see king Nala depicted as a model king, although he and his people were probably[31] of non-Aryan descent. In theory, class distinctions were nowhere so strong among Indo-European

---

[30] Cf. further the Kassitic word *maryannu-* "warriour on chariot", which could be of Indo-Aryan origin (:OI *marya-* "young man, warriour"?).

[31] This is traditionally held because the Niṣādas are known from other literary sources to be forest-dwellers.

peoples as in India, but in practice[32] - at least if we can trust Sanskrit literature[33] - the rich and mighty, individuals, families and even whole peoples never had any serious problems in rearranging that.[34]

The ethnogenesis of the Greek people and the Indo-Europeanization of Greece is still a matter for lively discussion. There are scholars like Xirotiris (1986) who stress the probability of a purely autochthonous evolution there during the third and second millennium. According to them, there is no archaeological evidence for invasion by a foreign population. Others like St. Hiller (1986) speak of a massive but short invasion of a homogenous group of Indo-Europeans during the Early Bronze Age, i.e. around 3000 BC, in northern Greece and Macedonia and of later gradual spread through the rest of Greece. The so-called Dorian invasion is then a restructuring of different Greek ethnic elements within an already Indo-Europeanized country. For linguistic reasons, the Indo-European dialects forming the Greek language group must have been imported not later than around 2000 BC. For me this contradiction can only be solved by the assumption of small Indo-European speaking groups intruding upon, not invading, existing civilizations. The Indo-European intruders, adopting the local cultural elements, managed to gain political power. Once holding influential positions their language (*sermo castrensis*) became attractive to their retainers and gradually spread through the whole country. Characteristically enough, Homer mentions "ninety languages" in

---

[32] Cf. Rau 1957, 62ff. und Mylius 1972, 335f.

[33] Cf. kings of Brahmanic descent as well as army-leading Brahmans in the two epics, and Śudras as kings in the classical literature.

[34] Whoever, as ruler of a tribe, pays for the appropriate ritual thus accepting the cast system can reach by ritual at least the status of a Kṣatriya, and as an artisan, merchant or farmer that of a Śudra. There are examples for such processes even from recent history (cf. the dynasties of the Mahrattas). The founder of the dynasties of the Śuṁgas (2nd c. B.C.), Kaṇvas (1st c. B.C.) and Kadambas (4th c. A.D., South India) were all Brahmans. And where do all the conservative Brahmanic families in South India come from? - Thanks to Harry Falk, Freiburg, for helpful references.

Crete (τ 174f.), and writers of the Classical age mention villages in Attica still speaking non-Greek, i.e. probably non-Indo-European, languages.

Further arguments for the validity of the snowball system model are presented by the history of the Celtic languages. Whereas the main Continental Celtic language, Gaulish, keeps rather close to the traditional type of old Indo-European, the Insular Celtic languages show traces of heavy influence by other, probably non-Indo-European, languages.[35] Their literature, however, displays a striking fidelity to Indo-European customs and manners. The Indo-Europeanization of the British isles was therefore, after all probability, the work of a rather small but very influential group.

III. Limitations: the example of mythology

I have been asked by the editors to consider possible evidence for early contacts of Indo-European populations with non Indo-European ones in the field of mythology. Therefore, mythological items will be used in the following as an example to show the intrinsic limitations of any study of Proto-Indo-European history.

In India, all possibly non-Aryan mythical and religious material most probably stem from contacts of the invading Indo-Aryans with local populations. These contacts cannot be dated earlier than c. 1500 BC, and have therefore nothing to do with the period discussed here. It should be mentioned, however, that the Indra-Vṛtra-myth has earlier been interpreted as a reflex of historical combats between Aryans and the local populations. Comparative Religion sees it nowadays rather as a cosmogonial myth comparable to the separation of earth and water in other mythologies.

The Iranian mythology is fraught with many special problems: Zarathustra's

---

[35] See recently Wagner 1987 (with references).

teachings reflect, apart from his personal religious experiences, purely Indo-Iranian, i.e. Aryan concepts, and everything that may be regarded as of non-Indo-European origin, like e.g. the Anahita cult, the funeral rites, the custom of incestuous marriages in noble families (attested for the royal families of Elam[36]), and the rich mythological material found in Middle Persian sources (Bundahishn), appear only later: they might have been taken over at any time from non Indo-Europeans who had always lived among and between the different Iranian tribes. These contacts are therefore difficult, not to say impossible, to date.

As all other Indo-European peoples with the exception of Hittites and Greeks emerge considerably later, all theories which argue using material coming from their respective mythologies only must be rather weak. The mythology of the Hittites (and the other minor Indo-European peoples in Anatolia, if anything is left from them at all) seems to be non-Indo-European throughout.[37]
Greek mythology offers many mythological items clearly borrowed from autochthonous non-Indo-European or non-Greek Near Eastern sources. The date of the earliest borrowings is unknown, but there are no arguments for assuming any such contacts before the 3rd millennium.
Classicists[38] are convinced that the cosmogonical scheme underlying Greek mythology was taken over from Oriental neighbours. But none of the Greek theogonies can be derived directly from a foreign one, without assuming genuine

---

[36] And elsewhere, e.g. Egypt.

[37] E. Neu's interpretation of the Anitta text stating an "enge Verbindung zwischen hethitischem Königtum und altindogermanischer Religion" (1974, 131) and speaking of "alte Bindungen der Hethiter an die höchste Gottheit des idg. Pantheons" (ibid.) overemphasizes the scanty remains, viz. that *$di\underline{e}us$ is still the name of a god, not yet (as later in hitt. šiuš) the appelative for "god". Already for Anitta (around 1800 B.C.), the veneration of images - an absolutely non-Indo-European practice - was nothing strange (see line 11 of the same text).

[38] E.g. Hans Schwabl 1962, from which many of the following Greek items are cited.

Greek transformations. Here, some characteristic points will be briefly indicated.

The divine genealogy Okeanos-Uranos-Kronos-Zeus corresponds to the same fourfold succession in the Hittite (earlier Hurrian, partly still older, perhaps containing Sumerian elements) Kumarbi Epic (succession Alalu-Anu-Kumarbi-weather god) and the Phoenician myth as given by Philon of Byblos (Hypsistos-Epigeios-Elos-Demaros). Because of the close correspondence in many details (e.g. Uranos' castration by his son, Kronos' swallowing of his offspring, the parts played by feminine deities), a common origin of the myth must be assumed: for chronological reasons, this source cannot be Greek.

A widespread cosmogonical concept is the separation of heaven and earth by a violent act as contained in Hesiod's stories of Uranos and Gaia. The same myth is well known from Sumer and Egypt, it was even found in recent times among the Maori people.

Sometimes connected with the separation of heaven and earth, but also independent of that myth, is the concept of a primordial egg out of which the world was shaped. The Greeks probably took over this picture from some Near Eastern sources, but it can also be found elsewhere, e.g. in Aryan tradition[39] and the Finnish Kalevala.

The tale of the great flood as reflected in the Greek story of Deukalion and Pyrrha clearly resembles the Biblical deluge and the flood of the Gilgamesh Epic. It goes back to real submersions in Mesopotamia as archaeological evidence shows. But the story is also found elesewhere, even in America.

The motive of a primordial combat between a god or demiourgos and a monster underlies (in different contexts and versions) the stories of Typhon and Python. It has often been compared to the stone monster of the Hittite Ullikummi song. It probably also underlies (at least partly) the dragon-killing stories found all over

---

[39] As established by Karl Hoffmann (1957).

the world.[40] The serpent Ladon guarding the Hesperides' golden apples strongly resembles the serpent of Paradise in the Bible; it may be another aspect of the complex.

The veneration of sacred stones as explained by Hesiod's version of the founding of the sanctuary at Pytho = Delphi (Zeus sets up the stone once swallowed by Kronos in place of his child Zeus) closely resembles Old Testament stories and the pre-Islamic rite of venerating a meteor stone in Mekka taken over by Mohammad. The belief in supernatural powers embodied in stones is of course found in other parts of the world, too, and nothing specifically Near Eastern or Indo-European.

Similar to the veneration of sacred stones is the worshipping of trees, found not only in Greece, but also among many other Indo-European peoples. The custom is probably genuinely Indo-European, and possibly elementary human.[41]

The various stories of Zeus' marital unions with a large number of goddesses have been interpreted as reflecting the incorporation of local cults (perhaps fertility cults?) into the religious system of the newcomers. This is a sensible view, but difficult to prove.

The idea of the creation of the human race out of divine blood is hidden in the Greek story of the giants and nymphs sprung from Uranos' blood, and is paralleled by the Babylonian myth (Enuma Elish) where mankind stems from the blood of Kingu, the adverse god king.

At this point, I would like to finish this rather impressionistic list. Innumerable books have been written on the subject. As in every dispute of interpretation, reliable results and objective criteria are difficult to agree on. Historical linguistics, which is a far more solid field, has shown that Greek religion, for the most part, is not of Indo-European origin: most gods have non-Indo-European names or at least names without acceptable Indo-European etymology.

---

[40] See now Watkins 1987.

[41] Many facts have been listed by J. W. Taylor (1979). According to his remark on Armenian p. 126, he is, however, a complete foreigner to Indo-European Studies.

332 When Worlds Collide

Uranos:	Greek formation, perhaps "rainer" (:OI *varṣ-*); but not related to OI *Varuṇa-*!
Kronos:	without etymology, the meaning "old man", occurring only in names, is based on the mythology or on popular etymology (: χρόνος).[42]
Zeus:	inherited as name of the god of "bright daylight sky", = OI *Dyauṣ (pitā)*, Hitt. *šiuš* "god", L *dius* "day" (in *nudius tertius* "the day before yesterday").
Hera:	without convincing etymology (hardly "goddess of the year"), probably pre-Greek < non-Indo-European.
Athene:	unexplained, pre-Greek < non-Indo-European.
Aphrodite:	of unknown origin, pre-Greek, non-Indo-European; the name may be altered by Greek popular etymology.
Hermes:	of disputed origin; pre-Greek according to Schwyzer and Chantraine.
Apollon:	without acceptable etymology, probably of (non-Indo-European ?) Anatolian origin, cf. Lydian *Pλdans*, Luwian *Apulunas*, Hitt. *I.ap-pa-li-u-na-aš*.
Artemis:	no convincing etymology known ("bear goddess" ??); Lydian forms *Artimuś, Artimuλ, Artimu-k*.
Dionysos:	perhaps a Thracian name "son (?) of Zeus"; but in fact without etymology.
Poseidon:	from an older (or perhaps even wrongly archaized?) name form Ποτειδάϝων, meaning "Lord (husband) of the Earth"[43]

---

[42] It has been understood also as a Pelasgian (i.e a non-Greek, but IE language spoken once in Greece or the nothern Balkans) form corresponding to Greek γέρων.

[43] The name is quite problematic. Possible Pelasgian origin cannot be excluded (cf. Demeter below). His classical function as a god of water is probably secondary, and due to Zeus' growing to overlord of the whole pantheon.- According to Wagner 1981, 23, the name *Poseidon* is "itself a translation of the Sumerian *En-Ki*, 'the Lord of the Earth'", and he finds the same in **Dumnonos*, the hypothetical name of the ancestor-deity of the Celtic *Dumnonii*. I see,

Ares:	of unclear stem formation, probably belonging to ἀρή "damage, ruin". Not inherited from Proto-Indo-European!
Hephaistos:	without etymology, pre-Greek, probably non-Indo-European.
Demeter:	Indo-European "Mother Earth", though the details of the first member of the compound are not clear. A probable parallel is found in the name of the Messapic goddess *damatura*.

So, only two of the fifteen names of the main Greek gods can safely be said to have been inherited: "(Father) Sky" and "Mother Earth", four or five may be Greek (or at least pre-Greek Indo-European) formations, the rest are of unknown origin, i.e. probably non-Indo-European. This should be enough to ensure intensive early contacts between the forefathers of our Classical Greeks and other, probably non-Indo-European peoples.

Some Germanic mythological themes should be presented here, too, as promised in my abstract. Germanic mythology is best known from late, viz. Scandinavian sources dating from the High Middle Ages. But there are earlier testimonies by the Classical writers, especially Caesar and Tacitus, church historians like Paulus Diaconus and Adam of Breme, the runic inscriptions from the 4th c. on, and some tiny remainders of pagan thinking hidden in Old English and Old German literatures. All these various sources provide us with rather consistant information about Germanic religion and mythology. The most prominent theme in Germanic mythology which could perhaps reflect early contacts between Indo-Europeans and non-Indo-Europeans is the war between the two divine families, the Ases and the Vanes. It has often been understood as a reflex of the conflict between an invading(?) people of warlike spirit, venerating Asic deities, and a sedentary people living from agriculture and husbandry. The

---

however, no possibility of substantiating any genetical connexion between such striking resemblences.

compromise between the two divine families would then symbolize the fusion of the two ethnic components. Attractive as this interpretation seems at first glance, it overlooks the fact that Caesar's and Tacitus' Germans still live a semi-nomadic life, but already venerate the typical Vanic deity *Nerthus*. Middle Age Scandinavia is extremely warlike (the Vikings!) and at the same time completely agricultural. It was the same Icelandic farmers and cattle-breeders who venerated the Asic war god Thorr and the Vanic fertility god Freyr. Furthermore, the Ases-Vanes dichotomy cannot be compared with the struggle between Devas and Asuras in Indian mythology. Germanic *ansuz* is a term on whose linguistic background unanimity has not been reached.[44] There can be no close connection to the Indian

---

[44] The etymological identity of *ansuz (Goto-Latin *ansis* 'semideos', Jordanes 76,13; Old Norse *áss*, OE OSax *ós* "Ase, god") with the appellative noun "beam" (Gothic *anza* DatSg, Old Norse *áss*, etc.) was first claimed by J. Grimm (Deutsche Mythologie I³ 22), whereas the connection with Old Indian *ásura-*, Avestan *ahura-* was first suggested by Güntert (1923, 102). Polomé (1953, 38) proposed the inclusion of Hitt. *haš-*, *haššu-* "to beget" and "king" in the same familiy. Oettinger (1976, 24 note 8) reconstructs an IE *h^2onsu-* "lord" as foreform of Hitt. *haššu-*, Av. *ahū-* "lord" and Germanic *ansuz. Polomé is more specific in describing the meaning of IE *$H2n̥su-(ro-)$* as "controller of vital energy" (letter, 16.12.87). This, however, would fit much more the Germanic Vanes than their Asic opponents (even if members of both divine families can distribute "vital energy" in the Eddic literature of Middle Age Scandinavia).- Cf. further Feist 1939, 52-3, Mayrhofer 1956-76, I 65 and III 637, Schlerath 1968, 142-153, and again Mayrhofer 1987,148. - The old theory (with "beam") is still worth considering because of the archaeologically attested veneration of so-called pile idols (many examples found in swamps), see R. Meringer 1919, 107-123.

Asuras because these deities are not inherited from Proto-Indo-European but, as proven by their Iranian counterparts, only Aryan developments out of abstract moral concepts (*Varuṇa* "true word", *Mitra* "covenant", *Aryaman* "hospitality") as Antoine Meillet and Paul Thieme[45] have shown in many publications.[46] Other divine disputes in the mythology of Indo-European peoples mostly reflect generation conflicts within a cosmogonic model such as the Uranos-Kronos-Zeus complex mentioned above.

Among other Germanic concepts that have been suspected of being of non-Indo-European origin are the creation of the world out of parts of the body of a first gigantic being (*Ymir*), or that of the creation of mankind out of trees (*Ask* and *Embla*); the concept of a world column[47] (Old Saxon *irminsul*); and the rich mythological material on various kinds of giants[48] and dwarfs or other supernatural but not divine beings. It is rather unlikely that these should be seen as traces of an older, non-Indo-European population. Similiar mythologemes are found elsewhere within Indo-European, esp. in Old Indian.

On the other hand, the Irish mythical history as related in the Lebor Gabala or in the traditions about the Battles of Moytura is generally understood to contain vestiges of earlier populations. But here, as well as in Germany, nothing is certain, no real evidence can be found.[49] A typical Celtic mythological motif is the kettle

---

[45] Fundamental is Thieme 1938.

[46] On a different view, see Brereton 1981 and my review of this book (Zimmer 1986).

[47] Found also in Finnish and Hungarian mythology.

[48] Cf. the recent collections by Motz 1984 and 1987 (with references).

[49] Wagner 1981 argues for strong substratum influences to be seen in Celtic religion, and points to possible similarities in Germanic and Greek of equally non-IE origin.

of rebirth. If the Gundestrup cauldron were to be correctly placed in connection with this theme, it would be attested for Continental Celtic, too. It recalls Shamanistic practices, and is probably another argument for a strong non-Indo-European substratum in Western Europe.

The custom of head-hunting and of guarding the slaughtered heads as trophies is known from Gaulish sanctuaries (e.g. La Roquepertuse), from Caesar's writings and from Old Irish saga texts. I see no possibility of forming any hypothesis on the where and when of this custom's origin.

One cannot be cautious, and even skeptical enough in comparing mythological data. There is a nice example from a MHG lyric poet: Heinrich von Meißen, called Frauenlob, at the beginning of his Frauenleich ch. 11, makes Mary utter the following words: *der smit ûz Oberlande warf sînen hamer in mine schôz*, obviously meaning "God has made me pregnant". Since the 19th century, this passage was seen as a remnant of pagan ideas, and has been compared with the use of Thor's hammer as an instrument of fertility, and with various Germanic designations of "heaven" as "land above".[50] But closer inspection of this allegedly evident case of mythological continuity has shown that Frauenlob could not have had the slightest idea of Eddic poetry, and that in fact all possible sources of his image were based on ideas of theology and natural philosophy of the Christian Middle Ages which in their turn go back to the Classical tradition (Krayer 1960, 124-174). How many items in our mythological handbooks would turn out as equally accidental pseudo-parallels if only we had enough material to analyze them sufficiently?

IV. Conclusion

There is no such thing as a Common- or Proto-Indo-European mythology, and

---

[50] See Fritzner 1896, I 715, with references to the older literature.

what we know about Proto-Indo-European culture is but a scanty bit of rather incoherent information unsufficient to allow a reconstruction of the whole. Among them are many items which could stem from early contacts of the Proto-Indo-Europeans with non-Indo-European peoples, but there is no way to control such assumptions, or even to prove them. We should not ask the wrong questions, but interpret our material within the frame of the probable and sensible. Progress is seldom achieved by proudly putting foreward bold theories which are, in the end, no more than risky hypotheses. What we need is epistemological modesty.

Even in what is their proper theme, viz. explaining in a pre-scientific manner the riddles of existence by telling histories about gods and other superhuman beings and their relation to the world and to mankind, myths are never clear and explicit enough for the standards set by modern scientific thinking. How can we expect, then, that it would be possible to gain historical (in the modern sense of the word!) information from them, being bits of traditional lore transmitted and variated over and over again for thousands of years? Let us take them for what they are: fascinating religious and literary documents, but surely not records of Stone Age history!

For the time being, I can only offer the following summary of the results of Indo-European comparative grammar research on the problematics of Ursprache – Urvolk – Urheimat:

1. Phonological reconstruction of preforms common to genetically related languages is only possible by using the sound law methodology which implies the Stammbaum model.
2. Morphological reconstruction yields only fragments of grammatical systems and subsytems.
3. Lexical reconstruction yields only disparate and incoherent (bundles of) items which cannot be situated in space and time.
4. No unequivocal interpretation of the reconstructed word and its reconstructed meaning in regard to physical reality is possible.
5. Any deduction from the reconstructed vocabulary to the physical world of the postulated Urvolk is bound to remain purely hypothetical.
6. The only reliable source for Proto-Indo-European thought, the

fragments of common poetical language, is representative of a very restricted part of society only, viz. the richer adult (and perhaps partly also juvenile) males.

7. Characteristics of this Proto-Indo-European ruling class society (if it could be so called) are the system of mutual hospitality, and the ethical value of truth.

Further research is needed: Ethnology may gain further insight into the typology of primitive and ancient societies and then be able to say whether the results of comparative linguistics are specific enough to be called Indo-European or not.

Prehistory will further clear the archaeological concepts of migration vs. local development and the methodology of their possible evidence.

Indo-European Studies (which I can only see as a branch of Comparative Grammar) will continue to reconstruct details on every level, and to present, from time to time, hypotheses summing up all these details in a possible picture of Proto-Indo-European, its speakers and their way of life.

Let us hope that one day someone will be able to present a model acceptable to all parties interested in this fascinating question.[51]

---

[51] Many thanks to Edgar Polomé for his kind comments on an earlier version of this paper, and to David Lewis for looking through my English manuscript.

Bibliography

Benveniste 1969
: Émile Benveniste, Le vocabulaire des institutions indo-européennes, Paris 1969 (2 vol.)

Bökönyi 1987
: Sándor Bökönyi, Horses and Sheep in East Europe in the Copper and Bronze Ages, in: Proto-Indo-European: The Archaeology of a Linguistic Problem. Studies in Honor of Marija Gimbutas, ed. by S.N. Skomal and E.C. Polomé, Washington 1987, 136-144

Buchholz 1968
: Peter Buchholz, Schamanistische Züge in der altisländischen Überlieferung. Ph.D.-diss. Saarbrücken 1968 (108 pp., unpubl.)

Brereton 1981
: Joel Peter Brereton, The Ṛgvedic Ādityas, New Haven 1981 (=AOS 63)

Colpe 1974-82
: Carsten Colpe (u.a.), Altiranische und zoroastrische Mythologie, in: Wörterbuch der Mythologie, hrg. v. H.W.Haussig, Band IV, Stuttgart 1974-1982, 161-487

Dröge 1982
: Christoph Dröge, Ein irischer *saṃsāra*? Betrachtungen zur Frage der "keltischen Seelenwanderungslehre", ZCP 39.1982, 261-268

Dunkel 1982
: George Dunkel, Typology versus Reconstruction, in: Bono Homini Donum: Essays in Historical Linguistics in Memory of J. Alexander Kerns, ed. Y.L. Arbeitman and A.R. Bomhard, vol. 2, Amsterdam 1981 (published 1982), 559-569

Elfenbein 1974-82
: Josef Elfenbein, Mythologie der Balutschen, in: Wörterbuch der Mythologie, hrg. v. H.W.Haussig, Band IV, Stuttgart 1974-1982, 489-507

Feist 1939
: Sigmund Feist, Vergleichendes Wörterbuch der gotischen Sprache mit Einschluß des Krimgotischen und sonstiger zerstreuter Überreste des Gotischen, Dritte...Auflage, Leiden 1939

Fritzner 1896
: Johan Fritzner, Ordbog over det gamle norske Sprog, 2. Utgave, Christiania 1883-1896

Gamkrelidze-I.1984	Тамаз В. Гамкрелидзе & Вячеслав Вс. Иванов, Индоевропейский язык и Индоевропейцы. Реконструкция и историко-типологический анализ праязыка и протокультуры. С предисловием Р. О. Якобсона. 2 vols., Тбилиси 1984, cxvi + 1328 pp.
Gignoux 1979	Philippe Gignoux, Corps osseux et âme osseuse: Essai sur le chamanisme dans l'Iran ancien, Journal Asiatique 267.1979, 41-79
Gignoux 1981	id., Les voyages chamaniques dans le monde iranien, Acta Iranica 21 (=Monumentum Georg Morgenstierne I).1981, 244-265
Gignoux 1984	id., Der Großmagier Kirdīr und seine Reise in das Jenseits, Acta Iranica 23 (=Orientalia J. Duchesne-Guillemin emerito oblata).1984, 191-206
Gilman 1981	Antonio Gilman, The Development of Social Stratification in Bronze Age Europe, Current Anthropology 22.1981, 1-23
Gimbutas 1980	Marija Gimbutas, The Transformation of European and Anatolian Culture 4500-2500 B.C. and its Legacy, Journal of Indo-European Studies 8.1980, 1-2
Gimbutas 1986	ead., Remarks on the Ethnogenesis of the Indo-Europeans in Europe, in: Ethnogenese europäischer Völker, ed. Wolfram Bernhard and Anneliese Kandler-Pálsson, Stuttgart - New York 1986, 5-20
Güntert 1923	Hermann Güntert, Der arische Weltkönig und Heiland. Bedeutungsgeschichtliche Untersuchungen zur indo-iranischen Religionsgeschichte und Altertumskunde, Halle 1923
Henning 1978	†Walter B. Henning, The first Indo-Europeans in History, in: Society and History, Essays in Honor of Karl August Wittvogel, ed. G.L. Ulmen, The Hague-Paris-New York 1978, 215-230
Hiller 1986	Stefan Hiller, Die Ethnogenese der Griechen aus der Sicht der Vor- und Frühgeschichte, in: Ethnogenese europäischer Völker, ed. Wolfram Bernhard and Anneliese Kandler-Pálsson, Stuttgart - New York 1986, 21-37

Hoffmann 1957	Karl Hoffmann, Mārtāṇḍa und Gayōmart, Münchener Studien zur Sprachwissenschaft 11.1957, 85-103 = Aufsätze zur Indoiranistik, hrg. v. J. Narten, Wiesbaden 1976, 422-438
Körber-Grohne 1987	Udelgard Körber-Grohne, Nutzpflanzen in Deutschland, Kulturgeschichte und Biologie, Stuttgart 1987
Krayer 1960	Rudolf Krayer, Frauenlob und die Naturallegorese. Heidelberg 1960
Leist 1884	Burkhard Wilhelm Leist, Graeco-italische Rechtsgeschichte, Jena 1884
Leist 1889	id., Alt-arisches Ius gentium, Jena 1889 = Innsbruck 1978 (mit Vorwort von B. Schlerath und Indices von J. Gippert hrg.v. W. Meid)
Leist 1892	id., Alt-arisches Ius civile. 2 Bände, Jena 1892
Le Roux-G. 1986	Françoise Le Roux et Christian-J. Guyonvarc'h, Les Druides, Glossaire des termes gaulois et irlandais, Rennes, Ouest-France 1986 (4ème éd.)
Littauer-C. 1979	M.A. Littauer and J.H. Crouwel, Wheeled Vehicles and Ridden Animals in the Ancient Near East (Handbuch der Orientalistik 7.1.2.B.1), Leiden 1979
Markey 1985	Thomas L. Markey, The Totemic Typology, Quaderni di Semantica 6.1985, 175-194
Mayrhofer 1976	Manfred Mayrhofer, Kurzgefaßtes etymologisches Wörterbuch des Altindischen, Heidelberg 1956-76
Mayrhofer 1987	id., Etymologisches Wörterbuch des Altindoarischen, I.Band, Lieferung 2, Heidelberg 1987
Meringer 1919	R. Meringer, Indogermanische Pfahlgötzen, Wörter und Sachen 9.1919, 107-123.
Motz 1984	Lotte Motz, Gods and Demons of the Wilderness, Arkiv för Nordisk Filologi 99.1984, 175-187
Motz 1987	ead., The Families of Giants, ibid. 102. 1987, 216-236

Mühlmann 1962	Wilhelm E. Mühlmann, Homo Creator. Abhandlungen zur Soziologie, Anthropologie und Ethnologie. Wiesbaden 1962, part IV: Stämme und Völker, p. 301-358
Mühlmann 1964	id., Rassen, Ethnien, Kulturen. Moderne Ethnologie. Neuwied 1964
Mühlmann 1985	id., Ethnogonie und Ethnogenese. Theoretisch-ethnologische und ideologiekritische Studie, in: Studien zur Ethnogenese, Opladen 1985, 9-27
Mylius 1972	Klaus Mylius, Die gesellschaftliche Entwicklung Indiens in jungvedischer Zeit nach den Sanskritquellen, II Die Produktionsverhältnisse, in: Ethnographisch-Archäologische Zeitschrift 13.1972,321-365
Neu 1974	Erich Neu, Der Anitta-Text, Wiesbaden 1974 (= StBoT 18)
Neu 1985	id., Das frühindogermanische Diathesensytem. Funktion und Geschichte, in: Grammatische Kategorien, Funktion und Geschichte, hrg. v. B. Schlerath und V. Rittner, Wiesbaden 1985, 275-295
Oettinger 1976	Norbert Oettinger, Die Militärischen Eide der Hethiter, Wiesbaden 1976 (=StBoT 22)
Polomé 1953	Edgar C. Polomé, L'étymologie du terme germanique *ansuz* 'dieu souverain', Études Germaniques 8.1953, 36-44
Polomé 1982	id., Indo-European Culture, with Special Attention to Religion, in: id.(ed.), The Indo-Europeans in the Fourth and Third Millennia, Ann Arbor 1982, 156-172
Rau 1957	Staat und Gesellschaft im alten Indien nach den Brāhmaṇa-Texten dargestellt, Wiesbaden 1957
Renfrew 1987	Colin Renfrew, Archaeology and Language. The Puzzle of the Indo-European Origins, London 1987
Roider 1979	Ulrike Roider, De chophur in dá muccida, Innsbruck 1979
Schlerath 1968	Bernfried Schlerath, Altindisch *asu-*, Avestisch *ahu-* und ähnlich klingende Wörter, in: Pratidânam, [Festschrift]...F.B.J. Kuiper (= Janua linguarum, series maior

	34), The Hague-Paris 1968, 142-153
Schlerath 1973	id., Die Indogermanen. Das Problem der Expansion eines Volkes im Lichte seiner sozialen Struktur, Innsbruck 1973
Schlerath 1982	id., Ist ein Raum-Zeit-Modell für eine rekonstruierte Sprache möglich?, Zeitschrift für Vergleichende Sprachwissenschaft 95/2.1981(1982), 175-202
W.P.Schmid 1987	Wolfgang P. Schmid, 'Indo-European' - 'Old European' (on the reexamination of two linguistic terms), in: Proto-Indo-European: The Archaeology of a Linguistic Problem. Studies in Honor of Marija Gimbutas, ed. by S.N. Skomal and E.C. Polomé, Washington 1987, 322-338
Schmitt 1985	Rüdiger Schmitt, Dumézilsche Dreifunktionentheorie, in: Johannes Hoops (Founder), Reallexikon der Germanischen Altertumskunde, 2. Auflage, vol. 6/3-4, 276-280
Schwabl 1962	Hans Schwabl, Weltschöpfung, in: Pauly-Wissowa, Realencyklopädie der classischen Altertumswissenschaft, Suppl. IX, Stuttgart 1962, 1433-1582
Sommer 1947	Ferdinand Sommer, Hethiter und Hethitisch, Stuttgart 1947.
Szemerényi 1971	Oswald Szemerényi, The name of the Picentes, in: Sprache und Geschichte, Festschrift für Harri Meier, München 1971, 531-544 (=Scripta Minora, Innsbruck 1987, vol. II, 911-924)
Taylor 1979	J.W.Taylor, Tree Worship, The Mankind Quarterly XX,1-2.1979, 79-141
Thieme 1938	Paul Thieme, Der Fremdling im Ṛgveda, Leipzig 1938 (=AKM xxiii,2)
Thieme 1954	id., Die Heimat der indogermanischen Gemeinsprache, Mainz 1954 (=Ak.d.Wiss.u.d.Lit., Abh.d.geistes-u.sozialwiss.-Kl., Jg. 1953, Nr. 11)
Untermann 1985	Jürgen Untermann, Ursprache und historische Realität, in: Studien zur Ethnogenese, Opladen 1985, 133-164
Vajda 1959	Laszló Vajda, Zur phaseologischen Stellung des Schamanismus, Ural-Altaische Jahrbücher 31.1959, 456-485

de Vries 1961	Jan de Vries, Keltische Religion, Stuttgart 1961
Wagner 1981	Heinrich Wagner, Origins of Pagan Irish Religion, Zeitschrift für Celtische Philologie 38.1981, 1-28
Wagner 1987	id., The Celtic Invasions of Ireland and Great Britain. Zeitschrift für Celtische Philologie 42.1987, 1-40
Watkins 1987	Calvert Watkins, How to Kill a Dragon in Indo-European, in: Studies in Memory of Warren Cowgill, ed. id., Berlin-New York 1987, 270-299
Weisweiler 1939	Josef Weisweiler, Die Stellung der Frau bei den Kelten und das Problem des keltischen Mutterrechts. Zeitschrift für Celtische Philologie 21.1939, 205-279
Wiesner 1968	Joseph Wiesner, Fahren und Reiten (Archaeologia Homerica I, F), Göttingen 1968
Xirotiris 1986	Nikolaos I. Xirotiris, Die Ethnogenese der Griechen aus der Sicht der Anthropologie, in: Ethnogenese europäischer Völker, ed. Wolfram Bernhard and Anneliese Kandler-Pálsson, Stuttgart - New York 1986, 39-53
Zimmer 1978	Author, review of Georges Dumézil, Les dieux souverains des Indo-Européens, Paris 1977, in: Studia Iranica 7/2.1978, 301-303
Zimmer 1986	id., review of Brereton 1981, in: Orientalistische Literaturzeitung 81/1.1986, 69-75
Zimmer 1987	id., Indogermanische Sozialstruktur? Zu zwei Thesen Émile Benvenistes, in: Studien zum indogermanischen Wortschatz, hrg. v. W. Meid, Innsbruck 1987, 315-329
Zohary-Hopf 1988	Daniel Zohary - Maria Hopf, Domestication of Plants in the Old World, Oxford 1988

GIFT, PAYMENT AND REWARD REVISITED

T.L. Markey

For the Indo-European speech community, the institution of gift/exchange, its socio-economic implications and, of course, the vocabulary to express this phenomenon have all been repeatedly investigated.[1] The roster of investigators includes some of the most distinguished forces in the fields of historical linguistics and anthropology, but of all contingents, perhaps the French is the most distinguished.

To single out but a few of the more prominent and, for our purposes here, pertinent names, we recall Antoine Meillet's (1907) pioneering functional definition of Mitra; the very general *Essai sur le don* (1925) by Marcel Mauss, the intellectual forebear of Claude Lévi-Strauss; Emile Benveniste's *Don et échange dans le vocabulaire indo-européen* (1951), subsequently expanded and refined in that scholar's *Le vocabulaire des institutions indo-européennes* (1969:1.17-202); and the classic *mitra Varuna* (1940, 2nd ed. 1947) by Georges Dumézil, which that father of the triadic theory of Indo-European social, economic, and power structures fittingly dedicated to Marcel Mauss and Marcel Granet.

Despite these and numerous other perceptive and engaging inquiries, not even the well-trodden ground of the Germanic sector, much less that of Northern Europe, specifically the Northwest Block covered by Celtic, Germanic, and Balto-Slavic (or Baltic and Slavic), has been exhausted. This northern block, particularly its western, insular fringes, was presumably one of the last areas of Europe to have been settled by Indo-Europeans. It is also an area in which there must have been prolonged and intimate contact between Indo-Europeans and their non-Indo-European precursors, prominently the megalithic builders of the third millennium. This was the setting for a clash between what were apparently quite divergent cultures.[2] To assume that, say, the builders of Stonehenge were catatonic primitives and that their successors had no interaction with the Indo-Europeans who survived them defies derision. Whereas creolistics has continually searched for lingual substrata, it has become a disciplinary prejudice on the part of Indo-Europeanists not to seek substrata. It is on these western fringes of Indo-European settlement that the Celtic and Germanic peoples forged cultures that shared much, a give and take that is reflected in the reciprocities of their institutional lexicons, even in the dictions of their later epics, transcended as they are from a common heritage.[3]

Here, we shall concentrate on the evolution of both inherited and secondarily developed Germanic terms for the semantics of gift/exchange. After having articulated an evolutive hypothesis, we shall first review an early set of terms related by the force of indebtednesses in premonetary conditions of *communitas* and, subsequently, see how these structures were reshuffled, semantically recast, or even replaced within monetary economy conditioned by indebtednesses circumscribed by payment/reward. As Leach (1982:152-75) has diagrammatically contended, it is debt that innervates, prolongs, and expands the networking of what social anthropologists term both *restricted* and *generalized exchange*. The state and nature of debt and the shifting patterns of social relationships and power structures that debt orchestrates in manipulating gift/exchange on the one hand and *payment/reward* on the other hand supply thematic focus for the discussion that follows.

From the available evidence, comparatists long ago inferred that "commercial" vocabulary of an early Common Germanic must have been severely limited and that this department of lexicon was later fleshed out (1) externally by borrowing and/or (2) internally by phylum-specific morphosemantactic shifts and other redeployments just prior to and for some time after the emergence of the Germanic peoples in recorded history. This observation as hypothesis can now be restated as an evolutive claim: as a speech and a cultural community Germanic was comparatively later than its neighbors, particularly those to the south, in moving from a primitive, inherited form of gift/exchange to vastly more complicated system of payment/reward. In its initial records, Germanic appears far more archaic than its neighbors and more nearly reflects the anterior stages of Indo-European.

Germanic clearly lacked analogues of Latin expressions such as *fēnus, ūsūra, merces, solūtio*, all of which evidence economic notions that are well advanced beyond a gift/exchange *communio*, or the state of affairs that is recorded for the Germani by Classical observers and/or compilers even a century after contact: *mos est civitatibus ultro ac viritim conferre principibus vel armentorum vel frugum, quod pro honore acceptum etiam necessitatibus subvenit. gaudent praecipue finitimarum genitium donis, quae non modo a singulis, sed et publice mittuntur, electi equi, magnifica arma, phalaerae torquesque; iam et pecuniam accipere docuimus.* (Tacitus, *Germania* Ch. 15).

The three principal sources for Germanic "commercial" terms are:

(I). Latin/Romance, an enduring loan source, provided English with, for example, *bargain, interest, salary, pay*, etc., but the chain of lending is often lengthy, sometimes indirect, and not every link is altogether clear. Note *bargain* < Anglo-Norman *bargaine* < LLat. **barcāne-um* to LLat. *Barcāni-āre* (Capit. Charles the Bald).

(II). Celtic, which, for example, supplied uniquely Gothic *dulgis* (OIr. *dliged*, W *dlēd, dyled*), giving rise to the phrase *dulgis skulan*, thereby narrowing the scope of a particular application of skulan (otherwise passively neutral as *skuld ist* 'it is necessary'), see Feist (1939:128-9), Benveniste (1969:1.199-1) and note OSC *dlŭgŭ* < Goth. *dulgs* (attested only in the genitive *dulgis*): Germanic (Gothic) supplied much of the "commercial" lexicon of Slavic.

and

(III). Other (quite possibly pre-Indo-European) donors. In this category we find Goth. *skatts*, Germ. *Schatz*, etc., the one Pan- and Proto-Germanic form of minted coin, presumably silver. It may well be that *skatts*, from whatever misty source, originally signified 'cattle' and only later came to mean money/coin, just *Vieh* --> *Geld* under the influence of Lat. *pecunia*. Here, too, is *silver*, found only in Germanic, Baltic, and Slavic (e.g. OPr. *siraplis*, OCS *srebro*), albeit in varying shapes, all of which are dialectic-specific calques on some ultimately common source. Whereas Germ. (etc.) *kaufen* is most plausibly explained as having been formed to Lat. *caupō*, Engl. *buy* (<OE *byc3(e)an*), Goth. *bugjan*, OS *buggian*, OIc. *byggja* ('to purchase a woman') lacks a plausible etymology. Whether High German (Frankish, Alemannian, Bavarian) had a congener is unknown and unknowable. Recourse to Engl. *big*, which is known only from the end or the 13th century in Northumbria and north Lincolnshire (*byge, bygg(e), bigge*) and which points to a *bhugh-yo- is no solution, as this form is also opaque.

Examples of phylum-internal adaptive changes are the wholesale shift of *saljan as (give, sell) in North Germanic and Ingwaeonic and replacement by *verkaufen* in the south. Even in later Old English, *sellan (syllan)*, which is well known for the phonological problems it poses, marginally had the modern denotations, but not epically (e.g. in *Beowulf*), e.g. the Old English Gospels (John 12.5): *Hwi ne sealde heo pas sealfe wip prim hundred pene3on*, a significance that is generalized in the course of the 13th century at the total expense of the original 'give' value. OE *costian* 'try, prove, taste', cf Germ. *kosten*, link of necessity (e.g. *needes coste* 'necessarily', so Chaucer and contemporaries) in the course of the 14th century.

A highly aesthetic exercise that provides much insight into early Germanic notions of gift/exchange and its motivation by necessary debt is the comparatively late Icelandic *Ðáttr Auðunar Vestfirzka* (*Morkinskinna*, c. 1200, Codex Gamble kg. Saml. 1009 fol., c. 1275; also copied in *Flateyjarbók*), popularized by its inclusion in E.V. Gordon's *An Introduction to Old Norse* (the edition cited here for convenience). This story must have been widely circulated and certainly survived by its distinct charm, but the fact of the matter is, carefully controlled stylistically as it is, this *þáttr* is virtually a parabolic extension of the gift/exchange ethics specified by *Hávamál* proper (St. 39-46), that is, in the core of this Eddic poem that probably represents its most authentic extent.

This *þáttr* relates the "commercial" adventures of Authun, an Icelander of modest means who first set aside enough provisions for his mother and then went to Greenland, where he *gave* all that he had earned to *buy* (=*kaupa*) a polar bear, a great treasure (=*gørsimi mikla*, and thus characterized throughout the tale). He intends to give the bear to King Sveinn of Denmark. He first goes to Norway and visits King Harald, who offers to buy the bear for (1) what Authun had paid for it and, when refused, (2) for twice what he had paid for it and, when he refused, (3) asks if he might receive it as a *gift*, which Authun also refuses. Authun is then permitted to do what he wants, namely, to leave and *give* the bear to King Sveinn of Denmark. Despite the state of war between the two countries, King Harald permits Authun to leave and asks only that Authun, who may well be "a lucky man" (=*gaefu-maðr*), visit him on his return. At the Danish court, Authun, now destitute (*ok er þá uppi hverr penningr fjárins*), first meets the King's steward, Aki, who refuses to provide food for Authun or his bear unless he has sold (= *selja*) a half interest in the bear, which Authun does. Upon meeting King Sveinn, Authun tells how he had fared with King Harald, how he had intended to *give* Sveinn the bear, which, thanks to Áki, he now only owns half of. King Sveinn banishes Áki, and Authun remains at court. He tires of that, and then goes on a pilgrimage to Rome, whence he returns destitute to King Sveinn. He then wants to return to Iceland. Sveinn says that Authun may be "a lucky man" (=*giptu-maðr*) and prepares the *gift* of a fully provisioned boat for him to do so. Authun informs King Sveinn that he will visit King Harald. In Norway, King Harald questions how King Sveinn had rewarded Authun for his gift, and Authun replies: (1) he accepted the bear, (2) paid for his pilgrimage, (3) made him his cup-bearer, (4) gave him a ship with provisions, (5) a satchel of silver, and (6) a ring with the prescription that he only part with it when he had found a man worthy (noble) of such a reward (...,*nema ek aetta nǫkkurum tignum manni svá gott at launa, at ek vilda gefa.*). Harald says he would have ceased with item (4), the ship, feeling that sufficient payment for the bear. Authun thereupon gives the ring to Harald, for Harald had chosen the nobler alternative: he had let Authun go when he could have killed him and taken the bear. Authun then parts from Harald, who "*gaf Auðuni í móti góðar gjafir.*" Authun then leaves for Iceland in the summer, and was ever after considered the luckiest of men (= *inn mesti gaefu-maðr*).

Clearly, commercialism fares badly here: Authun will not stoop to it with Harald, and Aki who does with Authun is banished. Giving, particularly of patents royal (the ring), is the highest honor: here, *gift/exchange* is far preferable to *payment/reward*. Yet, the focal *gift/treasure/reward* of the bear is a little ridiculous, though the custom of such gifts persists among heads of state even today. What we have in this comparatively late text is a re-contextualized remembrance of the *gift/exchange* ritual between *comitatus* and a prince, the scene reviewed by Tacitus in the *Germania* as quoted above. There is, however, a play on words: the *giving* Authun is termed *lucky* = *gaefu-/giptu-maðr* lit. 'gift-man', i.e. fortunate he who gives, precisely as the pertinent stanzas in the *Hávamál* tell us. Reward is expressed by *launa* v., cf. Germ. *Lohn*, OE *léan* from *lau-na-*, cf. Lat. *Lū-crum*, OIr. *lóg, lúach*. But the real reward is the bear, characterized as a "treasure" = *gorsimi*.

The contrasted court scenes, first in Norway, then in Denmark, and finally in Norway once again, are obviously framing devices central to both the tale's progression and its message: fortunate (lucky) he who gives, which is left to the reader to infer. But the giving is strategic. Significantly, these frames stage host (donor/receiver) and guest (donor/receiver) reciprocities, the relations of exchange and the personification of hospitality, that is, a social equality temporarily formed by *mutual* compensations, the setting of Mitra: a personification of social contract. These courtly frames have their origins in a specific Indo-European cultural context, namely, the rite of *philó-xe(i)nos* 'having (making) the stranger (guest) one's own by temporary annexation.' The bear as treasure is an honorific charge, the symbol of contract by exchange that implies obligations in return, at once both gift/reward and source of indebtedness. Hospitality, as this *þáttr* clearly shows, is something sacred and is not to be confused with or tainted by mere commercialism.

The term for 'treasure' = *gǫrsimi* (*gersimi, gǫrsemi, gǫrsime*, etc.) is obviously a late, entirely secondary, and uniquely North Germanic creation. This compound was originally an *īn*-stem (fem.), and it is conserved as such in the singular, but the plural has analogically gone over to the *ō*-stems. The initial component is *gǫr(r)*, the unusual past participle (= a pure adjective 'ready, done, made, beweaponed') of *gǫra/gera* ' to do, make', while the second component derives from **sōmi > -sōēme > -seme > -simi* (*-simi*), cf. OIc. *sim-la* 'always, ever', see Noreen (1970:Arts. 82, Anm 3; 149) and, on the formation of *īn*-stems, see Brugmann (1906:317-8). Cf., further, ODa. *gǫrsum*, MdnIc.. *gersimi*. The word is exceptional in several ways ON *īn*-stems regularly lack plurals, even those that are analogically derived (or might be analogically derivable). The initial component contains a well known crux: NGmc. is unique among Gmc. dialects in displaying *gera/gǫra/gjǫra* (etc.) for 'to do, make' (elsewhere, with the exception of Gothic, we have *tun* and *machen*, as well as reflexes of a **tōw*, e.g. runic *tawido* 'made', which lacks extra-Gmc. analogues). A reconstructible Norse input for *gera/gǫra* = **garwjan* lacks a credible etymology: postulation of an underlying **gh(w)orw-yo-* leads to nothing plausible. This is seemingly yet another pre-Indo-European constituent of dialectal Germanic. The second component is transparently from *sómi* < **sām*, a well pedigreed term for 'honor, appropriateness, appropriate (to/for), becoming', etc., see Lindow (1975:135-43) for an admirable survey of the cultural staging of this term. This noun turned qualifying suffix supplied Engl. *-some*, functionally equivalent to Germ. *-bar*. The original semantics of *gorsimi* were probably something like 'doable, fitting, suitable thing', but its life outside North Germanic was highly restricted: OE *gersuma* > ME *gersume* is patently a Norse loan, one of many that did not survive to become incorporated into a later, post Anglo-Norman, standard.

The significant observation here is that North Germanic was apparently forced to innovate to supply a term for 'treasure' in the context of the courtly gift/exchange ritual. The term that regularly filled this slot (the environment for *treasure* as *reward* conferred by princes on members of the *comitatus*, or, conversely, by members of the *comitatus* on princes, cf. the citation from the *Germania* above) is ultimately derivable from a **moi-t-mo*: Goth. *maiþm-s* (1x Mark 7.11 = Gk. δῶρον Vlg. *dōnum*, Engl. *given*, OS *méthom* masc. *a*-stem, OE *māð(ð)um* masc. *a*-stem, both with anaptyctic vowel, OIc. *meiðmar* fem. *o*-stem, pl. only. This lexeme is unattested in Old, Middle, or Modern High German, nor is it attested in any period of Frisian, where **māthe/mēthe* (or the like) might well have coalesced with *mēde* (*mīde*), also *mēthe/mīthe* 'reward, rent' = Germ. *Miete*, and the possibility of such homophonous coalescence is also conceivable for High German, cf. the forceful separation of the two words in Old Saxon: *meðmo te mēdu* (Hel. 4482). Cf. OHG *mēta* (besides later *mieta*, *miata*), which was replaced by *Zins* < Lat. *census* beginning in the 7th century. Luther's *Miete, mieten, Mietling* were unknown to his Upper German contemporaries. On *Miete* (etc.) 'rent, reward' = Goth *mizdō*, see infra.

Although artificially revived in the modern period, OIc. *meiðmar*, found only in the plural, is sparsely attested. It is never found in prose, nor in skaldic poetry, and is actually attested but seven times in what are generally considered younger poems of the Eddic canon: *Þrymskviða* (23.1), *Siguðarkviða in skamma* (2.2), *Atlakviða in groenlenzca* (5.5), *Atlamál in groenlenzco* (95.2), *Rígsþula* (38.5), *Hlǫðskviða* (*Hunnenschlachtlied*) (11.3, 33.3). Of the seven occurrences, five (*Þrk*. 23.1, *Sg*. 2.2, *Am*. 95.2, *Hunn*. 11.3, 33.3) are the collocation *fjǫlð meiðma* 'much, a great store of treasure', which has exact parallels in *Beowulf* (*mādma fela* 36, cf. *mādma maenigo* 41, *manegum māðmum* 2103, *māðma menigeo* 2143) and the *Heliand* (*meðmo filu* 3292), *stórar meiðmar (Akv.* 5.5) is required by alliteration (*stórar meiðmar oc staði Danþar*), but also has the appearance of a fixed phrase. The remaining occurrence is a problematic line: *meiðmar oc mǫsma, mara svangrifia (Rb.* 38.5), where *mǫsma* should be restored to *mǫsmar*, the obvious difficilior reading for this masculine plural, a hapax that has remained etymologically opaque, though the line is usually translated as: 'treasures and jewels (treasures) and slim-flanked steeds'. Alliterative collocation of 'treasures' and 'steeds' is a stock item in *Beowulf* and has every appearance as such of being archaic: *Beo.* = *mēarum ond mādmum* 1048, 1898; *mēara ond mādmum* 2166; that is, in three out of a total of thirty-one occurrences of the simplex in the poem. Further indication of the fixed, frozen phrase nature of *meiðmar* is the fact that *Hunn.* 33.33 is a repetition of *Hunn.* 11.3: *fé oc fiǫlð meiðma, sem mic fremst tíðir,* and note that *meiðmar* is contrasted with *fe* as a different sort of wealth/treasure. Cf. *Beowulf* 470-472, where Hrothgar explains that the wergild he had paid for Beowulf's father's slaying of Heatholaf had consisted of both *feoh* and *māðum*:

siððan þā fǣhðe   feo þingode
sende ic Wylfingum   ofer waeteres hyrcg
ealde mādmas;   hē mē āþas swōr.

and *mādmas* thus forms part of a contractual agreement (signalled by *āþas*).

In both *Beowulf* and the *Heliand, māðum/mēthom* is frequently qualified as 'brave, bold, expensive, dear': *Hel.* = *diurie methmos* 1198, 1845, 3286, 4578; *diurrero mēthmo* 5889 (i.e. five out of a total of twelve occurrences in the poem); *Beo.* = *dēorum mādme* 1528, *dēore māðmas* 2236, *dȳre māðmas* 3131, cf. *māþme þȳ weorþra* 1902. This is additional evidence that what we are dealing with here was a stock item of epic composition, the sort of information Snorri later inventoried, an item the well-trained *scop* had to know. Even compounds are stock items, cf. *mēthomhord (Hel.* 1643, 1676, 3261, 3772) and *hordmāðum* (Beo. 1198, 1x), cf. *māðma hord* (Beo. 2799, 3011). This term did not simply specify 'gift', for otherwise compounds such as *mēthomgeƀo (Hel.* 1200) would be tautologies. Nor was this simply 'treasure, jewels', as the word is traditionally and misleadingly glossed; otherwise we would not find definitional collocations such as *meðmo gestriuni (Hel.* 1721). This is gift/exchange, originally in ritualistic contexts, even as wergild and commemoration (e.g. *māððum tō gemyndum* Beo. 3016), as well as 'reward', e.g. *meðmo te mēdu* (Hel. 4482). The semantics of *mēthom/māðum* could even express heirlooms, comparable, in North American terms, to giving medicine bundles at a potlach, cf. *ealde mādmas* (Beo. 472) and synonymous *ǣr-gestrēon* (Beo. 1757, where it references *mādmas* in the previous line, and again in 2232).

We may now summarize the dialectal and chronological distribution of **maiþm-*. It is as we noted, attested but once in Gothic, where 'reward (treasure)/payment/gift' is otherwise glossed by *fra-gifts, giba, mizdō, laun*. As we noted, too, it is not found in Frisian or High German, nor, for that matter, it is found in (Old Low) Franconian. In Continental Germanic, it is restricted to Ingwaeonic. In Old Saxon, it occurs only in the *Heliand* (12x = 1198, 1470, 1721, 1845, 1848, 3192, 3286, 3292, 4482, 4487, 4578, 5889, and *mēthomhord*, the only compound with this term, occurs four times = 1643, 1676, 3261, 3772) and *Genesis* (1 x 171), but never as a gloss, nor in any of the later, minor texts, e.g. the *Freckenhorster Heberolle* (neither K, now lost, nor M), which, as they are generally commercial in scope, might be expected to contain this word had it developed and survived with a decidedly commercial sense. In addition to the *Gnomic Verses, Metres of Boethius*, and Alfred's *Pastoral Care*, Anglo-

Saxon attests *maipm-* frequently and, as we have seen, revealingly in *Beowulf* (31x = 36, 41, 169, 385, 472, 1027, 1048, 1052, 1482, 1528, 1756, 1784, 1860, 1867, 1898, 1902, 2055, 2103, 2143, 2146, 2166, 2236, 2490, 2640, 2779, 2788, 2799, 2865, 3011, 3016, 3131, as well as in compounds: *dryht-* 2843, *gold-* 2414, *hord-* 1198, *ofer-* 2993, *sinc-* 2193, *wundur-* 2173). In *Beowulf*, it remains semantically distinct from its demi-competitors: *gift* f., *lac* nt., *ge-strēon* nt., *sinc* nt., *fraetwa, -e* f.. Nevertheless, given frequent definitional collocations with these demi competitors and compounds, which, if not equipollently composed, are non-tautological, one is left with the impression that *maiþm-* was hardly anywhere in active use by the 9th century, but was reserved for the composition of epics or isolated as a cultural artifact. This assumption is, as we have seen, definitely borne out by Icelandic which attests the word a mere seven times and only in younger portions of the *Edda*. However, it seems entirely incorrect to assume, as Mohr (1939: 193) did, that Icelandic borrowed the term from a common stock of West Germanic literary filigrees. If so then the borrowing must have occurred well prior to Ingwaeonic (the only West Germanic area that attests the word) monophthongization of Gmc. *ai*, that is well before the Anglo-Saxon *Landnahme*. Otherwise, we would expect *máðmar* (or the like). Mohr's judgments, like those of his near-contemporary, Hans Kuhn, were prejudiced by an era that wished to see Continental Germanic as *the* cultural heartland. This word represents a Pan-Germanic inheritance with clear roots in the protolanguage. In this, it differs from its demi-competitors: *sinc*, of unknown origin, is found only in Old Saxon and Old English; as a noun, OE *lāc* (which survives in wed-lock) was restricted to Anglo-Saxon; OE *fraetwa, -e* is a dialect-specific nominalization built on *(fra)-twa-jan* to *tōw-* 'do, make', cf. Goth. *usfratwjan*, OS *fratahōn* (another incident of Ingwaeonic -w-~-g-/-h-), see Feist (1939:531); OE *ge-strēon* is elsewhere reflected only in OS, OHG *gi-striuni*, none of which survive into the Medieval period.

It seems altogether clear that an inherited Gmc. **maiþm-* was the term *par excellence* of gift/exchange (treasure, reward, payment) in the setting of the *communitas* and a word from the lexicon of pre-Christian epic recitation, the 'reward/treasure' circumscribed by social contracts in a primitive economy in which value was determined by social standing rather than the inherent worth of an object, cf. Dumézil (1947:79-83, 118-24, 152-9). In short, **maiþm-* is the Germanic answer to the notions personified as **Mitra* in Indo-Iranian.

Association of **maiþm-* with the *communitas* concept is assured by its collocation with **gamaini* = OLat. (acc.) *co-moin-em*, cf. Germ. *Meineid*: OE *māþma gemǣnra* (Beo. 1784), *māþmas gemǣne* (Beo. 1860), cf. Mdn. Engl. 'a man of means'. In the wake of the socio-economic revolutions that attended the introduction of Christianity, **maipm* was displaced, albeit at different rates and at different times from dialect to dialect: it was regarded the term for 'reward' in a decidedly non-Christian setting. The one Gothic occurrence supports this assumption. It is uniquely employed in Mark 7.11 to gloss *kaurban* = *corban*, a rendering of the Hebrew term that underlies this approximation for 'offering, oblation', cf. Leviticus 2.1; Jehovah rebukes all who adopt this device (offering, obligation = *corban* = *maiþm-*) to escape the necessity of supporting their parents, cf. Benveniste (1969:1.91), who overlooked this contextual saliency. Wulfila had the advantage of a native pagan term, while both Greek (=δῶρον here) and Latin (=*dōnum* here) translators lacked his bicultural/bilingual perspective. Within the "new" Christian tradition, what had formerly been the favored term was transformed into a pejorative: **maiþm-* was ostensified as the false reward, the pleasure of the unbelievers. But, then too, as Benveniste (1969:1.167-8) astutely shows, *mizdō*, ultimately related to *maiþm-*, referenced wordly reward, while *laun* (cf. *launa-wargs*, *sigis-laun*) denoted providential or heavenly reward: in Gothic, *maiþm-* was displaced by *laun*, see the collocations in Matthew 6.1-2. Similarly, note the progressive displacement of Germanic terms for 'temple, cult site', see Markey (1972). Note, too, that Lat. *lucrum*, originally 'providential reward', later acquired a pejorative stigma, not only within (Ibero-) Romance, but also upon entering English (e.g. the frozen phrase *filthy lucre*), cf. ME *lukir, lukre*, etc., so at least as early as Wyclif's (ca. 1380) *worldy honour and lucre*. In the *Heliand*, *mēthom* usually denotes worldly treasure, reward and is periodically equated with *ōdwelo* 'wealth', but the transition is not complete. In *Genesis* (171) it refers to heavenly reward: *mēomo sō mildi*. Note, too, in a confusing and much discussed line, *māþoum for Metode* (Beo. 169), perhaps 'Grendel ought not approach God's throne, the treasure/reward', cf. Philippson (1929:184).

The dyadic, binary opposition between *laun* (heavenly/true reward) and *mizdō* (false/earthly reward) as an articulation of the contrast between sacred and secular, divine and profane respectively, that Benveniste (1969:1.167-9) so admirably succeeded in eliciting from Wulfila's text was, we firmly suspect, guided by a well established structuralist principle. This is, of course, the principle of complementarity, the very basis of any hierarchical dialectic, a principle that asserts that the reality of an item's existence or position (often construed as coterminous) is defined by the oppositions it erects. This is the sort of thinking that has long directed the bulk of modern social anthropological inquiry, so Leach (182:221-4). It is certainly the common argumentative thread that underlies the investigations of two of Benveniste's most distinguished and influential colleagues, namely, Claude Lévi-Strauss and Georges Dumézil. Note, for example, how Dumézil (1947:76) asserts that, in the first instance, the concept of the *brāhmaṇá* was defined by its opposition to *kṣatriyá*. Indeed, the process of lexical bifurcation, particularly for notions that are obviously institutional in scope, in effecting repartitions between the secular and the divine is a hallmark feature of Indo-European, and a structuralism which embraces complementarity principles has been highly successful in uncovering the conceptual patterns and their interleafing that lie at the core of early Indo-European acculturation. Note, for example, in the realm of the sacred, the opposition between Goth. *hails* (secular) and *weihs* (divine), or in the law, Lat. *jus* (secular) vs. *fas* (divine), see Markey (1985b:278).

Now, if, as seems highly likely, *laun* originally defined providential, divine reward/treasure in opposition to *mizdō* (and congeners) as the expression of secular reward/treasure, payment gained by contest, conquest, or work, then where does *maiþm-* fit into this continuum and what, if any was its relationship to *laun* on the one hand and or its formal sibling, *mizdō*, on the other hand? then, too, in addition to the exigencies of a conversion literature as outlined above, why did *maiþm-* vanish? Why, too on its deathbed in that literature, was it so readily ambiguous (both secular and divine) and unable to make a transition to one pole (*laun*) or the other (*mizdō*)?

We suggest that, as the original expression for courtly gift/exchange within the *communitas*, *maiþm-* occupied a pivotal position midway between totally {+secular/-divine} and totally {-secular/+divine}, indeed just as the princeps as communal leader (Goth *þiudans*) and addressee of the *maipm*-ritual occupied the same position:

laun	*maiþm*	*mizdō*
+divine	±divine	-divine

| -secular | ∝ secular | +secular |

Nevertheless, *maiþm-* was still the highest earthly reward so long as no divine reward was distinctly crystallized, as it was in Christian tradition. Yet, *maiþm-* remained closer to *mizdō*, as both were essentially earthly as opposed to *laun*, and could, even formally as we shall see, be confused with *mizdō*. As an intermediary, as a betwixt and between area of liminality, an interface between two categories, *maiþm-* defined a position of danger, the typical locus of ritual activity: Authun could be rewarded by King Harald or King Sveinn or he could forfeit his life. In the shared feelings generated by participatory gift/exchange *communitas*, however, the social differences between individuals could be forgotten, as are the social differences between Chaucer's pilgrims en route to Canterbury, see Leach (1982:158). This is the locus of the Christmas gift/exchange ritual, the modern analogue of heathen *maiþm-*. Due to its interstitial, Janus-like midway position, *maiþm-* became ambiguous (both secular and divine), as we have seen in the early conversion literature. However, as Christianity emphasized the polarities of the continuum at the expense of the middle, *maiþm-* became increasingly cloudy, increasingly in need of definitional collocations, particularly so as the institution that required it weakened, and it finally vanished altogether. Its lingering effects alone conjured forth new creations such as *gørsimi*, or plugged such new creations into the contextual slot *maiþm-* had once occupied. On the other hand, as *mizdō* → *Miete*, with a narrowing of semanic scope (the specific reward of 'rent, interest'), or, as was the case with related OE *mēd* f. > Mdn. Engl. *meed* (archaic), lost its foregrounding and became increasingly vague, this member was phased out of the continuum, thereupon leaving *Lohn/lønn* (the case with Modern German, Dutch and Scandinavian) to cover both poles of the continuum. For *laun* (= OE *lēan*), English was somehow compelled to borrow Norse *lān* > Engl. *loan*, which was assigned a specifically commercial sense of 'reward', cf. *Miete*. Deprived of a laun, as well as an effective *mizdō*, English borrowed Anglo-Norman/Northern French *(re)warder* = Mdn. French regarder, in turn a Germanic loan to French (viz. some dialectal ancestor of Germ- *warten*, cf. *erwarten*) to cover both poles and additionally borrowed the source of *pay* (see *supra*) for distinctly secular rewards.[4] With reference to more modern (e.g. King James, etc.), as well as the Greek Vulgate, translations of the collocations in Matthew 6.1-2, we can establish the following polar members of the continuum:[5]

	LAUN	MIZDŌ
Gk.	μισδὸυ	μισδὸυ
Vulg.	mercedem	mercedem
Germ.	Lohn	Lohn
Dano-Nw.	lønn	lønn
Engl.	reward	reward

With the elimination of a definitional contrast in the post-Christian period, what had been a 'reward'-continuum in earlier Germanic collapsed to a unitary set. In operational terms, the anisomorphism that had once obtained between Germanic and Greco-Roman cultural norms in this denotational field was removed; the semantic space of *laun* was extended to cover *mizdō*, precisely the converse of the Greek situation. Subsequently, laun was necessarily affixally qualified in particular contexts, e.g. Germ. *be-löhnen/Be-lohnung*.

A Gmc. **maiþm-* unambiguously points to an underlying **moi-t-mó* > pre-PGmc. **móitm-*, that is, a deverbative (<**mei-*, see Pokorny 1959:715) nominal derivation in *-*tmó*, a secondary compound suffix which began with the addition of -*mó* to originally vowel-final verbal roots extended with -*t*- (not -*tó*-), cf. OHG *brādam* < **bhrē-t-mó* and OE *beorma* 'leaven, yeast' < **bher-mó-*, so Krahe-Meid (1967:125-6). Here, one may recall the following analogues of *t*-extensions: Goth. *maidjandans* (1x II Corinthians 2.17), *ga-maiþs*, OIc. *meiða*: Lat. *mūtuus, mūt-āre, mūtuor, mūtuum (dō)* < **moit-*, cf. *commoetācula* (Festus 56.29) < **com-moita-clom*; Gk. (Sicilian loan from Italic) μοῖτος 'thanks, favor'; OHG *muzzōn* < Lat. *mūt-āre* (indirectly).

The incidence of such *t*-extensions is generally restricted to western dialects, not only Germanic and Italic as just indicated, but also Baltic and Slavic. Cf., for example, the following derivations from an underlying **meitu-* (or the like) in Baltic and Slavic: latv.. *miêtus* 'exchange, change', *mietuôt* 'to exchange, *mitêt* 'change' (refl. 'to cease, stop'), *mît* 'to exchange', *pamîšu* adv. 'alternatively'; OSC *mitě* adv. 'alternately', Bulg. *ná-mito* adv. 'across, slanting', Pol. dial. *mitus/mituś/* 'crosswise', cf. OSC *mĭstĭ, mĭstiti* v., Bulg. *mŭstĭ*, Russ. *mesti*, Cz. *pomsta, -mstiti* v., Pol. *mścić* v. 'revenge/avenge'. The relationship between an underlying participial adj. **mit-tó-* > *mitsto-* > Gmc. (Goth.) *missa-* (cf. Engl. *mis-*) and the Old Irish negative prefix *mís(s)-* (e.g. *mís-imbert* ' foul play, he abused them') is contested, perhaps a reformation of *mí-* (e.g. in *mí-imbert* ' deceit', cf. *mí-t·n-imret* 'that they deceive him'), see Thurneysen (1966:Art. 365.2), who equates *mí-* with the prohibitive negative = Gk.μή, Arm. *mi*, Skt. *mā́*, etc., suggests that this negator had become a compositional prefix, and points out that there is no by-form *mis-* in Old Irish. Otherwise, the *t*-extension is seemingly found only in Indo-Iranian. Note Skt. √*mith* 'alternate, altercate', e.g. *mithatī* (R-V), *mḗthati; mitha* adv. 'shifting, mutual, together' = Av. *miθō* adv. 'falsified'; Skt. *míthus, míthus, mithuyā* adv. 'wrongly, falsely', *mithyā́* adv. 'in vain' < **mithiya*, where semantic isolation of adverbials became more complete after loss of their corresponding noun. Skt. *míth-u*, adv. 'alternately': *mithuná-* 'forming a pair, copulation' = Av. *miθwana*, are in reality abstracts in -*wan* formed to a radical enlarged with -*t*-, so Benveniste (1935:115-6). Note, too, the corresponding *vṛdhhi* adj. *maithuná* 'being coupled, characterized by coupling, connected by marriage'. Most plausibly also here is *Mítra-* from a common Indo Iranian **mitra-*, besides younger, specifically Indic *mitrá-* 'friend' (masc.), 'friendship' (R-V nt.) 'the prince whose territory adjoins that of an immediate neighbor is called "a friend"'; *vṛddhi maitra* 'belonging to Mitra', *maitr-eya* adj. 'benevolent', *maitrī* fem. 'goodwill, intimate association, perhaps also Ir. (Yašt. 19.29) *fra-mita-*, see Mayrhofer (1963:633-6) s.v. *Mitráḥ, mináti*. It seems doubtful whether Hitt. *mutai-* 'avoid, remove, distance oneself from' is related.

Another prominent suffixation of **me/oi-* is with -*nó/-né-* (*ní-*). Cf. OIr. *moín* (*main, maen*) fem. *i*-stem 'gift, treasure, reward', *dag-moíni, maenech* 'rich' (*moenech* MS Rawlinson B505 fasc., p. 165a, 12th cent.), *moenigfid* (MS Harley 5280, fol. 44b-48a), all from **moi-ní-* vs. British Celtic **mei-nó-*, e.g. W *mwyn* 'worth, value', see Vendryes (1960:M69-60). Note, further, Lat. *mūnia, mūnus* < **moi-ne/o-s*; Gmc. **ga-maini-* (e.g. OE *gemǣne*) + OLat. (acc.) *co-moin-em*, cf. supra; Lith. *maínas*, Latv.. *mains* 'exchange'; OSC *měna* 'change, exchange'.

Suffixation of **me/oi-* with -*nó/-né-* is a general characteristic of Western Indo-European (Germanic, Italic, Celtic, Baltic, and Slavic), but is also found in Indo-Iranian, albeit in forms with the semantics of 'revenge, vengeance, punishment', the negative, pejorative side of gift/exchange, cf. the *vertauscht* → *verfälscht* connotation of related OHG *mein*, Germ. *Meineid*. Cf. Skt. *mēni-* fem. 'revenge', Av. *maēni-* fem. 'punishment'. Of course, suffixation with -*nó-/-né-* is relatively recent in Indo-

European; it is ignored by Hittite. It is of interest to note that, with the exception of Celtic, the dialectal distribution patterns of t-extension and suffixation with -nó-/-né- coincide: Germanic, Italic, Baltic, Slavic, and Indo-Iranian.

Before proceeding further, we must underscore the facts that *maiþm-* is an exclusively Germanic innovation which must stem from pre-dialectal stages of Common Germanic. A canonical shape anticipated for Indo-European would have been **moi-mó-*, see Hamp (1982-1983). The arresting and insufficiently stressed observation is that Norse lacks an analogue to both exclusively WGmc. **mēd-* (> **maδ̄-*) and a **mizdō-*, though it attests what we have presumed to be a native reflex of **maiþm-*, namely, *meiδmar*, albeith, as we have noted, but feebly attested and defective, as it occurs only in the plural.

Having canvassed the Germanic evidence for *maiþm-* and noted, particularly, its co-occurrence with **ga-maini-*, especially in the Beowulf epic as a cultural context for gift/exchange and the detritus of the original wording of that ritual process, we now seem justified in reconstructing a specific figura etymologica for Pre-germanic, namely, **móitmos gho-móinis* '(dutifully, communally) given gift/exchange', which corresponds (however approximately) to a Common Italic **dōnom da-/dō-* which Euler (1982) has retraced. We thus have the remnant of an o-grade nomen actionis in **-mó-* qualified by a participial adjective in a ready-made surface structure formula that is simultaneously a thematic synthesis of a highly prized feature of early North European culture, presumably on a par in its significance with other such sets retrievable from Ind-European *Dichtersprache und Dichtkunst*, e.g. the celebrated /śráva(s) ákṣitam uncovered by the venerable Adalbert Kuhn, **wékwos wekw-*, **wesu klewos*, **deiwos nmrtōs*.[6]

OE *mēd* fem. ō-stem 'meed/Miete' (OS *mēda*, OHG *mēta* (*miata, mieta* with "breaking"), OFr. *mēde/mīde/meide*, Langobardian *mēta* uniquely glossed 'bride price' (*Edictum Rothari, Leges Liutprandi*)) could speculatively be derived from **mēi-dh-* (see infra) and thus relatable to *maipm-* and distinct from Goth. *mizdō*, OE *meord*, so Wood (1899:261-2), who however, posited a Pre-Gmc. **mēitá-*. If we accept **mēi-*, then we can mechanically project a Theme I **meₐ₁-y-*, however tentative.

Now, as every comparatist knows, the precise nature of the relationship between a WGmc. *mēd-* an what underlines Goth. *mizdō*, OE *meord* (primarily Mercian alone and but feebly attested, this fem. ō-stem occurs only in Bede's *Historia ecclesiastica* and St. Gregory's *Dialogi*) has long remained a moot question.

We may begin by providing a survey of the reflexes of an underlying **mizdhō-* 'reward, wage' (as a convenient form with which to operate, so Pokorny 1959:746). This etymon is distinctly eastern in orientation. Both italic and Celtic lack analogues. In Germanic, only Goth. *mizdō* and OE *meord* point to a **mizdhō-*. It is totally lacking in Armenian, which, in fact, fails to show any traces of a **me/oi-* (or the like), or any derivatives of the putative *Wortsippe* in question (personal communication from John C. Greppin). Gk. μισθός 'wages, pay', from Homeric to Modern Greek, is well integrated in the lexicon: ρητός 'fixed wages', μισθῷ 'for hire', δικαστικός 'daily wages of a dicast or juror', cf. μισθόω 'I give or receive a wage, pay' with a present in -ow, and thus with the appearance of a factative made to complete the conjugation of a passive. CF. μισθοῖ 3rd sg., μισθοῖ 3rd sg. subj., μισθοῦν < *μισθόειν. μισθο- is the only Greek reflex of this *Wortsippe*. This etymon is widely attested in Slavic, from which it is borrowed *Wortsippe*. This etymon is widely attested in Slavic, from which it is borrowed by Rumanian as *mezde*, cf. OSC *mizda/mŭzda*, Slov. (west. dial.) *mèzda*

(~pláča), Bulg. *muzda*, Cz *mzda*, Upper Sorb. *mzda/zda*, Russ. *mzda*. This is yet another segment of the lexicon of a Balkan *lingua franca*. The word is also prevalent in Indo-Iranian: Av. *mižda-* nt. (e.g. Yašna 62.6), Osset. *mizd/myzd*, Mdn. Pers. *muzd*, Skt. *mīḍhá-* nt. 'reward, contest, battle, prize' (in collocations with *raṇa, yuddhá*) < **miẓḍhá-* < **mizdhó-* < **mis-dh-ó-*, parallel to *nīḍá-* < **ni-zd-ó-* 'nest', and note identical development of *gd* > *ḍ*. In Sanskrit it is restricted to vedic; it does not survive in the Classical period. Interestingly enough, this also holds for related *miyédha-* (Av. *myazda-*) 'sacrificial offering', cf. *infra*. *mīḍhá-* occurs but four times in the Ṛgveda; 1.100.11, 6.46.4, 9.106.12, 9.107.11, and the last two occurrences are in an identical formula = ...*mīḷhé sáptir ná vājayúḥ*. It consistently appears as *mīḷha-*, that is, with *ḷh* for *ḍh* in the extant recensions, and this *may* indicate that the word was already considered a non-standard (eastern) dialectal variant by the time of early codification (Pāṇini does not subscribe to *ḷh/ḷ* and refers to Vedic usages such as *saḍha, iḍa*), see Deshpande (1979:226-8). Note the related perfect active participle *mīḍhvāns* (said to be from *⌈mih*) in the weak forms *mīḍhúṣe ~ mīḷhúṣe* 'richly bestowing (gifts), bountiful'.

The distributional evidence alone points to a later, secondary, albeit immediately dialectal origin for **misdhó*: Germanic, Slavic (but not Baltic), Greek (but not Armenian, and this is the only form in Greek that contains **me/oi-*), and Indo-Iranian. Composition is perplexing. Specht (1947:249-50) correctly noted that *-sdh-* is not a legitimate Indo-European suffix, but then continued with the unfounded suggestion that what we ultimately have her is a collapsed phrase: **mis dhe-* 'was als Austausch dagegen gesetzt wird' with **mis* < **me/oi-* as in Skt. *máyate*, etc. A participial origin (<**midzdho-*) was compellingly discounted by Brugmann (1930:1.626, Anm. 1). An effective way to proceed is to segment **misdhó-* as *mis-dh-o-* and then to review the primordial value of suffixal *-dh-* in terms of Benveniste's (1935:188-210) cogent presentation.

With reference to Benveniste (loc. cit), the affix *-dh-*, originally with restricted incidence in pre-dialectal Indo-European, became utilized in a particular dialectal range: Baltic, Slavic, Germanic, Indo-Iranian, and, particularly extensively, Greek (north European IE ?). From its primordial deployment as a radical enlargement (affix without alternating shapes), *-dh-* was extended as a suffix (affix with alternating shapes: *-dh-//-dho-*), particularly in the verbal system. This affix primarily signified "state, especially an acheived, accomplished state," and was readily coupled with roots with a neutral or instransitive value, a significance that was re-enforced by addition of *-dh-*, which also evolved as a sign of the middle, even desinentially in the 1st and 2nd persons plural.

Secondarily suffixed elements are regularly joined to zero-grade roots, an assumption that provides a basic **mis-dh-ó-* as a point of departure (Indo-Iranian, Greek, Slavic, Germanic---- northern IE?). A basic **mis-* is itself necessarily construed as an enlarged form of a radical **m^e/oi-(I. méi-C-* : II. *my-éC-*), that is, **maiy-* 'exchange, trade, gift', and thence 'common gift/ exchange,' see Pokorny (1959:710, 713-15). Postulation of **m^e/oi-* and perception of *-s-, -t-,* and *-g^w-* as elementary enlargements of this radical to which suffixes (*-dh-/-dho, -ne-/-no-, -m-/-mo-*) were optionally added permit relationship of an otherwise seemingly disparate set of highly archaic terms for 'gift/exchange':

         mei-g^w-(Gk. *amoibos*)
         mei-t-(-tu-) (e.g. Latv. *miêtus*)
         m^e/o(i)s- -->   *mis-dho-*

mos-mo- (ON *mǫsmr sg., mǫsmar pl. a dialect-specific hybrid of uncertain origin, possibly contaminated with mosurr and the like, an *Entgleisungsform* pieced together from mo(i)-//mo(i)s-mo-//mo(i)-t-mo-, see Johannesson (1956:677).

moi-t-/moi-t-mo- (Gmc.*maiþm-)
moi-n^e/o- (e.g. Lat. *mūnus*)

Regular association of -s- with *e*-grade radicals isolates OIc. *mǫsmr(masc. sg.) as an *Entgleisungsform*, but both contextual semantics and reconstructible shape point to a relationship within this *Wortsippe*.

Hamp (personal communication and in various versions furnished me of his study of OHG *sezzal* and related matters intended for the Moulton *Festschrift*) convincingly argues for the following development of *misdhó-*in Germanic: *misdhó- *mizdo- → (feminized thematic denominal formation requiring guṇa *e*-grade vocalism)*meizdā->meizd->me(i)zd->mē²d- where the latter two shapes provide the sources of attested early reflexes e.g. OE *mēord* vs. *mēd* resp., cf. Sievers (1894:409), Janko (1906-1907:255), where Janko anticipates Hamp's derivation with his *mē²dō-* < *mē(z)dō-* < *mē(i)zdā-*.

The archaic deployment of congeners in the m^e/*oi* 'gift/exchange' group in portions of the Indo-European speech (as opposed to language) community has been detailed above. A firm presence of the group in northern Indo-European, what we may term the *apple/plow/pig/*-sector (see Markey 1989), is particularly noteworthy, as is the adduced formulaic collocation: *móitmos gho-móinis* 'dutifully, communally given gift/exchange,' specifically reconstructible for pre-Germanic, which may well have had far wider dialectal and geographical currency, perhaps throughout northern Indo-European and the pre-non-Indo-European community of the so-called "apple-continuum." A *móitmos* (or the like) may well have been a tribute extracted by a forceful minority operating within a clefted feudalism in northern Atlantic Europe, an area which may now view as integrating non-resident Indo-European with a resident non-Indo-European settlement, a composite grouping, see the contributions by Hamp, Gilman, and Zimmer in this volume, Polomé's references to non-Indo-European in this volume, and Markey's (1989:592) account of ritualized grain tributes.

Having uncovered fragments of a prehistoric gift/exchange process, the archaeologist should seek coordination within the artifactual record, and here we refer to studies such as those compiled by Champion and Megaw (1985).

At this particular point in our research, we should be asking essentially interdisciplinary questions: is the delineation of possible prehistoric tythe barns coterminous with the presumed distribution of a *móitmos (or the like) and some associated ritual?

Preliminary investigation suggests---at least from the fragmentary linguistic evidence recovered to date for non-Indo-European in northern Atlantic Europe that, at the end of the megalithic period, this area witnessed extensive acculturation among indigenous, non-Indo-European groups and Indo-European or Indo-Europeanied groups. As indicated by some retrievable social nomenclature (e.g. the *magus/mawi* problem, see Hamp in this volume, and *skalk*, calques in Engl. *marshall* ('horse servant?'); certain limited lexical categories such as terms for crustacea, fish, fishing, and seafaring/boats; the practice of totem/tabu as a non-IE expression vs. oath/ordeal as an IE institution; the indication of tythes or tributes as gift/exchange in a clefted feudalism defined by socio-ethnic origins; distinctly non-IE terms for flora and fauna; non-IE agricultural forms and cultivars (*pig/plow/apple*); certain culturally tagged semantic pairings (time and weather as synonomous for non-IE, e.g. *tempus*, vs. differentiated in Indo-European); emerging bits and pieces of the onomastic puzzle (e.g. non-IE dial. **mal-* 'stone' vs. non-IE dial. **kar-*'stone'); culturally significant vocabulary that is institutional in scope, but inconceivably Indo-European (e.g. **bhugh-* as a basis for 'to buy'), we are finally beginning to realize a socio-economic situation for the association of indigenous groups in northern Europe, a situation that stands in vivid contrast to a romanticized vision of an intrusively nomadic, uniquely patriarchal and belligerent, Indo-European onslaught such as that captioned by Maria Gimbutas, see her contribution to this volume. By linguistically sifting non-Indo-European from Indo-European (e.g. all those *b*-ful forms in northern Europe), we are beginning to see the roots of accommodation by apposite groups on the threshold of recorded history.

NOTES

(1) Of course, I assume all responsibility for the interpretive efforts that follow, but I would here like to thank my many colleagues who have influenced me in thinking about these lexical matters over the past decade, especially Eric P. Hamp and Edgar C. Polome, but also, at Michigan, Garry W. Davis, who, while still a graduate student accompanied me on numerous fieldtrips to the Sauk and Fox of the Mississippi in Iowa and participated in many discussions about this topic and related anthropological matters.

(2) Comparatists have long recognized the possibility of non-IE elements in the Northwest Block, e.g. the shape that underlies North European (Germanic, Celtic, Balto-Slavic) 'apple', and etymologically difficult forms that underlie 'plow', certain terms for 'pig', and so on. In a paper presented to The Seventh International Congress of Celtic Studies (Oxford, July 10-15, 1983), we attempted to indicate signs of the prior, substratal existence of a distinctly non-IE *totem/tabu* culture in the Block, as well as the complementarity between *oath/ordeal* (=IE) and *totem/tabu* (=non-IE) cultures and their contents, spelled out in Markey (1985a), the nucleus of which Claude Levi-Strauss (*per litteras*) greeted with approval.

(3) See Elston (1934) and recall Arbois de Jubainville's (e.g. 1891) now discredited thesis of Celtic overlordship. As examples of key institutional etyma shared by the two groups, note OS *nimid* (1x) = OIr. *nemed* 'sacred grove', Goth. *liuga* f. 'marriage' = OIr. *luge* (*luige*) nt. < **lugyom* 'oat (in contracts)', GMc. **aiþ-* = OIr. *ōeth* < **oito-*. With respect to the lexicon of contractual agreement, such an intimate association as that evidenced by Celtic and Germanic is perhaps found nowhere else in Indo-European. Terms considered archaic, exclusively literary, items of restricted distribution in the older Germanic dialects are sometimes the norm in Celtic. Such is the case with OE *folm(e)* f., OHG *folma* f. 'hand' (vs. *hand, Hand* resp., of course, in the modern period) and their Celtic (OIr. *lam*, W *llaw*) congeners < **plHa-mā*, so Hamp (1982-1983:175), who sees Lat. *palma* as the syncope product of a **palama*. Further examples could be cited in legion.

(4) According to the OED, 'reward' in its present sense dates from c. 1320: *That to 3ow byth rewarded....* Initial and non-final intervocalic Gmc. *w* (or, better, Franconain *w*) regularly evolved as *g* in French, e.g. *wis-* > *guise, want-* > *gant, wahta* > *gaite, *werra* > *guerre*. In Norman and Northern French, however, w lingered for some time, and even in the medieval period it occurred as an approximate in Norman, so *guarder, guardez* in the 13th century Anglo-Norman *Ornatus mulierum*.

(5) What we have obviously attempted here is a diachronic mapping (by comparing synchronous states) of the internal structure of a lexical sub-system covering the conceptual field of 'reward'. This is a procedure well known from its application by Jost Trier (1934) to chart replacement of MHG *list* by *wizzen* and the disappearance of courtly and social connotations from the *kunst-wizzen* duality, see Lyons (1963:37-50) for a discussion and critique.

(6) On Indo-European poetics, see Zimmer in this volume, Hamp's account of the Indo-European horse in this volume, and the admirable and instructive overview provided by Watkins (1982).

REFERENCES

Benveniste, Emile. 1935. *Origines de la formation des noms en indo-européen*. Paris: Adrein-Maisonneuve.

———. 1951. Don et échange dans le vocabulaire indo-européen. *Anné sociologiquee*.

———. 1969. *Le vocabulaire des instutions indo-europennes. 1-2*. Paris: Editions de minuit.

Brugmann, Karl. 1906. *Grundriss der vergleichenden Grammatik der indogermanischen Sprachen*. Bd. II, Teil I. Strassburg: Trubner 2nd ed.

———.1930. *Grundriss der vergleichenden Grammatik der indogermanischen Sprachen*. Bd. I. Zweite Hälfte. Berlin.: de Gruyter.2nd ed.

Champion, T. C. and J.V.S. Megaw, eds. 1985. Settlement and Society. Aspects of West European Prehistory in the First Millennium B.C. Leicester: Leicester University Press.

d'Arbois de Joubainville, Henry. 1891. Les témoignages linguistiques de la civilisation commune aux celtes et aux germains pendant le Ve et le IVe siècle avant J.-C. *Revue archéologique* III. Serie 17.187-213.

Deshpande, Madhav M. 1979. Genesis of Ṛgvedic Retroflexion: A Historical and Sociolingusitic Investigation. In: *Aryan and Non-Aryan in India*. Ed. Madhav M. Deshpande and Peter Edwin Hook. Pp. 235-315. (Michigan Papers on South and Southeast Asia, No. 14.). Ann Arbor: Karoma Publishers, Inc.

Dumézil, Georges. 1940. *Mitra-Varuna. Essair sur deux représentations indo-européennes de la souveraineté*. Paris: Gallimard. 2nd ed. 1947.

———.1947. *Loki.* (Les dieux et les hommes, Vol. 1). Paris: Maisonneuve.

Elston, C. S. 1934. *The Earliest Relations Between Celts and Germans*. London: Methuen.

Euler, Wolfram. 1982. *dōnom dō-. Eine figura etymologica der Sprachen Altitaliens. Innsbrucker Beiträge zur Sprachwissenschaft. Vorträge und Kleinere Schriften*, Bd. 29.

Feist, Sigmund. 1939. *Vergleichendes Wörterbuch der gotischen Sprache*. Leiden: E. J. Brill. 3rd ed. rev.

Gordon, E. V. 1957. *An Introduction to Old Norse*. Oxford University Press. 2nd ed. rev.

Hamp, Eric P. 1982-1983. Indo-European Substantives in *-mó- and *-mā́-. *KZ* 96.2.171-7.

Janko, Josef. 1906-1907. Über germanisches $\bar{e}^2$ und die sog. reduplizierenden Praeterita. *IF* 20.229-316.

Johannesson, Alexander. 1956. *Islandisches etymologisches Worterbuch*. Bern: Francke Verlag.

Krahe, Hans and Wolfgang Meid. 1967. *Germanische Sprachwissenschaft*. Bd. III. *Wortbildungslehre*. (Sammlung Göschen, Bd. 1218b). Berlin: de Gruyter.

Leach, Edmund R. 1982. *Social Anthropology*. (Fontana Paperbacks). Glasgow: W. Collins & Sons.

Lindow, John. 1975. *Comitatus, Individual and Honor. Studies in North Germanic Institutional Vocabulary*. (Universities of California Publications in Linguistics, Vol. 83). Berkeley-London: University of California Press.

Lyons, John. 1963. *Structural Semantics. An analysis of the Vocabulary of Plato*. (Publications of the Philological Society, XX.). Oxford: Blackwell.

Markey, T. L. 1972. Germanic Terms for Temple and Cult. *Studies for Einar Haugen.* Ed. by E. S. Firchow, D. Grimstad, N. Hasselmo and W. O'Neil. Pp. 365-78. The Hague-Paris: Mouton.
_____.1985a. The Totemic Typology. *Quaderni di Semantica* 6.1/175-94.
_____.1985b. The Grammaticalization and Institutionalization of Indo-European Hand. *Journal of Indo-European Studies* 13.3-4.261-92.
_____.1989. The Spread of Agriculture in Western Europe: Indo-European Evidence. In: *Foraging and Farming. The Evolution of Plant Exploitation.* Ed. by David R. Harris and Gordon C. Hillman. Pp. 584-606. London: Unwin Hyman.
Mauss, Marcel. 1925. Essai sur le don, forme primitive de l'échange. *Année sociologique* n.s. I. 30-186.
Meillet, Antoine. 1907. *Journal Asiatique*. 10.X.143-59.
Mohr, Wolfgang. 1939. Wortschatz und Motive der jüngeren Eddalieder mit südgermanischer Stoff. *ZfdA* 76.3-4.149-217.
Noreen, Adolf. 1970. *Altnordische Grammatik. 1.* Tübingen: Niemeyer. 5th ed.
Philippson, Ernst Alfred. 1929. *Germanisches Heidentum bei den Angelsachsen.* (Kolner anglistische Arbeiten, 4. Bd.). Leipzig: Bernard Tacuhnitz.
Pokorny, Julius. 1959. *Indogermanisches etymologisches Wörterbuch.* Bern-Munich: Francke Verlag.
Sievers, Eduard. 1894. Germanische Miscellen. *PBB* 18.407-16.
Specht, Franz. 1947. *Der Ursprung der indogermanischen Deklination.* Göttingen: Vandenhoeck & Ruprecht.
Thurneysen, Rudolf. 1966. *A Grammar of Old Irish.* Dublin: Institute of Advanced Studies. rev. ed.
Trier, Jost. 1934. Das sprachliche Feld. Eine Auseinandersetzung. *Neue Jahrbuch für Wissenschaft und Jugendbildung* 10.428-49.
Watkins, Calvert. 1982. Aspects of Indo-European Poetics. In: *The Indo-Europeans in the Fourth and Third Millennia.* Ed. by Edgar C. Polomé. Pp. 104-20. Ann Arbor: Karoma Publishers, Inc.

INDO-EUROPÉENS ET PRÉ-INDO-EUROPÉENS DANS LA PÉNINSULE IBÉRIQUE

F. Villar

Entre la fin du second et le debut du premièr millenaire a.C. commence pour la Péninsule Ibérique la Protohistoire. À propos de ces premières siècles nous n'avons que des nouvelles sporadiques sur la fondation de Gadir, les fabuleuses richesses du Sud, le commerce de l'étain, la route des voyages atlantiques...

Malgré l'existence d'un système local d'écriture et d'une rélative abondance de textes écrits dans les langues péninsulaires, la pleine entré dans l'histoire n'aura lieu qu'au moment où les intérêts des grandes puissances méditerranéennes entrent en collision dans le territoire hispanique. À partir de ce moment, surtout par l'intermédiaire de Rome, on commence à avoir d'abondantes nouvelles sur les peuples qui habitaient l'Espagne pré-romaine, si bien malheureusement pas si explicites que nous ne voudrions.

Tous les témoignages dont on dispose (information de géographes et historiens de l'antiquité, épigraphie péninsulaire, realité linguistique de l'Espagne actuelle) s'accordent pour nous assurer que la Péninsule Ibérique n'a pas été pleinement indo-européisée avant l'arrivée des romains, mais qu'au contraire elle était divisée *grosso modo* en deux zones principales: 1) L'Espagne non-indo-européenne à l'est et au sud, 2) L'Espagne indo-européenne au nord et à l'ouest, comm'on peux voir avec plus d'exactitude dans la carte no I.

Chaqu'une de ces aires présente a son tour un aspect complexe que je commence à examiner tout de suite.

I. - L'HISPANIA INDOGERMANICA
A. - Les Celtes

Parmi les éléments indo-européens de l'Espagne Prérromaine, les celtes sont celui que l'on connaît avec plus de certitude. La presence des celtes est garantie par le témoignage des historiens grecs et latins, par une toponomastique variée et abondante et par une épigraphie spécifique.

Le principal établissement celtique se trouve dans la region appelée Celtiberia par les historien grecs. Le nom de "celtibères", que l'on interprétait autrefois comme preuve de métissage[1], doit être interpreté aujourd'hui, selon toute vraisemblance, tout simplement comme synonyme de "ces habitants de l'Ibérie qui sont des celtes". Il semble prouvé que la Celtibérie a été l'établissement plus solidement et depuis plus longtemps occupé par les celtes. Et il y a certains indices qui nous donnent lieu de penser que c'est de la Celtibérie qu'ils sont partis pour s'introduire vers le sud et le nordouest[2].

La Celtibérie est délimitée au nord et nordest par le bassin moyen de l'Ebre (les provinces de Soria, Logrono et la partie suroccidental de Saragosse), quoique elle surpasse le fleuve vers le nord, et rentre dans Alava et Navarre pour atteindre Pampelune); au sud par les hauts bassins du Tajo et du Jucar (les provinces de Cuenca, Guadalajara et une partie de Teruel); à l'ouest elle occupe une partie des provinces de Madrid, Segovia et Burgos; et à l'est limite avec les ibères du Levant.

L'anthroponimie indo-européenne préromaine est abondante. Et quoiqu'il existe une tendance, vraisemblablement injustifiée, à la considerer exclusivement celtique, il est evident qu'à coté des noms de nature celtique indubitable, comme *Uramus* (de *Uperamus), il y en a d'autres qui n'ont aucun trait spécifiquement celtique, comme *Seneca*.

Une grande partie de la toponimie celtique de l'Espagne peut être classifiée dans des groupes caractéristiques. Bien significatifs sont les toponymes en <u>seg-</u> (Segovia, Segobriga, Segeda, Segontia, Segisamo), en <u>eburo</u> (Eburobriga, Eburobrittium, Ebura, Evora) et ceux qui sont formé avec le suffixe du superlatif celtique <u>-samo</u> (Uxama, Ledesma, Segisama). Mais l'élément plus abondant et caractéristique de la toponimie celtique péninsulaire est la forme *-briga*, qui s'étend un peu partout dans l'*Hispania Indogermanica*, quoiqu'elle surpasse cette frontière dans le sud-ouest et s'introduit dans le sud du Portugal, où l'on trouve une épigraphie non celtique et vraisemblablement non-indo-européenne.[3]

Même si les toponymes en *-briga* sont connus aussi dans d'autres établissements celtiques d'Europe, ils offrent dans la Péninsule Ibérique une plus grand abondance qu'ailleur. Au contraire, les toponymes en *-dunum*, qui caractérisent d'autres établissements celtiques, sont rares en Espagne (Verdú Verdun), et généralement ils sont le resultat de la pénétration plus ou moins tardive d'éléments gaulois.

On pense que la cause c'est qu'en Espagne les celtes n'ont pas reussi á dominer l'ensemble du territoire et ils ont été obligés de le partager avec des populations hostiles. Et en conséquence ils ont habité dans des lieux hauts et fortifiés *(briga)*, habitude profondément enracinée parmis les peuples indo-européens.

L'épigraphie celtique péninsulaire comprend plusieurs genres de documents: les monnaies, les stèles funéraires et les *tesserae hospitales* sont les plus caracteristiques. Mais au début des années '70 apparut un nouveau document d'importance capitale pour la connaissance du celtibérique: Le "Bronze de Botorrita", qui est véritablement un des plus importants textes en celtique continental.[4]

La langue celtibérique possède des traits essentiels de la celtité, comme la perte du /p/ initial et intervocalique, le développement d'une voyelle /i/ après le /r/ vocalique, le passage à sonores des anciennes sonores aspirées (ce dernier trait partagé avec plusieres autres langues indo-européennes). Mais il y a des aspects où le celtibérique diffère pas mal des autres langues cletiques.

Or, le celtiberique n'a, à mon avis, aucun vestige sûr de la lénition consonantique (malgré les affirmations entendues frécantment[5]). Les diphthongues n'ont pas été alterées[6]; la voyelle /e:/ non plus[7]; et la voyelle /o:/[8] seulement en partie. Il n'existe pas de double flexion verbale; les labiovelaires[9] sont conservées intactes; il a des postpositions au lieu de prépositions[10] (ce qui est un archaïsme remarquable, non seulement par rapport aux autres langues celtiques, mais aussi par rapport à la plus grande partie des langues indoeuropéennes): la désinence du génitif thématique n'est pas -i comme en vieux irlandais (ou en latin), mais en -o[11], probablement de l'ancien ablatif[12], comme en baltique et en slave[13].

Touts les traits differenciels de la langue celtibérique par rapport aux autres langues celtiques sont donc des archaïsmes, sauf le génitif en -o. Et en conséquence il faut se limiter à affirmer qu'il s'agit de la variété plus arcaïque du celte connue. Mais nous n'avons pas de critères pour l'attacher à aucune des branches dialectales traditionelles, gaélique ou britonnique.

Introduits dans la Péninsule Ibérique à travers les pas occidentaus des Pyrénées, selon on peut le déduir d'après leur emplacement historique, les celtes se sont établis au sud des hautes montagnes pyréneennes et ils ont resté isolés des celtes de la Gaule par l'intermédiare de populations pré-indo-européenes de nature basque-aquitanienne. Ainsi, ils sont devenus un "aire isolée", propice à la conservation des états lingüistiques archaïques.

B.-<u>La Langue des Lusitaniens</u>

Dans la Péninsule Ibérique, á coté de nombreux éléments linguistiques dont la celtité ne pourrait pas être mis en cause, il y en a d'autres munis de certains traits incompatibles avec ce que l'on prend normalement pour une langue celtique.

Entre les antroponimes nous avons *Plendius, Pisirus, Paramecus, Palarus, Paesica*. Parmi les etnonimes *Pelendones, Paesici, Praestamarci*. Et parmi les toponimes *Paramus, Bletisama, Poemana, Pallantia, Pisuerga*, etc.[14]

Tous ces noms ont comme trait commun qu'il conservent le phonème /p/, c'est pour cette raison qu'il n'est pas possible les considérer celtique sans plus. On trouve ces formes avec /p/ un peu partout dans l'Espagne Indo-Européenne. Mais évidemment la frequence est beaucoup moindre en Celtiberie et Carpetanie que dans les pays des *Vaccei, Vettones et Lusitani*, par exemple.

Malheureusement nous ne savons rien de la langue de la grande majorité des peuples de l'Espagne pré-romaine. Il n'y a aucune épigraphie des Astures, Cantabri, Callaici, Vettones, Vaccei, Carpetani, Pelendones, etc. Avant l'arrivée des romains, L'Espagne indo-européenne ne connaissait pas l'écriture, à une exception près: les celtibères qui l'avait emprunté des ibères du Levant, leurs voisins orientaux. Néanmoins, on possède quelques inscriptions provenant du territoire des lusitaniens, écrites en alphabet latin, qui correspondent à une époque tardive dans laquelle les procès de romanisation était déjà à moitié chemin.

Il s'agit des inscriptions rupestres, en général très breves, de nature votive. Une des mieux connues décrit une offrande a plusieurs divinités qui a l'air d'être un *suovetaurilia*[15].

Or, dans ces inscriptions on trouve quelques témoignages du /p/ conservé (*porcom, porgom, praisom, trebopala, toudopalandaigae*) et aucun du /p/ amuï à la façons celtique. En outre, il y a certains autres traits qui ne sont pas compatibles non plus avec la celtité, comme la copulative *indi* (en face de *kue, uta* en celtibérique), inconnue dans les langues celtiques et présent au contraire dans le germanique et l'indo-iranien. Et aussi le thème du present du verbe "donner", que l'on trouve dans la 3ᵐᵉ du pluriel sous la forme *doenti*.

Un des traits essentiels qui s'opposent au caractère celtique serait le passage des aspirées indo-européennes à fricatives sourdes, selon on pourrait déduire du mot *ifadem* "étalon" (dit d'un taureau). Mais malheureusement il n'existe que ce témoignage et son étymologie, quoique vraisemblable, n'est pas indiscutable. Mais, si on veut se faire une idée exact de la valuer de ce critère, il faut ajouter que le traitement contraire des aspirées (en sonores) n'est pas assuré non plus, puisque il n'en existe aussi qu'un seul exemple (*angom*), dont l'étymologie en partant de la racine **angh-* "étroit" doit à mon avis être rejetée par des raisons sémantiques et morphologiques[16].

A côté de ces arguments contraires, il en existent d'autres favorables au caractère celtique de la langue des lusitaniens. Nous avons d'un coté la distribution uniforme de la toponymie en *-briga*, qui ne se trouve pas seulement dans la Celtibérie, mais qui s'etend dans toute l'Espagne indo-européenne, y compris la Lusitanie[17]. En outre, l'uniformité de l'anthroponymie indoeuropéenne péninsulaire, un argument dont la valeur á été récemment quelque peu amoindrie par Gorrochategui[18] qui vient de souligner que malgré certains éléments communs à la Lusitanie et la celtibérie, il y en a d'autres différentiels. Et, finalement, la présence dans les inscriptions lusitaniennes de certains traits compatibles avec la celtité comme le nominatif de pluriel thématique en *-oi*[19] et, surtout, une certaine quantité de vocabulaire celtique.

La présence généralisée de la toponymie en *-briga* et l'uniformité de l'anthroponymie indoeuropéenne signifient, selon Untermann, qu'il n'a existé qu'une invasion indo-européenne dans la Péninsule Ibérique: celle des celtes. Comme nous avons déja vu, le celte péninsulaire est tres archaïque. Et Untermann arrive à la conclusion que la conservation du /p/ ne serait qu'un nouveau archaïsme du dialecte celtique qui est rentré en Espagne.

Je ne pourrais pas examiner ici en détail tous les arguments pour et contre la celtité de la langue des lusitaniens, ce qu'ont fait recemment Schmidt et Gorrochategui d'un coté et Untermann de l'autre[20]. Je vais me borner à une valoration d'ensemble.

Une grande majorité des traits celtiques présents dans les inscriptions lusitaniennes appartient au domaine du lexique (y compris l'anthroponymie et l'élément toponymique *-briga*). Or, comme on le sait très bien, on pourrait expliquer ces coincidences lexiques comme le resultat du contact entre deux langues indo-européennes qui ont vécu ensemble pendant des siècles à l'interieur de la Péninsule Ibérique.

En dehors du lexique, on trouve un argument morphologique dans le nominatif pluriel en *-oi* dans le substantif thématique. Mais ceci est loin d'être une preuve incontestable, puisqu'on trouve cette désinence dans la flexion nominal de plusieures autres langues, comme le baltique, le slave, le grec ou le latin). Et par contre, elle ne se trouve pas en celtibérique qui, une fois encore, conserve comme archaisme la désinence *-os*.

Dans le domaine de la phonétique on n'a que le resultat incertain des aspirées. Très peu pour considérer celtique cette langue[21].

Mais, de leur côté, presque tous les traits contraires à la celtité pourraient aussi être rejetés comme de possibles emprunts, fausses étymologies, etc. si on les envisageséparément. Mais si on les considere ensemble il parait peu raisonnable dénier la valeur de tous et penser que le hasard a réuni dans un ensemble de textes si limité autant de faux indices contre la celtité de la langue des lusitaniens.

Et en plus, il reste le problème du /p/. Si le celte de la Péninsule Ibérique est dépourvu de presque tous les traits qui ordinairement servent à caractériser les langues celtiques et a leur place il a les respectifs archaïsmes serait-il permis d'imaginer qu'il conserve aussi le /p/ comme un archaïsme et que, en conséquence, seulement une partie des envahisseurs celtiques l'ont perdu après s'être installé en Espagne? Et, en cas affirmatif, qu'est ce qui nous reste encore comme constitutif du celtisme linguistique? En poussant la question à l'extrême: quel raison aurait-on pour appeler une langue "celte" quand elle n'a pas encore acquis un seul trait de ceux qui carcatérisent ce type de langue indo-européenne?

Si la langue des lusitaniens est dépourvue de tous les traits essentiels de la celtité, quel argument pourrait-on avancer pour assurer que, malgré tout, ils sont des celtes? Aucun de nature linguistique qu'on puisse considérer solide, comme nous venons de constater. Peut-être, ce que veulent dire ces savants qui croient à la celtité du lusitanien c'est qu'il dérive de la même tradition linguistique qui, en developpant ses traits historiques, est devenue ailleurs le celtique. Mais une telle croyance tombe en dehors des possibilités de controle d'un linguiste, qui doit se borner à constater que la variété de l'indo-européen parlée par les lusitaniens, malgré le vocabulaire celtique qu'elle partage, ne se laisse pas classifier comme ce qu'on entend ordinairement par une langue celtique.

Or, si le lusitanien n'est pas celtique, il faut definir a quelle modalite de l'indo-européen il appartient. En laissant de coté l'opinion de quelques savants du passé (Abois de Juvainville, Jullian) qui la considéraient ligur, Tovar a pensé à un certain moment que c'était *Alteuropäisch*[22]. Schmoll a été le premier à supposer qu'il s'agissait d'une nouvelle branche de la famille indo-europénne qu'il a appelé *Galläkisch*[23]. À présent ceele-ci est l'oppinion generale parmis ceux qui ne la considèrent pas celtique, mais c'est le nom "lusitanien" tout court qui s'est imposé[24].

Et quelle est la position dialectal du lusitanien dans l'ensemble des langues indo-européennes? Il semble évidnet qu'il s'agit d'un dialecte occidental ou peut-être *sudoccidental*. Mais il n'est pas facile pour le moment de préciser d'avantage. Par exemple l'aproximation au grec proposée par K.H. Schmidt[25] parait peu fondé en attachant trop de valeur au prétendu résultat /o/ de la laryngale dans la troisième pluriel *doenti*.

C. - <u>Le Alteuropäisch</u>

Nous avons donc examiné deux dialectes indoeuropéens: 1)Celui avec voyelles /o/ et /a/ différenciées et /p/ amuï (c'est à dire, le celte), et 2)Celui avec voyelles /a/ et /o/ différenciées et /p/ conservé (c'est à dire, le lusitanien).

Or, il y a vraisemblablement un troisièmè dans lequel le /p/ est conservè mais les voyelles /a/ et /o/ sont confondues en /a/. De cette troisième langue indoeuropéenne il ne subsistent que des toponymes, surtout des hydronymes, qui sont pourvus des mêmes traits phonétiques et morphologiques que ceux qui ont mené Krahe à sa théorie de l'Alteuropâisch[26].

L'étude de cette espèce d'hydronymie péninsulaire a été faite par de Hoz. Les racines plus fréquemment utilisées sont *ab-, *ad-, *alm-, *ar-, *arg-, *kar-, *nar-, *sal- et *sar-, toutes présentes comme appellatifs dans l'une ou l'autre des langues indo-européennes, avec la signification "fleuve", "fontaine", "eau" et d'autres notions pareilles.

Les vides qu'on trouve dans la catre ne doivent pas être pris trop rigoureusement, puisqu'ils pourraient être dus à une documentation insuffisante d'où puiser l'information plutôt qu'à une manque réelle de cette hydronymie. Tout de même, l'absence absolue dans le coin sudoccidental ne saurait être le fruit du hasard. Vraisemblablement, les populations centre-europeennes responsables de cette hydronymie sont entrées du nord vers le sud, de même que leurs successeurs plus recents, les celtes, et n'ont jamais atteint ces regions lointaines, trop écartées ou mieux défendues.

L'identification de ces éléments indo-européens dans l'hydronymie péninsulaire et la reconnaissance de leur antiquité n'implique pas l'acceptation des idées de Krahe sur l'Alteuropäisch. A mon avis, le *Aleuropäisch* ne doit pas être compris comme la langue commune de laquelle dérivent les langues indo-européennes occidentales, comme voulait Krahe. Et encore moins toutes les langues indo-européennes, selon préfère W.P. Schmid[28]. Vraisemblablemente cette hydronymie doit être consideré plutôt comme la preuve de la présence d'une strate indoeuropéenne dans la Péninsule Ibérique (et dans toute l'Europe occidentale) à une date anterieure à l'arrivée d'une autre strate plus récente d'où derivent les peuples indoeuropéens historiques de l'Europe (celte, germanique, lusitanien, etc.) Le trait phonétique de l'indistinction de /a/ et /o/ est vraisemblablement un archaïsme, au contraire de ce qu'on pense ordinairement, comme j'ai essayé de montrer ailleurs[29]. Et cela est en harmonie avec la plus haute antiquité de cette hydronymie dans toute l'Europe.

Il existe, paraît-il, certaines données archéologiques qui pourraient renforcer l'idée d'une pénétration indo-européenne dans l'Espagne long temps avant l'arrivée des celtes. Dans le gisement de "La Hoya", près de Vitoria, on a trouvé des matériaux typiquement centre-européens, parmis lesquel ils ne manquent pas des signes solaires comme la *svastika*, dans une strate datee comme appartenant au XVème siècle a.C. Ces groupes, arrivés de l'autre coté des Pyrénées, sont entrés en contact avec les communautés des cultures mégalitiques du cercle du Vase Campaniforme qui existaient déjà dans ce territoire. Et il y a des preuves d'échanges culturels entre les deux groupes.

Dans d'autres niveaux plus récents du même gisement, qui correspondent au XIIIème siècle a. C. on décele de nouvelles entrées de gens de l'Europe centrale qui amènent avec eux de nouveaux types de construction. Je ne peux pas apporter plus des détails sur ces trouvailles archéologiques parce que les resultats de la fouille, dirigé au présent par Armando LLanos, n'a pas encore été publiée et il n'en existe qu'un bref resumé[30].

En somme, nous avons été capable d'établir trois strates indo-européennes dans la Péninsule Ibérique, qui peuvent être distinguées par de critéres linguistiques. Mais il serait une simplification supposer que seulement dans trois occasions des éléments indo-européens sont rentrés dans l'Espagne.

César (BC I.51) raconte que quand il était en Espagne, près d'Ilerda, un groupe de chevaliers gaulois est arrivé près de son armée. Ils étaient 6.000 guerriers qui menaient avec eux leurs esclaves, femmes et enfants. Peut- être 20.000 personnes dans l'ensemble. Sans doute ils cherchaient des terres pour s'y installer.

Des faits pareils ont dû avoir lieu d'innombrables fois, sans que le hasard les ai tmises à la portée d'un historien qui ait pu nous en prêter son témoignage. Comme Garcia y Bellido a dit[31], il ne faut pas s'imaginer autrement le procès d'indoeuropéenisation de la Péninsule Ibérique (et pourrait-on ajouter: peut-être aussi de toute l'Europe).

Nous pouvons déduire, donc, que pendant 1500 années au moins une lente pénétration d'éléments indo-européens a eu lieu en Espagne qui a changé petit à petit sa composition linguistique. La populaiton n'a pas dû être trop nombreuse et ainsi les indo-européens et les pre-indo européens on pu partager le territoire dans de petites communautes imbriquées entretenants des rélation qui on du arriver fréquemment jusqu'au bilinguisme.

Avec le temps, les éléments indo-européens se sont imposés dans le nord et l'ouest, là où peut-être ils ont trouvé la moindre résistance, Dans l'est et le sud ils ont dû trouver dès le début de plus grandes difficultés, vraisemblablement parcequ'ils se sont heurtés à des cultures supérieures (le Argar, Tartessos). Et là les élements pre-indo-européens ont pu subsister jusqu'à l'arrivée des romains.

+++++++++++++++++++++

II.- L'HISPANIA NON-INDO-EUROPÉENNE
A.- Les Ibères

Sans doute l'élément le plus caractéristique de l'Espagne pré-romaine c'est le peuple ibérique, avec sa langue hermétique, son système d'écriture particulier et son art dont le caractère original ou imité du grecque on discute encore.

1) La Toponimie

La Péninsule Ibérique apparait divisée par une ligne, tirée il y a quelque temp par Untermann[32], qui délimite une région sud-occidental où dominent les toponymes en *Il- (Iltir-, Iltu-, Ili-)* et une autre nord-occidentale avec des toponymes en *briga*.

Comme on le voit sur la carte I, cette ligne ne coïncide pas avec celle qui separe l'Espagne indo-européenne de l'Espage non-indo-européenne. Les formes en -*briga* surpassent la division et pénètrent dans le coin sud-occidental du territoire non-indo-européen.

La toponymie en *Il-* est celle qui caractérise le domaine ibérique, mais elle surpasse de son côté les Pyrénées et s'étend vers le sud de la France jusqu'à la ville d'Enserune.

Malgré notre méconaissance de la langue ibérique, il ne parait pas hasardeux si l'on suppose que l'élément toponymique *Il-* est la racine ou une des racines ibériques pour exprimer la notion de "ville" ou quelque achose pareille.

2) L'écriture

L'Espagne pré-romaine disposait de son propre système d'écriture, d'inspiration vraisemblablement phénicienne[33], dont l'existence a été connue dès le Moyen Âge, au fur et à mesure qu'on a rencontré des monnaies frappées dans l'antiquité.

Sa lecture ne fût, malgré tout, possible jusqu'aux années '20 de notre siécle, quand Gómez Moreno[34] a réussi à la déchiffrer. Il s'agit d'un système mixte, moitié syllabaire et moitié alphabétique, qui avait derouté les savants pendant des siécles.

Tout en restant le même pour l'essentiel, ce système a des variantes locales, pas toutes complètement déchiffrees. La mieux connue est celle du Levant. Et celle qui nous offre le plus de problèmes est celle des inscriptions tartessiques. L'aire d'utilisation de chaq'une des ces variétés peut être examinée sur la carte.

Ce système d'écriture est foncièrement celui des peuples non-indoeuropéens, l'Espagne indo-européenne etant analphabétique. Mais dans le bassin moyen de l'Ebre, dans la région où était établie la frontière entre les Ibères et les Celtibères, les celtes ont enprunté ce sustème, comme nous avons déjà vu.

L'épigraphie en langue ibère dont nous avons connaissance est géneralment dans ce système. Mais il y a un groupe de documents en alphabet grecque, ce qui a facilité énormément le déchiffrement de l'écriture locale.

3) La Langue

Nous avons trois espèces de documents plus fréquents dans la langue des Ibéres: des monnaies, des inscriptions funéraires et des *plombs*[35]. Ces derniers sont les textes les plus longs; mais nous ignorons toujours quelle est leur nature et teneur.

Malgré le fait que soixante ans se sont déjà écoulés depuis le déchiffrement de l'écriture, la langue des Ibères défie encore les efforts qu'on fait pour arriver à la comprendre. D'elle nous ne savons presque rien avec certitude. Et le peu que nous savons appartient au domaine de la phonétique.

La langue ibère avait 5 voyelles (a/e/i/o/u); un système de 5 consonnes occlusives (-/b, t/d, k/g) où il manque le /p/; 3 nasales (m/n et une troisième dont la nature est inconnue; deux vibrantes; deux laterales; et deux sifflantes[36]. Les vibrantes, comme il arrive dans pas mal de langues, ne peuvent pas être le phonème initial de mot.

La structure syllabique est soumise à de différentes restrictions. La voyelle ne peut être précédée que par une seule consonne. Il n'existe même pas le groupe *muta cum liquida*. Par contre, elle peut être suivie d'un nombre indéterminé de consonnes, à l'unique condition qu'elles suivent un ordre d'ouverture descendante (U+R+S+T). Les phonèmes /y/ et /w/ consonantiques sont rares ou peut-être inexistants au début de syllabe.

Une structure syllabique semblable a été imaginée par Michelena pour la prehistoire de la langue basque[37]. Et nous verrons dans ce qui suit que des ressemblances pareilles entre le basque et l'ibérique ne font pas défaut. Plus tard j'essayerai d'en faire une valoration d'ensemble.

Après certains thèmes on trouve en ibère une alternance des éléments -n/-r/-o, mais on ne sait même pas s'il sagit d'un fait phonétique ou morphologique. Je laisse de coté l'étrange ressemblance avec l'hétéroclise indo-européenne, et souligne par contre que dans cette occasion aussi on trouve dans le basque un fait semblable, remarqué par Tovar[38]: *egu-n* "jours" (avec /n/) / *egur-aldi* "temps atmosfphérique (avec /r/) / *egu-berri* "Jour nouveau" (dit de Noël) (avec O).

Beaucoup moins et beaucoup moins sûr est ce que nous savons sur la morphologie et la syntaxe. Je vais faire mention de quelques hypothèses.

A. Tovar et L. Michelena[39] ont vu, avec des différences dans le détail, que le suffixe *-en* servait à exprimer la relation déterminant-déterminé entre deux noms, avec un ordre GN: *Iltibirkis-en seltar* serait probablement "la tombe d'Iltibirgis". Une fois encore, on trouve un parallèle dans le basque, où il existe un suffixe possessif *-en*.

Mais l'ibère aurait aussi, selon Michelena[40], un autre moyen pour exprimer la même fonction: la juxtaposition de deux noms sans aucun morphème dans l'ordre déterminant-déterminé: *kalun seltar* " la tombe de Calun". Si bien cette possibilité de juxtaposition n'existe pas dans le basque contemporain, c'est encore Michelena qui l'a reconstruit pour la prehistoire du basque[41].

Dans les monnaies on a des formes avec une espèce de désinence *-(s)cen*, qui sont le parallèle des génitifs pluriels latins ROMANOM, grecs EMPORITOM, celtibérique KONTEBAKOM, etc. Tout naturellement, il y a pas mal de savants qui se sentent attirés à voir dans cette désinence le morphème de génitif pluriel. Et une fois encore cela rappelle la désinence basque de génitive pluriel *-en* dont l'accentuation exige une contraction préhistorique de la voyelle à partir d'une possible forme *-*agen*[42].

Dans les monnaies ibériques, la désinence *-(s)cen* alterne dans la même fonction avec *-(e)tar*, qui trouve aussi un parallèle basque dans le suffixe *-(t)ar* qui sert à former des noms éthniques comme vizcaitarra, etc.

De Hoz[43] a suggéré l'existence en Ibère d'un morphème *-ka* avec la valeur d'ablatif et/ou datif d'intérêt. Et dans un travail récent Untermann[44] a proposé l'identification de plusieurs morphèmes: *-ka* serait un ergatif; *-te* un datif; *-ar* un possesif; etc. Même si ces morphèmes et leur fonction sont purement hypothétiques, comme Untermann a lui même signalé[45], il faut rappeler qu'encore une fois il existe un parallèle en basque dont le morphème d'ergatif est, comme tout le monde le sait, *-k*.

Dans le domaine du lexique, si on laisse de côté le mot voyageur pour désigner l'argent, que nous trouvans en ibère sous la forme *salir*[46], nous ne savons pratiquement rien sur le vocabulaire ibérique. Dans une inscription funéraire on trouve *are tace*, suivi de la formule latine HEIC EST. Mais on ne peut pas être sûr si les mots latins sont la traduction des mots ibères.

Pour se faire une idée du dégré d'incertitude de nos démarches, il suffira si je cite le cas du mot *eban(en)*, présent dans des inscription funéraires. Pour Tovar elle signifie "Pierre, tombeau". Pour Michelena c'est le nom pour "fils". Et finalement pour Untermann ce serait un verbe qu'il faudrait traduire par "curauit".

B.- LE BASQUE

En tant que langue qui a réussi a survivre après l'indo-européensiation en général et apres la romanisation en particulier, le basque est une langue parfaitement connu, ce qui m'épargnera de longues explications sur sa structure. Je vais me limiter à quelques remarques sur sa situation dans l'époque pré-romaine.

Le nom avec lequel nous connaissons au present ce peuple et sa langue est l'héritier de celui d'une de ses anciennes tribus, les Vascones, qui occupait les alentours de Pampelune, la capitale de la Navarre.

Les basques eux mêmes ils appellent leur langue "Euskara" et leur pays "Eskalherria", mot natifs que je vais employer désormais pour nommer l'ensemble de tribus qui parlaent cette langue dans l'antiquité.

Selon Tovar[47], à l'interieur de la Péninsule Ibérique, outre les Vascones, il y avait d'autres groupes qui parlaient aussi euskara, comme les Autrigones, Caristii et Varduli vers l'ouest jusqu'au Nervion et la ville de Bilboa; et peut-être les Airenosii et les Andorsini vers l'est. Et de l'autre côté des Pyrénées, il faut tenir pour démontré, d'apres les travaux de Michelena[48] et Gorrochategui[49], que la langue des Aquitains était aussi Euskara. Quand même, il y en a d'autres (comme de Hoz) pour qui dans le territoire des Varduli, Caristii et Autrigones il n'y a qu'une chose de sûre: que là dedans on parlait une langue indo-européenne (sans qu'on puisse déterminer quel dialecte). Et on ne saurait pas assurer si cette langue indo-européenne a partagé le territoire avec des populations pré-indo-européennes, euskariennes ou autres.

Sans doute, l'Euskara est la langue d'un peuple essentiellement pyrénéen, qui s'étend sur l'un et l'autre versant de la chaîne. D'après tous les indices il a dû occuper ce territoire au moins à partir du néolithique. Et là il s'est vu pressé par plusieurs peuples envahisseurs dès le premier instant où nous trouvons des traces dans la Proto-Histoire.

Peut-être un des traits qui caractérisent le plus la langue euskarienne c'est exactement celui-la. Toujours, à partir des premiers moments connus ou entrevus, elle a été une langue pressée et une langue en retraite en face d'autres langues de culture et organization sociale supérieures. Mais elle a réuissi à survivre malgré tout, même si elle a dû payer comme prix une profonde pénétration dans sa substance des langues qui ont agicomme adstrate et superstrate.

<u>Les relations entre le basque et l'ibère</u>

La thèse la plus étendue encore aujourd'hui parmi les savants non spécialistes est peut-être celle du Basco-Ibérisme qui consiste à supposer que dans l'Espagne pré-romaine (peut-être aujourd'hui faudrait-il dire "indo-européenne") il n'existait qu'une langue, l'Ibère, dont le Basque contemporain n'est que la survivance.

Cette croyance existait déjù parmi les savants espagnols depuis le Moyen Âge. Et elle s'est perpétuée, considerée un fait acquis mais restreine à l'ambiance espagnole, jusqu'au XIX s., quand elle a recu credit international grace au prestige de von Humboldt qui lui avait prêté son approbation. Comme ca la thèse du Basco-Iberisme s'est répandu dansr toute l'Europe.

Les preuves qui ont convaincu von Humboldt n'étaient ni trop nombreuses ni trop solides, quoiqu'elles étaient bien attrayantes. Le savant allemand a été frappé par l'identité de *Iriberri* "Ville neuve" (basque)/*Iliberri(ibere)*, et il en tira son principal argument.

Nous pourrions ajouter que parmi l'onomastique euskarienne et l'onomastique ibère il y a de nombreux parallèles. Dans l'une et l'autre langue les anthroponymes sont bâtis sous la forme de composés de deux éléments qui peuvent être mélangés de plusieures facons, comme il arrive aussi dans l'onomastique indo-européenne. Mais les paralleles ne se limitent pas au procédé abstrait de la composition. En plus, ils s'entandent aussi aux éléments concrets qui rentrent en composition. Ces éléments se retrouvent dans l'onomastique ibère, dans l'onomastique aquitaine et parois ils sont aussi présents dans l'euskara comme des appellatifs:ib *beles*, aquitain *Belex* eusk. *beltz* "noir"[51].

En outre, il convient de se rappeler que la lecture en haute voix d'un texte ibérique produit l'impression qu'il sagit d'un texte euskarien.

Mais, malgré tout, les spécialistes les plus qualifiés, ceux qui s'y connaissent le mieux à la fois en euskarien et en ibérique, sont généralement sceptiques par rapport à tout degré de relation génétique entre les deux langues. Et ils ont pas mal de raisons.

Tout d'abord, l'euskarien n'aide pas á comprendre un seul mot des textes ibérique. Il semble que si le basque était la forme moderne de l'ibère il pourrait aider au moins dans une modeste mesure. Il faut rappeler que ce sont presque mil mots ibériques que nous possédons déjà et, en laissant de côté l'onomasstique, il n'y a aucun qui puisse être interpretée par le basque. Le basque n'a même pas servi á identifier les pronoms personnels, les termes qui expriment les rélation de famille, les numeraux ni, en général, le vocabulaire plus stable des langues.

Le système verbal du basque ne trouve aucun reflet en ibérique. Et le nominal non plus, si l'on exclu quelques faits plutot isolés et hautement hypothétiques, déjà mentionnés.

Ces drôles de relations entre le Basque et l'Ibère nous paraissent plutôt déroutantes. Car elles sont trop limitées pour en déduire une relation génétique, mais trop nombreuses pour ne pas mériter une explcation. Là dessu Michelena a dit[52]:

> Et c'est ici, dans ce sous-ensemble di-sons onomastique, que l'on a trouvé la plupart des coincidences entre ibère et basque. Il y a, cela ne fait pas de doute, des accords, dont le nombre est trop élevé pour qu'on puisse les attribuer aux seuls jeux du hasard..."(1979, p.37). "Mais en faisant sa part au hasard, les coincidences sont remar-quables en nobre et en qualite. On hesitera donc a y voir des empruts massifs".

Sans prendre une position plus nette, Michelena a suggéré l'explication qui suit pour les coincidences onomastiques entre le Basque et l'Ibère, qui à son avis sont les plus importantes, selon on peut déduire de ses mots:

> "On dirait donc qu'ibère et euskarien avaient formé une espèce de pool onomastique, qu'ils possédaient un stock un grande partie commun d'éléments et de procédés de formation, dans lequel ils puisaient avec une grande liberté. Il n'est pas dit pour autant que ces éléments devaient être homogènes quant à l'origine".

S'il s'agit, comme actuelement pensent la plupart des savants, d'une relation de langues en contracte, il n'est pas hardi si on pense que la plupart des traits communs entre le basque et l'ibère ont dû passer de l'ibère au basque plutôt que dans le sens contraire, car l'ibère était la langue d'une culture supérieure, qui avait un système d'éciture et qui avait des rapports avec les grandes civilisations méditerranéennes[53].

Relations entre le basque et les langues indo-européennes péninsulaires

La mesure de la pression exercée des l'antiquité par les langues indo-européennes sur le basque trouve son reflet dans le fait, anecdotique si l'on veut, que le premier temoignage écrit du nom des VASCONES apparaît sur des monnaies, vraisemblablement de l'atelier monnaitaire de Pampelune, dans lesquelles on peut lire BASCUNES, avec un nominatif pluriel indo-européen, plus exactement celtibérique, puisque Pamelune était limitrophe entre les territoires celtibères et euskariens. Tout de même, il faut remarquer que selon Untermann[54] sur ces monnaies, dont il existe une variante BARSCUNES, on aurait le nom d'une ville celtibérique, dont l'evidente ressemblance avec le nom des VASCONES serait purement fortuite.

L'indoeuropéanisation du vocabulaire basque est profonde, à partir surtout du latin et des langues romanes. Mais il existe sans doute une couche anterieure de type celtique, pas toujours facile a séparer[55]. Michelena soulignait qu'un mot comme *errege* "roi" pourrait être un emprunt au celte aussi bien qu'au latin, puisque dans le celte péninsulaire la /e:/ n'a pas été fermée en /i:/.

Le basque, outre l'indo-européanisation de son vocabulaire, partage avec d'autres langues de la region plusieurs traits dont l'origine n'est pas facile à établir. Il a le même système vocalique (a/e/i/o/u) que l'espagnol, l'ibère et quelques dialectes gascons. Il a deux vibrantes, comme l'espagnol et l'ibère, différenciées par le nombre des vibrations. Et, de même que l'espagnol, il a deux réalisations différentes pour les occlusives sonores: occlusives au début de mot/fricatives entre voyelles.

C.- LA RÉGION MERIDIONALE

Dans le sud de la Péninsule Ibérique, dans ce qui est aujourd'hui la moitié occidentale de l'Andalousie et le sud du Portugal, on trouve une toponymie non indo-euoropéenne, mais différente de la toponymie ibérique déjà examinée.

Deux racines sont caractéristiques de cette toponymie: 1) *ip-/-i(p)po* et 2)*obu-/-uba*. L'une et l'autre peuvent apparaître, avec de petites modifications, comme premier et comme second élément des composés toponymiques.

Pour le premier, nous avons *Ollispo, Colipo, Baesippo, Ventipo, Orippo, Iptuci*. Normalement on établit un rapport avec des toponymes du nord de l'Afrique comme *Hippo Regius, Hippo Diarrhytus*.

Pour le second nous trouvons *Oba, Obulco, Corduba, Onoba, Ossonoba, Salduba*. Et il n'existe, dans la mésure de ma connaissance, aucun parallele en dehors de l'Espagne.

D'ordinaire on considère que les deux genres de toponymes appartiennent à une même couche de population, quoique il n'en existe aucune preuve. On a, c'est vrai, un exemple où les deux apparaissent unis: *Iponuba*. Mais ca ne prouve rien, parcequ' on a pas mal de toponymes d'hybridation évdente, comme *Augustrobriga, Juliobriga*. D'autre coté, même si les deux éléments se recouvre en partie, ils n'ont pas une distribution tout à fait uniforme, puisque -*i(p)po* surpasse la zone commune et penètre assez au nord de Portugal avec *Olisippo* et surtout *Collipo*.

Mais ce ne sont pas les seuls éléments toponymique de l'Andalousie. Dans la region suroccidentale on trouve aussi *Bae-* dans des noms comme *Baelo, Baetis* (le fleuve), qui réapparaît ailleurs dans la Péninsule, et qui parfois se trouve associé à un des autres éléments précités, comme *Baesippo*.

Un type d'anthroponymie pré-indo-européenne, exclusif de cette région péninsulaire, coincide *grosso modo* avec l'aire de diffusion de la toponymie méridionale.

Ce sont des noms formés avec la racine *Sis-*, toumours préfixée: *Sisiren, Siseanba, Sisen, Siseia*, etc.[56]

Il est naturel si l'on associe ce type d'antroponymes avec les toponymes en -*i(p)po* et -*uba*, puisqu'ils partagent le même territoire. Et puisqu'ils ne sont pas ni indo-européens ni ibériques, on pense à un troisieme peuple qui aurait occupe vraisemblablement l'Andalousie occidentale avant d'etre envahie par des iberes a l'est (avec des toponymes comme *Ilipa, Ilipula*) et par des celtes au nord-ouest (avec des toponymes comme *Nertobriga, Ebora*).

Enfin, dans le coin suboccidental de cette région on trouve pas mal de documents, inscrits dans la moins claire des varietés d'écriture ibérique et rédigés dans une langue différente de l'ibère.

Le plus grand nombre de ces textes appartiennent au sud du Portugal. Mais on en a quelques-uns en Andalousie occidentale et même en Estrémadure.

Il faut y ajouter les monnaies trouvées à *Salacia*, petite ville du Portugal, à moitié chemin entre les fleuves Guadiana et Tajo. Elles sont inscrites dans la même variété d'alphabet, mais rien peut nous assurer pour le moment que dans ce système d'écriture il n'y ait qu'une seule langue.

Sauf les monnaies de Salacia, toute cette épigraphie est funeraire[57]. L'écriture prend la forme concentrique et elle manque de procedés pour séparer les mots. C'est pourquoi, le premier problème consiste à diviser les textes en unitées successives. Le second dérive de la méconnaissance de certains signes. Et le troisième c'est d'établir la date de ces textes, quoique aujourd'hui il paraît qu'il s'est imposée l'opinion qui attribue cette épigraphie aux siecles VII et VI a.C.[58].

Tout le monde sait qu'à cet endroit et a cette époque florissait le royaume de Tartessos. Et c'est pour cela que quelques savants croient que ces inscriptions funéraires mettent dans nos mains la langue de ce mythique royaume. Autres, au contraire, prefèrent la prudence d'appeler tout ce material tout simplement "épigraphie sudoccidentale", ou quelque chose comme ca.

De Hoz (communication personnelle) croit que l'épigraphie du sud de Portugal pourrait mêttre à notre portée la langue des *Conii*, tandis que les inscriptions dans le même alphabet trouvées en Andalousie pourraient être rédigées dans la langue de Tartessos. Salacia, de sa part, serait une colonie tartessienne et ses monnaies devraient etre mises en raport avec les inscriptions et la langue de l'Andalousie. En fait, il ne pourrait être le fruit du hasard que l'anthroponymie en *Sis-* soit présente aussi à *Salacia*. Probablement ce'st un indice en faveur de l'association de cette onomastique en Sis- et la langue des inscriptions de l'Andalouisie.

De tout ce qui precède se dégage le fait que les inscriptions tartessiennes restent indéchiffrable. Mais, malgré tout, quelques savants croient pouvoir isoler certains éléments qui constituent la formule funéraire et ont proposé pour eux une traduction.

En fair, la formule *bare nabe keenti* se repete dans un bon nombre d'occasions, si bien le troisième mot offre quelques variantes, comme *keeni*. Wikander[59] croyait avoir trouvé un parallèle dans des inscriptions funéraires liciennes, dans lesquelles on lit *sijeni* "situs est". Il s'agit de la racine **kei-* "être couché", "gésir" (cf.gr. *keimai*, ai.*sate*) avec le même suffixe que les verbes hittites du type *ijannai*. Quant aux varianges *keeni/keenti*, il croit y découvrir la différence singulier/pluriel, selon la conjugaison hittite en -*hi*.

Il parait que les idées de Wikander sont partagées par Correa[60]. Et ce ne serait pas tout. Il faudrait y ajouter au moins un autre troit indo-européen: *nabe* serait un locatif avec la désinence -*bhi*. Ainsi, on devrait traduire la formule funéraire complète comme: "Il gît dans ce tombeau". Enfin, il serait aussi possible d'identifier une désinence de génitif -*el*, qui nous amène de nouveau aux langues antoliennes.

Si Wikander et Correa avaient raison, lalangue de Tartessos serait une langue indo-européenne de type anatolien. Et on aurait encore une fois une civilisation méditerranéenne, traditionnellement considérée pre-indoeuropéenne, comme il est arrivé auparavant avec le hittite et le micenien.

On soupconnait d'avance une certaine relation entre Tartessos et quelques éléments indo-européens, soi-disant celtes, d'après le nom du plus fameux des rois tartessiens.

Même si on laisse de coté tout ce qu'il puisse y avoir de symbolique de la part des historiens grecs pour appeler "Argantonios" le roi du pays mythique de l'argent, et on accepte qu'en fait le nom de ce roi aurait été vraiment indo-européennes, ca nous permetraitt tout au plus de supposer qu'il se serait produit une certaine pénétration indo-européenne dans le royaume de Tartessos qui aurait peut-être constitué une espèce d'aristocratie dominatrice, comme il s'est passé dans d'autres endroits.

Si les hypothèses de Wikander et Correa s'avérait exactes, et les inscriptions tartessiennes sont en fait rédigées dans une langue indo-européenne, il ne serait pas nécessaire de trop changer des idées précédentes. Il n'est que naturel que cette soi-disant aristocratie guerrière aurait utilisé sa langue pour ses habitudes funéraires, même si les couches plus anciennes de la population n'avaient jamais appris la langue de la couche dominate. Et ce serait à cette population pré-indo-eurpéenne qu'appartiendrait la toponymie qui caracterise la région.

Rien de tout cela est invraisemblable. Et d'autre côté, la possible origine anatolienne reste en parfait accord avec la chronologie du commencement du royaume Tartessos et la chute de l'empire hittite et l'exode subséquent.

Mais tout ce tableau, qui semble peut-être attractif et cohérent, a un gros côté faible: le caractere pour le moment spéculatif de l'interprétation de la formule funéraire et le petite nombre d'éléments sur lesquels l'hypotèse a été étayée.

NOTES

(1) Interprétation dèjá présente dans la tradition greco-latine, cf.Apianos *Iberia* 2; Diodoros S. V, 33. Parmi les savants modernes, l'idée a été très repandue après J. K. Zeuss 1837, p. 162 ss.

(2) Certains auteurs classiques parlent de l'origine celtibérique des *Celtici* de l'Andalousie (Plinius III, 13). Et l'archéologie la confirme (cf. W. Schüle 1969, I, p. 74 ss.). Estrabon III, 3-5 assure que les *celtici* du nord-ouest sont aussi proches parents de ceux du sud. Sur cet ensemble de problèmes cf. A. Garcia y Bellido 1953, pp. 60-66.

(3) *Ardobrica* et *Abobriga* dans la Galicie; *Nemetobriga* et *Tuatobriga* dans León' *Lacobriga* dans le nord de Palencia; *Flaviobriga* près de Bilbao; *Amallobriga* dans le Duero moyen; *Mirobriga* à l'ouest de Salamanque; *Caesarobriga*, *Augustobriga* et *Alpuebrega* dans le Tajo moyen; *Segobriga* dans la province de Cuenca; *Arcobriga*, c'est l'acutel Arcos de Jalón; *Mirobriga* et *Nertobriga* près d'Almadén; *Segobriga*, c'est l'acutel Segorbe, dans la province de Palencia; *Langobriga* et *Talabriga* dans la region de l'Aveiro; *Conimbriga*, l'acutel Coimbra; *Volobriga* et *Caeliobriga dans l'ouest* du Portugal: *Arabriga* et *Caetobriga* dans la region de Lisbonne; *Merobriga* dans le sud du Portugal; *Lacobriga*, l'actuel Lagos, dans l'Algarve, etc.

(4) I) MONNAIES: 1) *konteŕbia*; 2) *śekotias lakas*; 3) *konbouto*; 4) *kontebakom*; 5) *baśkunes*.

II) INSCRIPTIONS FUNÉRAIRES; *tiŕtanoś letontunoś ke belikioś*.

III) TESSERAE HOSPITALES: 1) Tessera de Paris: *luboś aliśokum aualo ke kontebiaś belaiśkaś*; 2) Tessera de Luzaga: *aŕekoratikuboś kaŕuo kenei / koŕtika lutiakei aukiś baŕasioka / eŕna uela tikeŕseboś śo / ueisui belaikumkue / keniś karikokue keniś / śtam koŕtikam elasunom / kaŕuo tekes śa koŕtica / teiuoŕeikiś*.

IV) BRONZE DE BOTORRITA (edición de J. de Hoz 1981, p. 298):

Face A

378 When Worlds Collide

1. tiŕikantam: beŕkunetakam: tokoitośkue: śaŕnikio: kue: śua: kombalkes: ne litom.

2.- nekue: eŕtaunei: litom: nekue: taunei:litom: nekue: maśnai: tisaunei: litom: śos auku.

3.- aŕe[.]ta[.]o: tamai: uta: ośkues: śtena: ueŕsoniti: śilabur: śleitom: konśkilitom: kabiseti.

4.- kantomśankiliśtaŕa: otanaum: tokoitei: eni: uta: ośkues: bouśtomue: koŕuinomue.

5.- makaśimue: ailamue: ambitiśeti: kamanom: uśabitus: osaś: śueś: śailo: kuśta: bisetus: iom.

6.- aśekati: ambitinkoiunei: śtena: eś: ueŕtai: enteŕa: tiŕiś: matuś: tinbitus: neito tiŕikantam.

7.- eni: onsatus: iomui: liśtaś: titiaś: sisonti: śomui: iom: aŕsnaś: bionti: iom: kuśtaikoś.

8.- aŕsnaś: kuati: iaś: osiaś: ueŕtatośue: temeiue: ŕobiśeti: śaum: tekametinaś: tatus: śomei.

9.- enitousei: iśte: ankioś: iśte: eśankioś: use: aŕeitena: śaŕnikiei: akainakuboś.

10.- nebintoŕ: tokoitei: ioś: uŕantiomue: auseti: aŕatimue: tekametam: tatus: iom: tokoitośkue.

11.- śaŕnikiokue: aiuisaś: kombalkoŕeś: aleiteś: iśte: ikueś: ŕusimus: abulu: ubokum.

Face B

luboś:	kouneśikum:	melmunoś:	bintiś	
letondu:	litokum:	abuloś:	bintiś	
melmu:	baŕausako:	leśunoś:	bintiś	
letondu:	ubokum:	turo:	bintiś:	lubinas
aiu:	beŕkantikum:	abuloś:	bintiś	
tiŕtu:	aiankum:	abuloś:	bintiś	
abulu:	lousokum:	uśeisunoś:	bintiś:	akainas
letondu:	uikanokum:	śueśtunoś:	bintiś	
tiŕtanoś:	śtatulikum:	leśunoś:	bintiś:	nouantutaś
letondu:	aiiankum:	melmunoś:	bintiś	
uśeisu:	aiankum:	tauŕo:	bintiś	
abulu:	aiankum:	taŕuo:	bintiś	
letondu:	letikum:	abuloś:	bintiś:	..kontas
letondu:	eśokum:	abuloś:	bintiś	

(5) Ceux qu'on présente ordinairement comme des cas de lénition ne sont que des sonorisations des occlusives sourdes itervocaliques: *porcom/porqom, touto-/touto-*, etc. La sonorisation seule n'est pas encore lénition. Une sonore n'est pas une sourde affaiblie. Mais, malgré tout, A. Tovar 1961, p. 93 ss. a interprété ces faits comme lénition et on repète fréquemment son opinion sans critique. En plus, ces sonorisations se trouvent d'habitude dans le lusitanien et dans le nord-ouest, tandis qu'elles sont pratiquement inconnues en Celtiberie.

(6) *tokoitei, bouśtomue, śailo*, etc.(dans le bronze de Botorrita): *teiuoreikiś* (dans le bronze de Luzaga).

(7) *tekes* (Luzaga), vraisemblablement de la racine **dhe-* (cf. J. Gil 1977, pp. 162-63; J. de hoz 1986, p. 75. En tout cas il n'y a auncun exemple de /e/ devenue /i/.

(8) Devenue regulièrement /u/ dans le nominatif singulier des thémes en -n: *abulu, letondu, tiŕtu, aiu, uśeisu* (Botorrita). Parfois conservée, parfois alterée dans le génitif pluriel :*aŕebasikom* (graphite de Numantia), *kontebakom, śekaisakom* (dans des monnaies), etc., en face de *alisokum* (tessera de Paris), *atulikum* (tessera d'origine inconnue), *belaiokumkeu* (Luzaga), *eśokum, letikum*, etc. (Botorrita). régulièrement conservé dans le génitif singulier des thémes en o/e: *tauŕo, tuŕo,* (Botorrita), *aualo* (tessera de Paris), etc. Sur cette désinence de génitif singulier cf. infra. En syllabe initiale on n'a que *tatus* (Botorrita A 8 y 10) comme possible temoin du passage /o/ > /a/.

(9) cf. la copulative *kue*, fréquente à Botorrita.

(10) *tokoitei eni* (Botorrita), *tiŕikantam eni* (Botorrita).

(11) *tauŕo, tuŕo,* (Botorrita), *aualo* (tessera de Paris), etc.

(12) J. Untermann 1967; K. H. Schmidt 1977.

(13) E. Hamp 1971, p. 225.

(14) Dans la carte de J. Untermann (1987, p. 72) on trouve l'inventaire complet des formes à /p/ conservé avec l'emplacement précis.

(15) 1. <u>Lamas de Moledo</u>
rufinus et / Tiro scrip-/ serunt / veaminicori / doenti / angom / lamaticom / crouceaimaca / reaicoi petranioi r- / adom porgom iouea[s] / caeilobrigoi.

2. <u>Caveco das Fráguas</u>
oilam. trebopala / indi. porcom . laebo / comaiam . iccona . loim / inna . oilam . usseam / trebarune indi . taurom / ifadem / reue /.

(16) A. Tovar 1961, p. 92 (cf. K. H. Schmidt 1985, p. 321 y 325). L'étymologie n'est pas vraisemblable pour des raisons morphologiques puisqu'elle suppose un dérivé radical thématique (o/e) de la racine *angh- qui, quoique theoriquement possible, en fait n'est atesté dans aucune des langues historiques (cf. Pokorny pp. 42-43). Elle n'est pas vraisemblable nom plus du point de vue sémantique: il s'agit d'une offrande à un ou plusieurs dieux dans laquelle on identifie un cochon (*porgom*). Et il n'a pas de sens que l'on offre une "vallée" à un autre dieu, comm'on traduit ordinairement le mot *angom*. Dans une inscription parallele (Cabeco das Fraguas) on puet indentifier avec toute vraisemblance trois animaux (brebis, cochon, taureau). Finalement, il faut rappeler que la lecture même n'est pas sûre. Cf. K. H. Schmidt 1985, p. 335 n. 49; J. Gorrochatequi 1987, pp. 83-87.

(17) J. Untermann 1962; 1987, où l'on trouve des réferences à la bibliographie antérieure.

(18) J. Gorrochategui 1987.

(19) Mais, quad même, en celtibérique les nominatifs pluriel son en -*os*, pas en -*oi* (*lutiakoś, aŕkailikoś śekiśamoś* (sur des monnaies). C'est pour cela que ce trait pourrait être employé autant pour que contre l'appartenance du lusitanien au celtique péninsulaire.

(20) K. H. Schmidt 1985, J. Gorrouchategui 1987; J. Untermann 1987.

(21) Sur les implications phonétiques de indi cf. A. Tovar 1985, p. 239; J. Untermann 1987, p. 62.

(22) A. Tovar 1966-67; cf. 1985, p. 251.

(23) U. Schmoll 1959 (cf. la carte qu'on trouve à la page 125).

(24) A. Tovar J de Hoz; K. H. Schmidt; J. Gorrochategui; etc.

(25) K. H. Schmidt 1985, p. 338.

(26) H. Krahe 1954 et 1964.

(27) J. de Hoz 1963; 1965.

(28) W. P. Schmid 1968.

(29) F. Villar (sous presse).

(30) *La Hoya. Un poblado del I milenio antes de Cristo* (6eme ed.), Victoria 1983.

(31) A. Gracia y Bellido 1953, pp. 60-61.

(32) J. Untermann 1961, cartes 2, 3 et 4.

(33) J. de Hoz 1983.

(34) Les différents travaux qui ont quelque rélation avec le déchiffrement ont été reunis dans M. Gómez Moreno 1949.

(35) MONNAIES: 1) iltiŕaŕker, 2) auśesken, 3) iltiŕkesken.

(36) L. Michelena 1979.

(37) L. Micheleena 1979, p. 26.

(38) A. Tovar 1962.

(39) A. Tovar 1961, p. 64. De son côté, L. Michelena 1979, p. 34 dit:"D'autres, dont moi-même, inclineraient à y voir un indice de génitif du type basque ou kartvélien ou, ce qui revient au même, un suffixe de dérivation, formant une nouvelle base nominal qui peut à son tour recevoir d'autres suffixes casuels".

(40) L. Michelena 1979, p. 34.

(41) L. Michelena arrive plus loin sur le parallélisme entre l'ibère et le basque dans le domain de la détermination quand il assure: "Il ne serait pas téméraire de croire que l'ibère était, tout à fait comme le basque, une langue où la distinction entre substantif et adjectif (faut d'accord, etc.) n'était pas très nette ou, si l'on veut, une langue où cette transposition catégorielle trouvait peu d'obstacles".

(42) L. Michelena, p. 34.

(43) J. de Hoz 1981/a, p. 482.

(44) J. Untermann 1987/a.

(45) J. Untermann 1987/a, p. 51.

(46) A. Tovar 1979, pp. 475-82.

(47) A. Tovar 1987, pp. 19-20.

(48) L. Michelena 1954.

(49) J. Gorrochategui 1984.

(50) J. de Hoz 1981.

(51) L. Michelena 1979, p. 38.

(52) L. Michelena 1979, p. 37.

(53) J. de Hoz, p. 56.

(54) J. Untermann 1972-1974.

(55) J. Gorrochategui (sous presse).

(56) J. Untermann 1965, p. 163 (carte 70).

(57) 1) koreli[...]nakiibuuoirauarbaa/tiirtoosnebaanaberkeeni(Fonte Velha). 2) akoosiosnabekeeti (Almoroqui, Cáceres).

(58) J. A. Correa 1985, p. 378.

(59) S. Wikander 1966.

(60) 1985, 1987.

BIBLIOGRAFIA

Correa, J. A. 1985. "Consideraciones sobre las inscripciones tartesias" *Actas del III Coloquio sobre Lenguas y Culturas Paleohispanicas*, Salamanca, pp. 377-96.

Correa, J. A. 1987. "El signario tartesio" *Actas del IV Coiloquio sobre Lenguas y Culturas Paleohispanicas*, Vitoria, pp. 275-84.

De Hoz, J. 1963. "Hidronimia antigua europea en la Peninsula Iberica" *Emerita*, pp. 227-42.

De Hoz, J. 1965. "La hidronimia antigua europea: origen y sentido" *Emerita* 33, pp. 13-22.

De Hoz, J. 1987. "La epigrafia celtiberica" *Epigrafia Hispanicade epoca romano-republicana*, Zaragoza.

De Hoz, J. 1981. "El Euskera y las lenguas vecinas antes de la romanicacion" *Euskal Linguistica eta Literatura*: Bide Berriak, Bilbao, pp. 27-56.

De Hoz, J. 1981/a. "Algunas precisiones sobre testos metrologicos ibericos ibericos" *APL* 16, pp. 475-86.

De Hoz, J. 1983. "Origine ed evoluzione delle scritture ispaniche" *AION* 5, pp. 27-61.

De Hoz, J. 1986. "La epigrafia celtiberica" *Epigrafia Hispanica de epoca romano-republicana*, Zaragoza, pp. 43-102.

Garcia y Bellido, A. 1954. *La Peninsula iberica en los comienzos de su historia*, Madrid.

Gil, J. 1977. "Notas a los bronces de Botorrita y Luzaga" *Habis* 8, pp. 161-74.

Gomez Moreno, M. 1949. *Miselanea, Historia, Arte, Argueologia*. Madrid.

Gorrochategui, J. 1984. Onomastica Indigena de Aquitania, Bilbao.

Gorrochategui, J. 1987. "En torno a la clasificacion del lusitano" *Actas del IV Coloquio sobre Lenguas y Culturas Paleohispanicas*, Victoria, pp. 77-92.

Gorrochategui, J. Sous presse "Vasco-Celtica".

Hamp, E. 1971. "Fils et fille en italique, Nouvelle contribution" *Bsl* 66, pp. 213-27.

Krahe, H. 1954. *Sprache und Vorzeit*, Heidelberg.

Krahe, H. 1964. *Unsere ältesten Flussnamen*, Wiesbaden.

Michelena, L. 1954. "De Onomastica Aquitana" *Pirineos*, 10, pp. 409-55.

Michelena, L. 1979. "La langue ibere" *Actas del II Coloquio sobre Lenguas y Culturas de la peninsula Iberica*, Salamanca 1979, pp. 23-39.

Schmid, W. P. 1968. *Alteuropäisch und Indogermanisch*, Akademie Mainz, Abhandlungen der Geistes und Sozialwissenschaftlichen Klasse, Nr, 4.

Schmidt, K. H. 1977. "Zum Problem des Genitivs der o-Stämme im Baltischen" *Commentationes Linguisticae et Philologicae Earnest Dickmann*, Heidelberg, pp. 335-44.

Schmidt, K. H. 1985. "A contribution to the identification of Lusitanian" *Actas del III Coloquio sobre Lenguas y Culturas Paleohispanicas*, Vitoria, pp. 319-41.

Schmoll, U. 1959. *Die Sprachen der vorkeltischen Indogermanen Hispaniens und das Keltiberisch*, Wiesbaden.

Schule, W. 1969. *Die Meseta-Kulturen, mediterränische und eurasische Elemente in früheisenzeitlichen Kulturen Südwesttteuropas*, Berlin.

Tovar, A. 1961. *The Ancient Languages of Spain and Portugal*, New York.

Tovar, A. 1962. "Fonologia del Iberico" *Estructuralismo e Historia, Miscelanea Homenaje a Martinet III*, La Laguna, pp. 171-81.

Tovar, A. 1966-67. "L'inscription du Cabeco das Fraguas et la langue des Lusitaniens" *EC 9*, pp. 237-68.

Tovar, A. 1979. "Notas linguisticas sobre monedas ibericas" *Actas del II Colquio sobre Lenguas y Culturas do la peninsula Iberica*, Salamanca, pp. 475-82.

Tovar, A. 1985. "La inscripcion de Cabeco das Fraguas y la lengua de los Lusitanos" *Actas del III Coloquio sobre Lenguas Paleohispanicas*, Salamanca, pp. 227-53.

Tovar, A. 1987. "Lenguas y Pueblos de la Antigua Hispania" *Actas del IV Coloquio sobre lenguas y Culturas Paleohispanicas*, Vitoria, pp. 15-34.

Untermann, J. 1961. *Sprachräume und Sprachbewegungen im vorrömischen Hispanien*, Wiesbaden.

Untermann, J. 1962. "Personennamen als Sprachquelle im vorrömischen Hispanien", *II, Fachtagung für indogermanische und allgemeine Sprachwissenschaft*, Innsbruck, pp. 63-93.

Untermann, J. 1965. *Elementos de un atlas antropoinimico de la Peninsula Iberica*, Madrid.

Untermann, J. 1967. "Die Endung des Genitiv singularis der -o-Stämme im Keltiberischen" *Beiträge zur Indegermanistik und Keltologie J. Pokorny zum 80 Geburstag gewidmet*, 1967, pp. 281-88.

Untermann, J. 1972-74. "Zu keltiberischen Munzlegenden" *Archivo Espaffol de Arqueologia* 45-47, pp. 469-76.

Untermann, J. 1987. "Lusitanisch, Keltiberisch, Keltisch" *Actas del IV Coloquio sobre lenguas y Culturas Paleohspanicas*, Vitoria, pp. 35-56.

Villar, F. Sous presse "The indo-european vowels /a/ and /o/ revisited.

Wikander, S. 1966. "Sur la langue des inscriptions Sud-Hispaniques" *Studia Linguistica* 20, pp. 1-8.

Zuess, J. K. 1937. *Die Deutshue und ihre Nachberstämme*, Manchen.

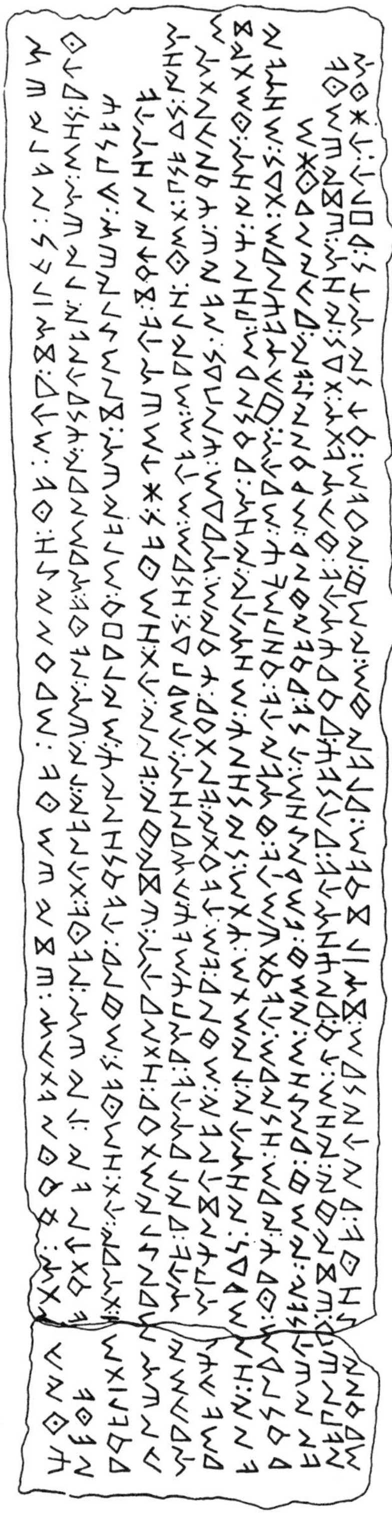

FIGURE 1 (a)

LE BRONZE DE BOTORRITA (FACE A)

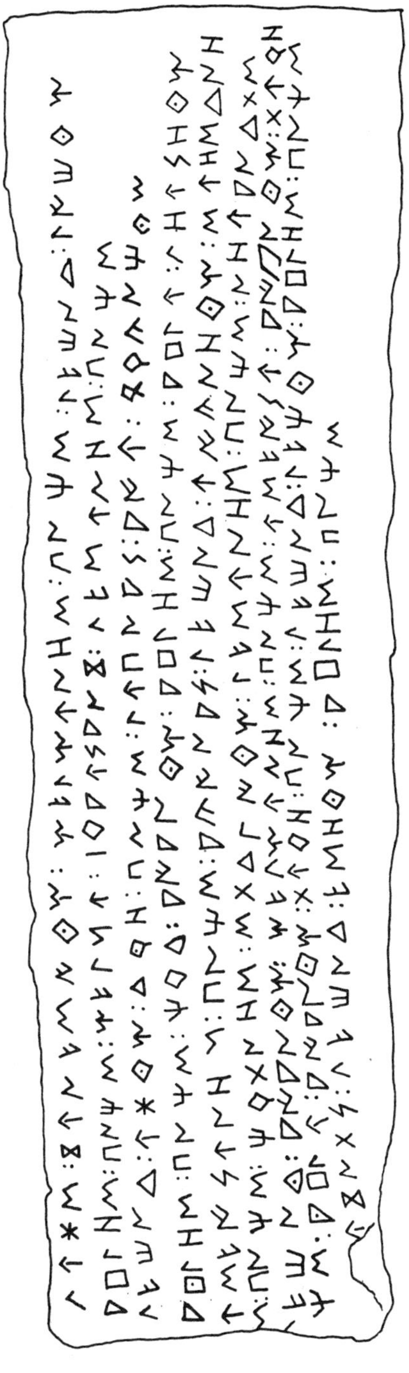

FIGURE 1 (b)

LE BRONZE DE BOTORRITA (FACE B)

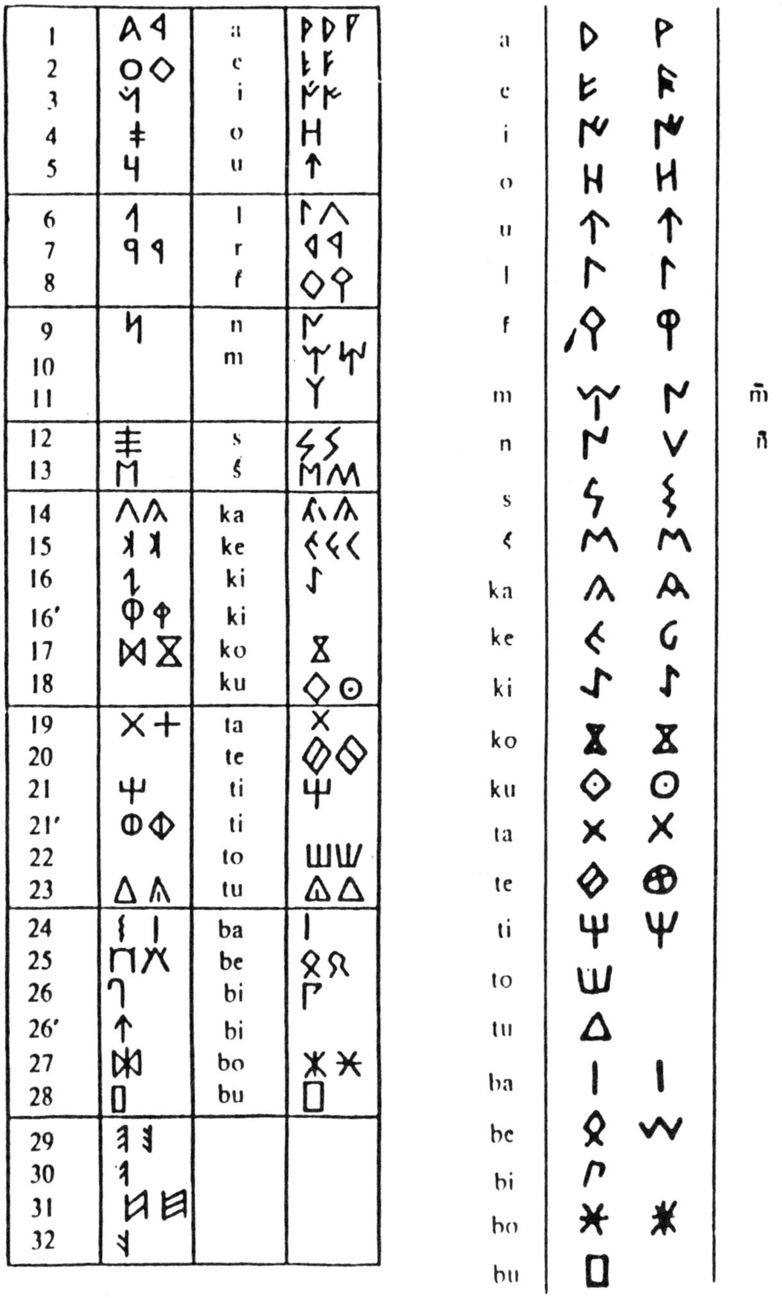

Écriture meridional et orientale
(a)

Écriture celtibérique
(b)

FIGURE 2

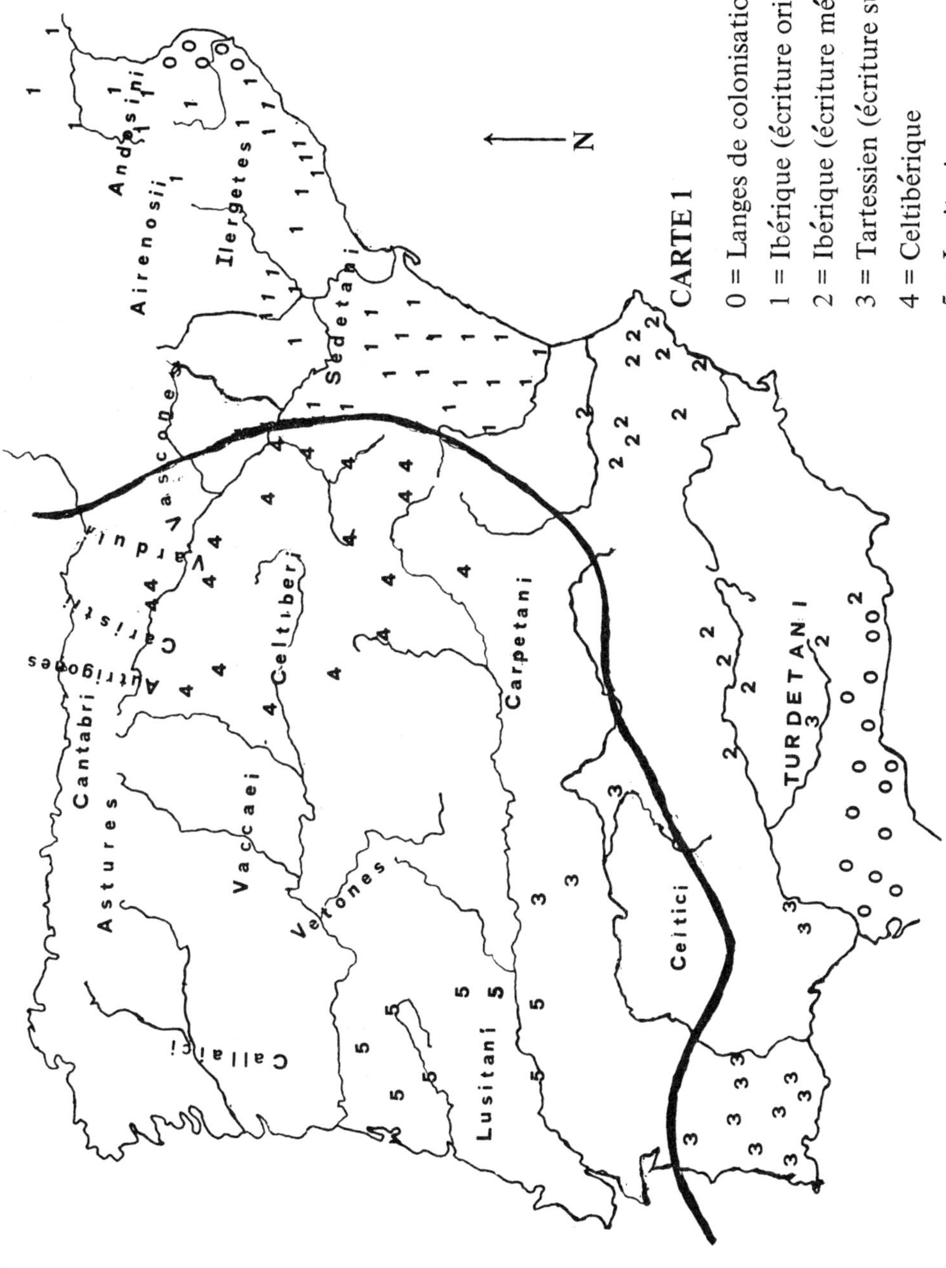

CARTE 1

0 = Langes de colonisation
1 = Ibérique (écriture orientale)
2 = Ibérique (écriture méridionale)
3 = Tartessien (écriture suroccidentale)
4 = Celtibérique
5 = Lusitanien

390 When Worlds Collide

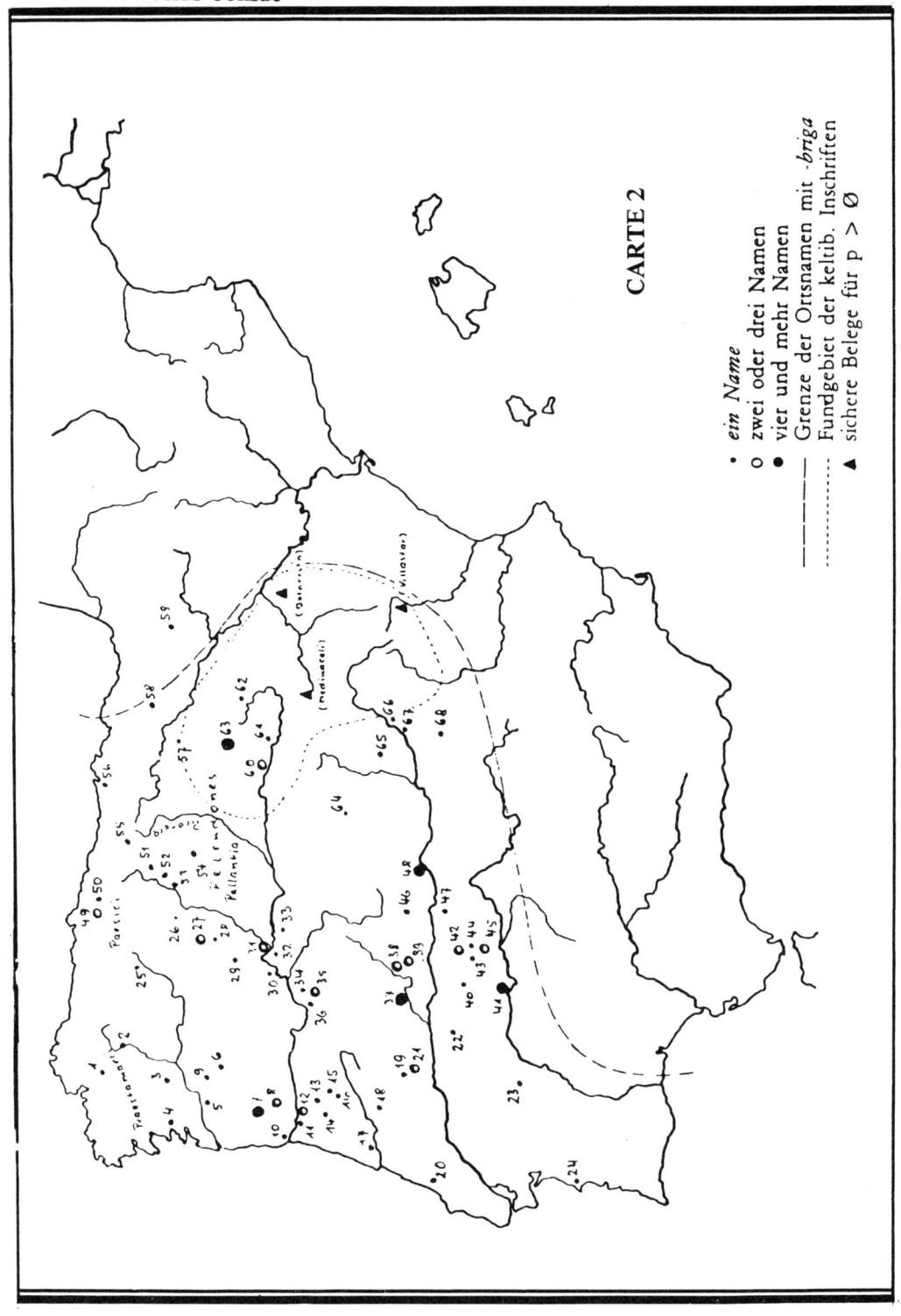

CARTE 2

- · ein Name
- ○ zwei oder drei Namen
- ● vier und mehr Namen
- —— Grenze der Ortsnamen mit -*briga*
- ······ Fundgebiet der keltib. Inschriften
- ▲ sichere Belege für p > ∅

KARTE 1. *Orts-, Personen- und Götternamen mit p im Anlaut oder in Inlaut zwischen Vokalen im indogermanischen Hispanien.*

1. Guitiriz: *Parraq(um)*
2. Lugo: *Poemana* GN.
3. Reádegos: *Paramaecus* GN.
4. El Padrón: *Pintavi*
5. Paderne: *Pentu*
6. Chaves: *Pictelancius*
7. Braga: *Apil., Paugenda, Pelisius, Pinarea*
8. Caldas de Vizela: *Peicana, Pintamus*
9. Ginzo de Limia: *Praenia*
10. Porto: *Pintamus*
11. Pombeiro: *Pugius*
12. Carquere: *Peda, Pistmus*
13. Penalva do Castelo: *Pacius*
14. Vouzela: *Paisiciecus* GN.
15. Lamas de Moledo: *Pisirus*
16. Viseu: *Peiniticis* GN., *Pellius*
17. Penacova: *Picera*
18. Oliveira do Hospital: *Picus*
19. Capinha: *Progela*
20. Porto de Mos: *Pellius*
21. Idanha-a-Velha: *Pintamus, Piscinus, Pucus*
22. San Vicente de Alcántara: *Pelsinus*
23. Vilaviçosa: *Pacina*
24. Santiago do Cacem: *Pagusicus*
25. Villablino: *Propeddus*
26. León: *Petonus*
27. Astorga: *Pelgus, Pellius, Pentili*
28. Fuente Encalada: *Pelusius*
29. San Vitero: *Pistirus*
30. Duas Egrejas: *Apilicus*
31. Villalcampo: *Pentius, Pintovius, Pistira*
32. Moral de Sayago: *Pintovius*
33. Tardobispo: *Apia*
34. Saldeana: *Pintovius*
35. Yecla de Yeltes: *Pacidus, Pentavi, Pistirus*
36. Hinojosa de Duero: *Apanus*
37. Coria: *Apinus, Perecaius, Pisinus, Pisira, Pisocia*
38. Caparra: *Gapeticorum, Pellius*
39. Plasencia: *Pellius, Pisira*
40. Cáceres: *Pelliocus*
41. Mérida: *Pintamus, Pintana, Ponius, Pusinca*
42. Trujillo: *Pellius, Ponceia*
43. Ibahernando: *Apaia*
44. Alcollarín: *Pellus*
45. Abertura: *Pintamus, Patia*
46. Candeleda: *Pintolanq(um)*
47. Villar del Pedroso: *Apinus*
48. Talavera de la Reina: *Apinus, Pellicius, Pentiniq(um), Pisitric(um)*
49. Cangas de Onís: *Pembelorum, Pentius*
50. Cofiño: *Peniorum*
51. Barniedo: *Palari*
52. Aleje: *Pallisi*
53. Cistierna: *Pendieginorum*
54. Velilla de Guardo: *Pentovius*
55. Luriezo: *Pentoviecus*
56. Castro Urdiales: *Purana*
57. Pancorvo: *Plandida*
58. Salvatierra: *Plendia*
59. Aoiz: *Peremusta* GN.
60. Coruña del Conde: *Pitana, P[ ]i-gancom*
61. Osma: *Pusinca*
62. Santervás de la Sierra: *Pusinc(um)*
63. Lara de los Infantes: *Paesica, Pedolus, Petelius, Plandica*
64. Segovia: *Protenius*
65. Alcalá de Henares: *Pusinca*
66. Sacedón: *Pelicus*
67. Illana: *Pentilia*
68. Cabeza del Griego: *Pindusa* GN.

Die Belege finden sich bei Albertos, *Onomástica*, «Organizaciones» und bei Untermann, *Elementos*.

CARTE 2
EXPLICATION

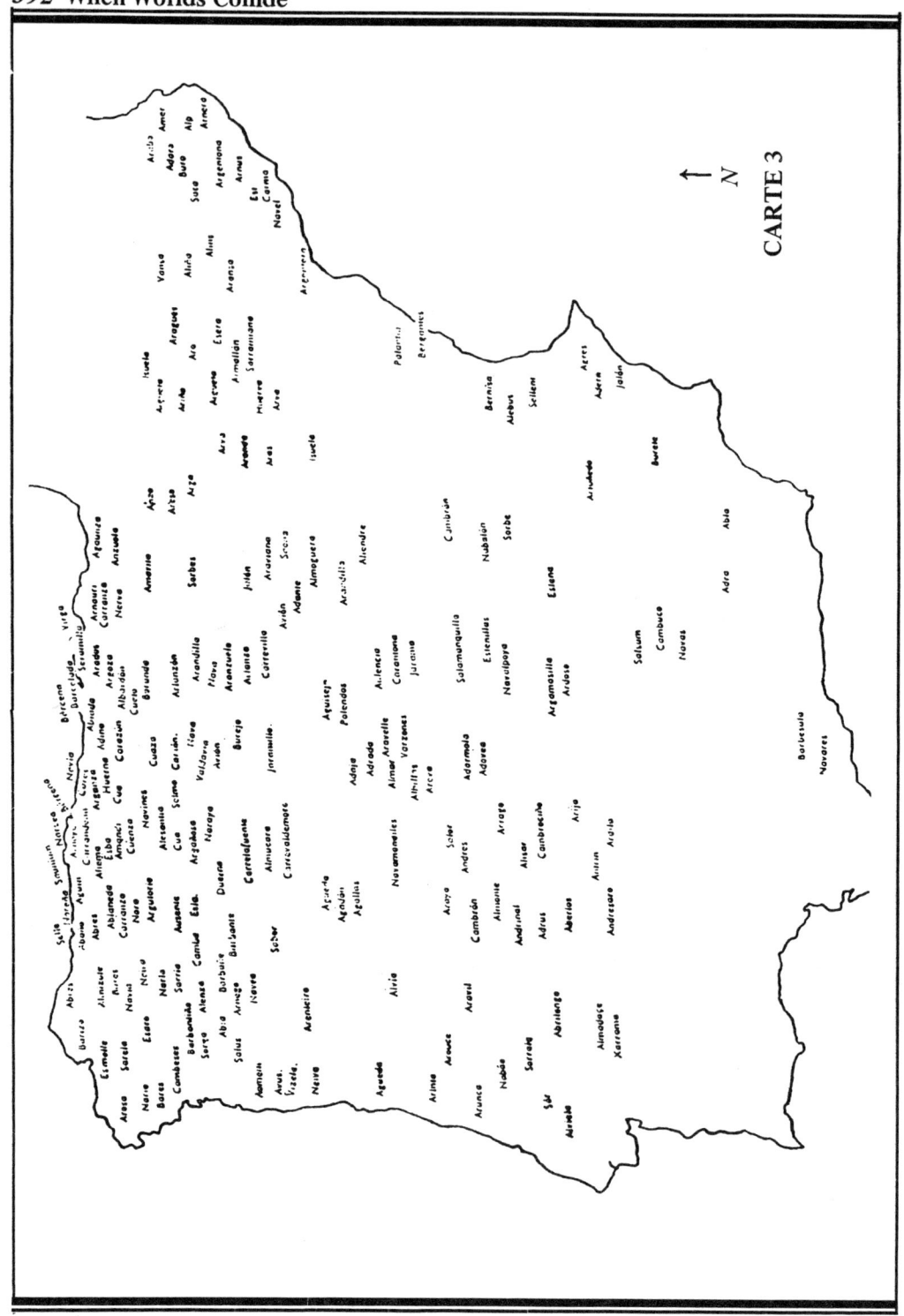

CARTE 3

	-a (-o-)	-l-	-k-	-l-	-m-	-n-	-nt-	-r-	-s-	-st-	-t-
*av- o *ab-	Avus	Abia	Ablanquejo	Abla		Aboño	Vansa	Aberios	Ausente		Abiada
*ad-	Ade	Adaja		Adaja	Adarmola	Adino	Adante	Adaro			Adarda
*al (-m)-		Alenza	Almucara		Aliena	Aliña	Almonte	Alerra	Alsie	Alest	
*ar-	Ara	Araya	Arnego	Arija	Armallán	Arnus	Arinta	Arnela	Areso		Arados
*arg-	Arga	Argoza			Argamasilla	Argentona	Arganza	Argentera	Argañosa		Argoza
*kar-	Carre (la fuente)	Carrión		Caralio	Carma	Carrandena	Carranzo				Carazón
*nar-	Nora	Nario	Narcea	Naria		Noreña					
*sal-	Salo	Salia	Salamanquilla	Seliolo	Selmo		Salamanquilla	Salor	Salsum		
*sar-	Sara	Sarria	Sorga	Sarela	Sarrauiana	Sarrauiana		Sardoira			Sardoira

CARTE 3
Explication

CARTE 4 ↑

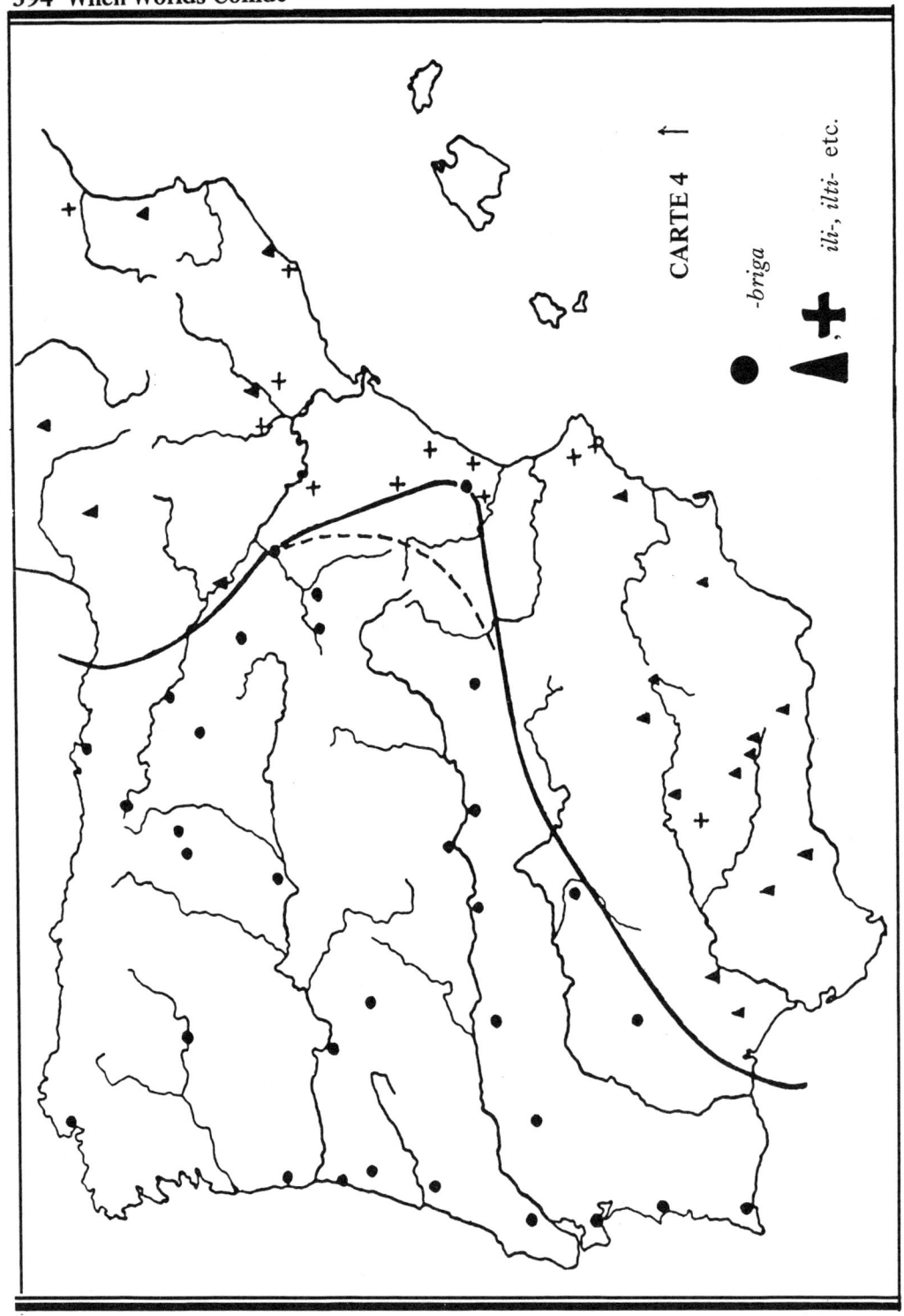

● -briga

▲,+ ili-, ilti- etc.

DISCUSSION

Editors:

The following is but a brief sampling of the transcribed taped discussion from the conference. Some tapes were defective; particularly unfortunate, was that of Edgar Polome's detailed critique of Colin Renfrew's presentation. The following, which conveys the flavor of the lively give-and-take of the conference, is exerpted from the general discussion that followed Colin Renfrew's presentation.

Edgar C. Polome: May I just say something? It is a fact that there were Mesopotamian colonies as early as 1930 BC in Asia Minor, very close to the end of the period you indicate. If this kind of people had been there, then why wouldn't there have been any mention of such people?

Colin Renfrew: I think there is. I have understood that there were reflections of Hittites.

Edgar C. Polome: Yes, of Hittites, but not of others.

Colin Renfrew: But what are we talking about here, the Luwians, and so on? I don't think I see any problem here. It's in the early period that we have a parenthesis, and then in the historical period we have Luwian and Palaic and Hittite, and these are reflected in the writings of Boghazköy and earlier.

Eric P. Hamp: But two of them only secondarily.

Colin Renfrew: But I'm not asserting that there was a greater variety. This is the very point Professor Villar is raising. I'm not suggesting that there were more than two or three groups and more interesting and more difficult, I quite agree, there is the fact that the non-Indo-European Hattic group was also surviving at that time.

Thomas V. Gamkrelidze: But why, then, did Hattic have no writing at all, the cultural writing of a small group?

Charles Burney: Might I inject a small point? While my real questions are on tradition, I must add here that there are texts which refer to writing on tablets of wood, but that wouldn't take us back to the time to which you are referring.
    Could I raise one or two more points?
    I would willingly settle for a fairly orthodox view of farming spreading from Anatolia to Europe, even though sad to say perhaps, from some points of view that would be an implied spread from west to east into the steppes. But I must say that, from the point of view of the origin of the farm, this is, in a way, an ultra-diffusionist point of view. It could be right about the Indo-European population in Central Anatolia, but I think we must distinguish between Central and Eastern Anatolia. I think that the arguments we heard from Heiner Eichner yesterday and the linguistic

picture militate against much here: Colin Renfrew simply cannot be right about the eastern zone in the wider economic sense. The fact is that there is fairly good evidence for goods production in Western Iran at earlier periods, though not as early as Jericho and places like that. We are now talking about the 17th and 18th millennia, the 17th millenium in Western Iran. That arrow on Renfrew's map showing arrows going across Iran (Fig. 8.4, p. 207 in Renfrew 1987) is, I think, a flight of fantasy, at least from my point of view anyway. As far as Eastern Anatolia goes, climatic, that is, environmental factors there seem to me rather hostile to a homeland there for the Proto-Indo-Europeans, point is that the mountains start from a plateau level of five to six thousand feet above sea level. It is what the Turks call a winter country, very inhospitable, and those arrows which are central, I suppose you could call them Anatolian, are on the periphery. So I think you should probably be a bit careful about putting blobs on the map, and that also applies to a reconstruction. I see that area -- alright, it's my own stomping ground, as a defensive zone in a sense, not a zone from which great movements, whether by "Wave of Advance" or whatever model, come. I do think, finally, that this approach is essentially a European approach. That alone doesn't invalidate it, but one has reservations whether the spread of farming goes with the Indo-Europeans to Europe.

Colin Renfrew: What I'd like to say is that it seems to me that the Eastern side of things is a little less clear, I mean lingusitically less clear. It seems to me not inconceivable, I just leave it as a question, that the first farmers of Turkmenia might also have been speaking an Indo-European language. In which case, we have no problem with all of the orientalist early sites in the highlands of Iran, the plateau of Iran.

Daniel Zohary: Two comments. One just to make an addition. I'm also not very enthusiastic about the eastern highlands. You are talking about the continental part of anatolia, and then when you climb from the plateau up to the mountainous area of Eastern Turkey, then you are coming from a region in which wheat and barley can survive in the wild into a region in which they are totally out of the ecological picture. It is the same as we know, for instance, that in Europe the agriculturally rich higher mountains of the Alps were rather late to be colonized compared with the colonization of the main lowlands, especially the loess soil lowlands. I would use this same argument with respect to the higher plateaus of Anatolia. I feel that this is secondary in terms of time: you have to have developed types of cultivars that could survive there, maybe only relatively later, or even secondary things such as bread wheats which are reproductive under such conditions.

Now, the second thing I would like to add is that I think that one should realize that, ecologically, farming was not only rain dependent farming, as we find it in Europe, but very early on serious wheat and barley farming was also successful in warmer places with the addition of irrigation water: the Jordan Rift Valley, some areas in Mesopotamia --- certainly some 1000 to 1500 years later in the main basin, and a little bit later on the Nile. I think that when we are talking about the establishment of farming in the east, then we are talking not so much about rain dependent farming, but on irrigation based agriculture, and the important fact to realize is that this started very, very early. If you ask me, I still cannot give you the answer to whether or not the initiation of wheat and barley domestication was due to the start of irrigated agriculture, or vice versa, in places, let's say, like the Nile Basin as far as Aswan, where we have the first indication of wheat domestication, which, if I remember correctly, is 7600 BC, or where, near Jericho, we find domesticated barley in the 8th millennium, and in the earlier part of the 8th millennium BC there were cereals which were cultivated with or without the aid or irrigation. So this dichotomy in agriculture (rain dependent vs. irrigation dependent) is very, very early, and one should take it into account. Maybe those who are based in Europe are more impressed by types of farming which are typical for that ecological zone of the globe and not by the warmer fringe which was actually able to support very successful civilizations very early, at the beginning.

Eric P. Hamp: I would just like to perhaps strike a balance to some of the statements which we have heard from Professor Renfrew.

First of all, I think that we have to give our predecessors their due on what they have said. I can illustrate this by seizing on a straight statement by Winfred Lehmann: I can only say from what I heard Professor Renfrew say that that statement reflects either ignorance or inattention. A knowing Indo-Europeanist, I think, who attends to his material at all would never have claimed this. Certainly, in the pages of Otto Schrader (b. 1855 - d. 1919: *Reallexikon der indogermanischen Altertumskunde,* 1901), or someone like that, you won't find any argument that the Indo-Europeans were pastoralists innocent of agricultural matters. After all, in the debate about the Indo-European base *$*seH1-$* 'to sow, cast, let fall,' as we find it in English, for example, the argument is not whether the Indo-Europeans were agriculturalists, or ever planted anything, the question is rather -- and Emmanuel Laroche has said the most decisive thing so far on this base which we find notably in every branch of Indo-European except Helleno-Armenian, whether the Indo-Europeans sowed by broadcast method, or whether they pushed seeds into the ground in planting that way. No one, in other words, doubts the mixed agricultural/pastoral economy that Indo-European reconstructions, at least from the linguistic point of view, leads to.

Secondly, you mentioned that we must imagine Europe as comprised of not just a few dialects yielding the few branches that we happen to have by the historical accident of writing, things that you have already alluded to in the case of Anatolia, but rather that there should be a relatively unknowable number of possible fragmentations of groups. Every Indo-Europeanist that I know of who thinks at all about how languages develop and break up takes that as axiomatic. We must imagine that Europe in, let's say, 2000 BC was a speckle of potential groups, probably three quarters of which failed to survive, just as has happened in more recent times and is happening yet today. After all, in every nation we know, in every area, and under no matter what conditions, we have dialects dying off, being gobbled up by others. This is the history of Aragon in Castile in one social setting; the history of things in the Hindu Kush with its little languages around; and so on. This is what we must understand as the natural state of affairs. Then, if I understood correctly, you suggested that Celtic sprang from some widespread uniformity. That's unrealistic from anything we know about languages simply because it is almost impossible, particularly if you have slower transportation than in modern times. It's almost impossible to get a uniform language variety spread over a large territory, unless there is a mechanism to carry it back and forth. The Algonquians provide us with a good model for having widespread uniformity, but then we also know that they were widespread, and this might have been true of the Celts at some point, overlaying other groups. We know, for instance, that certain Algonquian tribes in Quebec form a population that for several centuries now has filtered back and forth, across and through, French Canadian farmers. The Cree, of course, occupy a large territory: they have a dialect extent from Labrador to the Rocky Mountains, but they have a considerable dialectology. To get something like a Celtic family describable as we have it, you have to get that coming from a small compact area of people, which perhaps have been but one among ten other varieties. We don't deny that there may have been other para-Celts, if you like, around, nine out of ten of which all died off.

Colin Renfrew: First of all, the point about fragmentation is agreed. I only made that point in response to a remark that Tim Champion made. I think we are all agreed that there was great variety in the languages that have died out. That's not the original point anyway. It is simply that I think Tim Champion thought I hadn't sufficiently emphasized it in my book, and I accept that, and I think we're agreed on that. On the question of the emphasis which historical linguists and archaeologists have put on the pastoral, rather than on the agricultural, I'm very surprised that Professor Hamp doesn't have this impression. Wherever I read in historical linguistics or, indeed, in archaeology about the Indo-Europeans, we keep on being told that the Indo-Europeans are pastoralists. And why is this? Well, the only reason for thinking of them as pastoralists is some inferences made from the proto-lexicon, and if we're all happy to abandon the notion that they were pastoralists, well, I'm the first to be happy to abandon the notion also. So that is absolutely fine by me.

Tom Markey: There seems to be a bias here that says that any hunting and gathering culture is fragile, but, with reference to your agrarian "Wave of Advance" model, once you've achieved agriculture, then you're on the way, and all that follows is the steady onslaught of agriculture: there's never a need for price supports, never a crop failure, and never a dust bowl effect. There seem to be no glitches in the system. But, in fact, we know that even in the United States, where agriculture is a massive, technologically refined industry and supposedly highly sophisticated, it is actually very, very fragile. Such fragilities may, indeed, have opened the door to the sort of social gloss subsumed by Antonio Gilman's Mafia Hypothesis. This was a fragility to be protected, and one had to husband one's limited resources from time to time.

Colin Renfrew: These are different points, I think, from the ones which Professor Hamp and I were discussing.

Tom Markey: No, not really, as I am trying to provide a rationale for a mixed pastoral/agricultural economy. This crop failed, so let's now do a little nomadic pastoralism, and, should that fail, then let's return to agriculture.

Colin Renfrew: The point was about the Indo-Europeans having been originally pastoralists, and I was simply asserting that that seems to be a widespread preconception, but if it isn't a widespread preconception, and perhaps I'm wrong in this, then I'm very happy to abandon it. Again, I'm not saying they were pastoralists, but I am indeed suggesting that they were agriculturalist. However, I think that agriculturalists suffered their vicissitudes, and they have their environmental disasters. At the same time, there are a few cases I can think of where significant tracts of the world have gone over to an agricultural economy and then moved back from that to a hunting/gathering economy.

Eric P. Hamp: The Maya.

Colin Renfrew: There you've got a collapse of a civilization, not of an agricultural society. They're still living by agricultural products. It's simply that there you've got a collapse of a state society. It's not a case where the present occupants of Maya lands are hunter/gatherers, for many of them are not.

I'd like to speak to the Celtic point, and then I'll surrender the floor again. The notion that Celts had to come from a very compact homeland is obviously a linguistic issue where I don't have the standing to speak, but it seems to me that if the Indo-Europeans have dispersed from a compact homeland, then, on the basis of that model, in France and adjacent lands you would no doubt have people speaking a range of dialects who shared a common origin. Then one has to arrive at the crystallization, as it were, of languages which we now think of as Celtic languages. I think that Antonio Tovar ('Indogermanisch, Keltisch, Keltiberisch', in Karl Horst Schmidt (ed.), *Indogermanisch and Keltiberisch*, Wiesbaden: Ludwig Reichert, 44-66) wrote about this, I thought effectively. If every time we have a language emerging, it always has to emerge from a restricted geographical area, then, to be sure, that's a limiting model and surely we can expect the same language being spoken with essentially the same ranges of dialects, and then surely we are talking ourselves into a very restricted approach spatially.

Alice Harris: In giving your talk, you mentioned that you thought that there was no conflict between Map 1 (fig. 7.7 in Colin Renfrew, *Archaeology and Language. The Puzzle of Indo-European Origins*. London: Jonathan Cape, 1987. P. 160) and Diagram One that Professor Hamp has set up for subgrouping. I wonder, then, how, in fact, do you reconcile the two? From your map it looks as though Italic developed out of Greek, and Balto-Slavic developed out of Greek, and Germanic developed out of Balto-Slavic, and Celtic out of Germanic. Now, there are a lot of things we don't know very clearly in linguistics, and there are a lot of details about subgrouping that are in conflict, but there is one thing that we can really be sure of in linguistics and that is the overall subgrouping picture, and it's pretty clear that Italic didn't develop out of Greek.

Colin Renfrew: First of all, one thing that I'm not quite at ease with in the matters we discussed this morning, and that's Prehellenic. I think we were to call it Pelasgian, but I think when you look at the map, one really has to imagine....

Eric P. Hamp: It's *Pelasgian*, by which I avoid arguments with my Albanian friends.

Colin Renfrew: Well, I see. Thank you very much. I think if we're looking at the map, one really has to imagine the time depth, imagine this for whatever model is used for the development of the Indo-European languages from a homeland. There are limitations. You start with an apex, as it were, and there you have Proto-Anatolian spoken by their ancestors just a couple of generations ago in Anatolia. And then quite rapidly you have people moving into the Balkans and into Central Europe by well before 5000 BC, people who were no doubt speaking related languages. Now, the

Greek language would emerge millennia later from that source, so that when we look at Professor Hamp's diagram, right at the apex we have a point of source from which, ultimately, the later Anatolian languages are derived. Then comes the next divergence. On the one hand we have the European languages and Greek, while on the other hand we have Indian and Iranian. That is fine, and that divides a divergent east and west. Then, very appropriately, we have Armenian diverging off, which in terms of the spatial logic of the model I'm putting forth, is the ancestor of Armenian. On the other hand, we have the ancestor of Greek, and then further down comes the next divergence, which is a single point divergence as given on this diagram and which gives the various languages of Europe. So there is no suggestion that they share, which includes the ancestor of Greek.

Alice Harris: But it's the European part that I was focusing on, not the part to the east; it's the part beginning with Greece, as I don't think the parts you took care of are a problem. It's the parts after that.

Colin Renfrew: Well, on Professor Hamp's diagram we have Armenian out of the discussion for the moment, would therefore be around 6500 BC in Greece, where this is the interesting thing, and either I may be right or I may be wrong, but it's concrete: in Greece around 6500 BC you had people speaking what is still a Proto-Indo-European language, and then some of them stayed there.

Eric P. Hamp: Why in Greece?

Colin Renfrew: Well, let me answer my point while I'm giving you an idea, and you can question whether it's right or not. Some of them stayed there and their descendants continued to speak the languages that developed into the Greek language. Meanwhile, and here the focus moves a little further, at this point you now have the ancestor to the remaining languages of Europe. So, I think that simply all I'm saying is that there is no error in logic there: had Professor Hamp given a more complicated tree arrangement, rather than emerging from a single point there, I might have been able to have them match up, but he was making a general point, and so, too, am I and there is really no conflict in logic.

Eric P. Hamp: No. May I just make two corrections in the interpretations?
First of all, that diagram (Diagram One) is not a branching diagram of geographic location at all. It is a diagram of the abstract logic that returns reconstructions, so that actually that point where the Greeks and all those other languages are together, that might, for all we know, have been in Turkestan, let's say, and it denotes a possible divergence anywhere, including Mars. However, there was a time after some people had departed you might say, when there was a common language. So they weren't necessarily Greeks.

Colin Renfrew: But it doesn't exclude that they were in Greece, and it is still conceivable that they were in Greece.

Eric P. Hamp: No, because my diagram is independent of geography. And the second correction is that I do not make these directions so to speak obligingly: I refuse to make branching nodes until I have evidence of how they branch. Unfortunately, in some instances, I can only branch one or two very tentatively; otherwise I'd say that we don't yet know how to subbranch.

Colin Renfrew: Well, that's the only reason I'm able to give an answer to Dr. Harris.

Alice Harris: But your arrows suggest otherwise.

Colin Renfrew: No, I don't think that's fair. The arrows are showing, if you like, the movement of what are still Proto-Indo-European speakers across Europe, and that's all those arrows are indicating.
They're not suggesting that Greek is ancestral to Bulgarian or something. They are saying, and they're saying this in quite concrete terms, that we have Proto-Indo-European speakers in Greece who are in fact ancestral to Proto-Indo-European speakers in the Balkans, who are ancestral to Proto-Indo-European speakers in central Europe. In each case there will no doubt be some linguistic transformations through time which will be part of the process which leads to languages that are later observed. Concerning any of the models that have been offered for the origin of the Indo-European languages, when you get down to concrete terms, then the relationships between languages as observed by lunguists do not in fact correlate very well with the geography of their ultimate location. That is a general difficulty which I think we all face.

REFERENCE

Renfrew, Colin, 1987. *Archaeology and Language*. London: Jonathan Cape. 1st printing.